SHAKESPEARE AND
AESTHETIC

Shakespeare and Impure Aesthetics explores ideas about art implicit in Shakespeare's plays and defines specific Shakespearean aesthetic practices in his use of desire, death, and mourning as resources for art. Hugh Grady draws on a tradition of aesthetic theorists who understand art as always formed in a specific historical moment but as also distanced from its context through its form and utopian projections. Grady sees *A Midsummer Night's Dream*, *Timon of Athens*, *Hamlet*, and *Romeo and Juliet* as displaying these qualities, showing aesthetic theory's usefulness for close readings of the plays. The book argues that such social-minded 'impure aesthetics' can revitalize the political impulses of the new historicism while opening up a new aesthetic dimension in the current discussion of Shakespeare.

HUGH GRADY is Professor of English at Arcadia University in Glenside, Pennsylvania. He is the author of *The Modernist Shakespeare: Critical Texts in a Material World* (1991), *Shakespeare's Universal Wolf: Studies in Early Modern Reification* (1996) and *Shakespeare, Machiavelli and Montaigne: Power and Subjectivity from Richard II to Hamlet* (2002). He is editor of *Shakespeare and Modernity: From Early Modern to Millennium* (2000) and co-editor (with Terence Hawkes) of *Presentist Shakespeares* (2007).

SHAKESPEARE AND IMPURE AESTHETICS

HUGH GRADY

CAMBRIDGE
UNIVERSITY PRESS

CAMBRIDGE UNIVERSITY PRESS
Cambridge, New York, Melbourne, Madrid, Cape Town,
Singapore, São Paulo, Delhi, Tokyo, Mexico City

Cambridge University Press
The Edinburgh Building, Cambridge CB2 8RU, UK

Published in the United States of America by Cambridge University Press, New York

www.cambridge.org
Information on this title: www.cambridge.org/9781107404205

First published 2009
Reprinted 2011
First paperback edition 2011

A catalogue record for this publication is available from the British Library

Library of Congress Cataloguing in Publication Data
Grady, Hugh.
Shakespeare and impure aesthetics / Hugh Grady.
p.   cm.
Includes bibliographical references and index.
ISBN 978-0-521-51475-0
1. Shakespeare, William, 1564–1616–Aesthetics.   2. Shakespeare, William,
1564–1616–Knowledge–Art.   3. Art in literature.   4. Aesthetics in literature.
I. Title.
PR2986.G73 2009
822.3′3–dc22
2009018063

ISBN 978-0-521-51475-0 Hardback
ISBN 978-1-107-40420-5 Paperback

To Constance Claire Grady

The first in time and the first in importance of the influences upon the mind is that of nature. Every day, the sun; and after sunset, Night and her stars. Ever the winds blow; ever the grass grows. Every day, men and women, conversing – beholding and beholden. The scholar is [s]he of all men [and women] whom this spectacle most engages.
                              Ralph Waldo Emerson, 'The American Scholar'

Contents

Acknowledgements

My first debt is to my wife and intellectual partner, Susan Wells, who has shared the passion for politics, family, art, and nature which has sustained both of us for our adult lives and to which this book bears witness. We have shared, discussed, and debated the issues of this book over many decades.

I want to thank also the other two members of a small reading circle of Theodor Adorno's *Aesthetic Theory* in 2004–2005 – Rachel DuPlessis of Temple University and Mary Hawkesworth of Rutgers, without whose insights my study of Adorno would have been both slower and more labored.

My thanks also to readers of individual manuscript chapters who gave me valuable comments and encouragement: Susan Wells, Terence Hawkes, Charles Whitney, Kathleen McLuskie, Philip Alperson, David Hawkes, Avi Oz, and Ewan Fernie. The book has also benefited from conversations and emails with many interested scholars and critics over the years of its gestation: My thanks especially for this stimulation go to John Joughin, Madalina Nicolaescu, Terence Hawkes, David Hawkes, Dick Wertime, and John Drakakis. I am grateful for specific information and commentary on some issues supplied by Dan Traister, Christopher Norris, Lynne Bruckner, Ewan Fernie, Don Hedrick, Sharon O'Dair, Stephen Cohen, Simon Jarvis, and Heather DuBrow.

The final versions of chapters 2 and 4 were shaped in part in response to comments by readers for the journals *Shakespeare Studies* and *Shakespeare Quarterly*, which each published a compacted version of one of these chapters. Chapter 3 on *Timon of Athens* is a revised, expanded, and re-contextualized version of an earlier essay on the play in Richard Dutton and Jean Howard (eds.), *A Companion to Shakespeare's Works*, Vol. 1: *The Tragedies* (Oxford: Blackwell, 2003). The final draft responds to the astute comments of two anonymous readers for Cambridge University Press.

Portions of drafts of this book were presented at seminars of the Shakespeare Association of America; at the 2005 Annual Conference of the West Virginia Shakespeare and Renaissance Association; at a talk sponsored by the English Department, Royal Holloway, University of London, UK, August 31, 2005; at the 2006 Ropes Lecture at the University of Cincinnati, Cincinnati, Ohio; at the 2006 World Shakespeare Conference at Brisbane, Australia; at the 2007 Conference on Shakespeare, les français, les France (UFR d'Études anglophones, Université Paris Diderot, Paris); at Arcadia University Faculty Spotlight lecture in 2008; at the 2008 International Shakespeare Conference, at Stratford-upon-Avon and at the Autumn 2008 Conference of the Deutsche Shakespeare-Gesellschaft, Mainz, Germany. Audiences in all those venues gave valuable reactions and suggested ideas, some of which are incorporated in what follows.

The initial research and drafting were facilitated by a Summer Stipend (2004) from the National Endowment for the Humanities and from the Arcadia University Ellington Beavers Award for Intellectual Inquiry, 2004; a sabbatical in 2004–2005; and Arcadia University Faculty Development Awards for the summers of 2006, 2007, and 2008.

CHAPTER I

Introduction: impure aesthetics

The purely aesthetic is in other words indissolubly linked to the requirement that it be ultimately impure.[1]

Fredric Jameson

Art perceived strictly aesthetically is art aesthetically misperceived.[2]

Theodor W. Adorno

To speak of the aesthetic in the early twenty-first century within English studies is to risk multiple misunderstandings. The word has been a suspect one in recent years and has served as the subordinated member of key binary opposites in contemporary critical practice. For nearly a generation, in an era dominated by French poststructuralist theory, the aesthetic has been the opposite of the political. It identified the discredited critical practice of Northrop Frye and the New Critics before him; it meant discussing literature decontextualized from its larger social milieu, purposes, and intertextuality.[3] As John Joughin wrote, 'For most radical critics, aesthetics still tends to be discarded as part of the "problem" rather than the "solution."'[4] For many recent radical critics, art has been understood either as a version of ideology,[5] or as an

---

[1] Fredric Jameson, *A Singular Modernity: Essay on the Ontology of the Present* (London: Verso, 2002), 160.

[2] Theodor W. Adorno, *Aesthetic Theory*, eds. Gretel Adorno and Rolf Tiedemann, trans. R. Hullot-Kentor (Minneapolis: University of Minnesota Press, 1997), 6.

[3] Indeed, one can still find approving usage of the term in this sense in contemporary works – see Harold Bloom, *Shakespeare: The Invention of the Human* (New York: Riverhead, 1998), 9 and Jonathan Bate, *The Genius of Shakespeare* (London: Picador, 1997), 320–21.

[4] John J. Joughin, 'Shakespeare, Modernity and the Aesthetic: Art, Truth and Judgement in *The Winter's Tale*', in Hugh Grady (ed.), *Shakespeare and Modernity: Early Modern to Millennium* (London: Routledge, 2000), 61–84; 61.

[5] This position can be found in Communist-influenced critical writings like Norman Rudich, 'Coleridge's "Kubla Khan": His Anti-Political Vision', in Norman Rudich (ed.), *Weapons of Criticism: Marxism in America and the Literary Tradition* (Palo Alto, Calif.: Ramparts, 1976), 215–41; and in structuralist Marxism like that of Etienne Balibar and Pierre Macherey, 'On

irrationalist practice through which contemporary Postmodernist critics have undermined rationality.[6]

There have been a number of critics, however, and fortunately some major ones, who have resisted this reductive binary thinking in their use of the concept of the aesthetic. Fredric Jameson is one example, and a major influence on this book. Terry Eagleton recovered from an early anti-aesthetic phase to write the appreciatory, if flawed *The Ideology of the Aesthetic* and the more recent *Sweet Violence: The Idea of the Tragic*. And Stephen Greenblatt has also consistently kept the aesthetic an important and autonomous category for critical analysis and for understanding the interactions of the work of art and its larger social and cultural context.[7]

All of these critics knew something that had escaped many of their contemporaries: that the Marxist tradition – and German post-Kantian philosophy generally – contained an extensive, appreciative archive of writings on the aesthetic which valued art as a highly significant human practice in itself and, in the case of Marxist aesthetics, specifically refused to reduce art to ideology.[8] At the same time, this pro-art current within Marxism – there is as well a pronounced 'art-as-ideology' tendency – resisted the many extant versions of Romantic aesthetics emphasizing art as transcendent, mystical, or quasi-religious. Theodor Adorno has been exemplary in both regards, writing, for example, that 'Art is rationality that criticizes rationality without withdrawing from it; art is not something prerational or irrational, which would peremptorily condemn it as untruth ... Rational and irrational theories of art are therefore equally faulty.'[9]

For many people, of course, aesthetic discourse is invariably a discourse about beauty and unity, and this narrow conception gives the

Literature as an Ideological Form', in Terry Eagleton and Drew Milne (eds.), *Marxist Literary Theory* (Oxford: Blackwell, 1996), 275–95.

[6] Christopher Norris, *The Truth about Postmodernism* (Oxford: Blackwell, 1993); see especially pp. 60–64.

[7] See particularly Stephen Greenblatt, *Shakespearean Negotiations: The Circulation of Social Energy in Renaissance England* (Berkeley, Calif.: University of California Press, 1988), 1–20. I will return to this essay below.

[8] See Mikhail Lifshitz, *The Philosophy of Art of Karl Marx*, trans. Ralph B. Winn (1938; repr. London: Pluto, 1973); Theodor Adorno, *Notes to Literature*, ed. Rolf Tiedemann, trans. Shierry Weber Nicholsen, 2 vols. (New York: Columbia University Press, 1991, 1992); Maynard Solomon (ed.), *Marxism and Art: Essays Classic and Contemporary* (New York: Vintage,1974); Terry Eagleton, *Ideology: An Introduction* (London: Verso, 1991); Herbert Marcuse, *The Aesthetic Dimension: Toward a Critique of Marxist Aesthetics*, trans. Herbert Marcuse and Erica Sherover (Boston, Mass.: Beacon, 1978); Fredric Jameson, *Marxism and Form: Twentieth-Century Dialectical Theories of Literature* (Princeton University Press, 1971); Louis Althusser, 'A Letter on Art in Reply to André Daspre', in Louis Althusser, *Lenin and Philosophy and Other Essays*, trans. Ben Brewster (New York: Monthly Review Press, 1978), 221–27. Other relevant works will be cited as the discussion develops.

[9] Adorno, *Aesthetic Theory*, 55.

term a certain *fin-de-siècle* mauveness, a radical separation from reality that denies rather than challenges existing reality. But 'aesthetics' as used here contains the ugly as well as the beautiful, and references rather than denies reality while acknowledging an element of domination within it as well as one of emancipation. Again Adorno is eloquent on this point:

> The definition of aesthetics as the theory of the beautiful is so unfruitful because the formal character of the concept of beauty is inadequate to the full content … of the aesthetic. If aesthetics were nothing but a systematic catalogue of whatever is called beautiful, it would give no idea of the life that transpires in the concept of beauty.[10]

And while the unity of the artwork was a highly valued characteristic among all the classical aesthetic writers, contemporary Postmodernist art and contemporary critical theory have constructed an aesthetics of disunity, of incompleteness, and fragmentation; and aesthetic theorists like Walter Benjamin have challenged the notion that what the Romantics called 'organic unity' is the sole form aesthetic productions can manifest. It was Benjamin's friend and intellectual partner Theodor Adorno who most memorably criticized received ideas of the sanctity of the idea of unity when he parodied Hegel's dictum 'The whole is the true' by insisting, 'The whole is the false'.[11]

Unavoidably the term 'aesthetic' in what follows will be a polysemous one, but I want to declare from the outset that the main meanings of the word as I understand it devolve from an expansion of the term beyond its traditional attributes, the purely beautiful and the organically unified. The older classical emphasis on unity tended to create an Apollonian aesthetic, one that imposed order by suppressing or marginalizing the Dionysian, 'dangerous' content of art. Jonathan Dollimore has argued that it is precisely the relatively recent development in critical practice of a hermeneutics which celebrates disunity that has opened the text up to reveal its fissures, its faultlines, its 'other'[12] – and this amounts to a shift from one kind of aesthetics to another. A challenge to this idea of aesthetic unity is basic to my argument here. In fact, one way to think about 'impure aesthetics' is to understand such aesthetics to be possible only in our Postmodernist present, when the various new critical methodologies of our times have permitted

---

[10] Ibid., 50–51.

[11] Theodor Adorno, *Minima Moralia: Reflections from Damaged Life*, trans. E. F. N. Jephcott (London: New Left Books, 1974), 50. Many critics prefer the rendering, 'The whole is the untrue.'

[12] Jonathan Dollimore, 'Art in Time of War: Towards a Contemporary Aesthetic,' in John J. Joughin and Simon Malpas (eds.), *The New Aestheticism* (Manchester University Press, 2003), 36–50; 42–49.

us to think of the artwork as disunified, as constituted by internal clashes of discourse and by the insubordination of repressed materials.[13] In that sense the whole array of new critical approaches of the last thirty years has been based on a shift of aesthetic perception.[14] The 'impure aesthetics' I am elucidating thus can be seen as a part of the 'new aestheticism' defined and exemplified in several varieties in John Joughin and Simon Malpas's 2003 collection of essays, *The New Aestheticism*, including Dollimore's contribution just mentioned. It also has affinities with one strain of a largely American movement that has been called 'the new formalism' and which was recently championed by Marjorie Levinson[15] – a subject to which I will return briefly in the Conclusion.

The aesthetic, it is important to emphasize, can and does often have political effects and intentions; indeed, a major line of aesthetic practice from the Romantics to Baudelaire, through Rimbaud, through critical realism and Modernism, through surrealism up to contemporary writers and artists, takes many of its central concepts and much of its justification from political ideals of several kinds, often revolutionary, socialist ones. Although Theodor Adorno voiced criticism of a certain conception of political art,[16] I would argue that finally Adorno's argument for detached rather than committed art is a variation within this larger political tradition, inasmuch as it affirms a broad socially critical role for all art worthy of the name, while warning against artists' falling into over-simplifying ideologies based on short-sighted commitments. Above all, his is a conception of the aesthetic as always already distanced from the empirical and as such always already an implicit critique of the empirical.

I understand the aesthetic, as a concept, to be a product of modernity;[17] indeed, as Walter Benjamin and Theodor Adorno each argued, it is a concept

---

[13] The idea of an aesthetics of fragmentation, however, goes back at least to Benjamin's theory of the allegory from the 1920s in his *The Origin of German Tragic Drama*, trans. John Osborne (London: New Left Books, 1977), to be discussed in detail below in Chapter 4. However, the theory languished in obscurity until the 1970s.

[14] I argued a version of this thesis in Hugh Grady, *The Modernist Shakespeare: Critical Texts in a Material World* (Oxford: Clarendon, 1991), 204–11.

[15] Marjorie Levinson, 'What is New Formalism?', *PMLA* 122.2 (March 2007), 558–69. In early modern studies its major developers include Heather Dubrow and Mark David Rasmussen. See the Conclusion below for further discussion.

[16] For example, Adorno, *Aesthetic Theory*, 103–5, 123, and 246–48.

[17] This focus on modernity continues a line of argumentation I began in the 1990s on the ideas of modernity and presentism in Shakespeare studies: Hugh Grady, 'Renewing Modernity: Changing Contexts and Contents of a Nearly Invisible Concept', *Shakespeare Quarterly* 50. 3 (Fall 1999), 268–84 and 'Introduction: Shakespeare and Modernity', in Hugh Grady (ed.), *Shakespeare and Modernity: From Early Modern to Millennium* (London: Routledge, 2000), 1–19. More broadly it is continuous with my three previous books in Shakespeare studies, all of which address differing aspects of those issues.

intertwined very closely with the development of commodity-production under capitalism, simultaneously a mirror-image of and a site of resistance to it. Not coincidentally, the reception of Shakespeare, especially in late eighteenth-century Germany, has been intimately entangled within the production of the idea of the aesthetic as well.

To be sure, in one sense the category of the aesthetic seems to be as old as the human race itself. But in other and central ways, it is of recent origin, and one symptom of this relatively recent birth of the aesthetic is that the word itself and several important senses of the term only came into existence in the mid-eighteenth century. The age of Shakespeare, in this connection (among many others), is a very transitional one.

The idea of the aesthetic emerged during the Enlightenment in the same societies which also experienced the economic 'take-off' during which a recognizably capitalist economy, with banks, stock exchanges, and investment funds, had come into being. To note this connection, however, is not the same thing as reducing aesthetics to a simple reflex of a capitalist economy. The idea of the aesthetic has its own history, its own complications – and its own potential for contributing to human liberation. In sketching some of the crucial ideas of what I am calling 'impure aesthetics' – based primarily on concepts from Frankfurt School theorists Theodor Adorno and Walter Benjamin, but including contributions from several other sources as well – I want to look briefly at the development of aesthetic ideas in Western Europe, with special attention to the seminal aesthetic theory of Immanuel Kant who, perhaps surprisingly, remained an important source of aesthetic ideas for Adorno, despite Kant's largely ahistorical approach to the issue. Then I will continue the historical sketch with a brief look at how Hegel and Marx (and very briefly Nietzsche) contributed to aesthetics. The Introduction continues with a sketch of how Walter Benjamin and Theodor Adorno developed several of the ideas of Kant, Hegel, and Marx into the most consequential version of the broad project of 'impure aesthetics' at issue here and then situates this critical approach in contemporary Shakespeare studies.

KANT AND 'PURE' AND 'IMPURE' AESTHETICS

Some forty years after Alexander Baumgarten coined the term 'aesthetics' in his 1750 *Aesthetica*,[18] Immanuel Kant published what would prove to

[18] Baumgarten based the word on the Greek *aisthesthai*, 'to sense', and used it to argue for the idea that sensory perceptions could produce a kind of knowledge or cognition. In the second volume of the work, he extended the term to refer to sensory perception of the beautiful, and this became

be the most consequential and influential formulation of aesthetic theory in his so-called 'Third Critique,' the *Critique of Judgment* (1790) – a work which completed, as he notes in the introduction, the trilogy begun by his *Critique of Pure Reason* (1781) and *Critique of Practical Reason* (1788) – and thus inaugurated a central discourse of modern philosophy.

Because Kant is not often associated with the Marxist tradition of the Frankfurt School, I want to describe Kant's crucial contribution to the idea of the aesthetic and bring out what proved to be essential and what proved misleading in the subsequent formation of impure aesthetics. Both his strengths and his weaknesses are crucial to this subsequent development.

Kant's initial assertions about aesthetic experiences are surprisingly simple, but they entail a raft of complications and ramifications. He is struck by the singularity of what he calls 'this strange ability we have' to make judgments of taste, or aesthetic judgments – the non-verbal decision constituted by our pleasurable reactions to a beautiful object, like a rose.[19] According to Kant, we judge, without any conscious thinking about it, that what we have just perceived is beautiful, through a feeling of pleasure. Unlike Baumgarten and a number of subsequent theorists, Kant insists that there is nothing cognitive or intellectual about this judgment in itself. But, following the British skeptical empiricist David Hume (in this as in many other matters), he asserts that the judgment does have a cognitive implication. The truly beautiful, Kant says, will be universally perceived as such by all human beings if they are not disabled by some prejudice, interest, or handicap. And it is at this point that his argument begins to ramify into various complexities.

Kant argues that we have to distinguish between the truly beautiful (in principle universal) and the merely attractive (a quality of an object that is desirable to us because of some merely subjective interest). This argument constitutes Kant's notorious doctrine of aesthetic disinterest, and he soon finds himself disallowing the 'lower senses' of taste, touch, and smell; sexual or erotic desire; and any merely subjective associations. Furthermore, because the truly aesthetic is non-cognitive for Kant, it must exclude any conceptual dimension or 'teleological' pre-conceptions

---

the meaning that entered into Enlightenment philosophical discourse, in tandem with the other key words of French, British, and German aesthetic Enlightenment writings – 'taste', 'the beautiful', and 'the sublime' – discussions of some of which had pre-dated Baumgarten's coinage.

[19] Immanuel Kant, *Critique of Judgment* (1790), trans. Werner S. Pluhar (Indianapolis, Ind.: Hackett, 1987), § 31; 144. Subsequent references will, like this one, include the number of the section of the treatise from which the quotation or summary is taken as well as the page numbers from this edn.

(by which he means a judgment that something is a perfect specimen of its type – an excellent horse or human figure, for example). Such judgments, he writes, often accompany aesthetic pleasure in the perception of some object, but he insists they are logically separate.[20]

In other words, Kantian aesthetics is 'pure.'[21] Stripped of any erotic or personal charm, its content deemed irrelevant to its aesthetic purity, Kant's aesthetic is primarily a formalism (with the understanding that form involves a peculiar kind of non-utilitarian 'purposiveness'): 'A *pure judgment of taste*', Kant writes, 'is one not influenced by charm or emotion (though these may be connected with a liking for the beautiful), and whose determining basis is therefore merely the purposiveness of the form.'[22] The discussion of the sublime later in the argument complicates this, but Kant argues that because it lacks specific cognitive content and creates a pleasurable aesthetic feeling, the sublime is in the same category as the beautiful.[23]

The great bulk of Kant's ingenious argumentation consists in making the necessary distinctions and exceptions to keep aesthetics pure. To be sure, Kant recurs from time to time to the thesis, announced in his introduction, that aesthetics constitutes a kind of 'bridge' between pure and practical reason, between epistemology and morality. He argues that the beautiful is the 'symbol' of the morally good: in aesthetic pleasure we become conscious of a certain 'ennoblement' or 'elevation' above the mere pleasure of sensations, thus inculcating a kind of humanizing training or discipline analogous to that of the moral order.[24] But these claims of Kant have been among the least satisfactory ones to subsequent aesthetic theorists.[25] It has been Kant's separation of knowledge into three separate categories, rather than his attempt to link them, that has proved most fruitful for subsequent thinkers, notably including Adorno, for whom the autonomy of art from the other 'spheres' gives it much of its critical, negative, power.

For Kant, aesthetic experience is a crucial enough aspect of modern life that it demands to be defined as a third area of human judgment,

---

[20] *Ibid.*, § 2; 45–46 and throughout.
[21] Cf. Pierre Bourdieu, *Distinction: A Social Critique of the Judgement of Taste*, trans. Richard Nice (Cambridge, Mass.: Harvard University Press, 1984), 485–500. However, Bourdieu's critique amounts to a dissolution of the aesthetic into (some of) its social functions and involves no positive appreciation of it.
[22] Kant, *Critique of Judgment*, § 13; 69.
[23] *Ibid.*, § 23; 97–98.
[24] *Ibid.*, § 59; 225–32.
[25] See John J. Joughin and Simon Malpas, 'The New Aestheticism: An Introduction', Joughin and Malpas (eds.), *The New Aestheticism*, 1–19; 10–11.

along with 'pure' and 'practical' (i.e. ethical) reason – each constituting a separate sphere of human interaction with the world. And although Kant tried to link the aesthetic with pure and practical reason, it remains extraordinarily autonomous, uncontaminated by judgments of right or wrong (the matter of practical reason) or of truth or falsity (the matter of pure reason) – and, as noted, in many ways uncontaminated by thought itself.

There is, however, some give in these claims. Although aesthetic judgment in itself is non-cognitive, it can involve what Kant calls 'aesthetic ideas'.[26] Thus, poetry, although it uses language and concepts, is essentially aesthetic because such ideas are 'inner intuitions to which no concept can be completely adequate'. But aesthetic experience leads, crucially for Kant, into a *consciousness* of our cognitive abilities, a kind of awareness of our own powers, and it is pleasurable in itself.[27] This quality in turn allows Kant to say that the aesthetic experience thus harmonizes the whole person,[28] laying the basis for Kant's disciple Friedrich Schiller to claim in his *On the Aesthetic Education of Man* that aesthetics should therefore be at the heart of humanistic education – and subsequently providing to the young Karl Marx a concept to help define an ideal of all-round human development.

Kant's aesthetic theory was thus more than an attempt to conceptualize the specific states of mind associated with the beautiful and the sublime in Enlightenment culture. As Andrew Bowie argues, Kant became taken with the aesthetic in an attempt to 'save' a concept of freedom and of subjecthood from the imperializing encroachments of the developing natural sciences. In effect, Kant's notions of subjectivity and aesthetics could act as a counter to the agenda of empirical science, which threatened to turn nature and human subjectivity into mechanistic, rule-bound assemblages of serialized empirical data. Aesthetic judgment was fascinating to Kant because it operated outside of a narrow, rule-bound rationality and because it intuited a unity and a teleology within the object – say a poem or painting – for which there was no purely *cognitive* ground.[29] It thus appeared to be a kind of non-cognitive knowledge, and this is a concept of art which will prove central to both Benjamin and Adorno.

The idea of non-cognitive knowledge in turn raised the issue for Kant as to whether this unifying and teleological principle had the status of the transcendental *a priori* he had famously defined in *The Critique of Pure*

---

[26] Kant, *Critique of Judgment*, § 49; 182.   [27] *Ibid.*, § 9; 61–64.

[28] *Ibid.*, § 59; 228–30.

[29] Andrew Bowie, *Aesthetics and Subjectivity: From Kant to Nietzsche*, 2nd edn. (Manchester University Press, 1990, 2003), 24–32.

Reason. Kant stopped short of granting aesthetic judgement this status – as would the Frankfurt School theorists. But Romantic artist–philosophers would go beyond Kant in this, making the (aesthetic) Imagination the most truth-revealing mental capacity. But Kant himself argued that '(Independent) natural beauty carries with it a purposiveness in its form, by which the object seems as it were pre-determined for our power of judgment, so that this beauty constitutes in itself an object of our liking.'[30] That is, the beautiful creates a delightful 'as if', a premonition which reason cannot confirm, of the permeability of nature to human perception, as if the world had achieved its end in being apprehended as beautiful by us. Aesthetic judgment, then, constitutes a wholly fictive realm where natural objects are humanized and whereby human perception is made completely adequate to noumena. Of course Kantian transcendental philosophy was founded on the notion that the thing-in-itself remained categorically beyond the realm of human perception. Kant's 'as it were' is crucial in conveying this fictionality of the aesthetic.

This claim of Kant's is an important one, and one easily misconstrued. Terry Eagleton, for example, has argued in reference to this passage that this notion turns Kant's aesthetics into 'the very essence of the ideological'. Even though Kant's premise is self-consciously figurative or fictional, Eagleton says, 'it is the kind of heuristic fiction which permits us a sense of purposiveness, centredness, and significance, and thus one which is of the very essence of the ideological'.[31]

But because in the Marxist tradition the concept of ideology always raises suspicion, implying a 'false consciousness' produced under the influence of power and interest, Eagleton's use of it in this context disables him from seeing the utopian quality of Kant's description central to Frankfurt School aesthetics. Precisely because modern cultures fragment human experience into separate spheres and privilege individuality over collectivity, both ideology and the aesthetic come into existence in the strict sense only within modernity. But perhaps what is most germane here is the way Eagleton passes over the very *fictionality* of Kantian aesthetic perception, its counter-factual status. What kind of ideology, we might ask, is held permanently suspended, to be tentative, hypothetical – to be enjoyed and played with rather than uncritically assumed and identified with? Kant's notions of fictionality and playfulness are among the most valuable aspects of his seminal theory, still valuable precisely in

---

[30] Kant, *Critique of Judgment*, § 23; 98–99.
[31] Terry Eagleton, *The Ideology of the Aesthetic* (Oxford: Blackwell, 1990), 84–85.

this emphasis on beauty as an idealized representation of the intimate link between the human and the natural. It is this quality, in fact, which makes Kant an important source for 'green criticism' or Ecocriticism – a topic to which I will return briefly in the next chapter and in the Conclusion. It is possible to move this insight into a concept of the utopian, making art not a model for a really existing human world, but instead an idealized space from which the real can be measured and judged, not least in terms of humanity's relation to the natural world.

Kant's theory is considered by most historians of aesthetic discourse to be of founding importance. It is, wrote Eva Schaper, a contribution without which 'aesthetics would not exist in its modern form'.[32] Despite the earlier work of Baumgarten, Leibniz, Shaftesbury, Hutcheson, Burke, and Hume, among others, Kant's is the first work to incorporate aesthetics into a larger philosophical system, and it is almost every aesthetic theorist's starting point because it raised the issues and defined the terms still discussed today.

But for all that, it is also important to note that Kantian aesthetics today cannot stand without considerable supplementation. The doctrine of aesthetic disinterestedness, so crucial to Kant's entire theoretical edifice, has in particular struck any number of twentieth-century commentators as indefensible.[33] The elaborate attempts to keep aesthetic experience non-cognitive by separating it from 'teleological judgments' and by insisting that only form is truly aesthetic, with content a complete irrelevancy, found a formidable critic in G. W. F. Hegel and several subsequent theorists.[34] In our own time, it seems, only 'impure' aesthetics are viable, and Kant's achievement seems in many ways one of having raised the issues which others have had both to criticize and develop. As Fredric Jameson wrote, generalizing beyond Kant to the entire discipline of philosophical aesthetics of which Kant's writings are a formative discourse, 'what gives

---

[32] Eva Schaper, 'Taste, Sublimity, and Genius: The Aesthetics of Nature and Art', in P. Guyer (ed.), *The Cambridge Companion to Kant* (Cambridge University Press, 1982), 79; quoted in David E. Cooper, *Aesthetics: The Classic Readings* (Oxford: Blackwell, 1997), 94.

[33] Adorno, *Aesthetic Theory*, 10–11; Bourdieu, *Distinction*, 485–500; John Dewey, *Art as Experience* (New York: Minton Balch, 1934), 252; Henri Lefebvre, *Critique of Everyday Life* (1947), trans. John Moore (London: Verso, 1991), 138–39. I am indebted to Isobel Armstrong, *The Radical Aesthetic* (Oxford: Blackwell, 2000), n. 4, 81, for this collection of Kant critics, to which Armstrong, 32–37, should herself be added.

[34] This point is well developed in Alan Singer, *Aesthetic Reason: Artworks and the Deliberative Ethos* (University Park, Penn.: Pennsylvania State University Press, 2003), 5. Aesthetic theorists, Singer notes, can be divided into two camps: those who view the aesthetic as cognitive or with cognitive dimensions (Baumgarten, Herder, Hegel, Fichte, and Adorno) and those who view the aesthetic as essentially non-cognitive (neo-Platonists, Shaftesbury, Francis Hutcheson, and, ultimately, Kant).

these texts [of philosophical aesthetics] their power, from Kant's *Third Critique* all the way to Adorno's *Aesthetic Theory* – is the way in which they blow up the field in which they sought to work, in which they undermine the very framework which justified their project'.[35]

A case in point is Kant's utopian notion of the aesthetic as a realm of shared human understanding and as a harbinger of a possible human reconciliation with the natural – a doctrine which emerges in our era as a potent protest against the social alienation and domination of the natural world with which we now live. And Kant's understanding that post-Cartesian philosophy's split between subject and object has necessitated a differentiation of culture into the three autonomous spheres of science, ethics, and art remains fundamental.[36]

The utopian dimension of Kant was grasped and developed by the poet–philosopher Friedrich Schiller, whose *On the Aesthetic Education of Man* is a bridge, first to Hegel's and then to Marx's critiques of Kantian aesthetics and thus contributes indirectly but importantly to the Frankfurt School's version of impure aesthetics. While Schiller declared himself to be merely a faithful disciple of Kantian aesthetics,[37] he inserted Kant's aesthetic realm into a historical-ethical theory of human development through three sequential but separate stages of interaction with the realm of nature. He charts a process of increasing humanization and justice, a progress of humanity from a merely instrumental relationship to nature, to a recognition of its beauty, to a final stage of morality, or 'the sacred realm of laws', through which humanity will achieve justice and harmony. This final, culminating stage is, however, reached only by going through the *Bildung* of aesthetic education, a phase necessary to overcome the bonds of the merely physical relation to nature of the first stage.[38]

[35] Fredric Jameson, *The Cultural Turn: Selected Writings on the Postmodern, 1983–1998* (London: Verso, 1998), 101.
[36] The view that the three Kantian domains of the scientific, the ethical, and the aesthetic are fundamental to modernity is a constant of Frankfurt School theory from Horkheimer and Adorno through Habermas; see Jürgen Habermas, *Knowledge and Human Interests*, trans. Jeremy Shapiro (Boston: Beacon, 1971) and Jürgen Habermas, *The Philosophical Discourses of Modernity*, trans. Frederick Lawrence (Cambridge, Mass.: MIT Press, 1987).
[37] See Paul de Man, *The Rhetoric of Romanticism* (New York: Columbia University Press, 1984), 283–90, for an analysis emphasizing what de Man sees as Schiller's misreading of Kant.
[38] Friedrich Schiller, *On the Aesthetic Education of Man: In a Series of Letters*, trans. Reginald Snell (New York: Ungar, 1965), Letter 25; 119–23.

Schiller thus constructed one of the clearest arguments for the place of aesthetics in a world of increasing rationalization and the colonization of nature by technology: it is an alternative both to instrumental reason and to capitalist commodification. This is the context in which the idea of the aesthetic takes on its richest meaning for us, and it is a context of actualized modernity. For Schiller the aesthetic heals the split of the original subject–object divide because it involves both 'realms', that of the sensual, and that of the intellectual.[39] In addition it unites society by appealing to what is common to all, creating a realm of equality which can serve as a political model.[40] Schiller's highly Romantic claims for the educative value of aesthetic experience have been called into question numerous times, not least by the glaring case of cultivated Nazi supervisors of genocide. But his insights into an aesthetic mode of perception with the capability of superseding a merely instrumental approach to nature and existence will be taken up and developed by others and remains a crucial notion for our own times.

AESTHETICS IN HEGEL AND MARX

Both Hegel and Marx were attentive readers of Schiller's utopian and Romantic development of Kant, and they both internalized and further developed the new attitudes toward the aesthetic that had developed in the wake of the new paradigm of organic unity. Following up on earlier ideas of Herder, both Hegel and Marx inserted the individual, organic artwork in a larger historical context, so that the work's organic form was conceptualized as imprinted by the historical moment of the artwork's origins. Hegel found Schiller's historicizing impulse a decisive move forward from Kant's unhistoricized formalism, and he didn't hesitate to re-think the aesthetic completely in terms of his own historicizing system. In effect, he conceptualized art through a focus on the artwork itself rather than on the state of mind of its perceivers as Kant had done. For Hegel art was one of the three chief means, along with religion and philosophy, through which *Geist* (Mind/Spirit) articulated itself over a long series of dialectical developments in history. Since the content or subject matter of art could be nothing but *Geist* in some of its aspects – 'art makes everyone of its productions into a thousand-eyed Argus, whereby the inner soul and spirit is seen at every point', he writes[41] – content was

---

[39] *Ibid.*, Letter 27; 135, 138.   [40] *Ibid.*, Letter 27; 140.
[41] G.W.F. Hegel, *Aesthetics: Lectures on Fine Art*, Vol. I, trans. T. M. Knox (Oxford: Clarendon, 1975), 153–54.

an essential part of the aesthetic for Hegel – again unlike Kant. The history of art was, in large scale, a history of *Geist*'s attempts to discover forms adequate to contain and express itself.[42] Hegel thus laid the basis for both the history of ideas and art history, and in 1860 one of his many disciples (the German university system of the mid-nineteenth century was dominated by Hegelianism), the Swiss-born Jacob Burckhardt, made an epochal contribution to both these fields in his *The Civilization of the Renaissance in Italy*, supplying cultural categories which have been essential to the academic study of literature and culture ever since, for better or worse.[43]

The young Karl Marx, another product of the German Hegelian educational apparatus, having become convinced that only a radical socio-economic re-settlement could solve humanity's problems, famously 'inverted' Hegelianism, re-conceptualizing history in terms of material rather than spiritual–mental development – albeit leaving his numerous followers the problem of how then precisely to define the relation of the material and the intellectual.[44] Aesthetics was never a priority for Marx – he day-dreamed over the years of a book on Balzac which he never attempted. Nevertheless there was something aesthetic about his philosophical project from the beginning.[45] 'The world has long dreamed of something of which it only has to become conscious in order to possess it in actuality,' he wrote in a letter to his friend Arnold Ruge.[46] As noted briefly above, when in the *1844 Manuscripts* he needed a standard against which to measure the alienated labor of the nineteenth-century proletariat, it was, implicitly but recognizably, to Schiller's aesthetic that Marx turned. For Marx, labor in its essence was continuous with art but became distorted by the private-property system, with its differentiation of capital and labor, and of mental labor from physical. In the terms of the young Marx, the laborer under capitalism was estranged, both from her own labor process and

---

[42] *Ibid.*, 1–14.

[43] Jacob Burckhardt, *The Civilization of the Renaissance in Italy* (1860), trans. S. G. C. Middlemore (Harmondsworth: Penguin, 1990).

[44] The famous Marxian metaphor describing an economic 'base' over which was erected a 'super-structure' of law, politics, and culture in Karl Marx, *A Contribution to the Critique of Political Economy*, ed. Maurice Dobb, trans. S. W. Ryazanskaya (New York: International, 1970), 20–21, has been in the center of a multi-generational contest of interpretation. As Jameson, writes: '"base and superstructure" is not really a model, but a starting point and a problem', *The Cultural Turn*, 47. One of the best summaries and critiques of the terms is provided in Raymond Williams, *Marxism and Literature* (Oxford University Press, 1977), 75–82.

[45] Cf. Edmund Wilson, *To the Finland Station: A Study in the Writing and Acting of History* (1940; repr. Garden City, NY: Doubleday, 1953), 111–19; and Solomon (ed.), *Marxism and Art*, 3–21.

[46] 'Marx: the Utopian Reflex,' from Letter to Arnold Ruge, in Solomon (ed.), *Marxism and Art*, 58.

from the product of her labor.[47] One corollary of this, which Marx never spelled out, but which subsequent developers have emphasized, is that one of the chief forms of surviving unalienated labor was art – now, however, a highly specialized and differentiated activity that was also a commodity on the market in its own right.[48] Thus, Marx in effect borrowed Hegel's view of art as an expression of human cultures evolving over time, but unlike Hegel he emphasized its materiality and its links to labor.

Through these arguments, Marx and his later developers established a central connection between the aesthetic and the political. Aesthetic practice contains within it elements of human potentiality which are repressed within capitalist modernity. Aesthetic theory thus helps set an agenda for liberation.[49]

As mentioned, Marx himself really never developed these insights into a systematic aesthetic theory. That task was left to subsequent generations, and the results have been mixed indeed. Nowhere, perhaps, was the theoretical and spiritual poverty of Leninist and Stalinist Marxism more on view than in the Communist movement's dogmatic theory and tyrannical practice in regards to art and culture, the dissenting – or extenuating – works within this tradition of Trotsky and the older Lukács notwithstanding. Fortunately in this regard, a constellation of 'unorthodox' Marxists (a partial list would include Mikhail Bakhtin and his circle, Antonio Gramsci, the French surrealists, Bertolt Brecht, the Frankfurt School and its successors) has provided a rich counter-current, one drawing from a larger dissident archive of writings, most significantly from Nietzsche and Freud, but also from Kant, Hegel, and the German philosophical tradition generally. For this variegated tradition, art serves as both a collective memory of older stages of human history and a collective prophecy for newer ones, beyond regimes of pure instrumentality. In addition, art's sensuousness and playfulness allow it to interrogate the practices of the present and its iron cages of distorting ideology. Art's very playfulness allows it to be a means of political, social, and cultural critique.

[47] Karl Marx, *The Economic and Philosophic Manuscripts of 1844*, ed. Dirk Struik, trans. Martin Milligan (New York: International, 1964), 106–19.

[48] While Marx stops short of making this explicit, any number of his followers in subsequent generations did so; see Lifshitz, *The Philosophy of Art of Karl Marx*; Walter Benjamin, *The Arcades Project*, ed. Rolf Tiedemann, trans. Howard Eiland and Kevin McLaughlin (Cambridge, Mass.: Belknap, 1999), 651–70; Williams, *Marxism and Literature*, 151–57; and Adorno, *Aesthetic Theory*, 16–45.

[49] Bowie, *Aesthetics and Subjectivity*, 85–88, shows that the linkage of aesthetics and politics was a major theme of early German Romanticism, particularly for Friedrich Hölderin (1770–1843).

The archive of writings on the aesthetic of the last 250 years has to be approached critically, as I have tried to indicate. A useful start in this critique was produced by Terry Eagleton over a decade ago in his *The Ideology of the Aesthetic*, but, as my remarks above on Eagleton's interpretation of Kant might suggest, his is hardly the last word on the subject. A more positive, more detailed, better informed and altogether more useful approach to the same set of issues – and a key text for British New Aestheticism – is the revised edition of Andrew Bowie's *Aesthetics and Subjectivity*, cited previously – the new edition, in fact, is strongly endorsed by Eagleton in a blurb on the book's dust-jacket. Bowie shows that far more than an ideological gap-filler, the post-Kantian aesthetic responds to real problems in the philosophical texts of a Western world still attempting to come to terms with the collapse of traditional, theocentric worldviews in the Renaissance and Enlightenment. In addition, as he argues convincingly, recent poststructuralist and Postmodernist approaches to these problems have re-invented without surpassing insights from the discussion of the aesthetic within German philosophy from Kant to Nietzsche. In the light of Bowie's argument, then, it is necessary to qualify the claim of Isobel Armstrong that Derrida and de Man in effect have cleared the field of literary and cultural studies of many false starts through their related critiques of Romantic notions of the aesthetic as a privileged mode of knowledge of the unity of Self and Other.[50] Instead, it appears, what they have cleared are over-simplifying and misleading characterizations of important notions of Romantic aesthetics – albeit, many of the 'received' ones.[51]

Thus, at the same time as we take another look at Kantian aesthetic theory, it is important as well to confront this theory with elements of Hegel's and Marx's critique of Kant (explicit and implicit). One such decisive intervention is the Hegelian idea that aesthetics is a historically variable concept, with a history (as Burckhardt in particular argued) implicated in the production of modernity. A second is Marx's theory of the commodity, which later Marx-indebted theorists have linked to artworks through an often hidden interaction or dialectic. And finally, Nietzsche will provide an important epistemological afterword to this discussion.

---

[50] Armstrong, *The Radical Aesthetic*, 56.
[51] In addition to Bowie, *Aesthetics and Subjectivity*, see also Andrew Bowie, *From Romanticism to Critical Theory: The Philosophy of German Literary Theory* (London: Routledge, 1997) for an argument that, far from having been disabled by deconstruction, German Romantics like Novalis and Schlegel shared several of deconstruction's ideas and had prescient insights into its problems. Bowie sees them as beginning a tradition culminating in Theodor Adorno's aesthetic theory that offers the best hope of moving forward after deconstruction.

AESTHETICS, MODERNITY, AND THE CIRCULATION
OF COMMODITIES

The rise of the aesthetic depended on some of the basic conceptual differentiations comprising intellectual modernity, particularly that between subject and object. Kant articulated the most influential conceptualization of the barrier between the human subject and the external world of noumena – or between external reality and human perception – in his 1781 *Critique of Pure Reason*. This was, however, a classic instance of the coming of the owl of Minerva at twilight. Descartes, as the traditional narrative goes, had founded modern philosophy a century and a half earlier with his thought-experiment of a radically isolated human subject seeking to confirm objective, external reality. Literary and art historians have traced the subject–object split earlier still, whether to the arrival of 'objective' perspectivism of Italian Renaissance painting, or to the Petrarchan lyric's celebration of subjectivity in itself; to Machiavelli's new instrumental, value-free political analysis; or Galileo's epochal declaration of the autonomy of scientific research from religious authority. For Christopher Marlowe, William Shakespeare, John Donne, Francis Bacon, and any number of their peers, the world came to be conceptualized as a fragmented, objectified, alien realm indifferent or hostile to a separate human subjectivity which was accordingly immersed in a crisis of meaning and self-definition. Indeed in a long list of English Renaissance masterpieces such as *Dr. Faustus, 1 and 2 Tamburlaine, 1 and 2 Henry IV, Hamlet, Othello, King Lear*, and so on (it would be difficult to know which of Shakespeare's works from 1595 on could safely be excluded from such a list); in Donne's great love, religious, and satirical poems; and more blithely and optimistically, in Bacon's world-opening perspectives for scientific rationality – the spiritual crisis of an alienated subject in a hostile world is the main subject matter, as it continues to be for much of the art and culture of our times, and for the epoch in between. The differentiation of culture into separate, autonomous spheres, codified in Kant's three great critiques but established in Western art, literature, and philosophy well before Kant's time, is the enabling Copernican revolution for the complex intellectual condition we have (rather blandly) called 'modernity'. The culture of modernity is differentiated and fragmented, not a unitary culture,[52] and this differentiation is a crucial pre-condition for the idea of the aesthetic to emerge.

---

[52] I am drawing here from a number of Frankfurt School writings on this theme, notably Max Horkheimer and Theodor Adorno, *Dialectic of Enlightenment: Philosophical Fragments* (1944),

This is a point which, as I have argued elsewhere, was not always well appreciated in the synthesis of Foucault and Althusser which dominated the first formulations of cultural materialism in the eighties.[53] It was instead a contribution from the early sociology of Max Weber, deepened and radicalized by Frankfurt School members and affiliates Adorno, Horkheimer, Benjamin, and Marcuse, and further developed by Jürgen Habermas and his followers. It defines a culture with a permanent crisis of meaning, and it is this crisis which is the ground from which the modern concept of the aesthetic emerges.[54]

To understand this last point, we might consider, for example, the culminating canto of Dante's *Commedia*, that last revelation of the Celestial Rose and of the love which moves the stars. It is the completion of the revelation that has accumulated in our long journey through the three spiritual realms of the cosmos, with their web of connections to the minutia of secular life. From a modern perspective, we have to say, it is an aesthetic vision of a totality, a rounded, meaningful, and teleological vision of a world saturated with divine love – though one not without its own moments of self-negation and dissonance. But such a characterization would never have occurred to Dante or those sharing his vision, precisely because its playfulness and artificiality serve, as Dante put it in reference to his love for Beatrice in the *Vita Nuova*, as 'a screen to the truth'.[55] In this context, the term 'aesthetic' could only diminish the visionary claim asserted throughout the work. Even if we were to think of Western pre-modern writings on less ambitious works of the ancient or medieval world – say Plautine comedy or medieval romances – we would find them being conceptualized either as profane vanities or, as in Aristotle's much-quoted definition, 'imitations of nature' serving recreational, political, and/or moral purposes. We might find premonitions of the modern concept of the aesthetic, but nowhere any definitive elaboration. The poetry of pre-modern cultures is aesthetic for us, but not for the members of the cultures which produced it.

ed. Gunzelin Schmid Noerr, trans. Edmund Jephcott (Stanford, Calif.: Stanford University Press, 2002); and Jürgen Habermas, *Society and Human Interests*, trans. Jeremy Shapiro (Boston, Mass.: Beacon, 1971). For my attempt to map these differentiations onto the developing culture of the early modern, see Hugh Grady, *Shakespeare, Machiavelli, and Montaigne: Power and Subjectivity from 'Richard II' to 'Hamlet'* (Oxford University Press, 2002), esp. 109–25.

[53] Hugh Grady, 'On the Need for a Differentiated Theory of Subjectivity,' in John J. Joughin (ed.), *Shakespeare and Philosophy* (London: Routledge, 2000), 34–50.

[54] Cf. Mark Robson, 'Defending Poetry, or, Is There an Early Modern Aesthetic?', in Joughin and Malpas (eds.), *The New Aestheticism*, 119–30.

[55] Dante Alighieri, *La Vita Nuova*, trans. D. G. Rossetti, *The Portable Dante*, ed. Paolo Milano (New York: Viking, 1947), 552.

Another way to think about this differentiation is to consider the impact on cultural production of a growing commodity culture, culminating in a full-fledged, self-reproducing capitalist economic system in the eighteenth century. Fredric Jameson has recently suggested a thought-experiment of testing how often the term 'modernity' could be adequately replaced by the term 'capitalist' as a way of underlining the profound impact of capitalism on modernity.[56] However, the very earliest portions of modernity, including the age of Shakespeare, pose the greatest problem for the success of this experiment, inasmuch as anything like a modern capitalist economic system, with banks, free capital flow, and industrial manufacture, is at best embryonic until well into the eighteenth century.

There was, however, a thriving mercantile economy dealing both in the traditional cloth trade and in the sale of numerous new imported items.[57] The circulation of commodities on a broad scale has social consequences of its own. As Karl Marx famously wrote, the commodity 'appears, at first sight, a very trivial thing, and easily understood. Its analysis shows that it is, in reality, a very queer thing, abounding in metaphysical subtleties and theological niceties.'[58] The circulation of commodities in a money economy creates a vast social network and a universalizing system of valuation. The concrete, sensuous qualities of the commodity are subordinated to its monetary value. Things that have little or no intrinsic connection – say books and iron ore – are made equivalent by the magical abstraction of exchanging them for the quantities of abstract exchange-value symbolized by money. The concrete human labor which had produced the commodity is occluded by its monetary or exchange-value. A relation between people, Marx writes, is expressed fantastically as a relation between things. Commodities become fetishes or idols, worshiped by a humanity which had itself created their value.[59] Or as Walter Benjamin put it, everything in the world becomes allegorical, empty symbols of monetary value and the vast human network that creates it.[60]

---

[56] Jameson, *A Singular Modernity*, 215.
[57] See Jean-Christophe Agnew, *Worlds Apart: The Market and the Theater in Anglo-American Thought, 1550–1750* (Cambridge University Press, 1986); Douglas Bruster, *Drama and the Market in the Age of Shakespeare* (Cambridge University Press, 1992) and Jonathan Gil Harris, *Sick Economies: Drama, Mercantilism and Disease in Shakespeare's England* (Philadelphia, Pa.: University of Pennsylvania Press, 2004).
[58] Karl Marx, *Capital: A Critique of Political Economy*, Vol. 1, ed. Frederick Engels, trans. Samuel Moore and Edward Aveling (New York: International, 1967), 71.
[59] *Ibid.*, 71–83.
[60] Walter Benjamin, 'Paris, Capital of the Nineteenth Century: Exposé "of 1939"', in Benjamin, *The Arcades Project*, 22.

One of the most consequential characteristics of money's abstract quality is its bottomlessness, its unlimitedness. You cannot have too much of it. This is a quality already evident in the age of Shakespeare and Jonson, but even more apparent as the medium of money has evolved over time into the fantastic panoply of financial instruments of our own day. And once this unlimitability is established, a never-ending process of capital-formation becomes possible. The difference between ordinary money and capital for Marx is really only a reversal of ends and means. Ordinary money is obtained from the sale of commodities – one's labor-power or its products – in order to use the money to obtain other commodities essential to life, like food, shelter, and clothing. Capital can be said to exist when money is exchanged for commodities in order to produce more money.[61] Capital is that thing which Aristotle and a whole religious tradition condemned as unnatural, the perversion of money into a pseudo-living-thing able to reproduce itself.[62] As a result, there is no limit to capitalist expansion. It is a self-perpetuating, autonomous system which is also autotelic – that is, capital is an end in itself, ultimately serving no higher purpose than its own economic reproduction and expansion.

For Benjamin, the simultaneous emergence of the idea of the autonomous artwork – a quality eventually crystallized in the nineteenth-century slogan of art for art's sake – in the same era, and in the same societies which saw the development of an autonomous commodity economy, is more than coincidental. In order to see the context for this issue, it is necessary to return to the schema of modernity I was outlining earlier. As noted, if we look to understand some of the causes for the split between subject and object characteristic of the cultures of European early modernity, there are several well-known possibilities and likely contributing causes. For example, since Hegel and Weber, the Protestant Reformation has been seen as helping to create a new kind of subjectivity with its emphasis on the soul's individual, unmediated relation to God and on the individual interpretation of Scripture. The development of the modern scientific method objectified nature in a new way. The discovery of America challenged received notions of history and fostered new objectifying relations between Europeans and newly subjected races. But the development of mercantile capitalism, particularly in England, as it sought to catch up with and

[61] Marx, *Capital*, Vol 1, 146–55.
[62] This basic insight of Marx has been very consequentially and concretely applied to a variety of works of early modern English literature by David Hawkes in two recent books: *Idols of the Marketplace: Idolatry and Commodity Fetishism in English Literature, 1580–1680* (New York: Palgrave, 2001) and *The Faust Myth: Religion and the Rise of Representation* (New York: Palgrave, 2006).

surpass Italian city-state commerce and hold its own in the conquest of
new lands in the New World, is not the least among them.[63] Commerce
contributes to the decentering of European culture from its medieval unified worldview by separating the accumulation of wealth from traditional
feudal power structures and from traditional morality.

We don't have to re-construct this development for Shakespeare's age.
We only have to read *The Jew of Malta*, *The Merchant of Venice*, *Timon of
Athens*, *The Alchemist*, or *Volpone* to see this theme in florid exhibition.
Mercantile capitalism was perceived as corrosive of social solidarity and
social morality. Along with the Machiavellianism of power politics, it was
seen as the great corruptor of the life of the commonwealth.

What all of these long-term social processes constituting 'modernity'
had in common was the quality of *reification* – the creation of self-
perpetuating systems functioning according to their own laws
independently of the consciousness of their participants, who tend to see
power and commerce individually, not systemically, and so remain largely
unaware of the way the system functions to reproduce itself regardless
of who wins and who loses.[64] As more and more areas of traditional life
are affected or absorbed by power and commerce, daily life seems to be
drained of meaning. Things – and other people – become objects for the
pursuit of wealth and power; individuals become obsessed with their own
accumulation of wealth and power without regard for the social polity of
which they are a part – or they were immiserated, cut off from traditional
feudal agriculture and its support networks, becoming atomistic and
alienated subjects in a reified world. The Kantian split between meaning-
giving subjectivity and malleable objects develops.

As eighteenth-century philosophers worked to conceptualize, directly
and indirectly, these new social realities, they began to be taken by
the odd case of aesthetic pleasure. Such pleasure seemed to be merely
subjective, but it also seemed to be universal. Where could it be placed
in a world divided radically between subjects and objects? Was art
a commodity, to be measured by the exchange-value it acquired in
the market place? Or was it an anti-commodity, one that defied the
abstractness and cultural leveling of the market and gave access to a
more authentic, genuine realm of market-transcendent values? Could it

---

[63] An excellent updating and discussion of these multiple, interacting contributions to modernity
is Stuart Hall, Introduction to 'Formations of Modernity', in Stuart Hall, David Held, Don
Hubert, and Kenneth Thompson (eds.), *Modernity: An Introduction to Modern Societies* (Oxford:
Blackwell, 1996), 3–18.

[64] Hugh Grady, *Shakespeare's Universal Wolf: Studies in Early Modern Reification* (Oxford:
Clarendon, 1996), 26–57 and throughout.

produce knowledge of this external world and simultaneously begin to give it meaning? Could it function in the new, reified world somehow to bring back into modernity the sense of meaning that was characteristic of pre-modern culture? All of these possibilities began to be discussed in an unsystematic way in the new field of aesthetics – and to be enacted directly within the re-functioned cultural practices of painting, music, and poetry. The aesthetic was autonomous, fictive, merely imaginary, but it seemed to give access to meanings and secrets that objectifying, instrumental thought could not dream of. It was a new kind of religion for a decentered, secular world.

Of course religion proper thrived in the early modern as well. The documents and history of the Protestant Reformation and Catholic Counter-Reformation provide an impressive record of earnest, life-altering reconfigurations of religious life which provided havens, meaning-enabling worldviews, for millions. But this earnest striving also produced unprecedented warfare and ferocity in sixteenth-century France and the Netherlands and in seventeenth-century England and *Mitteleuropa*. When the victors consolidated the religious situation in Europe in the second half of the seventeenth century, it began to appear that art, not any specific confessional faith, would have to provide a new cultural community for Europe. The stage was set for the Enlightenment definition of the aesthetic in a religiously divided but relatively tolerant Europe. In this context, Kant belatedly argues that three separate realms of public rationality were required – scientific-philosophical, practical or ethical, and aesthetic. Religion was – in principle, for 'advanced' thinkers – now a private matter.

Thus, the idea of the aesthetic, like all our concepts, is a social construct, a signifier whose signified derives from a series of intricate networks, within itself, and with the fragmented world of a complex new, 'modern' society. For these reasons, I am arguing, the aesthetic is intrinsically 'impure' – it is a place-holder for what is repressed elsewhere in the system; it develops as an autonomous practice but participates in the market economy, the social-status system, the political world, the religious communities, and private life. In its pre-Freudian phase, at any rate, while it is a form or container of erotic energy, it tends to sublimate libido in a way that often disguises libido's imprint. And it is, as several theorists have insisted, intimately connected to human mortality, to mourning and to a longing for death.

But let Nietzsche have the last comment on the construction of the aesthetic as a category within modernity. In his very earliest work, *The*

Birth of Tragedy, he focused on the important relation of the aesthetic to rationality, defining its two opposing tendencies as the Apollonian and the Dionysian, both crucial aspects of the aesthetic perfectly balanced in the tragedies of Aeschylus and Sophocles. But as the argument develops it becomes clear that in important ways the Apollonian – the mode of order, logic, rationality, and visual images – is an illusion while the Dionysian – the surging passion, the will-to-power at the heart of Being – is the reality.[65] And this is an insight that has been picked up and ramified in the Postmodernist mentality which provides an important facet of the version of impure aesthetics I am working with here. Art in this conception is a revelation of Dionysian forces uneasily contained in Apollonian forms.

THE ORIGIN OF WESTERN MARXISM: LUKÁCS, BENJAMIN, AND ADORNO

Impure aesthetics in the sense I am defining it here is primarily a product of 'Western Marxism', above all of Walter Benjamin and Theodor Adorno (some of whose key themes I have just been summarizing). However, there are many other theorists relevant to it – like Mikhail Bakhtin, Raymond Williams, Herbert Marcuse, Georges Bataille, Jacques Derrida, and Fredric Jameson – who have made important contributions to its development, as well as a number of contemporary critics exploring its application to contemporary scholarship.[66] Benjamin was most notable for defining the new aesthetic paradigm of early modern drama (see Chapter 4 below) and for his later charting of the intricate choreography enacted by those unlikely partners, the work of art and the commodity. Adorno explored this and also issues of art's utopian and truth-asserting functions in an increasingly bleak world of almost complete colonization of the lifeworld by commodification.

While anything like a full treatment of the theoretical contributions of these theorists of impure aesthetics is far beyond the scope of this book, a short summary of the content and development of the theory is in order to orient readers unfamiliar with them. I described briefly above some of the aesthetic implications of Marx's philosophical and economic writings,

---

[65] Friedrich Nietzsche, *The Birth of Tragedy*, trans. Francis Golffing in Friedrich Nietzsche, *The Birth of Tragedy and The Genealogy of Morals*, trans. Francis Golffing (New York: Anchor, 1956).
[66] In Shakespeare studies the work of Kiernan Ryan has long advocated greater use of Frankfurt School concepts, particularly the idea of the utopian, in a number of works. For a summary statement of his positions, see Kiernan Ryan, *Shakespeare*, 3rd edn. (New York: Palgrave, 2002).

noting how they remained undeveloped insights for the most part. In the nineteenth century figures like William Morris, Antonio Labriola, Franz Mehring, and Karl Kautsky all attempted to push forward varying aspects of Marx's ideas relevant to theories of art and literature.[67] But a cornerstone in the long-range project was laid early in the twentieth-century by the remarkable Hungarian philosopher and critic Georg Lukács in a series of works charting his evolution from a Hegelian theorist of literature to a Marxist theorist and critic. The older Lukács's long and depressing series of theoretical tap-dances in response to changing Communist 'lines' on art and literature should not be allowed to obscure his seminal initial work. Although there is value in his later discussions of European realism (alongside an untenable anti-Modernism), the Lukács who today matters most is the Lukács who wrote the 'Hegelian' *Soul and Form* and *Theory of the Novel*, and then his 'Marxist' *History and Class Consciousness*, which is in many ways the founding document of Western Marxism. These works matter in the context of the present study because they were intellectually formative for both Benjamin and Adorno, each of whom traveled a similar path that combined aspects of Hegelian and Marxist philosophy into previously uncharted territory. However much each moved beyond Lukács's specific positions, his early work was a milestone example of how to move the legacy of Marx out of the orbit of the bureaucratic, dogmatic, and undemocratic Party organizations that attempted to control it. And Lukács showed as well how much of Hegel was still implicit in Marx, especially in matters of aesthetic theory. As Benjamin was to say later of his own early Plato- and Hegel-influenced theory of the allegory, all that was necessary to re-contextualize it in a more Marxist frame was to connect the 'emptiness' of allegorical space to the rise of the commodity form (see below, Chapter 4).

In *Soul and Form* Lukács turned to issues of literary form connected to ideas of collective historical development – specifically, in the essay most relevant here, to the case of tragic form. In *The Theory of the Novel*, he used the theory of tragedy to help develop a new approach to distinguishing the modern novel from the ancient and medieval epic tradition. In both works he developed the essentially Hegelian idea that literature manifested in its inner form the specific problem of meaning endemic to the age in which it was created. Using Hegelian methods, Lukács constructed ideal types of literary forms rather than empirical examples, though he

[67] See Solomon (ed.), *Marxism and Art*, 3–159, both for a generous sampling of remarks on art by Marx and Engels and excerpts from the works of their first interpreters.

thought the Homeric poems embodied the epic's type well and singled out *Don Quixote* and a few others for the case of the novel. For Lukács what mattered was the novel's 'inner form', defined in terms of the relation of its protagonist to the meaning of the world. In his discussion in the last essay of *Soul and Form*, 'The Metaphysics of Tragedy', he is explicit that the work of art's relation to its historical moment is profoundly different from that of a simple mirror, different from mimicking in the simple sense of the word: 'the reality of such a world [the world of a tragedy] can have nothing in common with that of temporal existence'.[68] Tragedy expresses life's privileged or 'great' moments, those rare points where one's Being coincides with one's Idea.[69] The greatest tragedies – and these alone count for Lukács – are explorations into how the soul finds meaning in its existence in the world. The 'form' of the work, for Lukács, is precisely the answer to this question, and he takes pains to show how neoclassical theories of the unities of time and place are badly formed partial insights into the profounder work of the tragedy in achieving a representation of a Self coinciding with its essence. The idea of the separateness of the work of art from empirical reality – its 'autonomy', its status as a 'semblance' (*Schein*) or appearance – is a central tenet of the impure aesthetics developed by both Benjamin and Adorno, and it was one emphasized both by Nietzsche and the early Lukács.

However, the relationship of the autonomous aesthetic form to the world from which it emerges changes as societies give way one to the other and as history develops, as Hegel had emphasized and as Lukács argues as well. The tragic hero was possible for the Greeks and Shakespeare, and may be possible again in the future, but it is much more difficult in the bourgeois age, Lukács argues. That is instead the age of the novel: 'The novel is the epic of a world that has been abandoned by God.'[70]

Perhaps most important of all was the formulation developed by Lukács as he redefined himself and his method as Marxist and confronted the 'orthodox' Marxism developed by the theorists of the Socialist and Communist Internationals, both of which interpreted Marxism as an economic determinism in which an economic 'base' determined and dominated a 'superstructure' of art, law, and politics. It was a formula open to various mitigating interpretations, but clearly it implied that the 'superstructure' was in some sense lesser, determined, delusive – in short,

[68] Georg Lukács, *Soul and Form*, trans. Anna Bostock (Cambridge, Mass.: MIT Press, 1974),159.
[69] *Ibid.*, 156.
[70] Georg Lukács, *The Theory of the Novel: A Historico-Philosophical Essay on the Forms of Great Epic Literature*, trans. Anna Bostock (Cambridge, Mass.: MIT Press, 1971), 88.

'unreal' – in contrast to the solidity of hammering and sawing, bolting and melting – the material processes of capitalist economic activity. Inevitably in such a philosophy art and its 'ideological' cousins would be de-valued and subordinated to something deemed more 'real'.

Lukács, instinctively, avoided this trap by his dictum – the central idea of his series of essays – 'It is not the primacy of economic motives in historical explanation that constitutes the decisive difference between Marxism and bourgeois thought, but the point of view of totality. The category of totality, the all-pervasive supremacy of the whole over the parts is the essence of the method which Marx took over from Hegel and brilliantly transformed into the foundations of a wholly new science.'[71] There are of course innumerable further ramifications, and, ironically, it was precisely Lukács's central concept of 'totality' which first Benjamin, then Adorno, rejected in the complex process of working out 'negative dialectics'. Similarly, Lukács's series of attacks on Modernism provided a later, extremely consequential parting of the ways of Adorno and Benjamin from the Lukács who cast his lot with the institutions of Stalinist Communism. But without Lukács's vindication of Hegel and rejection of 'base-and-superstructure' Marxism, their further work would be unimaginable.

Benjamin, as we will see below in Chapter 4, expresses his debt to Lukács explicitly in his 1928 *The Origin of German Tragic Drama*, and I will discuss Benjamin's similar development from idealist to materialist phases in the introduction to that chapter. Suffice it to say here that Benjamin experienced modernity in terms very similar to the motifs of 'emptiness' and evacuation favored by the young Lukács, that he saw such a perception as basic both to the baroque art of the seventeenth-century *Trauerspiel* he studied, to Shakespeare's *Hamlet*, and, eventually, to the Modernist works of his own day. Something of the uniqueness of his thought is caused, as Susan Buck-Morss and a number of other students of Benjamin have argued, by his inspired up-dating and application to aesthetics of the hermeneutics and visions of the Jewish mystical work the Kabbalah. The close dialectical connection in his thought between despair and redemptory hope owes something important to this source. Adorno, a younger man than Benjamin, was also steeped in German philosophy – he started his philosophical studies as a teenager reading Kant's *Critique of Pure Reason* with a tutor, Siegfried Krackauer, and he studied

---

[71] Georg Lukács, *History and Class Consciousness: Studies in Marxist Dialectics*, trans. Rodney Livingstone (Cambridge, Mass.: MIT Press, 1971), 27.

philosophy later under the German neo-Kantian Hans Cornelius. His philosophical studies were intertwined with intensive training in classical music as both critic and performer, and these musical studies also formed an important part of his unique intellectual *Bildung*. He had his own encounter with Lukács's *Theory of the Novel*, which became formative for his later understanding of the mutually critical interrelationship of culture and society. When he read *The Origin of German Tragic Drama* (1928), he was struck by Benjamin's originality and by the many parallels in their thinking, and he arranged a meeting with Benjamin almost immediately. Thus began the extraordinary intellectual collaboration of these two thinkers, a collaboration of mutual critique embedded in a larger sense of a shared intellectual project, which lasted until Benjamin's untimely death in 1940 – though in a real sense it was to continue until Adorno's own death in 1969, as Adorno continued the dialogue with a now-silenced partner for all of his career.

Because of the influence of the milestone 1977 New Left Review Editions anthology *Aesthetics and Politics*, which presented a multi-facetted debate about Marxism and realism involving Benjamin, Adorno, Brecht, Bloch, and Lukács – including a sharp exchange between Adorno and Benjamin – we are used to thinking of these two as independent, even antagonistic theorists – and indeed each maintained his own theoretical autonomy. But the more recent publication of the complete correspondence between the two from 1928 to 1940 is an important corrective to this perception, showing as it does the close friendship and the mutual support and shared perspectives of the two even when they disagreed. As the editor of the correspondence Henri Lonitz wrote:

The correspondence reveals the enormous significance of the practical and cultural solidarity which Benjamin and Adorno shared with one another during the period of their intellectual isolation – the one [Benjamin] an alien body amongst the French literary élite … The other [Adorno], forced at Merton College in Oxford, 'to lead the life of a mediaeval student in cap and gown', as Adorno puts it in one of his letters to Benjamin, maintaining a vital outlook which a conventional middle-of-the-road wisdom could easily interpret as one of ruthless critique. This ruthlessness with regard to the essential questions – and the authors regarded every one of their individual works as a contribution to a shared project of theoretical importance – expressed precisely that solidarity of criticism which is equally and simultaneously a form of intellectual self-criticism.[72]

---

[72] Henri Lonitz, 'Editor's Afterword', in Theodor W. Adorno and Walter Benjamin, *The Complete Correspondence, 1928–1940* (Cambridge, Mass.: Harvard University Press, 1999), 343–46; 344.

We can hear something of this sense of solidarity in a 1935 letter from Adorno to Benjamin in which he comments on Benjamin's Arcades Project:

Considering the crucial importance which I ascribe to this work, it would be blasphemy to express any particular praise for it. But I cannot resist the temptation here of singling out some of the things in it which have affected me most profoundly. In the first place there is your theory of *nouveauté* and your insight into the enormous significance of this category which you quite rightly compare to that of allegory ... And then there is the passage on fetishism which served once again to remind me just how closely our thoughts on this matter still correspond in spite of our two year separation.[73]

Benjamin is, if anything, more effusive than his somewhat reserved younger friend in an earlier comment on Adorno's inaugural academic lecture, 'The Actuality of Philosophy': 'There is no doubt that the piece as a whole succeeds in its aim, that in its very concision it presents an extremely penetrating articulation of the most essential ideas which we share, and that it possesses every quality "pour faire date", as Apollinaire put it.'[74]

The most important connection to Lukács in these writers is the idea of art as an autonomous semblance whose form – which causes it to be different from empirical reality – is nevertheless based on the moment of cultural development which produced it. The form, in other words, expresses the age in which it was produced, but in mediated ways that can only be understood through a study of the history of aesthetic forms and their relation to the history of other cultural and physical phenomena. Adorno liked to say that the artwork is a kind of 'monad', referring to Leibniz's idea of a peculiar interrelationship of created things to all other things in creation: 'Now this interconnection, relationship, or this adaptation of all things to each particular one, and of each one to all the rest, brings it about that every simple substance has relations which express all the others and that it is consequently a perpetual living mirror of the universe,' Leibniz wrote.[75] All things in Leibniz's philosophy are 'monads', independent beings which nevertheless 'mirror' within themselves the rest of the universe. Adorno thought that the formula happily captured both the autonomy and the interconnections of the artwork with its social context, and he used it

---

[73] Theodor W. Adorno, Letter to Walter Benjamin, 5 June 1935, in Adorno and Benjamin, *The Complete Correspondence*, 93.
[74] Walter Benjamin, Letter to Theodor W. Adorno, 17 July 1931, in Adorno and Benjamin, *The Complete Correspondence*, 8–9.
[75] Gottfried Wilhelm Freiherr von Leibniz, 'The Monadology', in *The Rationalists* (Garden City, NY: Dolphin, 1960), 464.

throughout his writings on art and literature. The contradictory qualities of the artwork captured by this philosophical borrowing and refunctioning – that an artwork is separate from reality but at the same time is connected to it by means of its form – is a crucial one for Adorno's aesthetic theory. Because the artwork is separate from the empirical reality which imprints itself on the work's form, the artwork can produce utopian visions which negate the real and its ideologies and clarify human needs and human desires, providing a point of perspective from which to conceptualize and to know the empirical reality in which we are otherwise entrapped.

Rather than attempt an impossible synopsis of theories which explicitly resist systemization, I will instead isolate four 'motifs' of the most relevant aspects of the Frankfurt School aesthetic theory and its most important sources, as I have construed them for purposes of this study: autonomy and form, aesthetic subtexts, art as labor, and art and the reconciliation with nature.

AUTONOMY AND FORM

Central to Adorno's aesthetic theory is what he calls the 'autonomy' of art, what a more contemporary idiom might call its 'alterity', its otherness from the social reality from which it is produced. This is a quality of the aesthetic for which we are indebted primarily to Kant's insights, and it can be said to come into existence when a conceptual or mental space – it of course can have a physical manifestation, as the stage in drama – is created for the inscription of specific contents organized into artful forms. Aesthetic space is thus radically differentiated from 'the real', assuming a stance of Other to lived experience and in that sense 'autonomous', existing in a world of its own. At one point in human history (and in religious loci up to the present), this effect was a religious one, creative of sacred space and ritual objects. But the aesthetic is specifically a secular idea, differentiated from the 'really' sacred. The differentiation of the aesthetic from the sacred, in fact, is a decisive moment in its history, and for many theorists it is the most crucial of a number of other differentiations involved in its creation (for example, from the economic, the domestic, the merely decorative, etc.). I will return briefly to this issue in discussing the third of the four motifs in play here.

The autonomy of the aesthetic is of course relative, not absolute. As we will see in a moment, the separation of art from the real is in fact the enabling basis for a myriad of connections to it. But it is important to highlight art's fictive, imaginary, and playful status. While art makes its own assertions in its uniquely aesthetic mode, it does not make direct, conceptual truth-claims. Precisely because of this special status, as I will argue in a moment, the aesthetic becomes an arena for all kinds of 'dangerous' material, but it achieves its license to do so because it is socially constituted as harmless, playful, dreamlike. It is a free zone and a privileged zone in regard to content – one with ideological limits, to be sure, but with a meaningful freedom within these limits.

We can see this effect at work (unevenly) in the poetic productions of the Elizabethan and Jacobean eras as well as our own. Philip Sidney famously replied to critics of poetry who deprecated it for its counter-factuality, its 'feigning', by distinguishing aesthetic space from that of daily life: 'What child is there that, coming to a play, and seeing *Thebes* written in great letters on an old door, doth believe that it is Thebes?', he wrote.[76] That is to say, everyone knows that theatre is make-believe, unreal, so it should be exempt from criticism for a kind of truth-value it never claimed. In *A Midsummer Night's Dream*, Shakespeare gives the anti-poetic discourse with which Sidney is quarreling a voice in his character Theseus, in famous words comparing poetry to madness and love, to which I will turn in the next chapter. But even in this deprecation, we should recognize, is a kind of freedom or license. The imagination can perform its strange, delusive functions safely there, in that space. In short, in Shakespeare's age and our own, the aesthetic is, up to certain ideological limits at any rate, a licensed discourse, precisely because it is deemed to be in a special kind of cultural zone or space, exempt from the truth-claims implied by ordinary discourse.

This special, privileged aesthetic space also creates a distancing and framing effect, one not quite the same as Kantian disinterest but more a matter of the perceiver's ability to distinguish the artwork's content from 'reality' and disengage from a sense of immediacy into a more contemplative mode of reception. In such a mode the perceiver becomes aware of *aesthetic form*, which is to say that the perceiver is invited to distance herself from the immediacy of the artwork, contemplating its artificiality and shaping. As noted, such distancing is not necessarily disinterested in Kant's sense. It is often seamlessly continuous with ideologies, political passion, sexual desire, private memories, and so on. It is rather an awareness of the Otherness of the artwork from lived reality. We can thus think of aesthetic form as a kind of framing device which signals the autonomy of the art work, its special privileged status within modern culture. We can see this effect at work, for example, in the case of found art or *l'art*

[76] Sir Philip Sidney, *A Defence of Poetry* (1595), in Brian Vickers (ed.), *English Renaissance Literary Criticism* (Oxford: Clarendon, 1999), 336–91; 370.

trouvé. When Marcel Duchamp famously created his work 'Fountain' by exhibiting a urinal in an art show, he was (besides shocking the bourgeoisie and radically estranging the idea of art) underlining the creative function of aesthetic space, its ability to induct the audience into a different mode of perception from that of ordinary life, one open to form rather than mere function. We will see Shakespeare doing something similar in *A Midsummer Night's Dream* with the plebeian play-within-the-play.

AESTHETIC SUBTEXTS: DESIRE AND DEATH IN ART

As we have seen, cultural productions labeled aesthetic are exempt from many ordinary forms of ideological policing[77] – think of the thoroughly respectable status of public nudity in painting for example – an exemption directly tied to the ideas that art is fictive and imaginary, not real, and that its proper reception is one of disinterested aesthetic pleasure, a highly specialized state which ostensibly neutralizes the artwork's content in favor of its form – or to put it another way, creates a space of denial in which transgressive subtexts can be safely experienced.

These qualities lead to the second characteristic of the aesthetic I want to highlight here – it is dependent on the first characteristic of the separation of aesthetic and worldly space – the idea that the aesthetic is a place-holder for displaced, or repressed materials, both political and psychic. It is, as Freud famously argues, and as Shakespeare himself suggests in the title of the work just mentioned, like a dream, a text with a surface level requiring a hermeneutics of suspicion to uncover subtexts which are implied but not explicit. Thus, as Freud suggests and as Shakespeare as well often seems to imply, the aesthetic is libidinal, containing desire which has been displaced and projected elsewhere – for example, onto the flowers, bowers, and secret places of the woods, or, more openly, on the figures of Oberon and Titania. It is often, as we will see in *A Midsummer Night's Dream* and in other plays, a container as well for violence, aggression, and death. Art, in other words, contains in disguised form elements of the sacred – taboo confluence defined by Georges Bataille, including bodily functions of sexuality, excrescence, and putrefaction in death.[78] As Bataille

---

[77] The fact that in our own time conservative politicians have sought ways to control the perceived obscenity of some art and that some artists have delighted in pushing the envelope of acceptability really strengthens rather than alters the general point – although it also suggests that there are political consequences to the Postmodernist tendency to efface the distance between 'high' art and the popular.

[78] See Georges Bataille, *Erotism: Death and Sensuality*, trans. Mary Dalwood (San Francisco, Calif.: City Light Books, 1957). The larger theory in which this work is situated is explicated in Bataille, *The Accursed Share*, trans. Robert Hurley, 3 vols. (New York: Zone Books, 1991, 1993). See also

argued (in the aftermath of Freud), we can see residues of the bodily in the central aesthetic categories of comedy (sex), tragedy (death), and satire (excrement) – aspects of human activity to which we will return.

In addition to these classically unconscious materials, however, the artwork can include consciously formulated allegories, symbols, and metonymies, as well as social subtexts not repressed into an unconscious so much as marginalized or displaced within the conscious ideological discourses of a culture – what Fredric Jameson analogically called the political unconscious.[79] The aesthetic lives with ideology – but it is crucial to see that it can negate ideology, distancing itself from it, as both Adorno and Althusser wrote.[80] But Adorno went much further than Althusser and spoke of art's powers of *mimesis*. Although the word is of course Aristotle's in *The Poetics* (usually translated as 'imitation'), Adorno, developing an early essay by Benjamin,[81] means something Aristotle never thought of: the idea that the sensory and extra-linguistic properties of art allow it to represent aspects of reality which denotative language – and therefore all forms of the ideological – allow to escape through its nets.[82] This power of artistic *mimesis* is the rational kernel of the long tradition which has seen poetry and art as divine, inspired, mystical, in touch with aspects of reality transcendent of ordinary rationality. However, as Adorno argues in a passage quoted above, aesthetic knowledge is an extension of rationality, an enlargement of reason, not its negation. But aesthetic rationality, as Kant suggests, is not wholly a conceptual one.

ART AS LABOR

Third and briefly – I develop this topic more extensively in the discussion below of *A Midsummer Night's Dream* – art should be conceived of as a form of labor, of a human transformation of given materials through mental and physical efforts, as any number of Marx's developers have asserted. It exhibits this status of labor in the 'madeness' or 'construct-edness' of the aesthetic object, in the transformation of its material medium into a new signifying system. Art is, as the Russian archivist and Marxist aesthetician Mikhail Lifshitz puts it in a hagiographic but

---

the discussion of Bataille in Susan Zimmerman, *The Early Modern Corpse and Shakespeare's Theatre* (Edinburgh University Press, 2005), 3–4.

[79] Fredric Jameson, *The Political Unconscious: Narrative as a Socially Symbolic Act* (Ithaca, NY: Cornell University Press, 1981).

[80] Althusser, 'A Letter on Art in Reply to André Daspre'; Adorno, *Aesthetic Theory*, 134 and throughout.

[81] Walter Benjamin, 'On the Mimetic Faculty', in Walter Benjamin, *Reflections: Essays, Aphorisms, Autobiographical Writings*, ed. Peter Demetz (New York: Harvest, 1979), 333–36.

[82] Adorno, *Aesthetic Theory*, 54.

pioneering survey of the young Marx's views on aesthetics, a form of specifically human labor, distinguishable from animals' work by its inclusion of conscious imagination and planning.[83] The constituting split of what we might call aesthetic from purely economic labor was a consequence of commodification and reification, one which created the split between two forms of value (of which Shakespeare was well aware, as we will see below in the discussion of *Timon of Athens*), economic and aesthetic. The result was the specialization of 'art' as a unique, still unalienated form of labor and the production of increasingly alienated, mechanized forms of labor associated with industrial manufacture in fully developed capitalist societies – a split which of course occludes the continuing connections between the two.

The idea of art as labor helps ground a number of its 'impure' qualities. It highlights, for example, the notion of artistic production as a transformation of the given – not as creation *ex nihilo*. All forms of art draw on the resources of the natural and cultural worlds, using forms and techniques developed in a complex historical process of collective social interaction. The soaring visions and transcendent claims of artworks are always anchored by their materiality and sensuousness, their status as constructed through skill and craft. Here again the rude mechanicals, those 'hard-handed men … / Which never labored in their minds'[84] are, beneath the layer of condescension toward them which the audience is seemingly inducted into, affirmative conveyers of this level of aesthetic production.

It was his insight into this hidden labor of the innumerable anonymous sources and predecessors of every artwork – and of the enabling labor of the rest of the artist's society represented in the work – that Walter Benjamin was evoking in his famous dictum: 'There is no document of culture which is not at the same time a document of barbarism.'[85] As Benjamin explains in a comment given just before this dictum: 'The products of art and science owe their existence not merely to the effort of the great geniuses who created them, but also, in one degree or another, to the anonymous toil of their contemporaries.'[86]

[83] Lifshitz, *The Philosophy of Art of Karl Marx*, 77–84.
[84] William Shakespeare, *A Midsummer Night's Dream*, *The Norton Shakespeare*, ed. Stephen Greenblatt et al. (New York, Norton, 1997), 5.1.72–73.
[85] Walter Benjamin, 'Eduard Fuchs, Collector and Historian', in Walter Benjamin, *Selected Writings: Volume III, 1935–38*, ed. Howard Eiland and Michael W. Jennings, trans. Edmund Jephcott, Howard Eiland, and Others (Cambridge: Mass.: Belknap, 2002), 260–302; 267.
[86] *Ibid*. See Howard Caygill, 'Walter Benjamin and the Concept of Cultural History', in David S. Ferris (ed.), *The Cambridge Companion to Walter Benjamin* (Cambridge University Press, 2004), 73–96; 92–93, for further discussion of this issue.

Along with the bodily connections of art defined by Bataille, the idea of art as a form of labor can throw light on the difficult issue of defining the materiality of art, as well as what we can tentatively call its *content*. Kant, as we saw, tended to view art's content as irrelevant, *form* only constituting the essence of the aesthetic. Hegel rightly was suspicious of this claim, but his counter-argument that art was one of the forms in which human mentality and spirituality (*Geist*) expressed itself created a virtually indeterminate content for art (anything thought or felt can be aestheticized) and omitted precisely the material elements which limit and define art – not only the resisting materiality of the various artistic media that Adorno emphasized (paint, stone, words, sounds, etc.), but also its connections to human biology – its intimate relations with mortality, sexual desire, and excrement – the biological substrata, as it were, of tragedy, comedy, and satire defined by Bataille. For the convenience of exposition, and drawing on the precedent of Susan Zimmerman's discussion of the relevance of Bataille to the representation of death in early modern drama, I will refer to two major biological/bodily limits, sex and death, seeing excrement as strongly allied to the element of putrescence in death.[87]

How can we reconcile these limits with Hegel's insight into the great variety of human experiences represented in art? Hegel was not wrong, surely, to see the potential content of art as as limitless as human experience itself – modern art especially demonstrates this virtual universality for us. But he does not account for the most familiar patterns and proclivities of artistic content, which have always centered around sex and death as human ultimates. Indeed the many claims for the timelessness of artworks – a timelessness that will always turn out to depend on the 'now' in which the artwork is constituted – have their moment of truth in this fascination of art with these elemental human ultimates. If art is that specialized form of labor that strives to objectify specifically human perception and human imagination, to articulate/create the shared visions of cultures and epochs, it will necessarily probe and constantly re-invent the meanings of these quintessential biological limits, the death of the individual, the reproduction of the community. As we will see in the last chapter of this work, in his *Romeo and Juliet* especially, Shakespeare defines the aesthetic in terms precisely of these two themes, off-setting the tragedy of individual death with the (metaphorically erotic) pleasure of artistic immortality.

---

[87] Zimmerman, *Early Modern Corpse*, 3–6.

ART AND THE RECONCILIATION WITH NATURE

Fourth and last in this heuristic and provisional list, the aesthetic models for us a relation of humanity to the cosmos and to human society, exploring human *meaning* and in its utopian mode figuring for us an immediate meaningfulness unavailable in societies dominated by commodity-exchange and capital-accumulation. In post-religious sectors of modernity, aesthetics thus takes on many of the functions that religion once fulfilled, especially in providing patterns of (non-existing) ideality against which to measure our own empirical experiences. Even in the domains of modernity in which religion is a continuing force, art has established enough prestige to act as a supplement to religion proper and share in its idealizing tasks. Precisely because the idea of the aesthetic developed in relation to the increasing dominance of the instrumentalizing relationship to nature implicit in capitalist development, the aesthetic becomes both the means and the depository for enacting values of non-instrumental orientations to the natural. This was an idea, as Andrew Bowie has shown us, central to the concerns of post-Kantian German aesthetic theory,[88] and it has been preserved and re-inserted within a more sober estimate of the potentials for disaster as well as liberation inherent within modernity, by Theodor Adorno and his followers. In this art always coquettes perilously with ideology, and the attempt to separate the aesthetic from the ideological is always a major issue for critical interpretation. Thus, the aesthetic is, I believe, often an unthematized component of contemporary Eco- or Green criticism (and I will return briefly to this topic in the Conclusion).

The artwork's construction of a specific relation of the human to the natural is a quality connected as well to Kant's idea, discussed above, that in aesthetic experience it is as if there were a perfect epistemological 'fit' between subject and object, one that the author of *Critique of Pure Reason* knows flies in the face of his central doctrine of the inaccessibility to human perception of the thing-in-itself. Nevertheless, this aesthetic intuition of the porous boundary between subject and object is not the least part of aesthetic pleasure for Kant, forever uncertain as it is. Both Schiller and Marx developed this thought further, in a different direction, emphasizing the way in which aesthetic experience humanizes nature and naturalizes humanity. There is thus a larger context for the previous discussion of the 'dangerous content' of art, its ability to provide a locus for repressed materials, so that the aesthetic is also a site for fantasies of

[88] Bowie, *Aesthetics and Subjectivity*, 102–13.

all kinds, social as well as sexual. Benjamin and Adorno both emphasized art's depiction of the non-existent, including that which never was, that which has ceased to be, and that which perhaps will emerge in the future. We can see this quality most easily in Shakespeare's *A Midsummer Night's Dream*, and especially in the scenes of the chief 'rude mechanical' Bottom, who undergoes, as we will see in the next chapter, both an erotic and social fantasy in his treatment by Titania and her serving fairies that is perhaps the most important moment in the unfolding of the idea of the aesthetic in the play.

The four aesthetic qualities I listed above and which I am privileging in this book, then, connect with elements of an older Marxist tradition, and with the most recent generation of materialist critics in affirming a role for ideology in art. The artwork necessarily draws its materials from the larger social context, and these come into the artwork with ideological imprinting. However, precisely because aesthetic space is a playful, imaginary space, and because it is not entirely conceptual or cognitive, ideology can become distantiated and critiqued within it. And because art involves non-linguistic resources, it communicates in ways which do not map in a one-to-one correspondence with ideological discourses. To reduce art to ideology is to misrepresent and impoverish it, just as an attempt to render it as 'pure aesthetics' does – as Adorno stated in the quotation I used as a motto for this Introduction.

AESTHETICS AND THE NEW HISTORICISM

In the wake of the generational turn since about 1980 toward the idea of criticism as something like ideology-critique, early modern and Shakespeare studies have proceeded in a twenty-years-or-longer experiment in non-aesthetic interpretations of texts – which, however, have persisted in being classed as 'literary' against the grain of the theoretical tools being used for the interpretation. If, as I indicated in my opening remarks, aesthetics has of late been a pejorative word for contemporary theory, it is not because aesthetics has simply disappeared. Rather, many aesthetic themes have entered into contemporary cultural and literary theory obliquely. They have inhabited the margins, or were discussed through other words and other concepts (ideology, cultural poetics, artifact, or theatricality, for example) in discourses which otherwise declared the aesthetic a retrograde concept.

Two different impulses of early new historicism towards aesthetics can be seen, for example, in a contrast between two key early developers of the method, Stephen Greenblatt and Louis Montrose. As I indicated briefly above, Stephen Greenblatt stands out from many of his contemporaries in his appreciation for the concept of the aesthetic. Like so many Marxist-influenced critics before him, Greenblatt rightly targets the old idea of a transcendent artist as the sovereign creator of the work of art.[89] But he is equally insistent on the necessity for a boundary – shifting and unstable, but inevitable – between the artwork and its context:

> If the textual traces in which we take interest and pleasure are not sources of numinous authority, if they are the signs of contingent social practices, then the questions we ask of them cannot profitably center on a search for their untranslatable essence. Instead we can ask how collective beliefs and experiences were shaped, moved from one medium to another, concentrated in manageable aesthetic form, offered for consumption. We can examine how the boundaries were marked between cultural practices understood to be art forms and other, contiguous, forms of expression ... The idea is not to strip away and discard the enchanted impression of aesthetic autonomy but to inquire into the objective conditions of this enchantment, to discover how the traces of social circulation are effaced.[90]

This passage, especially with its interest in how art is enchanted at one level and disenchanted at another, is in truth a fair paraphrase of elements of Adorno on the relation of the artwork to its social context.[91] Greenblatt puts the emphasis on the worldly side of the art–world barrier, while Adorno characteristically reverses that procedure, but the two are very close, and Greenblatt has never made a secret of his debt to Marxist aesthetics.[92]

Louis Montrose, on the other hand (to whom I will return in the next chapter), while giving us much that is admirable in his attempt to negotiate the same boundaries, ends up attempting to efface the aesthetic entirely, annexing the aesthetic, in effect, into the world on which it reflects:

> The *meta*dramatic or *meta*theatrical dimensions of Shakespeare's plays, which have exercised the ingenuity of a great many academic Shakespeare critics during the past quarter century, are not incidental theatrical commonplaces nor symptoms of aestheticism. The metaphorical identification of the world and the stage is one of the reflective dramatic strategies by which Shakespeare shapes a dialectic between his profession and his society.[93]

---

[89] Greenblatt, *Shakespearean Negotiations*, 4–6.   [90] *Ibid.*, 5.
[91] Adorno, *Aesthetic Theory*, 45–61.
[92] See particularly Stephen Greenblatt, *Learning to Curse: Essays in Early Modern Culture* (New York: Routledge, 1990), 1–5.
[93] Louis Montrose, *The Purpose of Playing: Shakespeare and the Cultural Politics of the Elizabethan Theatre* (University of Chicago Press, 1996), 208.

In his attempt to deny an aesthetic function to the play-within-a-play of *A Midsummer Night's Dream* especially, as we will see in the next chapter, Montrose seems to me to be involved in special pleading:

The play-within-the play device calls attention to the theatrical transaction between the players and their audience. In the process of foregrounding the imaginative and dramaturgical dynamics of this transaction, *A Midsummer Night's Dream* also calls attention to its socio-political dynamics ... The social order of Theseus's Athens depends upon his authority to name the forms of mental disorder and his power to control its subjects. Theseus's analogizing of the hyperactive imaginations of lunatics, lovers, and poets accords with the orthodox perspective of Elizabethan medical and moral discourses. These insisted that the unregulated passions and disordered fantasies of the ruler's subjects – from Bedlam beggars to melancholy courtiers – were an inherent danger to themselves, to their fellows and to the state.[94]

Here, in sharp contrast to Greenblatt and Adorno, the aesthetic is dissolved – unless the reference to 'foregrounding the imaginative and dramaturgical dynamics' is meant to avoid this – into the kind of totalizing social power which Montrose elsewhere in the book from which this quotation is taken is at pains to deny. Passages like this, it seems to me, are signs of an unworkable repression of the notion of the aesthetic in recent criticism.

Nevertheless, in the 1980s, when criticism embodying anti-aesthetic assumptions began to become influential in Anglo-American English studies generally, and in Shakespeare and early modern studies in particular, the immediate result was bracing and refreshing. Precisely because the previous aesthetic criticism of the New Critics and Northrop Frye had made political and ideological issues taboo subjects within the professionalist discourse of mainstream English studies, the new wave filled a gaping hole in literary studies and defined the agenda for a generation. Twenty years later, however, this kind of political criticism has to some extent itself become domesticated and academicized, leaving behind an empty fetishism of depoliticized 'facts' and objects called 'new new historicism' or 'the new materialism'.[95]

And where aesthetics has not been marginalized in recent Shakespeare studies, it has instead been removed from the work of art itself and applied, *à la* anthropologist Clifford Geertz, to cultures as a whole, in effect effacing the distance between art itself and the society

94 Montrose, *The Purpose of Playing*, 191–92.
95 For more details, see Hugh Grady, 'Shakespeare Studies, 2005: A Situated Overview', *Shakespeare: A Journal*, 1.1 (2005), 102–20.

which produced it and thus threatening to rob the artwork of its critical stance vis-à-vis its socio-cultural context. The new historicism set
the terms for this trend, but perhaps Patricia Fumerton's 1991 *Cultural
Aesthetics* is the pioneering work in this regard. Fumerton used the term
'aesthetic' but defined it in a way that helped pave the way for the so-
called 'new materialism' of more recent years.[96] Developing one strand
of Greenblatt's writing, she however replaced Greenblatt's earlier term
'cultural poetics' with 'cultural aesthetics' – traditionally the distinction
has differentiated a theory of artistic production called 'poetics' and a
theory of artistic reception called 'aesthetics'. But Fumerton used 'aesthetics' to refer to the semiology of aristocratic ornamentation as
displayed in clothing, food, jewelry, household furnishings, and other
articles of daily life, investigating their kinship with and reproduction
within literary works, particularly allegorical ones. As brilliantly argued
and suggestive as this work is, it never, I believe, fully theorizes itself or,
most especially, the category of the aesthetic, which it takes for granted
rather than interrogates. At several points, Fumerton approaches, without seeming to realize it, a re-invention of Walter Benjamin's theory
of the allegory as an aesthetic space of disunified fragments in which
any object can mean anything else because the world is assumed to be
valueless and emptied.[97] But the anthropological lure of turning society
itself into an aesthetic space leads Fumerton to an abandonment of the
idea of aesthetic form as that which separates art from society proper,
and it leads her into a vertiginous operation of seeing commodities and
commodity-trade as empty and de-humanizing but at the same time
meaningful and intimately tied to the values of selfhood and identity.
While pre-modern societies always look 'aesthetic' to us as participants
in disenchanted modern cultures, there is a crucial case to be made
for maintaining the distinction between the artwork and the society
which produced it, and it is precisely that lack which undermines the
argumentation of Fumerton's exhilarating book.

  Within today's Shakespeare studies, the idea of the aesthetic is in
many ways still taboo – in part because it is a theoretical construct and,
especially in a field under the sway of the stagnating assumptions of 'post-
Theory', theoretical innovations have been in short supply of late. Speaking
generally, it seems that the newest developments from new historicism and
cultural materialism have depended on an occlusion of the theoretical and

---

[96] Patricia Fumerton, *Cultural Aesthetics: Renaissance Literature and the Practice of Social Ornament*
(University of Chicago Press, 1991).
[97] Benjamin, *The Origin of German Tragic Drama*, 157–235.

political edges of these earlier approaches, an emphasis on their empirical, positivistic side. The resulting 'new materialism' seems to have abandoned both the political and the aesthetic simultaneously in favor of a new form of positivism. We have seen innumerable studies in the last few years solely concerned with uncovering lost historical contexts and material practices in the absence of any larger political or aesthetic purposes. We have learned about mirrors, beards, codpieces, writing tablets, fruits, condiments, clothing, stage props, and any number of other commodities and artifacts in use in daily life in the early modern – sometimes in the vain belief that such detail will deliver us reality sandwiches, more often because such studies have become fashionable and therefore publishable.[98] There is, I believe, often a hidden aesthetic dimension in many of these studies – the fascination with objects embodying meaning evidences a pleasurable, aesthetic experience – and many of these works provide useful information about the social contexts of early modern texts. But for most of the writers of this kind of criticism, the aesthetic has simply not been thought through. Some proponents of the new materialism have claimed that it is following the lead of Walter Benjamin's minute investigations of daily life in Baudelaire's Paris in *The Arcades Project*. But Benjamin's project was a radically theoretical one, based on Marx's theory of the commodity, Benjamin's own theory of allegory, and a radically new non-teleological, Messianic vision of historical change and revolution. Little of Benjamin's enabling framework can be found in the works of the new materialism. They are examples of commodity fetishism, not critiques of it.

It is, of course, all too possible that the recent hegemony of an absolutizing, aesthetics-blind political criticism will give birth in one of those Hegelian ironies so common in intellectual history to a politics-blind new aestheticism. Fredric Jameson sees precisely such a process in progress in France and Germany and fears that a 'new aestheticism' will amount to a return of the most scholastic and socially isolated components of the philosophical aesthetic tradition I discussed above.[99] Rather, as I hope it is already clear, I believe that a reinvigoration of 'impure aesthetics' is a step towards a new appreciation of the specifically aesthetic content of Shakespearean drama and a deeper understanding of the imbrication of Shakespearean aesthetics with the social, the political, and the historical,

---

[98] See Jonathan Gil Harris, 'The New New Historicism's *Wunderkammer* of Objects', *European Journal of English Studies*, 4.3 (2000), 111–23; and Douglas Bruster, *Shakespeare and the Question of Culture: Early Modern Literature and the Cultural Turn* (New York: Palgrave, 2003), 191–205.

[99] Jameson, *The Cultural Turn*, 113–23, discerns precisely this development in recent European works by Karl-Heinz Bohrer and Antoine Compagnon.

in both its original context and in our own. It is possible, I think, to bring the concept of the aesthetic to the fore again, but with a different content from that of Kant, the New Critics, and Northrop Frye – and one that builds on, rather than abandons, the critical methods of the last thirty years. I am not alone in this belief. Both in the United States[100] and the United Kingdom,[101] a new interest in aesthetics has arisen within the last decade, often by critics determined not to lose criticism's engagement with the political since the 1980s. And this beginning of a new interest in the aesthetic comes, I believe, in part through a perception that non-aesthetic criticism has largely exhausted itself, or led into disconcerting dead-ends.

AESTHETICS IN THE AGE OF SHAKESPEARE

In the case of Shakespeare's writings, the pre-Enlightenment status of cultural practice is crucial. Many of the conceptual 'splits' constitutive of modernity were not yet constructed – or were very unevenly in the process of being constructed – in Shakespeare's lifetime. It is precisely this quality of the early modern that gives this era's art much of its fascination for us. When T. S. Eliot defined his famous 'unification of sensibility' for writers and artists before the mid-seventeenth century,[102] he was doing more than myth-making (he certainly was also myth-making). Eliot's famous essay was a part of a larger Modernist project of imagining alternatives to life in a degraded modernity, and he turned in this instance to cultural history rather than myth outright. The result was a kind of Paradise Lost, which will not stand up to much skeptical scrutiny. But he was also registering an important perception about the era of Donne and Shakespeare – its

[100] See, for example, George Levine (ed.), *Aesthetics and Ideology* (New Brunswick, NJ: Rutgers University Press, 1994); Singer, *Aesthetic Reason*; Stephan Regan (ed.), *The Politics of Pleasure: Aesthetics and Cultural Theory* (Philadelphia, Penn.: Open University Press, 1992); James Soderholm, ed., *Beauty and the Critic: Aesthetics in an Age of Cultural Studies* (Tuscaloosa, Ala.: University of Alabama Press, 1997); Michael Clark (ed.), *Revenge of the Aesthetic: The Place of Literature in Theory Today* (Berkeley, Calif.: University of California, 2000); Heather Dubrow, *A Happier Eden: The Politics of Marriage in the Stuart Epithalamium* (Ithaca, NY: Cornell University Press, 1990) and her *The Challenges of Orpheus: Lyric Poetry and Early Modern England* (Baltimore, Md.: Johns Hopkins University Press, 2007); Mark David Rasmussen (ed.), *Renaissance Literature and Its Formal Engagements* (New York: Palgrave, 2002); and Jonathan Loesberg, *A Return to Aesthetics: Autonomy, Indifference, and Postmodernism* (Stanford University Press, 2005).
[101] See Jay Bernstein, *The Fate of Art: Aesthetic Alienation from Kant to Derrida and Adorno* (Cambridge: Polity Press, 1992); Bowie, *From Romanticism to Critical Theory*; Armstrong, *The Radical Aesthetic*; and Joughin and S. Malpas (eds.), *The New Aestheticism*.
[102] T. S. Eliot, 'The Metaphysical Poets', in T. S. Eliot, *Selected Essays* (New York: Harcourt, 1950), 241–50; 247.

relative lack of cultural differentiation. Eliot got important details wrong, as he may have intuited when he abandoned Donne in favor of Dante as his great exemplar of unified sensibility.[103] For example, Eliot never discussed how both Donne and Shakespeare showed an awareness of the new, instrumentalizing mentalities and the new realities of mercantile capitalism and Machiavellian statecraft. As will become clear below, in the discussion of *Timon of Athens* especially, the question of the relation of the artwork to the commodity was a live one for Shakespeare – as was, more broadly, a profound crisis of meaning connected with the new ethos of money-for-money's sake. The mental worlds presented in Donne and Shakespeare's works were, as Walter Benjamin argued was the case for much seventeenth-century art in a book to which I will return below in Chapter 4 on *Hamlet*, in many ways already fragmented, though not precisely along Kantian lines. Donne was of course obsessed with attempts to construct unities between these disparate fragments of his lifeworld – pre-eminently between the service of God and the cultivation of the pleasures of erotic, passionate, subjective love. Adorno, had he known Donne's poetry, would doubtless have taken him to be one of the great aesthetic exemplars of the futile and glorious attempt to join the broken halves of a lost totality, producing a new combination which is nevertheless not (as Adorno puts it) a whole. In a similar way, Benjamin would have defined him as a baroque allegorist of a shattered culture.

Shakespeare, as we will see, is even more various and complex, and here I am focusing on aspects of his great *oeuvre*. As noted, I have tried to summarize the most crucial of Benjamin's and Adorno's insights for my purposes in the preceding sections of this Introduction. But this is not primarily an exegesis of their methods – it is, rather, a raiding of them for what is immediately useful, coupled with a willingness to take Shakespeare seriously as a proto-theorist of the aesthetic with insights of his own – some prescient of later theorists, others uniquely his. Chapters 2 and 3, then, will be devoted to an investigation of how Shakespeare himself presents (within the complex metaphoric and dialogic language of his dramas) acute conceptualizations of what will later be called 'the aesthetic'. In the first of these meta-aesthetic dramas to be discussed, *A Midsummer Night's Dream*, the elements of art's alterity and of its connections to erotic fantasy are highlighted. In a play written perhaps ten years later, but also set in Athens and its nearby woods, *Timon of*

---

[103] T. S. Eliot, 'Dante', in T. S. Eliot, *The Sacred Wood: Essays on Poetry and Criticism* (1920; repr. New York: Barnes and Noble, 1960), 159–71.

Athens, we can see another prescient investigation into the idea of the aesthetic. In this one, however, the emphasis shifts, and we are given an anatomy of the complex, dialectical interplay of the artwork's economic and its aesthetic value.

With that much established, Chapters 4 and 5 turn to what we might call the aesthetic as such, shifting emphasis away from meta-aesthetics to an investigation of how the theory of impure aesthetics can aid in the reading of plays less centrally engaged in meta-aesthetic theorizing – although the first case investigated, *Hamlet*, clearly has important meta-aesthetic dimensions to be explored briefly.

Broadly speaking, my thesis in the first half of the book is as follows. Before the idea of the aesthetic was formulated in the Enlightenment, an implied idea of 'impure aesthetics' emerges in Shakespeare, in part because the autonomy of separate cultural spheres was not yet fully established. 'Disinterestedness', in particular, as Charles Whitney has argued, seems alien in a culture whose educated members had been trained by rhetoric and religion always to seek 'applications' of cultural productions to their personal lives, to invest the self into works of the imagination rather than contemplate them as aesthetic wholes.[104] However, several other elements of the idea of the aesthetic seem to be clearly in place. Most notably, the disintegration of the pre-modern holistic worldview ('the Elizabethan world picture') was very much in process – such disintegration emerges clearly, I have previously argued, in central Shakespearean dramas, mirroring a world where the separation of instrumental or technical reason from ethical or practical reason was still novel and much discussed in the governing classes.[105] But the idea of a separate, autonomous aesthetic domain was so tentative that it existed only at suggestive moments in neo-Platonic critical theory like Sidney's and in lyric and dramatic texts – most prominently Shakespeare's.

The book's second half attempts to provide at least an initial answer to the question of how a theory of impure aesthetics contributes to the reading of plays which are less centered on meta-aesthetics than these two. If the first half of the book derives largely from the ideas of Adorno's *Aesthetic Theory*, the second half is more dependent on Walter Benjamin's enigmatic 1928 master-work *The Origin of German Tragic Drama*, an

[104] Charles Whitney, 'Ante-aesthetics: Towards a Theory of Early Modern Audience Response', in Grady (ed.), *Shakespeare and Modernity*, 40–60.
[105] Grady, *Shakespeare's Universal Wolf* (for *Troilus and Cressida*, *Othello*, *King Lear*, and *As You Like It*) and Grady, *Shakespeare, Machiavelli and Montaigne* (for the second historical tetralogy and *Hamlet*).

investigation of seventeenth-century German baroque dramas which, however, continually refers to *Hamlet* as a crucial instance of the dramatic form Benjamin calls the *Trauerspiel* ('mourning-play') and which he distinguishes sharply from the form of Attic tragedy.[106] Benjamin's investigations into German seventeenth-century drama's implied *mentalité* and its relation to the onset of modernity has, as he suggests, important applications to Shakespeare as well, and *Hamlet* is the key case in point. Benjamin's method has an important historicist dimension, one which has been observed and adopted in several of today's 'new materialist' critical productions. Less noted, however, has been his emphasis on issues of aesthetic form and aesthetic effect, and I attempt in Chapter 4 to expand the few passages in his *Trauerspielbuch* which reference *Hamlet* into a much fuller exploration of the play as an allegorical *Trauerspiel* with expressive aesthetic dimensions not previously defined.

In *Hamlet* the motifs of a fallen world evacuated of meaning and of death as an omnipresent reality of all human life come to the fore, and these issues are taken up again in a final chapter that balances the emphasis on eros and the aesthetic of Chapter 2 with a thematization of death and the aesthetic in *Romeo and Juliet*. This early play serves well as an occasion for reviewing some of the key qualities of Shakespearean aesthetics previously discussed. Finally, a Conclusion will attempt to locate the critical practice of this work in the larger context of a changing literary criticism as we approach the end of the new millennium's first decade.

---

[106] Benjamin, *The Origin of German Tragic Drama*, 57–157.

PART ONE

A Shakespearean aesthetic: into the woods outside Athens

CHAPTER 2

A Midsummer Night's Dream –
eros and the aesthetic

> In their relation to empirical reality, artworks recall the theologu-
> menon that in the redeemed world everything would be as it is and
> yet wholly other.[1]
>
> Theodor Adorno

> The work of art is beautiful to the degree to which it opposes its
> own order to that of reality – its non-repressive order where even the
> curse is still spoken in the name of Eros.[2]
>
> Herbert Marcuse

A Midsummer Night's Dream represents one of Shakespeare's fullest
explorations of aesthetic ideas and is a development of the genre of comedy
to unprecedented levels of aesthetic complexity and self-reflection. Its
subsequent history as a cultural artifact both reflects and intensifies these
qualities, as the play has enjoyed a long history of representation in painting,
music, and film in addition to its many and varied stage productions.[3] For
any post-Enlightenment reader or viewer, it seems to have things to say
about the idea of the aesthetic *avant la lettre*, and the post-history of the
play is a useful resource in understanding its meanings for us in the present.
Such interpretations raise the question, as always, as to whether the play's
original audiences could have had similar interpretations, even without the
benefit of the word *aesthetic*. As I have argued in previous work,[4] all our

---

[1] Theodor Adorno, *Aesthetic Theory*, ed. Gretel Adorno and Rolf Tiedemann, trans. Robert
Hullot-Kentor (Minneapolis, Minn.: University of Minnesota Press, 1997), 6.

[2] Herbert Marcuse, *The Aesthetic Dimension: Toward a Critique of Marxist Aesthetics*, trans. Herbert
Marcuse and Erica Sherover (Boston, Mass: Beacon, 1978)); orig. pub. as *Die Permanenz der
Kunst: Wider eine bestimmte Marxistische Aesthetik* (Munich: Karl Hanser Verlag, 1977), 64–5.

[3] See especially Jay L. Halio, *Shakespeare in Performance: A Midsummer Night's Dream*, 2nd edn.
(Manchester University Press, 2003) for a detailed selective survey, from early productions to
current film versions; and Gary Jay Williams, *Our Moonlight Revels: 'A Midsummer Night's
Dream' in the Theatre* (Iowa City, Iowa: University of Iowa Press, 1997) which concentrates on
stage productions up to the mid-1990s.

[4] See Hugh Grady, *Shakespeare's Universal Wolf: Studies in Early Modern Reification* (Oxford:
Clarendon, 1996), 15–25 and *Shakespeare, Machiavelli, and Montaigne: Power and Subjectivity*

perceptions of the past are presentist in the sense that we are always immersed in our own ideologies and aesthetics as we work to reconstruct the past, and the past reveals new facets to us as our own understanding changes and develops. In this case, there is an inescapable, enabling presentism in my use of a concept that was not named and crystallized, as I explained in the Introduction, until 1750. But the hindsight involved in this re-negotiation with the past allows us to interpret texts like *A Midsummer Night's Dream* in ways that bring new focus, but not necessarily completely anachronistic perception, into our reading. And that in fact is what I believe the situation is here. I am arguing that an interpretation of *Dream* as a play about the aesthetic (among other things) is not only presentist, but also historicist because the play implies such a concept – a concept 'defined' in poetic and dramatic forms rather than theoretical language, but one no less viable for all that. However, in our post-Freudian age, we can see and conceptualize, in a way the early audience probably could not, consciously a close linkage between the aesthetic and the erotic. This linkage is an anti-Kantian tenet of Frankfurt School aesthetic theory, and one which I believe this play markedly supports.

Both of these qualities of the play – its presentation of a prescient concept of the aesthetic (meta-aesthetics) and its linking of the aesthetic with sexuality – were defined by one of the play's most unusual and perhaps unexpected artistic interpreters, the pre-Freudian but post-aesthetic nineteenth-century French Symbolist poet Arthur Rimbaud (1854–91).

There are only one or two very brief references to Shakespeare in Rimbaud's letters, but one of his earliest productions was the poem 'Ophélie', a Romantic meditation on Shakespeare's Ophelia. However, his most interesting reference to Shakespeare occurs in the elusive prose-poem in *Les Illuminations* which he titled, in English, in an allusion to the play's chief rude mechanical, 'Bottom'. An examination of the poem's autograph reveals that this title replaced that of an earlier draft, 'Métamorphoses' – an Ovidian title which reflects the series of transformations described in the surreal narrative, and one that recognizes the Ovidian influence on *A Midsummer Night's Dream*:

La réalité étant trop épineuse pour mon grand caractère, – je me trouvai néanmoins chez Madame, un gros oiseau gris bleu s'essorant vers les moulures du plafond et traînant l'aile dans les ombres de la soirée.

from 'Richard II' to 'Hamlet' (Oxford University Press, 2002), 1–25. See also the closely related work of Terence Hawkes, *Shakespeare in the Present* (London: Routledge, 2002); and Hugh Grady and Terence Hawkes (eds.), *Presentist Shakespeares* (London: Routledge, 2007).

Je fus, au pied du baldaquin supportant ses bijoux adorés et ses chefs-d'oeuvre physiques, un gros ours aux gencives violettes at au poil chenu de chagrin, les yeux aux cristaux et aux argents des consoles.

Tout se fit ombre et aquarium ardent. Au matin, – aube de juin batailleuse, – je courus, aux champs, âne, claironnant et brandissant mon grief, jusqu'à ce que les Sabines de la banlieue vinrent se jeter à mon poitrail.[5]

[Reality being too prickly for my noble character, I found myself nevertheless in my lady's chamber, a big gray-blue bird flying up towards the moldings of the ceiling and dragging my wings in the shadows of the evening.

I was, at the foot of the rich canopy which supported her adored jewels and the masterpieces of her body, a big bear with violet gums and hair white with sorrow, eyes of sideboard crystal and silver.

All became shade and refulgent aquarium. In the morning – a battlesome June dawn – I ran to the fields, an ass, trumpeting and brandishing the wrongs done to me, until the suburban Sabine wives arrived to hurl themselves at my chest.][6]

Very probably Shakespeare's Bottom had endeared himself to Rimbaud for a number of different reasons. Throughout his work, Rimbaud presents the image of himself as a worker, a peasant, a barbarian, a dark-skinned 'inferior' coming to the French poetic tradition as an outsider from the lower strata of society, re-inventing poetry and inverting many of its cherished aesthetic assumptions. Bottom the Weaver is precisely such an intruder into the aesthetic from the lower classes – and one for good measure who was a prescient precursor, in his relation of 'Bottom's Dream', of Symbolist synesthesia and poetic hallucination:[7] 'The eye of man hath not heard, the ear of man hath not seen, man's hand is not able to taste, his tongue to conceive, nor his heart to report, what my dream was.'[8] Poetic synesthesia had its best-known development in the famous poem by Charles Baudelaire, 'Les Correspondances', which described a series of sensations, one from each of the five senses, which the poem asserts are all somehow equivalent to each other in a mysterious unity.

[5] Arthur Rimbaud, *Oeuvres*, ed. Suzanne Bernard (Paris: Garnier Frères, 1960), 302.
[6] This translation is my own, with some adaptations from the translations of Paul Schmidt, translator of Arthur Rimbaud, *Complete Works* (New York: Harper & Row, 1974), 166–67, and Wallace Fowlie, translator of Arthur Rimbaud, *Rimbaud: Complete Works, Selected Letters* (University of Chicago Press, 1966), 227.
[7] François Laroque, '"I see a voice": Les voix du *Songe*: De la synesthésie au mystère', in Claire Gheeraert-Graffeuille and Nathalie Vienne-Guerrin (eds.), *Autour du 'Songe d'une nuit d'été' de William Shakespeare* (Rouen: Publications de l'Université de Rouen, 2003), 119–35, notes use of synesthesia in Bottom's Dream (120) as part of a motif in the play of sound and acoustics, seeing synesthesia as a akin to the religious or visionary states alluded to in Bottom's dream indirectly.
[8] William Shakespeare, *A Midsummer Night's Dream*, *The Norton Shakespeare*, ed. Stephen Greenblatt *et al.* (New York: Norton, 1997), 4.1.214–17. All subsequent citations from Shakespeare's plays are from this edition and will be given in the text.

Most commentators have seen the equivalence as, in the first instance, a matter of shared affect – the sound of an oboe, for example, evoking the same kind of feeling as the color of grasslands (to take images from the poem). Clearly the technique is a development of a basic premise of eighteenth-century aesthetic theory: that music, painting, poetry, and others of what came to be called 'the fine arts' were all versions of one abstracted idea of aesthetic production and that they all produced 'aesthetic effects' by their organization of the elements of sensation – sound, vision, and eventually, because of the perception of poetry as an example of the aesthetic *par excellence*, of words as well. Following Baudelaire's example, the next generation of Symbolists all developed the technique of synesthesia in various ways, Rimbaud most famously in his early poem 'Les Voyelles' ('The Vowels'). But Rimbaud went further. In his much-discussed 'Lettre du voyant' ('Letter of the Visionary'), he described synesthesia and famously advocated 'the systematic derangement of all the senses' as one of the most necessary labors of any would-be poet,[9] and Bottom in the above passage seems to have undergone precisely such an exercise. Like a good Symbolist poet, too, Bottom is for Rimbaud one in flight from quotidian reality into the hidden truths of poetic vision: 'Reality being too prickly for his noble character', as Rimbaud suggests in his 'Bottom'.

The prose-poem 'Bottom' alludes to two other of Bottom's experiences as well: his entrapment by a sexual dominatrix and his metamorphosis into an ass. The speaker in Rimbaud's poem is trapped 'in my lady's chamber' ('chez Madame') and figures himself, first as a blue-gray bird unable to fly outside – a probable allusion to a French tale about a lover disguised as a blue-gray bird – and later as trapped in an aquarium. That the entrapment is erotic is clearly indicated by the shift in imagery to the lady's jewelry and body ('bijoux adorés et ses chef d'oeuvres physiques'; 'her adored jewels and the masterpieces of her body'). All this recalls Bottom's amorous submission to the Fairy Queen Titania in her woodland bower, as does the latter reference to a transformation into a braying or trumpeting ass – itself another figure of Bottom's experience of metamorphosis and abasement. Rimbaud's figure is turned into a synesthetic, hallucinatory bear, a figure not explicitly taken from Shakespeare's play, but one reinforcing Shakespeare's emphasis on Bottom's heavy corporality co-existing with his uncanny, comical, and drug-induced attractiveness to Titania.

---

[9] Rimbaud, Letter to Paul Demeny, 15 May 1871, in Rimbaud, *Oeuvres*, 344–50; 346.

The poem's dénouement, however, in its reference to the Sabine wives (the French *Sabines* is feminine) seems to leave Shakespeare behind, imagining not Bottom's final metamorphosis into his old form (with a new, aestheticized consciousness), but rather a final and ambiguous confrontation with importuning females. The Sabines were an ancient Italian tribe defeated by the Romans early in their history who famously became the source of kidnapped wives for their conquerors. After living with the Roman men for a time, the Sabine wives are described by Livy as imposing themselves and their babies between the Romans and Sabine warriors just as they were about to do battle, pleading for peace – the episode was often painted, famously by David. If Rimbaud's reference is to this episode, the ending would evoke a final feminine appeal blocking the protagonist's escape from domination (the Sabine wives were successful in their pleading). Alternatively, perhaps we are meant to imagine the Sabine wives culminating the abasement of the poem's speaker through an ahistorical but inverted attack or a rape, and the allusion to them in this context would suggest that we are meant to visualize the kidnapped Sabine wives, transported to an era of suburban living, as the perpetrators of Bottom's final undoing. But however unspecific the final image, it seems clear that at the poem's end its protagonist has discovered that his escape from entrapment was only momentary.

The poem thus shares in the remorseful mood of Rimbaud's longer set of verse poems and prose vignettes, *Une Saison en enfer* (*A Season in Hell*), a series of bitter self-accusations and self-punishments which call into question his poetic, pharmaceutical, and sexual experimentations – at the same time preserving and aesthetically framing them.

Symbolist poetry was thus in many ways the culmination of a developing idea of the aesthetic which, after its beginnings in British, French, and German Enlightenment philosophical discourse, began to influence works of art directly, first among the Romantics, then in the development in mid-nineteenth-century France of the idea of *l'art pour l'art*, a doctrine most consequentially taken up by Baudelaire and adopted by the other Symbolists, major and minor. Rimbaud was an ardent disciple of Baudelaire's poems (he never met him) who developed and extended that poet's practice into a politicizing aesthetic tradition received and developed by twentieth-century surrealists and other Modernist and Postmodernist authors from Hart Crane to Bob Dylan. Thus Rimbaud was one of the premier developers of the aesthetic-political link discussed in the Introduction, and his references to and interpretation of Shakespeare's *A Midsummer Night's Dream* are among the most interesting

of the several post-Enlightenment uses of the play to figure aspects of
the aesthetic, clearly suggesting that Bottom is the play's (working-class)
hero and one who achieves an aesthetic vision and sensibility inextricably
mixed with a complex, ambivalent erotic experience.

Much more recently, the 1999 film version of the play by Michael
Hoffman whimsically inscribes its filmic text with allusions to a
synesthetic notion of the aesthetic, inserting Italian opera and *tableaux
vivants* alluding to Italian painting, even floating phonograph disks
along the streams of its enchanted woods.[10] The play has also inspired
innumerable paintings, from William Blake and Henry Fuseli through
Richard Dadd to our own day. Mendelssohn's incidental music for it
is justly famous, and it has been adapted to opera by both Purcell and
Benjamin Britten – and in 2004 by Elvis Costello for a ballet. It is a
favorite for professional and amateur performances,[11] particularly in out-
door venues, becoming a fixture over the years at the Open Air Theatre
in Regent's Park in London, for instance. It seems to lend itself to
synesthetic interpretations.

A Midsummer Night's Dream is the comic leg of Shakespeare's three
break-through works of the *annus mirabilis* 1595, which also saw his
composition of the tragedy *Romeo and Juliet* and the tragical history
Richard II. Although James Shapiro has recently argued that 1599 was the
most significant turning point in Shakespeare's career,[12] I think a stronger
case can be made for 1595. With these three plays Shakespeare reached a
new level of artistic development, one establishing him as independent of
his English predecessors and one which would eventually make him not
only an English dramatist but a European and then a global one. This
break-through was multi-dimensional. I attempted to define something of
its intellectual and political dimensions in my previous book, *Shakespeare,
Machiavelli, and Montaigne.* Here I want to underline the central role of
a sophisticated concept of the aesthetic – while it is also an element of
Richard II, I will here focus on *A Midsummer Night's Dream* and come to
Romeo and Juliet below in Chapter 5.

---

[10] The details of the film's aesthetic whimsicality can be studied in a long, perceptive review by
MacDonald P. Jackson, '"A Wood Near Monte Athena": Michael Hoffman's *A Midsummer
Night's Dream*', *Shakespeare Newsletter* 49 (Summer 1999), 29, 37–38, 44, 48.
[11] Michael Dobson, 'Shakespeare as a Joke: The English Comic Tradition, *A Midsummer Night's
Dream* and Amateur Performance', *Shakespeare Survey* 56 (2003), 117–25, discusses the history of
amateur performances of the inset play 'Pyramus and Thisbe' as a much-repeated English joke
from 1646 to the present.
[12] See James Shapiro, *A Year in the Life of William Shakespeare: 1599* (New York: HarperCollins,
2005).

AESTHETIC UNITY AND *A MIDSUMMER NIGHT'S DREAM*

The first critics to appreciate *Dream* as something more than the hodge-podge which neoclassical critics saw in the play were influenced by the new ideas of the aesthetic which, as I discussed in the Introduction, were important currents in German and then international Romanticism. August Wilhelm Schlegel, the German translator of seventeen plays of Shakespeare, whose writings in turn provided the basic ideas for Coleridge, first defined an over-arching structural unity of the play,[13] unity being a privileged category in classical aesthetics. The traditional aesthetic idea of unity helped structure the approaches of innumerable mid-twentieth-century critics who attempted to find a harmony in the disharmony of the play's myriad materials and styles.[14] But this classical emphasis on unity tends to create an Apollonian aesthetic, one that imposes order by suppressing or marginalizing the Dionysian, 'dangerous' content of art.[15] Guided by such an aesthetic, a distressing number of these found that a Shakespearean–Elizabethan ideology of male chauvinism provided the aesthetic linchpin of the play,[16] and most of these New Critical readings achieved unity in terms of a hierarchical arrangement of the play's elements that almost inevitably supported aristocratic and male privilege.[17]

In contrast, recent criticism of this play has tended to deconstruct these hierarchies and has become overwhelmingly political and/or historicist, with foci on sexual politics, class division, popular culture, and even colonialism. This de-hierarchization and subsequent awareness of political subtexts are both relevant to impure aesthetics. However, a certain relocation of focus will be attempted here, a movement from 'outside' to 'inside' the aesthetic space of the play, while retaining a suspicion of hierarchical unity and the imprint of ideology (since what

---

[13] August Wilhelm Schlegel, *A Course of Lectures on Dramatic Art and Literature*, ed. A. J. W. Morrison, trans. John Black, rev. edn. (London: Henry G. Bohn, 1846; repr. New York, AMS, 1965), 379–99.

[14] See Dorothea Kehler, '*A Midsummer Night's Dream*: A Bibliographic Survey of the Criticism', in Dorothea Kehler (ed.), '*A Midsummer Night's Dream*': *Critical Essays* (New York: Garland, 1998), 3–76, for a very usefully organized history of criticism, to which I am indebted in what follows.

[15] As noted in the Introduction, this point is argued eloquently by Jonathan Dollimore, 'Art in Time of War: Towards a Contemporary Aesthetic', in John J. Joughin and Simon Malpas (eds.), *The New Aestheticism* (Manchester University Press, 2003), 36–50; 42–49.

[16] Examples include: George A. Bonnard, 'Shakespeare's Purpose in *Midsummer-Night's Dream*', *Shakespeare Jahrbuch* 92 (1956), 268–79; Paul A. Olson, '*A Midsummer Night's Dream* and the Meaning of Court Marriage', *ELH* 24 (1957), 95–110; R. A. Zimbardo, 'Regeneration and Reconciliation in *A Midsummer Night's Dream*', *Shakespeare Studies* 6 (1970), 35–50.

[17] This point is incisively argued by Barbara Freedman, 'Dis/Figuring Power: Censorship and Representation in *A Midsummer Night's Dream*', in Kehler (ed.), '*A Midsummer Night's Dream*', 179–215; 188–89.

is 'in' the artwork is in fact 'from' that society). 'Art is related to its other as is a magnet to a field of iron filings', writes Theodor Adorno.[18] By respecting the separation of the artwork from society, it becomes possible to analyze aesthetic qualities of Shakespeare's plays while retaining a suspicion of hierarchical unity and the imprint of ideology – indeed, it becomes possible to see the suspension of hierarchy and the resistance to ideology as integral to the work's aesthetics.

Interestingly an 'aesthetic' reading of the play is often assumed and alluded to, but never actually performed, in many recent critical works. In her brilliant study of the network of a set of words and puns in the play which extends out into the surrounding cultural and social context, for example, Patricia Parker writes: 'Apprehension of this play's famous metadramatic aspect would lead in this regard not to the purely formalist or self-reflexive, but rather to its linkages with the partitions and joints of other early modern structures, social and political as well as rhetorical, logical, and grammatical.'[19] Thus, the 'formalist or self-reflexive' reading remains a road not taken in a work which describes itself as self-consciously historicist. In a similar vein Louis Montrose, in the influential essay on the play discussed briefly in the Introduction, writes: 'That the play foregrounds the dramatic medium and the poetic process does not necessarily imply a claim for the self-referentiality of the literary object or the aesthetic act. I suggest, instead, that it manifests a dialectic between Shakespeare's profession and his society, a dialectic between the theater and the world.'[20] As I tried to emphasize in the Introduction, it is precisely this interplay between the enclosed work of art and the larger world from which it draws its material that constitutes the aesthetic situation as conceptualized in what I have been calling 'impure aesthetics'. But contemporary criticism has decidedly relegated the aesthetic to the margins. It is perfectly possible, however, to pursue ideology-critique and aesthetic analysis simultaneously.

AESTHETIC SPACE, FORM, AND AUTONOMY

The idea that aesthetic form enables a kind of 'relocation' of the materials of art from empirical reality to a wholly fictive 'space' in which unfolds the form proper – the arrangement of elements into an aesthetic whole or disjuncture – is implicit in Kant and was subsequently taken up by many

[18] Adorno, *Aesthetic Theory*, 7.
[19] Patricia Parker, *Shakespeare from the Margins: Language, Culture, Context* (University of Chicago Press, 1996), 113.
[20] Louis Montrose, *The Purpose of Playing: Shakespeare and the Cultural Politics of the Elizabethan Theatre* (University of Chicago Press, 1996), 204–5.

others'. A version of the idea existed in Renaissance discourses on poetry, as can be seen in Sidney's *A Defence of Poetry* (probably written 1580–81; published in two versions in 1595):[21]

Only the poet, disdaining to be tied to any such subjection, lifted up with the vigour of his own invention, doth grow in effect another nature, in making things either better than nature bringeth forth, or, quite anew, forms such as never were in Nature, as the Heroes, Demigods, Cyclops, Chimeras, Furies, and such like: so as he goeth hand in hand with Nature, not enclosed within the narrow warrant of her gifts, but freely ranging only within the zodiac of his own wit. Nature never set forth the earth in so rich tapestry as divers poets have done; neither with so pleasant rivers, fruitful trees, sweet-smelling flowers, nor whatsoever else may make the too much loved earth more lovely. Her world is brazen, the poets only deliver a golden.[22]

Since in our own time the boundary between the empirical context and the aesthetic space proper has been underplayed by most critics,[23] it is important to begin with the idea of the fictive or aesthetic space of this play – an idea, I should emphasize, that is fully compatible with disjunctive as well as unifying aesthetics, and one important to rescuing the aesthetic from the denial which now prevails in regard to it in contemporary criticism. Since the advent of new historicism and cultural materialism, critics have actively sought to abolish the boundaries between these two domains, the aesthetic and the empirical world.

In *A Midsummer Night's Dream*, the fictive space is highly complex, it is composed from very heterogeneous sources, and it mixes realistic and fairy worlds. Of course the use of fantastic, frankly counter-factual settings was not new.[24] But a thematization of this quality, and a playing with it – in short, a self-conscious signaling of fictionality, a kind of meta-aesthetics – is far rarer, a sign of modernity and a prerequisite for consciousness of the modern concept of the aesthetic.[25] And the playfulness of this drama's use of its 'sources' is particularly striking.

---

[21] Mark Robson, 'Defending Poetry, or, Is there an Early Modern Aesthetic?', in Joughin and Malpas (eds.), *The New Aestheticism*, 119–30; 125–26, also argues that Sidney's *Defence* represents an early modern concept of what would subsequently be called 'the aesthetic'.

[22] Sir Philip Sidney, *A Defence of Poetry* (1595), in Brian Vickers (ed.), *English Renaissance Literary Criticism* (Oxford: Clarendon, 1999), 343.

[23] An interesting if relatively brief exception is Kathleen McLuskie, '"Your Imagination and not Theirs": Reception and Artistic Form in *A Midsummer Night's Dream*', in Gheeraert-Graffeuille and Vienne-Guerrin (eds.), *Autour du 'Songe d'une nuit d'été'*, 31–43.

[24] The plays of John Lyly, for example, sometimes had similarly fanciful, mixed-chronology settings. See Leah Scragg, 'Shakespeare, Lyly and Ovid: The Influence of "Gallathea" on "A Midsummer Night's Dream"', *Shakespeare Survey* 30 (1977), 125–34. The use of various kinds of imaginary settings for lyric poetry and narrations is, of course, ancient in provenance.

[25] It requires, among other things, a critical sense of history as distinguished from legend and myth, and if this distinction had emerged to a certain extent in ancient historians like Herodotus,

In the opening scene the names of the characters and the allusions they make identify the setting as the ancient Athens of the mythical hero Theseus and the Amazon queen Hippolyta, known to Shakespeare and some of his audience from any number of Greco-Roman sources, including Shakespeare's oft-consulted Plutarch. But Theseus is, anachronistically, as in Chaucer's 'The Knight's Tale', 'Duke of Athens'; and the town of Athens is populated, as we learn in the play's second scene, by artisans with distinctly English names: Bottom, Snout, Quince, and Starveling, among others. Finally, and most radically, the play's woodlands are occupied by 'fairies' or 'spirits', imaginary beings alluding both to Greco-Roman mythology (Titania's name can be found in Ovid, as an alternate designation for both Diana and Circe) and, more centrally, to English folklore with its legends of mischievous and malignant fairies in enchanted forests.[26] In addition, it seems very likely that Spenser's phantasmagoric *The Fairie Queene* (Books I-III were published in 1590), that variegated tapestry of multiple and disparate cultural materials, mixing (like this play) ancient, medieval, and modern matter, is a 'deep' source for Shakespeare, as has sometimes been suggested.[27] Oberon's name appears in one passage of *The Fairie Queene* (2.10.vv.75–76) as one of the royal ancestors of Gloriana, the eponymous Fairy Queen of the poem, and since there seems to be a more general Spenserian influence at work in this play, Spenser may well be where Shakespeare found the name, rather than the c. 1260–68 French medieval romance, *Huon de Bordeaux* (translated into English c. 1534), where the name (spelled Auberon) seems to have originated[28] and which Spenser appears to have known.[29]

Thucydides, or Tacitus, it is hard to find in the medieval, and it is very unevenly established in the Renaissance.

[26] Cf. Terence Hawkes, *Meaning by Shakespeare* (London: Routledge, 1992), 23–27.

[27] See for arguments for a probable Spenserian influence on *Dream*, Robert L. Reid, 'The Fairy Queen: Gloriana or Titania?', *The Upstart Crow* 13 (1993), 16–32; and Maurice Hunt, 'A Speculative Political Allegory in *A Midsummer Night's Dream*', *Comparative Drama* 34 (2000–2001): 423–53. Hunt believes that the play involves a concealed allegory criticizing Queen Elizabeth's infatuation with her French suitor the Duke of Anjou.

[28] See Claire Vial, 'De la fée épique à la fée elfique: Oberon, de *Huon de Bordeaux* au *Midsummer Night's Dream*', in Patricia Dorval (ed.), *Shakespeare et le Moyen-Âge* (Paris: Société Française Shakespeare, 2002), 203–22, for the case that Shakespeare knew the English translation of *Huon de Bordeaux*.

[29] A fairy-king named Auberon was also alluded to in the entertainment for Queen Elizabeth given at Elvetham in 1591, the occasion which is a prime suspect for explaining the play's allusion to a 'Western vot'ress' as Queen Elizabeth – who was seated to the west of the water from which music played in the pageant. But the evidence is all circumstantial, the connection to Shakespeare uncertain. See C. L. Barber, *Shakespeare's Festive Comedy: A Study of Dramatic Form and its Relation to Social Custom* (1959; repr. Cleveland, Oh., Meridian, 1967), 121–22. A fairy-king Oberon also appears briefly in Robert Greene's *The Scottish Historie of James IV, Killed at Flodden*, which was not printed until 1598 but which was probably played around 1590.

This already complex neo-Spenserian space is itself soon subject to the even more complex aesthetic distancing brought into existence by metadramatic devices, including the play-within-the-play performed at the end by Bottom and his fellows in their over-the-top, comically inept production of Ovid's story of Pyramus and Thisbe. A similar self-reflective or meta-aesthetic effect is achieved by the several references to dreams – Titania's, Bottom's, those of the four lovers – highlighted, of course, in the play's title.

The complex fictive space is the container, as it were, of the play's unique – and elusive – aesthetic form proper. One aspect of form can be seen in the interaction of the play's four distinct plot-lines – the frame-plot involving the wedding of Theseus and Hippolyta, the fairy-land plot centered on the quarrel of Oberon and Titania, the main plot of the four lovers in their shifting allegiances, and the story of the rude mechanicals' planning and production of a play. This mixture constitutes an 'impure' form that alienated its neoclassical readers and viewers[30] since it seemed to them, because of its mixture of poetic styles and plot-lines, to lack 'unity of action'. To post-Romantics, however, up to the present generation, the complex architecture of the play's interacting plots is part of its glory, allowing the action to be presented from multiple viewpoints, its themes developed with significant variations and at more than one level, its representation of society more complete, including nobles, gentry, and craftsmen. And it is a form in which any aesthetic 'unity' is constantly threatened by the disjunctures of the constituting materials.

Another aspect of the play's form involves the contrasting poetic and prose styles, loosely connected with the different plots.[31] There is the familiar Shakespearean differentiation of a verse-speaking gentry and a prose-speaking lower class. But both the lovers' and the fairies' dialogue is often given further distancing and artifice-status through the use of rhyme, and Robin Goodfellow[32] is at times given shortened, trochaic

---

[30] Samuel Pepys, *The Diary of Samuel Pepys*, ed. Robert Latham and William Matthews, 11 vols. (Berkeley, Calif.: University of California Press, 1979), Vol III, 208, declared in 1662 *Dream* 'the most insipid ridiculous play that ever I saw in my life'.

[31] Several critics have studied the contrasting poetic styles and their relation to the play's over-all design. See especially David P. Young, *Something of Great Constancy: The Art of 'A Midsummer Night's Dream'* (New Haven, Conn: Yale University Press, 1966); and, for a study much more open to the discord rather than concord of the clash of styles, Christy Desmet, 'Disfiguring Women with Masculine Tropes: A Rhetorical Reading of *A Midsummer Night's Dream*', in Kehler (ed.), '*A Midsummer Night's Dream*', 299–329.

[32] A strong argument in favor of the name Robin rather than Puck was made by Barbara A. Mowat, 'Nicholas Rowe and the Twentieth-Century Shakespeare Text', in Tetsuo Kishi, Roger Pringle, and Stanley Wells (eds.), *Shakespeare and Cultural Traditions: The Selected Proceedings of the International Shakespeare Association World Congress, Tokyo, 1991* (Newark, Del.: University of Delaware Press, 1994). The use of the name 'Puck' goes back to Nicholas Rowe's

rhymed lines to contrast with the statelier iambic pentameters more often employed by his fairy superiors. The dramatic dialogue is continually enriched with 'set-piece' lyrical moments of great intensity – moments, we will see, which are often among the play's most aesthetically self-conscious ones. Paradoxically, the prose of the rude mechanicals complements these and signals their own aesthetic-self-consciousness as well, as I will discuss below. The contrasting styles, as well as the several plots, reinforce a dialogical structure with emphasis on contrasts and resistance to unification.

All plays signal their own artificiality, in the simple sense that they can't disguise their location in a theater or theatrical space before an audience assembled to be entertained. This play, with its mixed temporality and styles, levels of reality, and play-within-the-play, goes much further and causes us to become acutely conscious of its artificiality and of the multiple perspectives represented within it. Within this complex fictive space and multi-leveled form of *A Midsummer Night's Dream* we can see at work antagonistic discourses – most centrally for my purposes here an antagonism between two different representations of nature and of the relation of humanity to nature – creating a kind of dialogue of differing visions or perceptions of reality.[33]

In part, it is a matter of the kind of dynamic described in Northrop Frye's concept of 'green-world comedies'. *A Midsummer Night's Dream* is a canonical example of the form, beginning in a recognizable realistic setting, then undertaking a withdrawal from that society into the green woods to a kind of freedom from many of the oppressive social norms that had created the play's comic dilemma, and concluding by a return to the normal world after a solution to the conflict within the green world.[34] The idea of the aesthetic as a separate, idealizing, and self-reflecting space of imagination works itself out within this interaction in a paradoxical, mirrors-within-mirrors fashion.

Of course, *A Midsummer Night's Dream* is an aesthetic 'object' from beginning to end; it is a shaped semblance of reality in a complex relation of similarity to and difference from the world from which it draws its materials – but clearly distanced from that world through its defining

---

eighteenth-century edition of Shakespeare, but an attentive reading of quarto and folio texts clearly shows that Robin Goodfellow is the name of the character, while 'puck' is a common or generic noun, not a proper noun or specific name. Thus this character is 'a puck' (an evil or mischievous spirit), but is named Robin Goodfellow (as he tells us), not Puck.

[33] Freedman, 'Dis/Figuring Power', provides a lucid and insightful analysis of contrasting viewpoints and slippery textuality in the play.

[34] Northrop Frye, *Anatomy of Criticism: Four Essays* (New York: Atheneum, 1968), 182.

forms and idealizations. But some parts of it, as George Orwell might say, are more aesthetic than others. The play recreates in its fictionality the very relationship of the artwork to the world that it itself participates in as an artwork in the world. In this way it shares a self-reflective 'baroque' nature with such plays as Pedro de Calderón's 1635 *La vida es sueño (Life is a Dream)* or Pierre Corneille's 1636 *L'Illusion* – and has an affinity to the complex metadramatic and meta-aesthetic effects of the inset plays within Shakespeare's own *1 Henry IV*, *Hamlet*, and *The Tempest*. Not only does the play's own inset play 'Pyramus and Thisbe' produce this effect; so too do the highly charged lyric language and the charming images of the harmony of humankind and the natural world in the fairy segments of the play.

In contrast, the 'four Athenians' plot of the play represents in relation to the privileged or heightened material of the fairy plot the familiar world of human experience – in an idealized form and language to be sure, but clearly in a more 'realist' mode than the material of the fairy realm. In this way the play 'models' in its own aesthetic space an implied theory about the relation of (a certain mode of) the aesthetic to the larger social world. It is a mirror within a mirror, as it were, and this is the key to its meta-aesthetic quality. And although the difference between these two realms in the play is clear, the barrier between them, like the wall in the inset play, has chinks in it, and within each separate domain there are traces of its excluded Other.

Another way to describe this dynamic is in terms of the various characters' perceptive capabilities: the green world is seen quite differently by the human characters on one side and by the rulers of fairy-land, Oberon and Titania, on the other. Oberon's messenger, Robin Goodfellow, is a mediator between these two realms, but as we shall see, in one crucial area – that of vision – he is associated with the human rather than the fairy domain for reasons to be pursued below.

In the 'normal woods' perceived by the humans, the four lovers are blind to the magical forces that surround them, and their withdrawal from the ordinary social restraints and arbitrary laws of the town of Athens raises as many problems as it solves – at least at first. But Titania and Oberon see and experience a different green world – one not without its own problems, but one which is highly aestheticized and expressive of an idealized state of potential harmony between the natural and the human worlds. The fact that the world of Oberon and Titania is disrupted by a lovers' quarrel of course links it with the human world – desire is disruptive in both realms, and an ideology of patriarchy rules in both as well. At the same time, however, the humanized Oberon and Titania control the forces of nature and live in a fairy paradise of rare beauty distinct from the human world and with its own poetic stylization. They are personifications of the natural world even as they display human foibles.

This is not an unfamiliar combination. Shakespeare (and all educated Elizabethans) had seen something very similar to it in their beloved Ovid and in the other sources of Greco-Roman mythology. The Greek and Roman gods had exactly this combination of qualities – embodying and controlling powerful natural forces but still subject to all the human emotions and weaknesses – desire and jealousy prominent among them. The fairy realm is thus at one level a 'mirror' of human society, but at another level it is far superior to it. It is not heaven, nor is it Eden; it is more like Olympus.

In his discussion of the seventeenth-century German *Trauerspiel*, or plays of lamentation, Walter Benjamin had seen the survival of the ancient classical gods within the Christian era (mostly, as he writes, in diabolic forms) as crucial to the formation of the poetic mode he calls 'allegory' (see below, Chapter 4). Emptied of their original context and meaning, they survive as protean signifiers for the baroque vision of an empty, mechanical world of violence and misery[35] – a vision which Shakespeare explores in numerous of his tragic and historical works, as Benjamin was well aware.[36] In *A Midsummer Night's Dream*, however, Shakespeare puts these signifiers to work in an altogether different mode, aestheticizing them as emblems of a potentially harmonious relation between the human and the natural but displaying them as at odds with this potentiality at the same time.

Much recent criticism has seen the fairy realm as mirroring the human world, but it has neglected the ways in which it is also utopian, or aesthetic.[37] Despite the gods' quarreling, in this region of the green world we find the Kantian 'as if' structure of a place in which the human and the natural are permeable to each other – a harmony expressed allegorically,

[35] Walter Benjamin, *The Origin of German Tragic Drama*, trans. John Osborne (London: New Left Books, 1977); orig pub. as *Ursprung des deutschen Trauerspiels*, Berlin: E. Rowohlt, 1928), 167–200.
[36] *Ibid.*, for example, 136–9.
[37] Kiernan Ryan over a number of years has been an important exception to this generalization; see especially his *Shakespeare*, 3rd edn. (New York: Palgrave, 2002), 102–57. A notable exception from the previous critical generation is Barber, *Shakespeare's Festive Comedy*, 147: 'Part of the delight of this poetry is that we can enjoy without agitation imaginative action of the highest order. It is like gazing in a crystal: what you see is clear and vivid, but on the other side of the glass.' More recently McLuskie, '"Your Imagination and not Theirs"', in Gheeraert-Graffeuille and Vienne-Guerrin (eds.), *Autour du 'Songe d'une nuit d'été'*, 31–43, has argued for more attention to the aesthetic and utopian in the play.

as we will see, by the humanized 'spirits' themselves. This quality is not really ideological because it does not ask for belief (we can certainly find ideology at work in many other aspects of the text, particularly its representations of class, gender, and marriage).[38] Rather, it is utopian in Ernst Bloch's sense: it defines an ideal space, clearly designated as such, in which it is possible to represent and contemplate determinate human needs, wants, and desires in various stages of their satisfaction; to reflect on human needs and their impediments; and to imagine alternatives to the world as it currently exists.[39] 'In art,' Adorno writes, 'ideology and truth cannot be neatly distinguished from one another. Art cannot have one without the other.'[40] Thus, here as elsewhere in Shakespeare, the utopian space is itself open to interrogation and qualification within the play's dialogic structure. But it is an important locus within a more complex structure. This utopian aspect of the play expresses one of the crucial components of the idea of the aesthetic that informs it. Adorno puts it this way:

The iridescence that emanates from artworks … is the appearance of the affirmative *ineffabile*, the emergence of the nonexisting as if it did exist. Its claim to existence flickers out in aesthetic semblance; yet what does not exist, by appearing, is promised. The constellation of the existing and nonexisting is the utopic figure of art. Although it is compelled toward absolute negativity, it is precisely by virtue of this negativity that it is not absolutely negative.[41]

In *A Midsummer Night's Dream*, we see this quality of the artwork in one of its consummate forms.

---

[38] The ground-breaking work defining the play's ideological investments was Louis Montrose, "'Shaping Fantasies": Figurations of Gender and Power in Elizabethan Culture', *Representations* 1.2 (Spring 1983), 153–82, later considerably expanded and revised in Montrose, *The Purpose of Playing*, 109–205. Other valuable studies defining the play's ideological work include: Madelon Gohlke, "'I Woo'ed Thee with my Sword": Shakespeare's Tragic Paradigm', in Murray M. Schwartz and Coppélia Kahn (eds.), *Representing Shakespeare* (Baltimores Md.: Johns Hopkins University Press, 1980), 170–87; Laura Levine, 'Rape, Repetition, and the Politics of Closure in *A Midsummer Night's Dream*', in Valerie Traub, M. Lindsay Kaplan, and Dympna Callaghan (eds.), *Feminist Readings of Early Modern Culture* (Cambridge University Press, 1996), 210–28; Freedman, 'Dis/Figuring Power'; Stephen Orgel, *Imagining Shakespeare: A History of Texts and Visions* (New York: Palgrave Macmillan, 2003), 85–104; and Alan Sinfield, 'Cultural Materialism and Intertextuality: The Limits of Queer Reading in *A Midsummer Night's Dream* and *The Two Noble Kinsmen*', *Shakespeare Survey* 56 (2003), 67–78. Other ideology-disclosing works will be cited as the discussion develops.
[39] See Ernst Bloch, *The Principle of Hope*, trans. Neville Plaice, Stephen Plaice, and Paul Knight (Cambridge, Mass.: MIT Press, 1986), trans. of *Das Prinzip Hoffnung*, 3 vols. (Berlin: Aufbau-Verlag, 1954–59). See also Ernst Bloch, *The Utopian Function of Art and Literature: Selected Essays* (Cambridge, MA: MIT Press, 1988). I summarized and applied the concept to *As You Like It* in Grady, *Shakespeare's Universal Wolf*, 191–212.
[40] Adorno, *Aesthetic Theory*, 234.   [41] *Ibid.*, 233.

UTOPIAN VISION AND THE FAIRY REALM

Oberon and Titania thus live in an enchanted, aestheticized world which occupies the same space as the one mere mortals inhabit but which operates according to a different kind of reality or through a different form of perception – one that is utopian and aestheticizing.[42] This is an ability which the play presents as lacking in humans – and it appears, lacking as well in mere common fairies. Oberon tells Robin Goodfellow of the origin of the magic flower whose drops induce a state of amorous madness:

> My gentle puck, come hither. Thou rememb'rest
> Since once I sat upon a promontory
> And heard a mermaid on a dolphin's back
> Uttering such dulcet and harmonious breath
> That the rude sea grew civil at her song
> And certain stars shot madly from their spheres
> To hear the sea-maid's music?
> ...
> That very time I saw, but thou couldst not,
> Flying between the cold moon and the earth
> Cupid, all armed. (2.1.148–57)

There follows the lyric description of one of Cupid's shafts, which missed its target and landed instead on the western flower – lines which historicist critics since the eighteenth century have identified as performing 'local' and power-accommodating work in deference to Queen Elizabeth,[43] said to be the western vestal (2.1.158) or 'imperial vot'ress' (2.1.163) who is Cupid's target – but who is untouched by the love-inducing dart. Such a reference would help 'immunize' the play from an undesired 'infernal' interpretation of Titania – the Fairy Queen of this play – who might easily be seen, via Spenser's Fairy Queen, as an allusion to Elizabeth.[44]

---

[42] Renaissance writers generally thought that imagination, because it was influenced by desire, tended to corrupt vision; see the classic essay by R. W. Dent, 'Imagination in *A Midsummer Night's Dream*', *Shakespeare Quarterly* 15 (1964), 115–29; repr. in Kehler (ed.), '*A Midsummer Night's Dream*', 85–106.

[43] Stephen Greenblatt, *Will in the World: How Shakespeare Became Shakespeare* (New York: Norton, 2004), 47–53, is another in a long line of historicist critics discussing these connections. Unlike many of them, however, he also discusses the considerable aesthetic qualities of these lines as well. My thanks to Terence Hawkes for pointing out this passage to me.

[44] Montrose, *The Purpose of Playing*, 160, finds Elizabeth's *cultural* presence as a female authority central to the play, but a bit later in his discussion he adds that the play, for all its anxiety about female power, is not directly about Elizabeth and depends for its complex effects on her exclusion (176). Lisa Hopkins, *Writing Renaissance Queens: Texts by and about Elizabeth I and Mary, Queen of Scots* (Newark, Del.: University of Delaware Press, 2002), 104–7, also suggests that Shakespeare, here and elsewhere in his work, is employing a 'strategy of avoidance' vis-à-vis the Queen. Hunt, 'Speculative Political Allegory', suggests that a reading of Titania as Elizabeth

A reader in our own day, however, is likely not to notice this brief 'local' moment because of the lush lyric intensity of the verses. If Titania and Oberon constitute, as I believe, Shakespeare's homage to Spenser, these lines attest to one to Ovid.[45] As in *The Metamorphoses*, nature is populated by humanized gods serving as intermediaries between natural objects and human society. Dympna Callaghan has argued that of the many Elizabethan poets who made use of Ovidian motifs and allusions in their works, it was Shakespeare who best reproduced Ovid's subversive eroticism in an age rife with attempts to moralize and even Christianize his sophisticated, pagan verses. 'Totally unlike his predecessors', she writes of Shakespeare's epyllion *Venus and Adonis*, 'in eschewing didacticism, this new, more aesthetic and pagan conception of Ovid represents a breach with orthodox allegorical Christian interpretation of classical authors.'[46]

The same is true, I would argue, of *A Midsummer Night's Dream*. Mermaids, nymphs, fairies – all at one level personifications of natural places – inhabit an intermediate zone in harmony and intimate connection with the non-human. The mermaid on a dolphin's back might, as a number of historicist critics have argued, serve as a reference to Mary Stuart, but far more to the point here is that this 'sea-maid' is said to be singing in so lovely a manner that nature is moved at her song and responds sympathetically. The aesthetic act of singing allows for mutual communication between the natural and the human, and this mythical figure personifies that harmony and links it with the art of music. These lines are a microcosm of the aesthetic ambitions of the play as a whole, which represents to us an idealized aesthetic realm in complex relations to a realistic, human one. Even more unambiguously in Shakespeare than in Ovid, the gods and goddesses are figural, imaginary, aesthetic images evoking and standing for a certain privileged, desired, but non-existing harmony between the human and the natural worlds.[47]

The very essence of the play's aestheticizing strategy can be seen in its treatment of these mythological figures. In a classic move of the dialectic of enlightenment, supernatural beings are reconfigured as aesthetic,

---

may exist in the play for a small coterie (probably from the Essex faction) who may even have asked for such an episode. But Hunt emphasizes that if this were the case, Shakespeare disguised this level of meaning to give it 'deniability'.

[45] Barber, *Shakespeare's Festive Comedy*, 122–23, influentially linked Ovid to the play's depiction of the fairies. See also Leonard Barkan, *The Gods Made Flesh: Metamorphosis and the Pursuit of Paganism* (New Haven, Conn.: Yale University Press, 1986), 251–70; Hawkes, *Meaning by Shakespeare*, 20–23; Scragg, 'Shakespeare, Lyly, and Ovid'; and Dympna Callaghan, 'Comedy and Epyllion in Post-Reformation England', *Shakespeare Survey* 56 (2003), 27–38.

[46] Callaghan, 'Comedy and Epyllion in Post-Reformation England', 28.

[47] Cf. Greenblatt, *Will in the World*, 48.

fictional ones, 'emancipat[ing] themselves from mythical images', Adorno writes, 'by subordinating themselves to their own unreality'.[48] The aesthetic arises in this process of enlightenment precisely in a refusal simply to annihilate objects of the pagan past; instead the aesthetic attempts to recuperate their truth-value by re-functioning them as art, preserving something that had lurked in the mythology in mystified form. In Shakespeare's *A Midsummer Night's Dream*, the something has to do with the connection of the human and the natural as it might be and perhaps one time was. This connection is the very essence of the Kantian moment discussed in the Introduction, when aesthetic perception gives us a world that seems to be attuned to the human sensibility in a way that produces that mysterious power of a non-cognitive aesthetic pleasure – although of course Kant would have insisted that any erotic component of the charm is simply incidental.

The charm of Ovid, and of Shakespeare here, is so delicately balanced and evocative that one is tempted to acquiesce to this Kantian claim. We would finally be mistaken to do so, however, not only because of the pronounced erotic aura of the poetry, but also because there is a clear intellectual component to this aesthetic experience: the presentation for our delight of a world of our desires, a world of reconciliation and harmony – between the sexes, between humanity and nature, between imagination and reality. And, as we will see shortly, it is a conception which the play itself both reflects on and holds up for our scrutiny and interrogation, especially in Theseus's triple comparison between love, madness, and poetry – and in the inset play which concludes the action after all the other dramatic conflicts have apparently been resolved.

THE AESTHETIC AND THE IDEOLOGICAL

Part of Shakespeare's *hommage* to Spenser is his use of an allegorical method in his treatment of Oberon and Titania[49] – a poetic strategy found in a different form in some tragedies, as we will see below. The allegory has both utopian and ideological components. Louis Montrose and others have shown us in great detail how patriarchal anxiety in the face of female power permeates the play,[50] and we will see that the aesthetic and the ideological are in very

---

[48] Adorno, *Aesthetic Theory*, 86.
[49] Barber, *Shakespeare's Festive Comedy*, 122–24, thinks the method is more indebted to Ovid and that the fairies generally are 'embodiments of the May-game experience of eros in men and women and trees and flowers, while any superstitious tendency to believe in their literal reality is blocked' (124).
[50] Montrose, *The Purpose of Playing*.

close company in the treatment in this text of issues of 'mastery' between the sexes. Indeed, the 'layering' qualities of the allegorical method, in which one signifier stands for multiple signifieds, is highly conducive to such mixing. My point, however, is that Titania is much more than an object of displacement for anxieties aroused by the real Queen Elizabeth – although she signifies that as well. The weakness of anti-aesthetic, historicist/political criticism – even in writings as nuanced and insightful as Montrose's certainly is – is not a weakness of commission, but one of omission. We are now much more conscious of ideological influence in early modern canonical masterpieces than ever before, and this is positive. But a problem arises when ideology-critique constitutes the entirety of the archive of criticism on these works, as they have threatened to do recently. In the case of Titania, we need to see that she exists in *A Midsummer Night's Dream* as more than a marker in a power struggle. For instance, she is importantly a kind of personification of natural fertility and its associated properties of sexuality and maternity; she is, as C. L. Barber saw, a kind of fertility and love goddess,[51] and these qualities constitute a profound and not merely ideological connection of humanity and the natural. These significations become apparent in her famous speech to Oberon explaining why she refuses his request to give up the human boy to be Oberon's 'henchman':

His mother was a vot'ress of my order,
And in the spicèd Indian air by night
Full often hath she gossiped by my side,
And sat with me on Neptune's yellow sands,
Marking th'embarkèd traders on the flood,
When we have laughed to see the sails conceive
And grow big-bellied with the wanton wind,
Which she with pretty and with swimming gait
Following, her womb then rich with my young squire,
Would imitate, and sail upon the land
To fetch me trifles , and return again
As from a voyage, rich with merchandise.
But she, being mortal, of that boy did die;
And for her sake do I rear up her boy;
And for her sake I will not part with him. (2.1.123–37)

The fertility attributes here are not all focused onto the figure of Titania herself; they are 'distributed', some to her votaress, some to the big-bellied

51 *Ibid.*, 137–39; Shirley Nelson Garner, '*A Midsummer Night's Dream:* "Jack Shall Have Jill;/Naught Shall Go Ill"', in Kehler (ed.), '*A Midsummer Night's Dream*', 127–43, agrees with Barber on this diagnosis and rightly emphasizes the way in which Titania is also implicated in an ideology of male supremacy, but largely ignores aesthetic implications.

sails, some to the boy himself. In this they all interplay to create a poetic interconnectedness which colors the theme of sexual reproduction with a surface beauty not unlike the kind Spenser gives us in his erotic landscapes, but more concentrated, more enabled by the imagery's affect and less by one-to-one correspondences between the details of the poetic surface and the abstract signified. Indeed, one is tempted to say that there is no allegory at all here, that all is poetic aura. Nevertheless, taking into consideration the larger context, the parallel with Spenser is clear, and the allegorical effect created for Titania not hard to see. She 'stands for' and focuses the dispersed poetic field of erotic aura which surrounds her in this passage, not unlike Spenser's character Amoretta, who grows up and learns 'true feminitee' in the Garden of Adonis,[52] absorbing, as it were, the dispersed qualities of the eroticized and ideologized landscape. The references to India constitute a subtext connecting to the colonializing mentality of the era,[53] and the charged affect surrounding the boy is suggestive of homoerotic components of the poetic aura as well. But these allusions are 'translated' into the play's aesthetic space and made to serve atmospheric, erotic, and aesthetic functions as well as ideological ones.

Oberon is less well developed as an allegorical figure, but he shares some of Titania's functions. The connection is defined when Titania identifies the quarrel between the two of them as the cause of the disordered seasons of the natural world and thus clearly links Oberon to her own signification of the forces of nature and Eros, designating both as personifications of a natural world out of kilter. Their reconciliation is allegorized as the restoration of natural order to the seasons of the year, a disorder which 'comes / From our debate, from our dissension. / We are their parents and original' (2.1.115–17). And their disunion takes a specifically sexual form. Titania says of Oberon, 'I have foresworn his bed and company.' Nature is disordered because the fairy King and Queen have suspended their amorous consort. Natural harmony, it seems, is a matter of frequent conjugal relations between the fairy King and Queen. And this sexual symbolism is clearly connected to the agricultural human world, in a series of details mentioned by Titania:

> The ox hath therefore stretched his yoke in vain,
> The ploughman lost his sweat, and the green corn

[52] Edmund Spenser, *The Faerie Queene*, ed. Thomas P. Roche and C. Patrick O'Donnell (Harmondsworth: Penguin, 1979), 3.6.51.5.
[53] See Margo Hendricks, 'Obscured by Dreams: Race, Empire, and Shakespeare's *A Midsummer Night's Dream*', Shakespeare Quarterly 47 (1996), 37–60; and Shankar Raman, *Framing India: The Colonial Imaginary in Early Modern Culture* (Stanford, Calif: Stanford University Press, 2001).

Hath rotted ere his youth attained a beard.
The fold stands empty in the drownèd field,
And crows are fatted with the murrain flock.
The nine men's morris is filled up with mud,
And the quaint mazes in the wanton green
For lack of tread are undistinguishable. (2.1.93–100)

The emphasis is on re-establishing boundaries and distinctions and re-imposing order so that the land's fertility can be renewed – although it should be noted that 'order' in this case conspicuously includes May-games and country dancing. The human–natural connection is virtually seamless, and we are invited to re-imagine ourselves within it. Read from a distance of 400 years, in our own de-humanized and de-naturalized world, the poignancy is deep and the poetry compelling. This is in many ways a reading of 'green criticism',[54] but to the extent that the idea of the aesthetic is centrally concerned with the relation between human perception and the natural world, it is a crucial aesthetic notion as well.

But it seems clear, as recent feminist criticism has underlined, that 'natural' sexuality in this play involves female submission.[55] 'Do you amend it, then', Oberon tells Titania. 'It lies in you' (2.1.118). Just give in, in other words. And Titania of course refuses – until she has undergone the humiliation of falling in love with Bottom, a 'torment' as Oberon terms it, that cures her of insubordination as it dazzles Bottom with indescribable visions. Nor, of course, is the motif of female submission confined to this plot. Hippolyta was an Amazon queen conquered and wooed with Theseus's sword. Hermia is made to undergo comic humiliation in the woods, and her humiliation continues even when she is the object of the ardent desire of her beloved rather than his scorn. Lysander, Demetrius, and especially Bottom have their moments of abasement as well, so that domination is not always a case of male over female. But male superiority is the only form that is coded 'natural'. From a twenty-first-century point of view, then, the aesthetic harmony achieved in such satisfyingly comedic knitting together of the plots at the end of Act 4 is tinged with the ideology of male supremacy.

---

[54] See Conclusion below for further discussion of the relation between impure aesthetics and green criticism.

[55] Notable examples would include: Gohlke, 'I Woo'ed Thee with my Sword'; Desmet, 'Disfiguring Women'; Garner, '*A Midsummer Night's Dream*'; Traub, 'The (In)Significance of Lesbian Desire in Early Modern England', in Jonathan Goldberg (ed.), *Queering the Renaissance* (Durham, NC: Duke University Press, 1994), 62–83; Dympna Callaghan, *Shakespeare Without Women: Representing Gender and Race on the Renaissance Stage* (London: Routledge, 2000), 146–60.

SEXUALITY AND HIERARCHY

In the current era, of course, the play's sexual politics have been discussed many times, but its aesthetic properties and aesthetic thematics are understudied while older aesthetic treatments are badly in need of updating. One of the central political-aesthetic issues of the play, as I have suggested, involves the complicated linkage of the fairies, the natural world, sexuality, and human attempts to govern sex. As mentioned, Titania is a key link in this chain, as is her consort Oberon – he is never called her husband, although he claims to be her 'lord' and she his 'lady'. And these off-hand references give us a certain insight into the family life of the fairy world which creates a dissonant subtext beneath the ideological affirmations of male supremacy. A marriage between Titania and Oberon is almost taken for granted, but never explicitly confirmed. This uncertainty creates an ambiguous 'place' for marriage in the ideal natural order as conceived by this play, and this is a difference that marks the distance of the play's utopian fairy-land from the human world under the aegis of the law. In the fairy realm, those figures of a fecund nature and natural sexuality, Oberon and Titania, are not monogamous but retain a certain autonomy from each other:

> OBERON: Tarry, rash wanton. Am not I thy lord?
> TITANIA: Then I must be thy lady; but I know
> When thou hast stol'n away from fairyland
> And in the shape of Corin sat all day,
> Playing on pipes of corn, and versing love
> To amorous Phillida. Why art thou here
> Come from the farthest step of India,
> But that, forsooth, the bouncing Amazon,
> Your buskined mistress and your warrior love,
> To Theseus must be wedded, and you come
> To give their bed joy and prosperity?
> OBERON: How canst thou thus for shame, Titania,
> Glance at my credit with Hippolyta,
> Knowing I know thy love to Theseus? (2.1.63–76)

And although there is a certain level of accusation in these assertions, these amorous indiscretions are not the source of the couple's discord: the disposition of the boy is. We should note as well that what occurs to Oberon as a fitting punishment for his estranged beloved is to set her up with a sexual liaison with a plebeian mortal. It seems that we are meant to understand that in the fairy realm, as in the kingdom of heaven described by Jesus, there is no giving and taking in marriage, that as non-humans, the fairies are as exempt from traditional moral injunctions to marital fidelity as are the animals of the woods – or, for that matter, as the gods of Greco-Roman legend. Thus, and with much the same implication, we could see fairy-land as an Olympian world where the gods marry but are not bound to marital fidelity. In either case, the fairy realm remains a sexually open, preternatural place – a quality which undermines that institutional keystone of the Elizabethan ideology of gender relations, marriage. The four lovers, in contrast, live in an all-too-human one where marriage is a necessity. Thus, whereas in Spenser there is a definite attempt to distinguish the wanton, alluring, but shameful lust of the Bower of Bliss from the allowed joys of sex with reproduction (presumably in marriage) of the Garden of Adonis, in Shakespeare the distinction is rather between a utopian or aesthetic sexuality unrestrained by the institution of marriage and a social, 'human' world where marriage is the only solution to the urgent problems of desire in unconstrained circulation.

The result is one of the fundamental possibilities of aesthetic representation: to distantiate us from the familiar human world, to lead us into imagining other modes of living and loving, to look critically into received ideologies of love and marriage.[56]

The implied allegorization of Oberon and Titania, then, works in two related domains. The two of them evoke the forces of nature, especially the rhythms and order of the growing seasons, with their impact on the fertility of the land and hence on the human world. And they evoke human sexuality, its power of attraction, its fertility, its pleasures, its involvement in sexual difference – a sexuality displaced to the love-drops unloosed by Oberon's orders on the unsuspecting young lovers. And these two levels, of course, function as mutually mirroring metaphors through a figure with an ancient lineage: the fertility of the land, the fertility of human sexuality. They are a sexual couple – but also allegorical figures whose (familiar, 'human') quarreling and mutual estrangement tropically constitutes and 'causes' a violation of the natural order.

An older, Apollonian aesthetics tended to the idea that male domination is part of the idealized natural world represented allegorically in this play – and a previous generation of critics reflected this tendency in many different readings of the play. In the light of the 'new' aesthetics of disunity and fragmentation, however, we are able to see this idea

---

[56] Sinfield, 'Cultural Materialism and Intertextuality' sees similar potential in the play, via a provocative reading 'against the grain' to find possibilities for homoerotic and other unconventional sexual liaisons in the play.

contested by the various forms of resistance to male domination throughout the play – the formidable, autonomous figure of Titania especially, as well as the independence of Helena and Hermia. In re-constituting the play for our own era, we can and should emphasize these subtexts and critique the ideology of male domination connected to the play's idea of the natural. With that done, the aesthetic implication of the Titania and Oberon allegory of the play is still clear: the force that through the green fuse drives the flower also drives the human heart and genitalia. This is the same force of nature, the play is at pains to show us, that can generate sexual violence and domination and subordination. But it is also the force that makes possible sexual pleasure and sexual generation, linking the human and the natural worlds.[57] In this play, in a phrase Adorno was partial to, sexuality is a kind of 'nature within', and a utopian vision of such a connection constitutes one of the chief aesthetic characteristics of the play, one that starkly contrasts an aestheticized vision of potential harmony with a familiar world of law and ideology – which, of course, the play also represents for us in the opening scenes set in Athens, as part of its 'modeling' of the construction of the idea of the aesthetic.

The allegorization of Titania and Oberon thus constitutes the presentation of an aesthetic, harmonious continuity between the natural and the human world – one subject to (comic) disruptions and unruliness, one with a continually visible subtext of potential violence, and one with a possibly disturbing linking of the human and animal. For all that, however, the play continually alludes to an Ovidian harmonization between the human and the natural – a possibility, of course, that is an artifact of desire rather than the real – but there is a continuity nevertheless. Lacanians would ground this region in Lacan's pre-linguistic Imaginary, and I have no argument with that labeling, so long as such a diagnosis does not reduce the richness of this motif to mere psychologism. A key point of this continuity, we will see, is the sexual production of children – a fundamental part of human life at once natural and ideological: the play ends with the fairies' blessing of the newly-weds' beds specifically against birth defects or abnormalities, and it is significant

---

[57] Two critics from an earlier generation strongly emphasized the insight that the play celebrates human sexuality as an impersonal power of nature. See Jan Kott, *Shakespeare Our Contemporary*, trans. Boleslaw Taborski (Garden City, NY: Doubleday, 1964), 207–28; and Barber, *Shakespeare's Festive Comedy*, 132–39. Barber sees this aspect of the play as influenced by the surviving 'pagan' associations of the rites of May and Midsummer's Night evoked several times in the play. I believe this diagnosis is correct; for my argument linking the holiday and carnival to the aesthetic, see Hugh Grady, 'Falstaff: Subjectivity between the Carnival and the Aesthetic', *Modern Language Review* 96.3 (July 2001), 609–23.

that the one irresolvable conflict between Titania and Oberon is over a child. But I will return to this issue below, in connection with the relation of sexual love with madness asserted by the play as well.

This play is clearly implicated in Elizabethan ideologies of love as a prelude to patriarchal marriage, as numerous critics have shown. But its aesthetic richness surpasses these ideological investments – without, however, erasing them. In the intensely imagined fairyworld, in the rich, lyric language of the play, in its complex dramatic interactions, *A Midsummer Night's Dream* discloses that *promesse de bonheur*, that image of a life beyond our present constraints, that is a crucial function of the aesthetic. And it embodies an Adornoan *mimesis* of sexuality and desire that is far from being merely ideological.

NATURE AS OTHER

There is another nature in the play, however, one not so idealized, aesthetic, or harmonious. It is the nature perceived by the four lovers and by Robin Goodfellow. This last rustic, plebeian fairy is, as we have seen in a passage quoted above, unable to see the god Cupid between earth and the cold moon, as Oberon does. He both perceives and is a figure for a nature in which sexual desire is troublesome and disruptive and where sexual violence is never very far away.[58] For this mode of perception, the woods outside Athens constitute a wilderness, not an enchanted forest. Demetrius warns Helena against this wilderness:

> You do impeach your modesty too much,
> To leave the city and commit yourself
> Into the hands of one that loves you not;
> To trust the opportunity of night,
> And the ill counsel of a desert place,
> With the rich worth of your virginity. (2.1.214–19)

As the argument builds, Demetrius threatens to leave Helena 'to the mercy of wild beasts' (2.1.228) – a clear sign that this nature is that of the Other. If we missed the contrast, Oberon soon appears to remind us of his quite different view of the green woods, with the celebrated, lyrical set-piece, 'I know a bank where the wild thyme blows' (2.1.249–56), a

---

[58] A number of studies have emphasized the subtext of sexual violence co-existing with comic lightness in this play – Theseus's conquest of Hippolyta, Demetrius's veiled threat of rape against Helena, Titania's coercion against Bottom, the story of Pyramus and Thisbe, and several details in the sources used. See Kott, *Shakespeare Our Contemporary*, 212–22; Levine, 'Rape, Repetition, and the Politics of Closure'; Callaghan, *Shakespeare Without Women*, 146–60; Orgel, *Imagining Shakespeare*, 87–97.

vision of the forest as a haven of beauty as well as a safe refuge for sleeping
and dreams, where, in contrast to Hermia's disturbing dream, snakes –
those traditional signifiers of sexuality – are aestheticized as supplying
'enamelled skin' to make fairy garments (ll. 254–55) and where everything is tranquil. But it is the human, fear-inducing nature (a nature of
the Other – in the Lacanian sense of the Other as the unconscious, the
repository for repressed psychic materials) that is the site for the play's
depiction of sexual desire among the four young lovers. When we think
about how desire is represented in this segment of *A Midsummer Night's
Dream*, we have to say that it is shown to be an urgent problem in
need of solution, a menace unleashed into the world. We see it at work
first in a purely realistic world, in the confines of the familiar space of
Latin comedy. An incensed father, Egeus, appears before Duke Theseus
demanding the enforcement of the law against the desires of his daughter
Hermia, who has spurned the father's preference for Demetrius in favor
of Demetrius's friend and rival Lysander.

To be sure, there is something distinctly unclassical in the warning
Theseus gives to Hermia concerning the alternative to the death penalty
which she is promised if she continues in disobedience:

> For aye to be in shady cloister mewed,
> To live a barren sister all your life,
> Chaunting faint hymns to the cold fruitless moon. (1.1.71–73)

Although the words are threatening, their lyric intensity also evokes one of
the modes of the utopian, a withdrawal from everyday life and a connection to a larger cosmos – in this case, the moon, the presiding, supremely
indeterminate image of this play – suggesting the possibility of an intimate, lived link between the human and the natural worlds in a women's
community.[59] But sexual desire, as we have seen, is slowly revealed, in the
complex unknotting of this play's multiple contradictions, as the mediating category most clearly linking the social and the natural, even though
it contains the destructive possibility of undermining the most fundamental social arrangements.

But in the opening of the play, we are far from any such commerce
between the human and the natural worlds. Desire, instead of representing
a mediation between them, is portrayed as a potentially deadly disruption
of the human social order. As in so many Elizabethan works, this one
seems to be preparing for what any number of recent critics of the play

---

[59] The play's depiction of female communities as positive is well described in Garner, '*A Midsummer
Night's Dream*', and Desmet, 'Disfiguring Women'.

have described as the play's chief ideological work: the mobilization of heterosexual desire and its eventual containment in the institution of patriarchal marriage. This ideological formation was complexly linked with Protestant Reformation re-definitions of marriage and family life and with Queen Elizabeth's specific pre-occupations and her court's cultural response to them.[60] But as Fredric Jameson argued long ago, any ideology has utopian dimensions, and aesthetic productions both incorporate and distance themselves from the (merely) ideological.[61] Sexuality is a problem for ideology precisely because it is potentially transgressive and disruptive of the social order and its property relations. And, since Freud, it is clear as well that desire is a component of all aesthetic forms, including the narrative and the lyric – both memorably mobilized in this play.

While typically in Elizabethan literature sexual desire is closely connected with – one might almost say disguised as – romantic love, this play inflects love in a more classical, unromantic manner – love as simply another word for desire. Throughout *A Midsummer Night's Dream* sexual desire is presented in the most unsentimental terms imaginable, undercutting its associations with romantic love although never quite breaking with them – but clearly emphasizing the 'blind' side of proverbial love. There is no question, for example, but that desire is presented as arbitrary and irrational.[62] Lysander makes this point quite inadvertently to Egeus when he argues for his virtual equivalence to Egeus's favorite Demetrius:

> I am, my lord, as well derived as he,
> As well possessed. My love is more than his,
> My fortunes every way as fairly ranked,
> If not with vantage, as Demetrius. (1.1.99–102)

Nothing in the play contradicts these assertions, and indeed, the effects of the enchanted flower-drops – indistinguishable from 'the course of true love', we should notice – bring this point home in hilarious fashion. And Hermia's consenting answer to Lysander's proposal that the two of them escape their social bonds and find a liberty outside Athens starts optimistically but ends in an ironic catalog of desire's arbitrariness and fickleness:

---

[60] An excellent resource for the study of these connections is provided in Gail Kern Paster and Skiles Howard (eds.), *A Midsummer Night's Dream: Texts and Contexts* (Boston, Mass. and New York: Bedford, 1998), 192–64, which reprints a number of contemporaneous historical documents relevant to these issues.

[61] Fredric Jameson, *The Political Unconscious: Narrative as a Socially Symbolic Act* (Ithaca, NY: Cornell University Press, 1981), 281–99, esp. 286.

[62] Cf. Orgel, *Imagining Shakespeare*, 87–89.

> I swear to thee by Cupid's strongest bow,
> By his best arrow with the golden head,
> By the simplicity of Venus' doves,
> By that which knitteth souls and prospers loves,
> And by that fire which burned the Carthage queen
> When the false Trojan under sail was seen;
> By all the vows that ever men have broke –
> In number more than ever women spoke –
> In that same place thou hast appointed me
> Tomorrow truly will I meet with thee. (1.1.169–78)

The appointed place, we learned earlier, was one in which Lysander had gone a-maying with his previous love (and Hermia's best friend) Helena.

Helena, too, argues for her essential similarity to Hermia:

> Through Athens I am thought as fair as she
> But what of that? Demetrius thinks not so. (1.1.227–28)

And she completes the enunciation of this theme in a set of measured couplets on the blindness and childishness of love/desire (ll. 232–45) – and illustrates the theme by her resolution to seek out Demetrius's favor even after this clear-sighted speech on his fickleness. In other words there seems to be a kind of economy of desire in which the love-objects are essentially equivalent, but in which they become wildly 'over-valued' by the caprice of an arbitrary desire.[63] There is clearly something fundamentally irrational about this set-up, and the play soon begins to catalog for us the various absurdities and dangers that this situation produces.

To see the danger of love-desire clearly, however, we have to get outside of its power of enchantment. We are led outside the charmed circle by Robin Goodfellow, the main articulator of this distanced, dispassionate view of erotic desire, as shown in his comments on the irrational absolutizing of the lovers' perceptions of each other:

> Shall we their fond pageant see?
> Lord, what fools these mortals be!
> ...
> Then will two at once woo one.
> That must needs by sport alone;
> And these things do best please me
> That befall prepost'rously. (3.2.114–21)

---

[63] This is related to but much more local and specific to this play than the 'sex/gender' system described by Gayle Rubin, 'The Traffic in Women: Notes on the "Political Economy" of Sex', in Rayna R. Reiter (ed.), *Towards an Anthropology of Women* (New York: Monthly Review Press, 1975), 157–210 and discussed by Montrose, *The Purpose of Playing*, 109 n. 1.

Robin is a fairy constructed from different cultural materials than those drawn on for Oberon and Titania, coming directly from English folklore, though sanitized a bit in the idealizing logic of this comedy. The term 'puck' with which Robin is associated was commonly applied to an evil spirit and sometimes identified as a devil. We are warned away from that interpretation in this play when Oberon tells the audience, 'But we are spirits of another sort' (3.2.389). Robin is a 'merry wanderer of the night', and 'merry' implies fun-loving and mischievous. We soon get a list of examples of his antics, including frightening maidens, misleading night wanderers and laughing at them, and spilling ale on an elderly drinker (2.1.32–57). He is more plebeian than aristocratic, a country spirit, a 'lob' (2.1.16), and he speaks in favor of the masculine world of his master Oberon and his desire to remove the changeling boy from a maternal world (where, from this point of view, he is being feminized with crowns of flowers and too much doting) to a male sphere of training for knighthood. We don't see Robin doing anything very harmful or frightening in this play. Instead he is a bungler, though he means to carry out his assignments. In terms of his affect, what most distinguishes him from Oberon and Titania is his apparent immunity from sexual desire. He is the anthropologist from Mars who observes the absurdities of sexual desire and its radical impact on perception with a distanced, unempathetic, merry scorn. Like all the fairies of the play, he seems an allegorical figure for the natural world and its powers, but he is on the 'all-too-real' rather than the idealized side of the natural world as it is presented in this play. Like Titania, he personifies libido, but as an alien and aggressive force from the Other, not, as in the case of Titania, as one who shows it to us from the inside.

As the fairies observe the shifting allegiances of the four young lovers, they clearly see (as the audience does) how dangerous desire can be: breaking hearts, destroying friendships, promoting jealousy and violence, undermining family stability. Desire does all that, but by the end of the play we see as well that, with a bit of guidance from without, it can produce harmony, beauty, reconciliation, and a stable base for raising the next generation. Just how this is managed, we will see, is the matter of discussion between Theseus and Hippolyta that provides the play's most startling and illuminating reflection on its own action and seems to re-open a commerce between the two realms of the play's green world closed before – in an aesthetic harmony that is, however, an unstable one.

Northrop Frye has it, as we have seen, that the green world is a kind of zone of transformation in which comic resolution is achieved outside of the normal world, then returned to it. And he points out that in Shakespeare especially this idealized realm is connected, however indirectly, to the pagan fertility rituals of the past, but also to the desire of the play's present:[64] 'the genuine form of the world', Frye says platonically, 'that human life tries to imitate'.[65] We would do better, as I have written previously in a discussion of the related green-world comedy, *As You Like It,* to perform a kind of materialist inversion of Frye through reference to the concept of the utopian as developed by Marxist theorist Ernst Bloch.[66] Bloch's utopia, like Frye's green world and like Barber's holiday world, is generated from desire, but instead of conceptualizing this as the timeless work of eternal myths of an eternal human condition, Bloch situates utopia in specific socio-material situations: utopia is the result of an experience of specific lacks caused by the inabilities of specific societies to meet human needs, both innate and historically generated. The fairy realm of this play – momentarily disturbed by Oberon and Titania's quarrel, but in principle a domain of the natural harmony of nature with human society – is an excellent example, structured specifically for a rapidly urbanizing society haunted by the memory of a rural, feudalistic past (which still in part existed in Shakespeare's time outside of London), and haunted as well, *pace* Montrose *et al.,* by the actual power of a female monarch.

But what we have to say about the green-world and utopian motifs of *A Midsummer Night's Dream* is that the green world in this play consists of two separate realms, a utopia and a dystopia – not, as in Thomas More's original transliterated-Greek pun, 'good-place' and 'no-place', but two places: one of them an idealized but momentarily disturbed aesthetic realm, the other a jungle of dangerous sexual desire. Both are realms of desire operating outside of civil society, in the de-socialized space of the woods outside the city, but one of them figures desire as embedded in the rhythms of the natural world, while the other shows desire from a different viewpoint, as a force disrupting the social.

As several critics have argued, the play poses for us the question, how do we make harmony out of discord, when Hippolyta famously praises the hounds of Sparta:

> Never did I hear
> Such gallant chiding; for besides the groves,
> The skies, the fountains, every region near
> Seemed all one mutual cry. I never heard
> So musical a discord, such sweet thunder. (4.1.111–15)

---

[64] Frye, *Anatomy of Criticism,* 183.   [65] *Ibid.,* 184.
[66] Grady, *Shakespeare's Universal Wolf,* 190–93.

In a similar vein, the rustic play put on by the workingmen of Athens and advertised to the court as 'very tragical mirth' (5.1.57) provides another discord, a contradiction which soon brings forth more oxymorons from Theseus, who concludes by saying, 'How shall we find the concord of this discord?' (5.1.60). The repetition of this formula in two otherwise dissimilar passages suggests it serves a thematic function. *Discordia concors* – the philosophical and rhetorical name for this figure – one perhaps more familiar to Donne than to Shakespeare scholars – seems to have been a familiar concept to Shakespeare as well, judging from these passages. And the structure of the play as well as the dialogue poses the question: how do we get from the nature of the Other to a harmonized nature, from the discord of unruly desire to the concord of a naturalized human world and a humanized natural world? The relation of the artwork to nature has been a fundamental one for aesthetics since Aristotle defined poetry as a *mimesis* or imitation of nature. But the problem has been re-formulated by aesthetic theorists of the modern era dissatisfied with Aristotle's relatively simple epistemology. The Romantics especially revolted against the notion that art was a copy of anything else rather than a vision in its own right. Adorno attempts a complex dialectical weaving among several of these theories, affirming that every artwork attempts and fails to enact a reconciliation with nature, that every kind of art involves a rationality of form and a *mimesis* of nature in a special sense of the word – *mimesis* as 'the nonconceptual affinity of the subjectively produced with its unposited other'[67] – that is, *mimesis* as the artwork's ability to re-produce within itself aspects of nature which conceptual thought as such, and certainly ideology, are blind to. *A Midsummer Night's Dream*, with its mixture of ideology and something that escapes ideology, would seem to be a prime example, and the play uses the motif of the dream as a surrogate for the unnamed concept of the aesthetic.

Thus, in *A Midsummer Night's Dream*, as in *As You Like It*, the answer to the question of how to achieve harmony seems to be: in our dreams – that is, in a counter-factual realm that can help clarify our unmet needs by conceptualizing their fulfillment in an artifactual, unreal form – in the realm of the aesthetic, figured here in the restored world of Titania and Oberon.

THE AESTHETIC SPACE OF DREAMS

When Titania awakens after Oberon administers her the antidote to the love-drops, she exclaims,

---

[67] Adorno, *Aesthetic Theory*, 54.

> My Oberon, what visions have I seen!
> Methought I was enamoured of an ass. (4.1.73–74)

Earlier, Oberon had foretold that all Bottom would remember of his experience is 'the fierce vexation of a dream' (4.1.66). And on cue, Bottom gives us his account of 'Bottom's Dream' in the form, as we saw earlier, that apparently endeared him to Arthur Rimbaud in the late nineteenth century. Clearly, one of the devices that helps unify the disparate materials of this play is the motif of the dream or the vision (a term which acts as a synonym for dream). Dreams have been linked to art and poetry many times, and Shakespeare seems to be involved in constructing a relationship between them throughout this play. 'Dream' is one of the many shifting place-holders for the absent term 'aesthetic'.

The four lovers are soon talking about dreams as well. After they are found in the woods sleeping near each other by the early-rising hunters Theseus and Hippolyta, they puzzle over their clouded memories, so oddly conjoint, without a clear understanding. Hermia says:

> Methinks I see these things with parted eye,
> When everything seems double. (4.1.186–87)

It is tempting to interpret this as a kind of metatheatrical allusion to the double vision of the green world I have been describing (Titania and Oberon's idealizing vision vs. the human vision of the rest), but its most immediate sense has to do with the mis-match between Hermia's confused memory and her sense of normal reality. And this apparent reference to a lack of coherence in her memory, like unfocused eyesight, is given a less optimistic interpretation by Helena:

> So methinks.
> And I have found Demetrius like a jewel,
> Mine own and not mine own. (4.1.187–89)

In this formulation, Demetrius is like some unexpected, surprising and valuable find, which, as a gift of chance too good to be true, may just as easily be lost once more. The world of harmony into which the four lovers have awakened may be only a dream. And this observation expresses a thought which many in the audience may have entertained in the face of the improbable simultaneous resolution of so many knots – that this concord may soon be lost again. Demetrius links that resolution to the space of dreaming, again confusing the experience of dreaming and that of being awake:

> It seems to me
> That yet we sleep, we dream. Do not you think
> The Duke was here and bid us follow him? (4.1.189–91)

They re-enter the civil life of Athens by following the Duke and Egeus back into town, their love problems sorted out, but, presumably, they also follow Demetrius's suggestion that on the way they recount their dreams (4.1.195).

It is just after this that Bottom tells the audience of his 'most rare vision', his 'dream past the wit of man to say what dream it was' (4.1.199– 201), the dream that created the synesthesia associated with the aesthetic by French Symbolists 300 years later. Because he cannot explain it, he will transfer it to (what we would call) an aesthetic realm, involving two media, song and drama, to be inserted at the play's climactic moment:

> The eye of man hath not heard, the ear of man hath not seen, man's hand is not able to taste, his tongue to conceive, nor his heart to report what my dream was. I will get Peter Quince to write a ballad of this dream. It shall be called 'Bottom's Dream', because it hath no bottom, and I will sing it in the latter end of a play, before the Duke. (4.1.204–210)

Significantly, then, Bottom's vision cannot be classified under any of the received categories of his own experience, and so it is 'translated' – to use a word also applied to Bottom himself when he is given the head of an ass – to the aesthetic realm. A number of critics have noticed that the terms of Bottom's speech echo the language of Paul's First Epistle to the Corinthians 2:9 (quoted here from the Geneva Bible), which alludes to the indescribability of Paradise: 'Things which eye hath not sene, and eare hath not heard, nether have entred into mans mynde, which thinges God hath prepared for them that loue hym.' But Bottom's parodic allusions to Paul's Epistle by no means suggest a literal claim for divine insight. It is the very nature of the aesthetic, Adorno argues, that 'its object is determined negatively, as indeterminable. It is for this reason that art requires philosophy, which interprets it in order to say what it is unable to say, whereas art is only able to say it by not saying it.'[68] In that sense, Bottom is being secular and true to aesthetics, rather than theological.[69] If anything, Bottom's inability to speak in determinate, rational concepts links his experience with the (pagan) 'divine frenzy' of the poet (a notion dear to neo-Platonism) to which Theseus (perhaps) alludes as well, as we shall see below. In both these two locations in Shakespeare's *Dream*,

[68] *Ibid.*, 72.
[69] See John J. Joughin, 'Bottom's Secret …', in Ewan Fernie (ed.), *Spiritual Shakespeares* (London: Routledge, 2005), 130–56 for a similar analysis of the passage which treats the unnamed category of Bottom's confused attempts at defining the indefinable as involving 'an epistemological and ontological transformation' (134) that is based on an '"aesthetic attitude"… [which] refuses to be prescribed by predetermined categories' (136). Joughin's analysis, however, is much more oriented to unearthing in the play attitudes akin to the religious than is my own.

I would argue, the veiled allusions to the divine serve as metaphors for an experience that is otherwise coded secular and natural, if marvelous: the concept-without-a-name, the aesthetic. And Bottom is the privileged vessel of this experience.

The almost theological negations of Bottom's description of his dream, in fact, implicitly invite the audience that has just witnessed his experience to try to get to the bottom of this dream in the very proclamation of the impossibility of doing so. We have seen a foolish, plebeian artisan, accidentally, by whim and circumstance, inducted into a fantasy-as-reality – and happily succumbing to it. He is brought into the enchanted, erotic, aestheticizing vision-world of Titania, with its fanciful surface of dainty, fairy artifices made from objects of sensuousness and natural beauty (with a slight undertone of violence):

> Feed him with apricots and dewberries,
> With purple grapes, green figs, and mulberries;
> The honeybags steal from the humble-bees,
> And for night tapers crop their waxen thighs
> And light them at the fiery glow-worms' eyes
> To have my love to bed, and to arise;
> And pluck the wings from painted butterflies
> To fan the moonbeams from his sleeping eyes. (3.1.148–55)

This moment of aesthetic concord with nature is followed by Bottom's attempt to befriend his servants in this new realm and make himself at home within it. And of course there is an undercurrent of sexual tension throughout this scene – the allusions to going to bed carry it here – giving the whole experience a distinctly erotic aura. Bottom is, of course, a prisoner of love, as Titania makes clear:

> Out of this wood do not desire to go.
> Thou shalt remain here, whether thou wilt or no. (3.1.134–35)

If there is any doubt about this,[70] it is expelled by Titania's exclamations at the opening of scene 4.1:

> Come, sit thee down upon this flow'ry bed,
> While I thy amiable cheeks do coy,
> And stick musk-roses in thy sleek smooth head,
> And kiss thy fair large ears, my gentle joy. (4.1.1–4)

[70] Kott, *Shakespeare Our Contemporary*, 207–36, helped open the eyes of readers to the 'brutal eroticism' of the Titania–Bottom scenes and influenced the milestone Royal Shakespeare Company production of the play directed by Peter Brook in 1970. Callaghan, *Shakespeare Without Women*, 146–62, amplifies and further develops the details of the eroticism, which is often carried by *double entendre*; and the point is emphasized and further illustrated by Orgel, *Imagining Shakespeare*, 85–97.

For his part, Bottom is relaxing into his gilded cage and creates his own version of the fairy-land aesthetic mode in good, plebeian prose:

Monsieur Cobweb, good monsieur, get you your weapons in your hand and kill me a red-hipped humble-bee on the top of a thistle; and, good monsieur, bring me the honeybag. Do not fret yourself too much in the action, monsieur; and, good monsieur, have a care the honeybag break not. I would be loath to have you overflowen with a honeybag, signor. (4.1.10–15)

He is soon calling for rustic music as well.

The running gag in all this comes from the audience's ability, seconded by Robin and Oberon, to see the ordinary, disenchanted, 'material' Bottom in utter disjunction from Titania's doting vision. Bottom's name itself is one important signifier of this materializing strand. When Robin Goodfellow says, in a quote given above, that he loves to see things 'That befall prepost'rously', Latin-savvy members of the audience could note the reference to 'bottoms' in the word 'preposterous' (etymologically, posterior-first). And the closeness of the word 'ass' to 'arse' (identical in American English) is another of these associations.[71] Lars Engle has argued that Shakespeare was in fact creating a distanced, symbolic version in these allusions of the close encounter with Alison's lower bodily stratum by the fastidious, love-sick clerk Absalom in Chaucer's 'The Miller's Tale'.[72] And Bottom's corporality is underlined when Titania, in her attempt to lure Bottom to stay with her voluntarily (after her announcement that he could not leave in any case), promises him:

> And I will purge thy mortal grossness so
> That thou shalt like an airy spirit go. (3.1.139–40)

The comic, preposterous concord of Bottom's corporality with airy spirits is not the least important of the several versions of *discordia concors* in the play, and like most of them, it is related to an implied concept of the aesthetic. The aesthetic, like Bottom, is sensuous, dependent on materiality for its very form and expression, and yet perceived as spiritual, signifying, and revelatory of human experiences without a definite name. The aesthetic is the 'rare vision' 'that hath no bottom to it' – no bottom because it lacks a determinate concept, no bottom because it suggests access to an unlimited world of new experiences, no bottom because it somehow transcends its own materiality – perhaps no Bottom because, in Rimbaud's famous and enigmatic dictum, '*I* is another' ('*Je* est un autre').[73]

---

[71] On this point see Annabel Patterson, *Shakespeare and the Popular Voice* (Oxford: Blackwell,1989), 66–68, and Parker, *Shakespeare from the Margins*, 20–55.

[72] Lars Engle, *Shakespearean Pragmatism: Market of his Time* (University of Chicago Press, 1993), 141.

[73] Rimbaud, Letter to Georges Izambard, 13 May 1871, in Rimbaud, *Oeuvres*, 344.

In Bottom, and in the rude mechanicals more generally, Shakespeare pays his homage to the aesthetic usefulness of the ugly, as a moment of discord which, as Adorno claims, both violates and confirms aesthetic unity, creating a dynamic tension which can incorporate anal pleasure and simultaneously affirm the lower ranks of society.[74] Bottom in this way completes the aesthetic as he is transformed by it.

'PYRAMUS AND THISBE'

The play-within-the-play that takes up most of Act 5 is the long and hilarious gloss on Bottom's dream. Bottom himself expresses a desire to incorporate the dream, once labored over by Peter Quince, into the play as a song to be sung at the moment of death of Thisbe (4.1.210–11). The song never in fact appears in the performance we and Theseus's court witness, but the connection to it has been made: the play itself embodies the same concept of the aesthetic that the dream does.[75]

There is, of course, a strong element of parody at work, and Hippolyta and the three men among the newly-weds keep up witty patter to drive the point home. The rustic players have had recourse to their own kind of allegory or personification in the production – just, as we have seen, this play personifies concepts via the allegories associated with the fairies. In the parody version, not concepts, but concrete objects are signified by Wall and Moonshine; the method is self-parodying, another call of attention to the techniques of the larger play it both represents and is a part of. The impersonators of Pyramus and Thisbe (Bottom and Flute) distantiate us both from the convention of using males to play female parts and from the craft of acting itself. Bottom especially is an obvious ham, and we see parodied precisely the kind of scenes of death and grief which in other contexts and plays like *Romeo and Juliet* are prime examples of the power of the stage to move audiences.

The result of the parodic elements is precisely the meta-aesthetic one of creating self-consciousness in the audience of the aesthetic space of illusion or fictionality in which it has been immersed and to show us in detail the materiality of the signifiers used to create the signification, or the illusion. This reminder of materiality is, as we saw previously, the function of Bottom throughout his erotic captivity by Titania, and so we have within the action of the drama the same parallel between love-desire and poetry that Theseus develops in the famous speech (to which I will turn shortly). This

[74] Adorno, *Aesthetic Theory*, 46, 48–49.   [75] Cf. Joughin, 'Bottom's Secret ...', 148.

insistence on the materiality of the aesthetic is one of the recurrent themes of Shakespeare's development of the implied concept throughout the play. It is a 'skeptical' point of view to the extent that it anchors the potentially extravagant claims of neo-Platonist poetics (to which the play indirectly alludes twice), poetics that claim a kind of divine or mystical power of insight for the poet. Theseus's skepticism is similar to this anti-idealist idea, and the play as a whole embodies it as well: nowhere in the play are we outside of a natural world – it has been poeticized and idealized through imagination, but never transcended. It is a world permeated, as we saw, with a quite human aura of Eros, not the supernatural celestial heights of a Dante.

However, there is another point of view in dialogue with the skeptical materializing thread embodied in both the parody and in Theseus, a dialogic strand that insists in reply that the material signifiers of aesthetic experience may not transport us to heaven, but they do transport us – in the sense of the word as used by Starveling in reference to Bottom's metamorphosis (4.2.3–4) – to the region where Bottom experienced his visions. And during the play we also hear evidence that Bottom is still involved in his post-transport synesthesia:

> I see a voice. Now will I to the chink
> To spy an I can hear my Thisbe's face. (5.1.190–91)

The confused sensory references clearly allude to Bottom's dream and imply that Bottom has brought back something with him from the aesthetic realm of the green world. The poet, Rimbaud had claimed, must be a *voleur de feu*, a thief of fire – Prometheus – a seer who mediates to the rest of mankind the harmonious realm of aesthetic imagination.[76] But it is not a propositional message communicable in utilitarian language, as we discover in Bottom's words to his fellows upon his return to Athens:

BOTTOM: Masters, I am to discourse wonders; but ask me not what. For if I tell you, I am no true Athenian. I will tell you everything right as it fell out.
QUINCE: Let us hear, sweet Bottom.
BOTTOM: Not a word of me. All that I will tell you is that the Duke hath dined.
(4.2.25–30)

In another of Rimbaud's poems, he describes a group of workmen out at four in the morning, when many lovers were just ending voluptuous nights. He fantasizes a gift of Eros to a subjected working class:

> Ah! pour ces Ouvriers charmants
> Sujets d'un roi de Babylone,

---

[76] Rimbaud, Letter to Paul Demeny, 15 May 1871, in Rimbaud, *Oeuvres*, 347.

Vénus! laisse un peu les Amants,
  Dont l'âme est en couronne.
  O Reine des Bergers!
Porte aux travailleurs l'eau-de-vie,
Pour que leurs forces soient en paix
En attendant le bain dans la mer, à midi.[77]

For these charming dabblers in the arts
Who labor for a king in Babylon,
Venus! Leave for a moment
  Lovers' haloed hearts.
  O Queen of Shepherds!
  Carry the purest eau-de-vie
To these workman while they rest
And take their bath at noonday, in the sea.[78]

Bottom is like one of Rimbaud's workmen who has had this wish fulfilled[79] – a Rimbaldian hero-worker visited by Venus who has bathed in her sea and imbibed her eau-de-vie. This transgressive experience of pleasure-for-pleasure's sake – a humiliation for Titania, but an ennoblement of Bottom the weaver – is a version of the Eros-suffused aesthetic celebrated in this play. Bottom is, as Rimbaud clearly recognized, the aestheticizing Symbolist poet of *A Midsummer Night's Dream*.

LOVE, MADNESS, AND THE AESTHETIC

The aesthetic theorist, on the other hand, is clearly Theseus, in the often quoted lines I alluded to above:

I never may believe
These antique fables, nor these fairy toys.
Lovers and madmen have such seething brains,
Such shaping fantasies, that apprehend
More than cool reason ever comprehends.
The lunatic, the lover, and the poet
Are of imagination all compact.
One sees more devils than vast hell can hold:
That is the madman. The lover, all as frantic,
Sees Helen's beauty in a brow of Egypt.
The poet's eye, in a fine frenzy rolling,
Doth glance from heaven to earth, from earth to heaven,
And as imagination bodies forth

---

[77] Rimbaud, *Oeuvres*, 155.   [78] Rimbaud, *Complete Works*, 144.
[79] Patterson, *Shakespeare and the Popular Voice*, 67–70, points out the insistence on Bottom's class as reinforcing his evocations of the bodily.

The forms of things unknown, the poet's pen
Turns them to shapes, and gives to airy nothing
A local habitation and a name.
Such tricks hath strong imagination
That if it would but apprehend some joy
It comprehends some bringer of that joy;
Or in the night, imagining some fear,
How easy is a bush supposed a bear! (5.1.2–22)

Although there have been critics who have seen Theseus's words as choral,[80] the critical consensus for many years has been that there is a strong element of irony at work in his statement, that his rationalism is too much in contradiction to the main themes of the play to merit acceptance at face value. My own view is that Theseus's rationalism should be taken as being in dialogic relation to the claims that the other characters (the lovers, Bottom, Hippolyta) are making about experiences which seem transcendent to them. While his rationalism is reductive, it also serves to put into question the kind of transcendent claims about aesthetic visions that Renaissance neo-Platonists (and later Romantics) made about aesthetic vision.

Certainly the comparison that he makes between lovers and madmen does not really strain the audience's credulity after it has witnessed the turmoil created by mobile desire, with its attendant jealousy, rage, fighting, and threats of killing. It is when he makes it a triple comparison, by bringing in the poet, that he raises our suspicions. We have been engrossed in a poetic feast so rich that Theseus's debunking rationalism, his confidence that the poetic is merely delusive, a form of madness, must make us give pause. Hippolyta's counter-argument (given the last word in this short scene) is an assertion that a shared dream, recounted consistently by four different dreamers, is surely something to be wondered at and perhaps beyond the ken of Theseus's narrow rationalism. If, as I argued above, the dream-space is one of this play's chief signifiers of the aesthetic, then Hippolyta's last word affirms a positive role for the aesthetic against Theseus's debunking.

The comparison between poetry and madness, as I indicated previously, is very likely an allusion to the Renaissance neo-Platonic doctrine (found, among other places, in Sidney's *Defence of Poetry*) of the poet's divine

---

[80] See John Vyvyan, *Shakespeare and Platonic Beauty* (London: Chatto and Windus, 1961), 77–91. The literature on this topic is summarized and critiqued in Claire Gheeraert-Graffeuille, '"Call you me fair? That 'fair' again unsay": La beauté et ses monstres', in Gheeraert-Graffeuille and Vienne-Guerrin (eds.), *Autour du 'Songe d'une nuit d'été'*, 257–74.

madness.[81] This doctrine was a re-interpretation of Plato's own excessively rationalistic disdain of poetry (in his *Republic*) as merely an imitation of an imitation that weakened the ideal republic by appealing to the non-rational, merely sensual and emotional, human faculties. Faced with this hostility of Plato's, Renaissance neo-Platonists like Ficino, Scaliger, and Sidney did to this text exactly what Augustine had urged Christians to do when faced with apparently offensive Biblical texts: if the apparent meaning of the text contradicts the received faith and morals of the Church's teachings, he wrote, then we are clearly interpreting the Bible incorrectly, and we should look to other possible meanings, including allegorical ones. Here Plato collided with hard-won truths of humanism, and he had to be re-interpreted; he was re-interpreted. The poet's kinship with madness, the neo-Platonists decided, was one of a noble transcendence of ordinary rationality, the achievement of a vision which, piercing the outer veils of mere experience, arrived at higher truths in much the same way that Plato himself, using Socratic dialectic instead of poetic inspiration, had done. Poetry and philosophy were harmonized, and Renaissance humanism never looked back. It was a doctrine, too, which German and English Romantic poets revived in dissatisfaction with Kant's insistence on the aesthetic as non-cognitive, its suggestions of a subject–object perfect fit not, as Kant thought, a happy and improvable hypothesis, but instead an insight into the deepest truths of reality. *A Midsummer Night's Dream*, and Theseus's speech in particular, have been interpreted as sharing in this view of the poet's divine madness.

What I would argue, however, is that divine madness is at work, not so much within poetry (to which I will return below), but within sexuality. There should be no great objection to the idea that this play presents love/desire as a kind of madness, as noted above. But why say it is a 'divine' madness? The answer is two-fold.

In the first place, the madness of love, the strength, even the delusion-creating properties of desire, can be channeled into marriage, as the Elizabethan ideology of marriage taught and as the nuptials in this play hammer home to us. And what, according to this play, can marriage do for us? It contains desire, keeps the peace between former rivals, and creates a safe locus for sexuality. Sexuality, in turn, creates children, and as Shakespeare had told us elsewhere, 'The world must be peopled.'[82] Unlike most romantic comedies, the link between sexual union and the production of children is not obscured in this play. We see the first such

---

[81] Sidney, *A Defence of Poetry*, 376.   [82] Shakespeare, *Much Ado about Nothing*, 2.3.213–14.

linkage in Titania's great love for her votaress's orphaned child and in Oberon's desire to have the child to himself. And we are left with this thought again at the very end, when the fairies re-appear as fertility figures blessing the beds of the newly-weds and warding off childhood abnormalities. Love is a madness, but it has served its profound purpose in creating the conditions for human reproduction.

The second reason that love and desire are divine is revealed, it seems to me, in the comparison of lover and poet, through the figure of the madman. For all its arbitrariness and fickleness, desire is capable of revolutionizing the perceptual world, of transforming the subject's evaluations of reality fundamentally. In that way it is like (as Theseus asserted in his skeptical mode) poetry or the aesthetic. The fairy love-drops are the magical/ material means of this revolution, and the poetic symbol of it.[83] We remember Oberon's descriptions of how the drops originated. Cupid had loosed an arrow toward the fair vestal of the West, but the arrow missed its target and landed instead on a wild flower: 'Before, milk-white; now purple with love's wound– / And maidens call it love-in-idleness' (2.1.166–67). In this delicate, erotic imagery, not only, as we saw, is Queen Elizabeth exempted from the plagues of desire, but more importantly the natural world is eroticized, human sexuality naturalized, and the end of virginity celebrated in one pleasing moment of aesthetic intensity. Thus, in this play, the aesthetic is erotic, and Eros itself is aesthetic.

This is a harmony that only Oberon and Titania fully grasp in this play, and they themselves endangered it with their willful quarreling. It is, of course, an ideal harmony. But it can be created in poetry – it is created in poetry in this lyric play through the ability the Renaissance called 'imagination' – the 'faculty' of the mind which is able to fashion images for the inner eye of thought – and even more vividly in dreams – including images which have no existence in the real world. This is why Theseus says that lovers, poets, and madmen are interrelated; they all have strong imaginations of the kind productive of unreal images. These images are illusions, and that is all that matters to Theseus.

But if we are spirits of another sort, we will be discontented with Theseus's Platonic reduction of poetry to the status of mere illusion.[84] To the extent we have allowed ourselves to share in the magic of *A Midsummer*

---

[83] Orgel, *Imagining Shakespeare*, 94–7, describes this double signification for the drops (as eros and as imagination), but he sees both as kinds of social control rather than as having dual effects, both enchaining and empowering.

[84] Cf. Gheeraert-Graffeuille, '"Call you me fair?"', in Gheeraert-Graffeuille and Vienne-Guerrin (eds.), *Autour du 'Songe d'une nuit d'été'*, 273–74.

Night's Dream, we have implicitly found a value in imagination, in an aesthetic experience. And yet there is little warrant in this play to elevate the concept of imagination to Romantic levels, to make it the privileged portal to the deepest reality of creation. The play's fifth act is mostly taken up with a farcical anatomizing of drama at its degree zero in the version of 'Pyramus and Thisbe' given by the workmen. As Robert Weimann puts it, 'what Bottom and the players blithely ignore is the most hallowed demand in the Renaissance poetics of representation, to narrow, if possible to eliminate, the gap between the object and the agency of representation, between the imaginary world in the representation and the material tools and means of rendering it'.[85] That is to say, the play-within-the-play high-lights the signifiers, the materiality of the theatre. In this inset play we see all its artifice – its rehearsals, its props and costumes, its calculations of audience reaction – on display before us. Just as the character Bottom never allows us to forget the flesh, materiality, and irrationality of love and desire, just as he shows us how the aesthetic, for all its spiritualizing effects, remains rooted in materiality, the play he performs in re-inforces this message in terms of the very medium we are witnessing. The aesthetic magic we have witnessed is based on nothing less material than can be, in unpolished, primitive form, but the same for all that, supplied by 'hard-handed men … / Which never labored in their minds till now' (5.2.72–73). The poet's eye, after all, as Theseus tells us, 'Doth glance from heaven to earth, from earth to heaven' in its fine frenzy. Its vision is not of the real, but of what the real lacks, what is desired, what we dream of. Desire, in short, is one of the crucial links between the poet and the lover, the engine, as it were, of the imagination. Rooted in a material world represented in this play by the civic life of Athens and by the play of destructive desire among the four lovers in the green world, desire has recourse to imagination to body forth from the airy nothing of lack the needs and wants that can potentially humanize the world, if the world could wake up to them and achieve them.

   All the magic, however, this play tells us, is at present theatricality, stage-illusion, aesthetics, wrought in a material world out of a motley collection of resources. It is a play which presciently constructs a modern concept of the aesthetic and at the same time shows us the constructedness of this concept, its relation not only to imagination and the artistic past, but to desire and labor as well. 'In artworks', writes Theodor Adorno, 'the criterion of success is twofold: whether they succeed in integrating

[85] Robert Weimann, *Author's Pen and Actor's Voice: Playing and Writing in Shakespeare's Theatre*, ed. Helen Higbee and William West (Cambridge University Press, 2000), 83.

thematic strata and details into their immanent law of form and in this integration at the same time maintain what resists it and the fissures that occur in the process of integration.'[86] In *A Midsummer Night's Dream*, we see Shakespeare engaged in precisely this double task. In the travesty that is the rude mechanicals' play, he presents us with the final truth of his own masterpiece – its madness, its materiality, its resistance to the artist's shaping fantasies. In case we missed it, Shakespeare ends the play with another plebeian voice (this time from the fairy realm), Robin Goodfellow, who speaks the play's epilogue – quite against the wisdom of the imperious rationalist Theseus, who had said to the artisans: 'No epilogue, I pray you; for your play needs no excuse' (5.2.340). Robin re-inforces Theseus in one sense, but in a mode which he expects will lead rather to applause than to skepticism:

> If we shadows have offended,
> Think but this, and all is mended:
> That you have but slumbered here,
> While these visions did appear;
> And this weak and idle theme,
> No more yielding but a dream,
> Gentles, do not reprehend.
> …
> Give me your hands, if we be friends,
> And Robin shall restore amends. (Epilogue 1–16)

It is a misleadingly self-deprecatory assertion of the purposeless purposiveness of aesthetic production, creative of a specialized 'place', a sphere where materials of the social text are re-functioned into an autonomously structured aesthetic realm made from, and imprinted with, all the cultural materials which new historicism has so persuasively demonstrated inform the autonomous artifact. *A Midsummer Night's Dream* is Shakespeare's paean to, and anatomy of, impure aesthetics.

[86] Adorno, *Aesthetic Theory*, 7.

CHAPTER 3

Modernity, usury, and art in Timon of Athens

The 'modern' is the time of hell ... To determine the totality of traits
by which the 'modern' is defined would be to represent hell.[1]

Walter Benjamin

The socially critical zones of artworks are those where it hurts;
where in their expression, historically determined, the untruth of
the social situation comes to light. It is actually this against which
the rage at art reacts.[2]

T. W. Adorno

In *Timon of Athens* Shakespeare[3] returned to the woods outside of Athens
a decade or more after writing *A Midsummer Night's Dream*, deciding
some time between 1605 and 1608 – perhaps in early 1606 as John
Jowett has recently argued[4] – to dramatize the story of the proverbial
misanthrope Timon. As was the case in *A Midsummer Night's Dream*,
he explores in *Timon* aspects of an unnamed concept of the aesthetic,
but in a very different aesthetic mode, a satirical one that situates the
aesthetic within the day's system of commodity exchange. *Timon* is thus
linked with plays with similar concerns – *The Merchant of Venice,* for
example, and his other Greek play, *Troilus and Cressida* – all three plays

[1] Walter Benjamin, *The Arcades Project*, ed. Rolf Tiedemann, trans. Howard Eiland and Kevin
McLaughlin (Cambridge, Mass.: Belknap, 1999), 544.
[2] Theodor W. Adorno, *Aesthetic Theory*, ed. Gretel Adorno and Rolf Tiedemann, trans. R. Hullot-
Kentor (Minneapolis, Minn.: University of Minnesota Press, 1997), 237.
[3] As will be discussed below, in the light of recent scholarship Shakespeare appears to be the author
of about two-thirds of the play, while the younger Thomas Middleton appears to have written
the rest.
[4] See John Jowett, Introduction, *The Life of Timon of Athens*, by William Shakespeare and Thomas
Middleton, ed. John Jowett (Oxford University Press, 2004), 3–9, for a judicious and persuasive
critical review of previous arguments about the date and a strong case for the proposed date of
early 1606. There is no external evidence to help date the play, but its style, its use of Plutarch as
a source, and its themes link it to the late tragedies *King Lear* (1605–06), *Antony and Cleopatra*
(1606), and *Coriolanus* (1608). Several different factors converge for early 1606 as the probable
date, Jowett argues.

with an interest in the corrosive effects of mercantile capitalism and other negative aspects of emerging modernity. *Timon* takes up the difficult formal problem of how to integrate these disparate impulses, the meta-aesthetic and the socially satirical, and achieves a kind of disjunctive aesthetic solution to this problem through an ending which has puzzled and challenged generations of critics.

Timon of Athens is an extreme play that poses difficult problems of interpretation. Early in the history of modernity, it comprehends the element of nihilism inherent in the new social and ideological arrangements of mercantile capitalism and attempts to deal with that nihilism without fully endorsing it, but without dismissing it out of hand either. In this play Shakespeare is occupying similar terrain as would Nietzsche more than two centuries later; and as with Nietzsche an idea of the aesthetic – a Shakespearean, not a Nietzschean conception, however – is part of the response to the challenge posed by nihilism.

The Western idea of the aesthetic emerged in a capitalist and post-mythological era – that is, one that had, in its hegemonic culture, endorsed scientific rationality and marginalized or segregated non-rational explanations of existence – but was committed to a new, ultimately irrational system of determining value through market dynamics. The aesthetic was thus an idea grounded in secularism and commodity culture and became one of the characteristic marks of a developing modernity. In the wake of Horkheimer and Adorno's *Dialectic of Enlightenment*, however, we can now see that the Enlightenment combination of free scientific inquiry and a reified commodity economy created its own mythology, leading to an often uncritical faith in both the market and a totalizing scientific rationality. Today that faith has largely lost its legitimacy, and nihilism – the absence of values, usually resulting from an inability to ground them – becomes a problem confronting our era.[5] A prescient perception of this predicament is somewhere near the center of *Timon of Athens*, and the play ties the new nihilism to the workings of the cash nexus.[6] Shakespeare, in a transitional period in which many

[5] See Max Horkheimer and Theodor Adorno, *Dialectic of Enlightenment: Philosophical Fragments*, ed. Gunzelin Schmid Noerr, trans. Edmund Jephcott (Stanford, Calif.: Stanford University Press, 2002), 1–34 and throughout.

[6] Kenneth Muir, 'Timon of Athens and the Cash Nexus,' *Modern Quarterly Miscellany* 1 (1947); reprinted in Kenneth Muir, *The Singularity of Shakespeare and Other Essays* (Liverpool University Press, 1977), 56–75, influentially argued for the centrality of the cash nexus as defined by Marx for the play. An earlier critic, John W. Draper, 'The Theme of "Timon of Athens"', *Modern Language Review* 29.1 (January 1934), 20–31, argued a similar position without reference to Marx. And see Terence Hawkes, 'Band of Brothers', in Hugh Grady and Terence Hawkes (eds.), *Presentist*

capitalist institutions were in embryonic form, is far from sharing any Enlightenment optimism towards the developing market economy, as this play above all others demonstrates clearly.

In order to explore the latent potentialities of this economy, Shakespeare 'bracketed' the central Elizabethan–Jacobean institutions of Church and State, and this allowed him to create a series of thought-experiments focusing on the abstracted dynamics of the market – and, in other plays, those of Machiavellian politics as well. Classical settings were one strategy for doing so, and the classical age in Shakespeare thus evokes an allegory signifying an emerging modernity. The Greek world in particular, as depicted in *Troilus and Cressida* and *Timon of Athens* – *A Midsummer Night's Dream,* as we saw, is from a completely different, much more heterogeneous register – held a special place in Shakespeare's allegorical use of antiquity to signify emerging modernity. But we have to get outside our own post-Romantic idealizations to understand how Shakespeare's age understood 'the glory that was Greece'. Classical Greek literature was known primarily by reputation and Roman references rather than directly, and in Elizabethan slang the associations of the word 'Greek' were anything but glorious. 'Merrygreeks' were rowdy, licentious revelers, for example.[7] And both *Troilus and Cressida* and *Timon of Athens* are excellent examples of these negative associations. Robert Miola in a useful 1980 article catalogued numerous instances of Renaissance humanists denouncing Athens as a decadent historical example, its democracy a frightening and ill-conceived aberration. Miola does less justice to the pro-republican discourse exemplified, for example, in Machiavelli's *Discourses* and widespread among his English admirers,[8] and he doesn't take into account Shakespeare and Middleton's treatment of Athens as a republic, not a direct democracy. But he clearly establishes the suspicion of Greek political forms rampant in Elizabethan and Jacobean England.[9] In short, for the case of Shakespeare's most satirical plays, we have to reverse exactly the terms which Hegel established for satire's geographical provenance: 'Now since what is disclosed in Satire is the dissolution of the Ideal, a dissolution prosaic in its inner content, we have not to look

---

Shakespeares (London: Routledge, 2007), 6–26; 18–19, for a discussion of some of *Timon*'s 'presentist' and Marxist resonances at different historical junctures.

[7] T. J. B. Spencer, '"Greeks" and "Merrygreeks": A Background to *Timon of Athens* and *Troilus and Cressida*', in Richard Hosely (ed.), *Essays on Shakespeare and Elizabethan Drama in Honor of Hardin Craig* (Columbia, Mo.: University of Missouri Press, 1962), 223–33.

[8] See on this subject the more recent works of Andrew Hadfield, *Shakespeare and Republicanism* (Cambridge University Press, 2005) and Willy Maley, *Nation, State and Empire in English Renaissance Literature: Shakespeare to Milton* (New York: Palgrave Macmillan, 2003).

[9] Robert S. Miola, 'Timon in Shakespeare's Athens', *Shakespeare Quarterly* 31 (Spring 1980), 21–30.

for its actual soil in Greece as the land of beauty. Satire in the forms just described belongs properly to the Romans.'[10]

Shakespeare's first 'Greek' play *Troilus and Cressida* was written about 1602 and is well known for its darkness and nihilism. It is a play with a relentless puncturing, deflating strategy, and what it deflates are two of the most valued themes of Western literature (and Elizabeth's court), romantic love and heroic chivalry. The Homeric heroes Shakespeare had apparently encountered through Chapman's translation of *The Iliad* are treated as vainglorious, contemptible, and brutal. The already dubious love between Troilus and Cressida which he discovered in Chaucer's poem becomes a sordid liaison between a self-deceiving, extravagantly idealizing Troilus and a realist, materialist Cressida at the mercy of the powerful, instrumentalizing men around her.[11] All is lechery and war, we are continually reminded by the play's satirical commentator, the Greek churl Thersites. He speaks a naturalistic, materialist discourse in which all values are diagnosed as in the service of those drives which a post-Freudian age calls aggression and sexuality. His characterization of the cause of the Trojan war, for example, is as follows: 'All the argument is a whore and a cuckold. A good quarrel to draw emulous factions and bleed to death upon. Now the dry serpigo on the subject, and war and lechery confound all.'[12]

The Trojans in this play fare somewhat better than the Greek camp, but only superficially. In one of the day's much repeated commonplaces, Troy was a figure for mercantile London, and the Trojans in *Troilus* speak a language fraught with mercantile terms and concepts. Troilus's extravagantly idealizing discourse is revealed to be not merely his, but that of all the Trojans. Their idealization is depicted as a product of the marketplace and its quantifying of the irrationalities of human desire in the form of the prices of commodities. Many critics (myself included) have concluded that *Troilus and Cressida* embodies an early critique of mercantile, proto-capitalist commodification.[13] In the end, the Trojans'

[10] G. W. F. Hegel, *Aesthetics: Lectures on Fine Art*, trans. T. M. Knox (Oxford: Clarendon, 1975), Vol. I, 514.
[11] See my earlier treatment of this play in Hugh Grady, *Shakespeare's Universal Wolf: Studies in Early Modern Reification* (Oxford: Clarendon, 1996), 58–94, and the secondary sources cited therein. For a related, more explicitly Presentist reading of the play, which sees it as coming into full comprehension only in the twentieth century, see Kiernan Ryan, '*Troilus and Cressida*: The Perils of Presentism', in Grady and Hawkes (eds.), *Presentist Shakespeares*, 164–83.
[12] William Shakespeare, *Troilus and Cressida*, *The Norton Shakespeare*, ed. Stephen Greenblatt *et al.* (New York: Norton, 1997), 2.3.65–8. Other citations from Shakespeare plays other than *Timon of Athens* are from this edition. and will be given parenthetically in the text.
[13] See, for example, Grady, *Shakespeare's Universal Wolf*, 58–94; Douglas Bruster, *Drama and the Market in the Age of Shakespeare* (Cambridge University Press, 1992), 97–117; Eric Mallin,

romantic discourses do not keep them from acting very much like the Greeks.

Ancient Greece, in short, is a very nasty place in *Troilus and Cressida*. It is clearly allegorical for contemporary London as well, and that helps give point and bite to the deflation so relentlessly pursued in the play. And in *Timon* ancient Greece in the form of classical Athens is evoked with similar affect and topical function.

Composed by Shakespeare and Middleton at least four years after *Troilus*, *Timon of Athens* re-presents the earlier play's picture of an ancient society dominated by instrumental reason and mercantile calculation, but it also recapitulates themes and motifs from Jonson's and Middleton's city comedies, with their evocations of contemporaneous London. Timon's Athenian society is hypocritical. It displays an exterior of entertainment, friendship, and (oddly female-less) domestic life, but it is actually organized to enrich a class of merchants and usurers, corroding the friendship it pretends to, as well as the ancient bonds of loyalty and service. Timon's transformation from an idealizing, generous patron to a bitter, railing misanthrope serves among other things as a vehicle to puncture Athenian/London pretensions to civility, much as was the case for Troy in *Troilus and Cressida*.

This play, however, is far more than a recapitulation of the critique of mercantile capitalism of *Troilus*. It explores not just commodification and capital (in the form of usurious loans); it probes that other form of autotelic human practice, the aesthetic, a socially critical form which simultaneously participates in the corruptions of commercialism as a commodity. And it follows Timon's denunciations of corruption to their logical extremes, only to subject Timon's critique to its own interrogations and assert at the very end of the play, in the idea of the aesthetic, an alternative to philosophical universalisms. *Timon* thus pursues issues of commodification, usury, reification, and cultural nihilism in a Shakespearean thought-experiment about the logical outcome of social interactions governed purely by economic exchanges, and its critique is devastating. But, in its opening and conclusion especially, the play highlights another aspect of emerging modernity – an unnamed concept of the aesthetic. Indeed, the conclusion gives the aesthetic the last word in this often under-valued play.

'Emulous Factions and the Collapse of Chivalry: *Troilus and Cressida*', *Representations* 29 (Winter 1990), 145–79 ; and Lars Engle, *Shakespearean Pragmatism: Market of his Time* (University of Chicago Press, 1993), 147–63.

SHAKESPEARE'S THEATER AND COMMODITY PRODUCTION

The dialectic between the two intertwined but antagonistic aspects of modernity – between commodification (in the sense of reducing the value of a thing to its price on the market) and aestheticization (the valuing of a thing for its beauty and/or form) can be discerned not only in this play, but within the very institution which dominated Shakespeare's adult life, the early modern London theater. Unlike ancient and medieval theaters, Shakespeare's was commercial, a privately owned, profit-making venture. In short, Shakespeare was in the business of creating commodities for exchange-value. The aesthetic goal of creating aesthetic pleasure was far from 'pure'; it was a matter of economic survival to create commodities which audiences would find pleasing.[14] As a number of cultural materialists and new historicists have argued, the status of the theater as a private business, making its poets relatively free of the need to find aristocratic patrons and putting them into immediate contact with a broad array of representatives of different social classes and strata, gives it a relative autonomy, a certain, if limited, exemption from direct social control.

To be sure, aristocratic and royal approval appears to have been courted, and censorship existed and can be seen at work in what is *not* attempted by Shakespeare or his peers – a head-on critique of the power structure of his society.[15] But the London theaters of Shakespeare's day exhibit many of the qualities of autonomy that I discussed in the Introduction. A figure like Shakespeare's Falstaff, for example, was allowed to strut his many hours on the stage, tweaking whatever sensibilities he tweaked, so long, we can surmise, as his name was not Oldcastle and he wasn't *explicitly* a satirical Puritan zealot. The theatrical space is not quite yet the public sphere of free discussion theorized by Jürgen Habermas as crucial to modernity and democracy, but it is perhaps a direct ancestor of it, with some of its crucial qualities.

---

[14] The play, as Don Hedrick has argued, was (and is) a peculiar kind of commodity, since not the playscript as a property, but the experience of viewing a single performance of it constitutes the commodity being sold. This is further complicated because the play's repeatability is limited and it is thus subject to the wear of use, like capital machinery. My overriding point here, however, is that in the playhouse a commodity is very definitely being sold, in the same way that services sold constitute intangible commodities, however evanescent the actual material form. See Don Hedrick, 'Male Surplus Value', *Renaissance Drama* 31 (2002), 85–124 and 'Advantage, Affect, History, *Henry V*', *PMLA* 118.3 (May 2003), 470–87.

[15] Cf. Annabel Patterson, *Shakespeare and the Popular Voice* (Oxford: Blackwell, 1989) and Jonathan Dollimore, *Radical Tragedy: Religion, Ideology and Power in the Drama of Shakespeare and his Contemporaries* (1984), 3rd edn. (Durham, NC: Duke University Press, 2004).

It is, however, already an aesthetic space, an autonomous sphere of fanciful, pleasure-giving cultural production that becomes an arena for the exhibition of licensed, dangerous materials, the contemplation of the relation of humanity to the universe, and the exhibition of craft and skill. In the iconoclasm of *Timon* we can see this relative autonomy on display, just as we can see an acute consciousness of the tension between writing for profit and writing for its own sake.

TIMON'S CRITICAL FORTUNES

One reaction to *Timon's* thematic complexities can be (and has been) a kind of throwing up of the critical hands, a dismissal of the play as an aesthetic failure. That such reactions are still common is suggested by two of the play's recent commentators, who, in the course of otherwise quite admiring general treatments, have asserted that the play is Shakespeare's single least popular one. *Timon of Athens*, writes Anthony Davies, 'enjoys the dubious distinction of being perhaps the least popular play in the Shakespeare canon'.[16] More recently John Jowett has echoed this assertion, writing, 'It is no coincidence that Shakespeare's least loved play is about a misanthrope'.[17]

Interestingly, neither writer offers much in the way of documentation for these assertions, and the diagnosis is at least at one level contradicted by a list of some of the play's ardent admirers, like Herman Melville, A. W. Schlegel, William Hazlitt, the German Hegelian Hermann Ulrici, Karl Marx, George Brandes, Wyndham Lewis, Kenneth Burke, and above all, G. Wilson Knight[18] – this last critic especially considered

---

[16] A[nthony] D[avies], 'Timon of Athens', in Michael Dobson and Stanley Wells (eds.), *The Oxford Companion to Shakespeare* (Oxford University Press, 2001).

[17] Jowett, Introduction, 1.

[18] Melville's appreciatory views on *Timon* (found in marginalia) are discussed in Harry Levin, 'Shakespeare's Misanthrope', *Shakespeare Survey* 26 (1973), 89–104. See also August Wilhelm Schlegel, *Lectures on Dramatic Art and Literature*, ed. A. J. W. Morrison, trans. John Black (London: George Bell, 1892), 417–18; William Hazlitt, *Characters of Shakespeare's Plays and Lectures on the English Poets* (London: Macmillan, 1903), 38–42; Hermann Ulrici, *Shakespeare's Dramatic Art; And His Relation to Calderon and Goethe*, trans. A. J. W. Morrison (London: Chapman, 1846), 239–44; Karl Marx, *The Economic and Philosophic Manuscripts of 1844*, ed. Dirk J. Struik, trans. Martin Milligan (New York: International, 1964), 165–69; George Brandes, *William Shakespeare: A Critical Study*, trans. William Archer and Diana White, 2 vols. (London: F. Ungar, 1963), 254–70; Wyndham Lewis, *The Lion and the Fox: The Role of the Hero in the Plays of Shakespeare* (London: G. Richards, 1927), 247–56; Kenneth Burke, *Language as Symbolic Action: Essays on Life, Literature, and Method* (Berkeley, Calif.: University of California Press, 1966), 115–24; and G. Wilson Knight, *The Wheel of Fire: Interpretations of Shakespearean Tragedy, with Three New Essays*, rev. edn. (London: Methuen, 1949), 207–39.

Timon a titanic masterpiece. And most recent critics – including Davies and Jowett – have generally been at least implicitly positive in their evaluations of its quality.[19] To be sure, one could create a list of commentators who see the play as a failure approximately as long as that of its admirers.[20] In terms of its overall critical history, then, *Timon* is, like several other plays (*Henry V* and *Measure for Measure* come to mind), an object of critical contention, with a very mixed but fairly evenly balanced reception history. It certainly has not been one of the most performed plays, but there have been some notable theatrical interpretations, and no play which attracted the talents of Duke Ellington (who wrote incidental music for the play used in 1963, 1991 and 1999 productions) can be said to be absolutely unpopular.[21]

The uneven appreciation of *Timon of Athens* has come about, as I have suggested, because of the thematic difficulties with which it confronts its readers and viewers. In my own experience with the text, *Timon* is a play well worth taking seriously. It presents its share of interpretational puzzles, but so do most of Shakespeare's plays. We can never be certain that our readings have solved the puzzles – but that is the eternal fate of all readers and play-goers. 'Artworks are enigmas', Adorno writes. 'They contain the potential for the solution; the solution is not objectively given.'[22] What we can say is that 400 years of developing capitalist modernity have made *Timon* more rather than less comprehensible in its main outlines, because the play comes alive as a prescient vision of a world dominated by the cash nexus in which one of the few avenues of human redemption is supplied by works of art.

[19] See, for example, Coppélia Kahn, '"Magic of Bounty": *Timon of Athens*, Jacobean Patronage, and Maternal Power', *Shakespeare Quarterly* 38. 1 (Spring 1987), 34–57; Michael Chorost, 'Biological Finance in Shakespeare's *Timon of Athens*', *ELR* 21 (1991), 349–70; and Ken Jackson, '"One wish" or the Possibility of the Impossible: Derrida, the Gift, and God in *Timon of Athens*', *Shakespeare Quarterly* 52. 1 (Spring 2001), 34–66.

[20] The most influential argument that *Timon* is an artistic failure – and an unfinished work as well – is Una Ellis-Fermor, '"Timon of Athens": An Unfinished Play', *The Review of English Studies* 18 (July 1942), 270–83. A sample of other critics who see the play as a failed or lesser work include: Samuel Taylor Coleridge, *Coleridge's Shakespearean Criticism*, ed. Thomas Raysor, 2 vols. (Cambridge, Mass.: Harvard University Press, 1930), Vol. 1, 108–11; G. G. Gervinus, *Shakespeare Commentaries*, trans. F. E. Bunnett, rev. edn. (London: Smith, Elder, 1877), 769–86; E. K. Chambers, *William Shakespeare: A Study of Facts and Problems* (Oxford: Clarendon, 1930), Vol. 1, 480–84; A. C. Bradley, *Shakespearean Tragedy: Lectures on 'Hamlet', 'Othello', 'King Lear', and 'Macbeth'*, new edn. (1904; reprinted Harmondsworth: Penguin, 1991), 226–28; Theodore Spencer, *Shakespeare and the Nature of Man* (New York: Macmillan, 1942), 177–202; and Peter Ure, *William Shakespeare, the Problem Plays: 'Troilus and Cressida', 'All's Well That Ends Well', 'Measure for Measure', 'Timon of Athens'*, rev. edn. (London: Longmans Green, 1964), 44–51.

[21] See Jowett, Introduction, 89–120, for a detailed performance history.

[22] Adorno, *Aesthetic Theory*, 121.

TEXT AND AUTHORSHIP

Another part of *Timon*'s public-relations problem stems from its unique textual provenance: the play has attracted as much attention because of the uncertainties surrounding its last-minute inclusion in the First Folio (and related textual and authorship issues) as it has for its dramatic qualities – albeit a new consensus on these issues seems to have taken place recently. A very strong case has emerged in the last thirty years that the play was co-written by Shakespeare and the younger playwright Thomas Middleton,[23] and although this case is not absolutely ironclad, it is strong enough that it is assumed here. In a dissertation completed in 1982 but still unpublished at the time of this writing, R. V. Holdsworth undertook a stylistic analysis of the play[24] which was more extensive than but which also corroborated independent studies by David Lake and MacDonald P. Jackson and a later one by Brian Vickers.[25] All these scholars found strong evidence of Middleton's hand in portions of the play. Holdsworth's stylistic analysis assigns Shakespeare the authorship of about two-thirds of the play – roughly speaking, the beginning and the end. Middleton apparently wrote the first banquet scene (1.2) and the scenes in the middle of the play (3.1– 3.6), with the exception of the middle section of 3.6). Thus, he is responsible for the scenes in which Timon interacts with his creditors while his steward Flavius denounces his profligate unthriftiness – and for the troubling scene of Alcibiades at the Senate (3.5). Aside from a few other stray passages (all associated with the character Flavius – apparently Middleton's favorite), Shakespeare wrote the rest and is clearly the primary author.

As John Jowett has pointed out, it is possible to see different emphases in the two portions: Middleton is a cultural Puritan, concerned above all

[23] See Brian Vickers, *Shakespeare, Co-Author* (Oxford University Press, 2002), 244–90, for an exhaustive and judicious survey of the discussion of the authorship question. The case for Middleton's co-authorship, Vickers argues, is virtually conclusive. However, Karl Klein, Introduction, William Shakespeare, *Timon of Athens,* ed. Karl Klein (Cambridge University Press, 2001), 61–65, remained unconvinced, whereas Jowett constructed his landmark 2004 Oxford edition around the assumption of co-authorship. The long-awaited new edition, Thomas Middleton, *Thomas Middleton: The Collected Works,* ed. Gary Taylor and John Lavagnino (Oxford University Press, 2007), assumes co-authorship, as does the Arden 3 edition (which appeared in the very final stages of revision of this work), Anthony B. Dawson and Gretchen E. Minton, eds., *Timon of Athens,* by William Shakespeare and Thomas Middleton, Arden Shakespeare Third Series (London: Arden, 2008).

[24] R. V. Holdsworth, Middleton and Shakespeare: The Case for Middleton's Hand in *Timon of Athens,* Diss., University of Manchester, 1982.

[25] David J. Lake, *The Canon of Thomas Middleton's Plays: Internal Evidence for the Major Problems of Authorship* (Cambridge University Press, 1975); MacDonald P. Jackson, *Studies in Attribution: Middleton and Shakespeare,* Jacobean Drama Studies 79, Salzburg Studies in English Literature (Salzburg: Institut für Anglistik und Amerikanistik Universität Salzburg, 1979); and Vickers, *Shakespeare, Co-Author,* 244–90.

with wastefulness and profligacy; Shakespeare, in contrast, is most passionate in depicting ingratitude, loyalty and disloyalty, and the philosophically central issues of misanthropy and its problems.[26] Most important here, Shakespeare introduces the theme of art as commodity and as a form of knowledge in the play's opening scene and returns to it at the end in a treatment with both subtlety and depth, while in Middleton's portions this theme goes unaddressed. Accordingly, a re-focus on the play's thematic and aesthetic qualities is in order, in this context particularly on the topic of the play's treatment of the nature of art and its relation to a developing and de-humanizing world of commodity production.

MONETARY AND AESTHETIC VALUE IN SCENE I.I

The play's first scene introduces four characters identified only by their trades: Poet, Painter, Jeweller, and Merchant.[27] For many readers or viewers in our own time, such a grouping must seem anomalous, a mixture of apples and oranges, of profit-seeking businessmen and profit-defying artists. The grouping of the four seems to link art and capitalism without as yet telling us the significance of the linking. But there is also a suggestion of a division in the group. Two of the characters, the Poet and the Painter, at first speak only to each other, while the Jeweller and Merchant pair off, presumably on the other side of the stage. These two pairings seem to support our own preconceptions. The Poet and the Painter are, by post-Kantian standards, engaged in creating intangible, unquantifiable value by producing fine art, a kind of protest in itself against a commodified world ruled over by monetary or exchange-value – that quantitative, economic abstraction expressed in terms of price in a marketplace. The other two, the Jeweller and the Merchant, are in contrast mere purveyors of commodities in search of profits. By grouping the four together, but pairing them separately, this carefully crafted scene seems to introduce an issue central to the twentieth-century aesthetic theories of Benjamin and Adorno: what is the relation between the two kinds of value associated with the artwork? How does the work's status as a commodity relate to its status as an

---

[26] Jowett, Introduction, 49–70. The argument was made earlier in John Jowett, 'Middleton and Debt in *Timon of Athens*', in Linda Woodbridge (ed.), *Money and the Age of Shakespeare: Essays in New Economic Criticism* (New York: Palgrave, 2003), 219–35.

[27] The Folio stage directions add a Mercer, deleted as an error by many editors including Klein in the edition followed here.

anti-commodity, a non-use value that seems to defy the laws of economics by having no particular purpose of its own?

There is much in the dialogue that clearly suggests something unusual about the specific commodities of the Poet and Painter – and perhaps the Jeweller's as well. For all their utility as articles of commerce, the products associated with their trades – painting, poem, and jewels – are also something else as well. And indeed we find the Poet and the Painter at moments discussing their arts in terms that have nothing to do with exchange-value, suggesting instead a kind of connoisseurship and the idea of art as a form of beauty and knowledge. The Jeweller shares in this as well, admiring the 'water' – the deep lustre or liquid appearance of the interior – of a jewel he intends to sell Timon. There is thus an aesthetic value, an appearance of beauty, in this object of nature worked over by labor to create two kinds of value – aesthetic and monetary.

The Poet is conscious of aesthetic value as well. For example, he praises the production of the painter:

> POET: Admirable! How this grace
> Speaks his own standing! What a mental power
> This eye shoots forth! How big imagination
> Moves in this lip! To th'dumbness of the gesture
> One might interpret.
> PAINTER: It is a pretty mocking of the life.
> Here is a touch; is't good?
> POET: I will say of it,
> It tutors nature; artificial strife
> Lives in these touches, livelier than life.[28]

Two aesthetic notions can be found in this dialogue, both of them tenets of post-Enlightenment aesthetic theories. First, in expressing his admiration, the Poet emphasizes that the images of the painting provide us with a kind of non-verbal knowledge or information – the 'dumbness of the gesture' which can then be interpreted verbally. The dumb images convey the spirit and the affect of their subject: a 'big imagination', a

---

[28] Shakespeare, *Timon of Athens*, ed. Klein, 1.1.31–39. I use this edition, despite what I take to be the superior scholarship of the Jowett edition, because it retains traditional post-Enlightenment act divisions; Jowett, to be faithful to the Folio's lack of act divisions, instead numbers scenes consecutively without reference to acts. But the scene-numbering is equally foreign to the Folio, and the lack of act divisions makes cross-references to other editions of the play inconvenient. In addition, Klein retains a Folio reading at a crucial point (1.1.22–23) to be discussed below. The Arden 3 edition (ed. Dawson and Minton, *Timon of Athens*) appeared too late to be used in this work. All subsequent citations of *Timon* are from Klein's edition and will be given parenthetically in the text.

'mental power'. Second, we see a certain inflection of the Aristotelian idea that the work of art is a mimesis, an imitation of nature, when the Poet glosses the Painter's claim that his work 'is a pretty mocking of the life', exclaiming that it goes beyond life and mere imitation: it 'tutors nature', it is 'livelier than life'. This is an interpretation of mimesis that emphasizes the artwork's separateness and alterity from the nature from which it takes its materials; it is closer both to post-Kantian aesthetics and to the neo-Platonic notions we found in the previous chapter in Sidney's *Defence of Poetry* than it is to Aristotle.[29] And, as discussed in the Introduction, this sense of the aesthetic as a separate realm with its own (relative) autonomy is a crucial one in the impure aesthetics I am using as an interpretive lens in this study. This idea of art's autonomy, brought up so casually in scene 1.1, will turn out to be crucial to this play's denouement, when it becomes time to assess the meaning of Timon's final resting place after his suicide. It is addressed late in this scene as well, in words of Timon which editors have often found obscure:

> The painting is almost the natural man;
> For since dishonour traffics with man's nature,
> He is but outside; these pencilled figures are
> Even such as they give out. (1.1.161–64)

This is a prescient assertion of the autonomy of the aesthetic from empirical reality and from the social context in which it exists as a commodity or other use-value. The Poet and Apemantus had conceived of the Poet's work in terms of patronage,[30] of a relation between a wealthy patron and a subservient poet seeking remuneration and succumbing to ideology and power in the process, thereby destroying the artwork's constituting autonomy. But Timon in these lines separates the artwork from reality. In the fallen world of commodity culture, 'dishonour traffics with man's nature'. The word 'traffic' is used just a few lines further as a synonym for trade, or the business of the merchant (1.1.237–39). This meaning suggests both commodity culture and a general tendency to 'dishonour'. In such a world, Timon continues, man is 'but outside' – that is to say, he is forced by the Machiavellian world of 'traffic' to conceal his interior life and intentions and act in the world showing a mere appearance – his

---

[29] Sir Philip Sidney, *A Defence of Poetry* (1595), in Brian Vickers (ed.), *English Renaissance Literary Criticism* (Oxford: Clarendon, 1999), 343.

[30] For an early discussion of Renaissance patronage of the arts evoked in this scene, see Patricia Thomson, 'The Literature of Patronage, 1580–1630', *Essays in Criticism* 2.3 (July 1952), 267–84.

'outside' – not the whole man. The idea echoes Hamlet's complaint that he alone of all the court does not know 'seems' – just before he is obliged by the out-of-joint times to undertake a stratagem of 'seems' in a world he realizes is an unweeded garden.

But in the world inside the painting, Timon continues, 'these pencilled figures are / Even such as they give out'. Being an appearance, the artwork can only be appearance, with nothing hidden underneath it. Art, precisely because it is not reality but a mere semblance, cannot lie, and this is in great contrast to the situation of the real world, as even Timon seems to realize here. Art, because it is not merely a passive mirror of reality, can reveal truths about human nature obscured in empirical reality. This is an aspect of art which Adorno in particular underlined,[31] and it is underlined here by Timon in words that are wiser than he knows. There is that within art which escapes its commodity status and offers an alternative to a world of commodity idolatry. As Adorno puts it, 'Artworks are plenipotentiaries of things that are no longer distorted by exchange, profit, and the false needs of a degraded humanity. In the context of total semblance, art's semblance of being-in-itself is the mask of truth.'[32] This is a notion to which Timon will return late in the play, when all else has lost its value.

The Poet is also aware of values implicit in his own work that go beyond economic ones, that assert the need for a critical distance between art and the world, as he converses with the Painter:

> When we for recompense have praised the vile,
> It stains the glory in that happy verse
> Which aptly sings the good. (1.1.16–18)

He is clearly referring to the possibility of corruption, of the Poet's susceptibility to a kind of bribery if, for the sake of monetary 'recompense', the Poet praises someone not deserving of such praise, with the result that all poetry declines in (non-monetary) value because of the corruption of some poems. Toward the end of the scene, the Cynical philosopher Apemantus accuses the Poet of being just such a flatterer – although there is also a familiar Shakespearean quibble about poetry being by definition a lie – without any rebuttal:

APEMANTUS: Art not a poet?
POET: Yes.
APEMANTUS: Then thou liest: look in the last work,
    where thou hast feigned him a worthy fellow.

---

[31] Adorno, *Aesthetic Theory*, 78–100 and throughout.   [32] *Ibid.*, 227.

POET: That's not feigned, he is so.
APEMANTUS: Yes, he is worthy of thee, and to pay thee for
thy labour. He that loves to be flattered is worthy o'th'
flatterer. Heavens, that I were a lord! (1.1.221–28)

Throughout the scene, then, the double face of the work of art is insisted
on. It is a token in a social game of flattery and patronage and an economic
commodity (the two categories often seeming to slide into each other in
the dialogue). And yet at another level art is, or should be, autonomous
from that society as a pure semblance in a relation of Other to the social
world in which it circulates, and because of that separation, it is able to
comment on and implicitly judge the world it negates.

THE ALTERITY OF ART IN *TIMON*

This dual status of the artwork is, here and elsewhere in *Timon*'s first scene,
a tension-filled one. In terms of twentieth-century aesthetic theory, the
issue is one of the relation of power and ideology to art. And in this play
art, like almost everything else, is subject to these corrupting influences.
The aesthetic can lose its distance from the world it reflects upon and
instead join it and its corruption. At one level this play depicts precisely
such a corruption, as we will discover when we meet the Poet and Painter
again, in the play's second half. In another way, however, the play affirms
art's autonomy by constituting itself, a work of art, as a fierce critique of
the existing world.

The distance from its social context of *Timon of Athens* is clearly of a
different sort than the kind I discussed in *A Midsummer Night's Dream*.
In the comedy the alterity of the aesthetic was figured by the fairy world
and fairy perception, giving us an idealized golden realm that mirrored
the human world in some ways but clearly excelled it in many others.
Timon is very different from this, more like one of the works rejected by
Duke Theseus on his wedding night as unsuitable to the occasion, 'The
thrice-three muses mourning for the death / Of learning, late deceased in
beggary', as Egeus calls it. Theseus replies:

> That is some satire, keen and critical,
> Not sorting with a nuptial ceremony. (5.1.52–55)

The same could be said, in spades, of this play, centered on a
misanthrope and featuring the railing rhetoric of the Cynical
philosopher Apemantus[33] and a train of corrupted and corrupting

---

[33] Apemantus's specific philosophical school is alluded to in the many references to dogs in the
language of those talking to and about Apemantus in the play. These allusions, along with

characters.³⁴ The fictional Athenian society depicted in this play is both an aesthetic device and a satirical signifier of the London of Shakespeare's day. The woods outside Athens are a kind of inverted green world – sharing with their comic counter-part the role of providing a space outside of society for its inhabitants to experiment with different kinds of behavior, value, and identities.³⁵ But when Timon discovers the hidden gold in his version of the green world, utopia can no longer keep society at bay, and he is visited by representatives of all the social types he had fled Athens to escape. One of the many ironies of this drama – which seems continually to turn in on itself – is that the green world turns out to be a different version of the city. Thus this satirical fictional space can be said to select and magnify features of the social real, mixing them into an aesthetic space in much the way the poet indicates he has done in his poem about the fickle nature of fortune, to which I will turn below. It is the kind of combination Adorno describes in his dictum, 'The nonexisting in artworks is a constellation of the existing.'³⁶ As a work with important elements of satire, it is a form of the aesthetic which emphasizes the ugly rather than the beautiful, dystopia rather than utopia, critical reflection more than imaginary invention. And yet, like the other forms of the aesthetic, it is more than, other than, a slice of the real. If it is a mirror to nature, it is one whose end is 'to show virtue her own feature, scorn her own image, and the very age and body of the time his form and pressure'³⁷ – that is, to stylize, thematize and evaluate the world, not merely mimic it. Satire in its negativity creates its own utopia in the implied space in which its jaundiced verdict on the real might be appreciated and affirmed. The

Apemantus's demeanor and argumentation, clearly indicate that Shakespeare had picked up from one of several possible sources a tradition of associating Apemantus with the Cynics, whose name derives from the Greek word for dog, which in turn was either a reference to a gymnasium where the sect developed or the nickname of its best known figure, Diogenes of Sinope (412?–323 BCE) – or perhaps, as Jowett suggests, a reference to the snarling style of earlier stage and print Cynics depicted by Marston and others (Jowett, Introduction, 74–77). However, Jowett does not treat Cynicism as a philosophical school with its own cogency. As will become clear below, I think Apemantus is a more positive figure in the drama than Jowett does.

³⁴ That *Timon* partakes of the spirit of Roman satire has been observed by a number of critics beginning with Charles Gildon, 'Remarks on the Plays of Shakespeare' (1710), in *Shakespeare: The Critical Heritage*, ed. Brian Vickers, Vol. II: *1693–1733* (London: Routledge, 1974), 226–62. See also Schlegel, *Lectures on Dramatic Art and Literature*, 417–18; Alvin Kernan, *The Cankered Muse: Satire of the English Renaissance* (New Haven, Conn.: Yale University Press, 1959), 192–246; Robert C. Elliott, *The Power of Satire: Magic, Ritual, Art* (Princeton University Press, 1960), 141–67; William W. E. Slights, '"*Genera mixta*" and "Timon of Athens"', *Studies in Philology* 74. 1 (1977), 36–62.

³⁵ Cf. Jowett, Introduction, 2.   ³⁶ Adorno, *Aesthetic Theory*, 135.

³⁷ Shakespeare, *Hamlet*, 3.2.20–22.

satirist is always an idealist, as the old saw has it, and it is a form which can create mirrors within mirrors, satires upon the satirist. Part of the 'selection' involved in creating the fictional space of the play, in its own day and in ours, constitutes what I have been calling a thought-experiment, a construction of an artificial world featuring what we recognize as prescient features of a slowly emerging modernity – separated out, as it were, from the much more religious and traditional society that Shakespeare lived in.

MYSTERIES OF THE COMMODITY

The opening scene of *Timon* clearly shows an awareness of the artwork as a specialized kind of knowledge and one capable of producing alternatives to the existing world even as it takes its place within it. But while the dialogue in the scene establishes a bond of artistry between the Poet and the Painter (one that was of course a commonplace dating back to Horace and beyond), it is still striking that all four tradesmen – Poet, Painter, Jeweller, and Merchant – are brought together in a common and explicitly economic enterprise, based in the pursuit of exchange-value or money. They are all drawn by what the Poet calls the 'magic of bounty', the flow of wealth from Timon's coffers to them and a herd of others. The Poet in fact gives us a memorable invocation of this attractive power when he personifies it and addresses it evocatively:

> See
> Magic of bounty, all these spirits thy power
> Hath conjured to attend! (1.1.5–7)

As Coppélia Kahn emphasized in her insightful reading of the play (at once psychoanalytic and new historicist), Timon's followers – and, until his disillusionment, Timon himself – fantasize an endless (and maternal) fecundity, the creation of wealth from nothing through magic.[38] We will discover later in the play the material basis of this illusion, created by the paradoxical, delusive properties of financial interest or usury as Shakespeare inevitably calls it, which becomes in Marx's sense no longer simply money but capital – that is, money expended not for other commodities to satisfy immediate needs, but for profits (see Introduction). For any post-Marxist reader, the figure of the 'magic of bounty', in the words of John Jowett, is a fantasizing figure for capitalism itself,[39] and it is a central issue in this play,

---

[38] Kahn, ' "Magic of Bounty" '.
[39] John Jowett, 'Shakespeare, Middleton, and Debt in *Timon of Athens*', Presentation, Annual Meeting, Shakespeare Association of America, April 2001, Miami, Fla. My thanks to Professor

intimately connected with the play's aesthetic ideas. It is one that draws not only the Merchant and the Jeweller, but the Painter and Poet as well.

No one who has read Shakespeare with an open eye should be surprised at his interest in the social effects of the emerging mercantile capitalist society of his day. He had made it a central issue, as mentioned previously, in the 1596–97 *The Merchant of Venice,* and it was a crucial part of the deluded Trojan society he had depicted in *Troilus and Cressida* (1602) – the play closest in many ways, as we have seen, to the corrosive spirit of this one. The issue of commodification exists as a background in many of the other plays and in the Sonnets as well.[40] Nowhere, however, is the tone of a Shakespearean play more bitter or caustic in its denunciations of the deleterious effects on society of the money economy than in *Timon.* Like the theme of art, this one too is introduced to us subtly in the first scene, where, as we have seen, we learn that art is not only a conveyor of aesthetic knowledge and pleasure, but also a commodity seeking its price on the marketplace. We could speak of Timon as a patron of the poet and painter, but they seem to think of themselves – and the opening scene seems to present them – as commodity-dealers, seeking a *de facto* sale, rather than as ornaments to society in search of patronage. The Jeweller at least is clear on this point:

> JEWELLER: I have a jewel here.
> MERCHANT: O, pray, let's see't. For the Lord Timon, sir?
> JEWELLER: If he will touch the estimate. But for that– (1.1.13–15)

But he never finishes his point because he is interrupted by the Poet, whose lines on the fragility of poetic integrity were just discussed. However, it seems clear that the shared assumption of all the speakers is that commodities, including poems and paintings, have monetary values ('the estimate'), and they will sell if offered an adequate price.

Early in 1.1 the focus shifts to the poem that the Poet appears ready to present to Timon for his approbation and monetary compensation – 'A thing slipp'd idly from me' (1.1.21), he says with a certain *sprezzatura,* but as we soon learn, it is one that has been meditated and worked over. Its production as described seems firmly rooted in what we know of Renaissance rhetoric and poetics: the poet has clearly mined traditional sources for material 'aptly' suited to a present situation. Despite these commonplace elements, however, to explain his work the Poet directs the Painter's attention to 'this confluence, this great flood of visitors' to

---

Jowett for providing me with a typescript of this presentation.
[40] See Grady, *Shakespeare's Universal Wolf,* 26–35 and 85–94.

Timon (1.1.43). He then indicates that his work has depicted a fictional character in precisely this kind of situation:

> I have in this rough work shaped out a man
> Whom this beneath world doth embrace and hug
> With amplest entertainment. (1.1.44–46)

The poem thus indicates two different kinds of materials incorporated into its shaping vision: the first, as I have been emphasizing, is the poem's and the play's social context. If you look around you, the Poet tells the Painter, you will see exactly the sort of scene my poem describes. The other source, however, is poetic tradition and allegorical technique, drawn on to give moral meaning and aesthetic shaping to the 'rough' material of the real:

> Sir, I have upon a high and pleasant hill
> Feigned Fortune to be throned. The base o'th'mount
> Is ranked with all deserts, all kind of natures
> That labour on the bosom of this sphere
> To propagate their states. Amongst them all,
> Whose eyes are on this sovereign lady fixed,
> One do I personate of Lord Timon's frame,
> Whom Fortune with her ivory hand wafts to her,
> Whose present grace to present slaves and servants
> Translates his rivals. (1.1.66–75)

There is even perhaps the faintest echo of the aesthetic vision of *A Midsummer Night's Dream* in the word 'translates', so strategic in that play in evoking movement from the real into the aesthetic and from one social station to another (see Chapter 2). As several critics have pointed out, this paraphrased poem-within-the-play, along with the elusive Masque of the Amazons in Middleton's scene 1.2, is the aesthetic equivalent of more famous plays-within-plays in *1 Henry IV*, *Hamlet*, *The Tempest*, and of course *A Midsummer Night's Dream*. It is, in Maurice Charney's much-cited characterization of the Poet's production, 'the central fable of the play'[41] – a miniature, as it were, of the whole, but embedded within that larger whole. What in Shakespeare and Middleton's play is a skillfully sketched turning point, stretching over several scenes, is in the poem a mere subordinate clause:

> When Fortune in her shift and change of mood
> Spurns down her late beloved, all his dependants
> Which laboured after him to the mountain's top

[41] Maurice Charney, Introduction to *Timon of Athens*, *The Complete Signet Shakespeare*, ed. Sylvan Barnet (New York: Harcourt, 1972), 1368; quoted in Kahn, "'Magic of Bounty'", 36.

> Even on their knees and hands, let him slip down,
> Not one accompanying his declining foot. (1.1.87–91)

This poetic précis does, however, provide us interpretive clues for evaluating the unfolding dramatic action ahead of us: Timon's fall is a caprice of fortune, that proverbial strumpet, not a richly deserved punishment for foolishness; and attention is focused on Timon's isolation after the shift of fortune, his desertion by all those who had previously shared in his good fortune. Finally, and most importantly from my point of view, the motif of an inset poem complements the aesthetic discussion of scene 1.1 and calls attention to the idea of art's participation within – while maintaining aesthetic distance and autonomy from – a world of wealth and power.

Both of these characteristics of the artwork are glanced at in the odd and elusive definition of poetry given by the poet as he describes the work he has produced in hopes of patronage from Timon, in lines which have troubled editors because of their obscurity:

> A thing slipp'd idly from me.
> Our poesy is as a gown which uses
> From whence 'tis nourished. The fire i'th'flint
> Shows not till it be struck. Our gentle flame
> Provokes itself, and like the current flies
> Each bound it chases. (1.1.21–26)

In an innovation followed by numerous subsequent editions of the play, including the new one of John Jowett, Alexander Pope emended 'gown' to 'gomme' or 'gum' and 'uses' to 'issues'. Samuel Johnson kept Pope's first change, but altered his emendation of 'uses' to 'oozes', producing the following, much reproduced wording:

> Our poesy is as a gum which oozes
> From whence 'tis nourished.

But in this Pope–Johnson reading, there is a subtle shift to an eighteenth-century, proto-Romantic notion of art as self-expression, as a kind of life-juice from the producer oozing out. However in the Folio's reading, the emphasis is on poetry as a kind of use-value, perhaps even a commodity, which can wear out through use, like a gown which, as it is repeatedly worn, frays and thins. The poem, we are told, 'slipp'd idly from me', and this verb is more consistent with the image of a loosely worn gown slipping off its wearer than with gum oozing from a plant. Much later in the play, we in fact hear of a gown which has slipped off its wearer when, in the tumult created by Timon's 'feast' of dishes filled with nothing but warm water, the guests have misplaced various articles of clothing. The Fourth Lord says, 'I have lost my gown' and then finds it lying on the ground (3.6.96–102). But the key to this textual crux lies in a meaning of the term 'uses' which editors have apparently never considered.

What could the Poet mean in claiming that the poem/gown 'uses/ From whence 'tis nourished'? One contribution to a solution to this conundrum was evoked in the opening lines of the play, when, in answer to the commonplace inquiry, 'How goes the world?', the Painter replies to the Poet: 'It wears, sir, as it grows.' The word 'uses', as a verb, can in fact be construed to mean either 'wear' (a common sense, albeit normally in the passive or with an agent, as in the idea of using something up) or, in the context of this play, to 'grow' (in the sense of a usurious loan's self-growth) – this last meaning evoked by a pun based on the term usury. Used as a verb like this, it evokes the practice of usury, a crucial motif in what follows. Aristotle's critique of usury, which had long been a part of received Christian teaching, and which is alluded to repeatedly in Shakespeare's *The Merchant of Venice* and in some of the sonnets, indicts the 'unnatural' practice of allowing sterile money to reproduce itself like a living thing. Applying this meaning of the term to the Poet's words, we could say that poetry 'uses' in the sense of money in an interest-bearing loan – that is, it gains in value of itself; hence it would be another instance of the 'magic of bounty' which the Poet had earlier proclaimed. There is a similar usage of *use* in a dialogue in *The Merchant* between Shylock and Antonio, when Shylock says:

> Methought you said you neither lend nor borrow
> Upon advantage. (1.3.65–66)

Antonio replies, 'I do never use it' (1.3.66),[42] with *use* clearly here referring to the practice of usury in lending. Given the prominence of usury to the story of Timon of Athens, a similar meaning is probably at work in the obscure line of the Poet. Although admittedly the Folio reading is not crystal clear, I think it is far superior to the unlikely common emendation to 'gum' and 'oozes'. In an example of a complex word unaccountably neglected by William Empson,[43] 'uses' would also suggest – without producing a completely coherent meaning in the process – the idea of being used up. Thus poetry, like a gown which can potentially grow in value due to various contingencies, can grow in value while it simultaneously diminishes in thickness due to wear. This double meaning of the word

---

[42] My thanks to John Drakakis for alerting me to this line from *The Merchant*.

[43] He did, however, discuss the myriad uses of the word 'dog' in the play – see William Empson, *The Structure of Complex Words*, 3rd edn. (London: Chatto & Windus, 1951), 175–84.

reproduces the double sense of value which keeps being highlighted in scene 1.1. The contradiction is one between the commodity's exchange-value and its use-value.

With this double meaning of *uses*, then, poetry is exactly like the world described by the Painter at the beginning of the scene: 'It wears, sir, as it grows' (1.1.3) – that is, it wears out at one level while it grows (the world in population, the gown/poem in value when presented to Timon, perhaps) at another. This second sense of self-growth is re-stated by the two following comparisons: poetry is like a 'gentle flame' arising of itself, not needing to be struck with a flint, and it is like a stream which overflows each barrier which tries to contain it. It is a craft, a mysterious self-arising, artistically arranged stream of words, autonomous from its author. And, along with painting, poetry is a usurious commodity which seems to possess the same kind of magical dynamic as Timon's out-stream of wealth – the 'magic of bounty'. Does this reference to the double nature of poetry apply to the play *Timon of Athens* as well?

Drawing on Donald Hedrick's discussion of the peculiar economic value of the commercial play as a commodity which I summarized above, we might imagine any number of situations in which a play could be said to use 'From whence 'tis nourished' in both senses of the term defined above. As an object in itself, it seems to arise magically and effortlessly (at least for Shakespeare, according to his fellow players), to produce itself. As a commodity, the play's value could be said to be increasing as it is repeatedly performed and draws in more paying customers – it would in that way be 'using' like a loan which will be re-paid with a greater sum than was originally given out. However, with each performance, the play uses up some portion of its potential audience, so that in realizing its profitability it also uses up its value. Old plays attracted scant attendance, and the players were aware of this, as we learn from the testimony given at Essex's trial in 1601, when the players said they feared that *Richard II* was 'so old and so long out of use as that they should have small or no company at it'.[44] Dramatic productions, as we saw, are like tools and 'wear' as their profitability is realized, although, from another perspective, they also 'use' – increase in value – in the sense of realizing what had been up until actual performances a mere potentiality. And poetry is just one in the long list of commodifications which this play will catalog for us, while it retains the potential of serving other functions as well.

---

[44] From the Examination of Augustine Phillips, 18 February, 1601, excerpted and reprinted in Greenblatt *et al.* (eds.), *The Norton Shakespeare*, 3333.

Usury in fact is a central issue in *Timon of Athens*. The theme of usurious loans is picked up and enhanced by Middleton in the following scene and given a new emphasis. First the disillusioned philosopher Apemantus, then the steward Flavius provide the voices for a characteristically Middletonian discourse on wastefulness which punctures the illusions about the magic of bounty we have witnessed in the first scenes (1.2.29–48; 186–89). This is the first indication of a situation on which Middleton's and Shakespeare's portions equally depend, that Timon's apparently limitless bounty is in reality finite and hence the 'magic of bounty' is an illusion. Just as important, we learn that he is now in debt to usurers, his lands collateral to his loans:

> He is so kind that he now pays interest for't;
> His land's put to their books. (1.2.188–89)

And later Flavius reports, 'The greatest of your having lacks a half / To pay your present debts' (2.2.138–39). Timon's private bubble economy has burst, and the text underlines two inter-acting causes. First, in passages by both poets, the worldly foolishness of Timon's self-deception and denial is emphasized. Shakespeare apparently wrote the lines of a Senator who realizes that the time has come to call in his earlier loan to Timon:

>   It cannot hold, it will not.
> If I want gold, steal but a beggar's dog
> And give it Timon, why, the dog coins gold.
> If I would sell my horse and buy twenty more
> Better than he, why, give my horse to Timon,
> Ask nothing, give it him, it foals me straight
> And able horses. No porter at his gate,
> But rather one that smiles and still invites
> All that pass by. It cannot hold, no reason
> Can sound his state in safety. (2.1.4–13)

Similarly, but with different emphasis, we read in one of Middleton's passages:

> When all our offices have been oppressed
> With riotous feeders, when our vaults have wept
> With drunken spilth of wine, when every room
> Hath blazed with lights, and brayed with minstrelsy,
> I have retired me to a wasteful cock,
> And set mine eyes at flow. (2.2.152–57)

In the history of criticism of this play, evaluating Timon's culpability in his own downfall has been a major issue. Terry Eagleton, for example, is sure how the audience should respond to Timon's generosity:

An obsession with strict exchanges is typical of middle-class utilitarianism; the aristocracy are traditionally more spendthrift. This is certainly true of Timon of Athens, one of the last of Shakespeare's big spenders, whose grotesque generosity to his friends is a subtle form of egotism, triumphantly trumping their own gifts by returning them many-fold.[45]

On the other hand, G. Wilson Knight has nothing but praise for Timon's generosity:

Timon is a Universal Lover, not by principle but by nature. His charity is never cold, self-conscious, or dutiful. He withholds nothing of himself ... If, as Shakespeare's imagery sometimes suggests, the lover sees his own soul symbolized in his love, then we can say that Timon projects himself into the world around him; mankind is his own soul; a resplendent and infinite love builds an earthly paradise where it may find complete satisfaction in the intercommunion of heart with heart, and gift with gift.[46]

Trying to go beyond the either/or thinking defined in these alternatives, Coppélia Kahn psychoanalyzes Timon and finds him to be, in his phase of generosity, identified with 'the seductively maternal female presence' – the 'bountiful mother'.[47] This unqualified maternal identification in turn lays the basis for its negation in Timon's misanthropy, based on a total 'dis-identification' with the mother, a totalizing rejection of all things human.[48]

In investigating some of the qualities of his early maternalistic phase, Kahn turns to the work on gift-giving of anthropologist Marcel Mauss[49] in an interesting re-thinking of the issues and compares Timon's actions to that of the subject of the ceremonial potlatch of Northwest Native American culture. While Kahn discusses potlatch as a paradoxical form of aggression and argues that Timon unwittingly plunges himself into a male world of competition and mutual aggression by undertaking his elaborate gift-giving, there are other dimensions of the practice to consider. Whatever its psychoanalytic motivations, potlatch also plays a crucial social function in the societies in which it prevails. It is a key device in differentiating social status from the accumulation of property and is thus an example of a non-capitalist economy that reverses the priorities of the economic system we wholly take for granted. Whether we see Timon's actions as motivated by noble generosity (as Knight does) or by unconscious aggression (as Kahn and Eagleton do) – or, of course, as a

[45] Terry Eagleton, *William Shakespeare* (Oxford: Blackwell, 1986), 83–84.
[46] Knight, *The Wheel of Fire*, 211–12.   [47] Kahn, '"Magic of Bounty"', 41.   [48] *Ibid.*
[49] Marcel Mauss, *The Gift: The Form and Reason for Exchange in Archaic Societies*, trans. W. D. Halls (New York: Norton, 1990).

combination of the two – we should acknowledge the affront to capitalist property ethics that they amount to.

Within a property system such as prevails in the fictional Athenian setting of the play, Timon's actions are foolish, and he indeed comes to grief because of them. This judgment on Timon – based on an uncritical acceptance of the rules of the property system – is most clearly expressed, as John Jowett has demonstrated, in Middleton's culturally Puritan, middle-class portions of the work. In Shakespeare's portions, however, another reaction to Timon's action prevails. In effect he acknowledges Timon's worldly imprudence, but places much more emphasis on the ingratitude and disloyalty of Timon's beneficiaries, the de-humanizing, unethical qualities of a money-dominated society. In the context of those Shakespearean values, Timon is less foolish and more other-worldly. He is at once neo-aristocratic and presciently radical, and from this point of view the play refuses to shift the burden of blame onto Timon's denial of the rules of property accumulation. Timon in the more properly Shakespearean context is a kind of (secular) holy fool in something of Falstaff's mode:[50] he lives in a self-created, counter-factual world based on the denial of the real but projecting an imagined reality ethically superior to the real – a non-capitalist realm where wealth is freely available to meet human needs and to create gratuitous aesthetic pleasures. This realm itself, we might say, is at least a partially aesthetic one, like Falstaff's Carnival world, *A Midsummer Night's Dream*'s fairy realm of erotic freedom, or that theater of unfixed subjectivity, the woods of Arden in *As You Like It*. It is most like the Carnival of *2 Henry IV*, however, because it will be brought into direct confrontation with the real and collapse in the process, producing the negative utopia of the play's magnificent second half.

THE PLAY'S CONDEMNATION OF A MONEY ECONOMY

Shakespeare had inaugurated the theme of commodities and their exchange-value in scene 1.1 subtly but decisively, as I argued above. The next scene by Shakespeare, 2.1, however, replaces subtlety with directness, using the philosopher Apemantus and an underdeveloped accompanying Fool to drive home the point. The moral bankruptcy of usury – and the society it creates – is assumed throughout the scene's caustic dialogue. The usurers' servants are said to be fools and bawds: fools for serving manifestly evil masters and

---

[50] Cf. Roy Battenhouse, 'Falstaff as Parodist and Perhaps Holy Fool', *PMLA* 90.1 (Jan. 1975), 32–52.

bawds for pandering to the wants of others with damaging relief. The dialogue here makes the first of many connections in the play between usury and the sex trade. The Fool works for a brothel and notes:

I think no usurer but has a fool to his servant. My mistress is one, and I am her fool. When men come to borrow of your masters, they approach sadly, and go away merry; but they enter my master's house merrily, and go away sadly. (2.2.96–99)

Shakespeare made a similar connection in another dark play, *Measure for Measure*, when the comic figure Pompey wittily says, ''Twas never merry world since, of two usuries, the merriest was put down, and the worser allowed by order of laws' (3.1. 263–64). In *Timon*, though, the 'second usury' – sex – is less than merry because it leads to venereal disease. Sexuality in this play is always presented in its commodity form, like the works of the Poet and Painter.

The practice of usury in *Timon of Athens,* then, is far more than incidental to the play's other concerns. It is a central motif, metaphorically connected to the play's other themes: art, commodities, prostitution, theft, venereal disease, gold, and politics. All these connections are made explicit in the play's stylistic highpoint, the great invectives of Timon in Act 4, when he has renounced the company of mankind in a rage and proclaims himself 'Misanthropos, hater of man'. Famously, the central passage – unmistakably Shakespearean in provenance – was also a favorite of Karl Marx. It occurs after Timon, digging for roots, discovers gold instead in the soil of the Athenian countryside:

> Gold? Yellow, glittering, precious gold?
> No, gods, I am no idle votarist.
> Roots, you clear heavens! Thus much of this will make
> Black, white; foul, fair; wrong, right;
> Base, noble; old, young; coward, valiant.
> Ha, you gods! Why this? What this, you gods? Why, this
> Will lug our priests and servants from your sides,
> Pluck stout men's pillows from below their heads.
> This yellow slave
> Will knit and break religions, bless th'accursed,
> Make the hoar leprosy adored, place thieves,
> And give them title, knee, and approbation
> With senators on the bench. This is it
> That makes the wappened widow wed again;
> She whom the spital-house and ulcerous sores
> Would cast the gorge at, this imbalms and spices
> To th'April day again. Come, damnèd earth,

Thou common whore of mankind, that puts odds
Among the rout of nations, I will make thee
Do thy right nature. (4.3.26–45)

Ben Jonson, in the opening scene of *Volpone*, had represented his title
character worshiping gold. Shakespeare here deepens by reversing
Jonson's opening, giving us not an ironic instance of gold-worship but
an impassioned, analytic denunciation of it.[51] As in Jonson the gold is
both literal and metonymic, invoking not just itself as legal tender but the
whole fantastic network of commodities, credit, capital, and the desire
underlying the whole system.

This theme has already been introduced earlier in the play, when
Apemantus casually alludes to the reifying effects of gold or money. In
scene 1.1 Timon is making conversation with his difficult friend and asks
in regard to a jewel, 'What dost thou think 'tis worth?' Apemantus replies,
'Not worth my thinking' (1.1.216). Similarly, a few lines further, Apemantus
spars with the Merchant in the following pointed trading of quips:

> APEMANTUS: Traffic confound thee, if the gods will not!
> MERCHANT: If traffic do it, the gods do it.
> APEMANTUS: Traffic's thy god, and thy god confound thee.
>
> (1.1.240–242)

The last quick verbal slash is a highly condensed allusion to the idea of
the artificiality of monetary value, one that Shakespeare had earlier developed in *Troilus and Cressida* and which he assumes throughout this scene.
A commodity's value in not intrinsic but depends on the social network of
commodity trade, the knitting together of individual desires into a social
network, and a projection of those abstracted desires onto the thing itself –
just like an idol's sacredness. Without the collective thinking/desiring
that creates value, the whole system collapses, and Apemantus is being
a principled abstainer from what Hector in *Troilus* calls 'mad idolatry' in
refusing to think the thoughts of commodity fetishism. In contrast, he
seizes on the fetishism of the merchant, who sees the vagaries of the commodity market as acts of the gods, to stigmatize him with another version
of idolatry: 'Traffic's thy god, and thy god confound thee', he concludes.

The new economic criticism has taught us much about the mechanics
of finance in Shakespeare's day, and we now know that gold itself, despite
the Spanish plunder of the native civilizations of the New World, was in
relative short supply. Elizabethan lords and sovereigns distributed much
of their wealth and benefits through a system of credit, which created

---

[51] Cf. Jowett, Introduction, 7–8.

obligations and networks of its own. We are a century or more from a modern, impersonal financial system of banks and stocks in England, and thus the credit system which Shakespeare and Middleton have in mind in their depictions of Timon's financial situation is still pre-modern and pre-capitalist in many ways, with most financial transactions taking place through credit, without an exchange of gold or money.[52]

Nevertheless, Marx's comments on the passage on gold are still of great relevance to our understanding of this play because it is the long-run, philosophical, system-creating properties of money that Timon denounces, and as Marx suggests, Shakespeare has got to the heart of the matter, giving us a description not just of his own day's financial follies, but of the logic of any commercial civilization under the sway of the circulation of capital. Of this and a later, related passage (4.3.381–92), Marx writes:

Shakespeare excellently depicts the real nature of money ... Shakespeare stresses especially two properties of Money: (1) It is the visible divinity – the transformation of all human and natural properties into their contraries, the universal confounding and overturning of things; it makes brothers of impossibilities. (2) It is the common whore, the common pimp of people and nations. The overturning and confounding of all human and natural qualities, the fraternization of impossibilities – the divine power of money – lies in its *character* as men's estranged, alienating, and self-disposing *species-nature*. Money is the *alienated ability of mankind*.[53]

The peculiar terminology used here in this 1844 manuscript is borrowed from the German philosopher of alienation Ludwig Feuerbach, and its relation to the work of the older Marx has been a much debated issue; however, Marx quotes Timon again at a climactic moment of *Capital*, and he again asserts something very similar in a more popular language, beginning with a hoarded quote from Christopher Columbus:

'Gold is a wonderful thing! Whoever possesses it is lord of all he wants. By means of gold one can even get souls into Paradise.' (Columbus in his letter from Jamaica, 1503). Since gold does not disclose what has been transformed into it, everything, commodity or not, is convertible into gold ... Just as every qualitative difference between commodities is extinguished in money, so money, on its side, like the radical leveler that it is, does away with all distinctions. But money itself is a commodity, an external object, capable of becoming the private

---

[52] See especially Marc Shell, *Money, Language, and Thought* (Baltimore, MD: Johns Hopkins University Press, 1982) and Craig Muldrew, *The Economy of Obligation: The Culture of Credit and Social Relations in Early Modern England* (Basingstoke: Macmillan, 1998).

[53] Marx, *The Economic and Philosophic Manuscripts*, 167–8.

power of private persons. The ancients therefore denounced money as subversive of the economic and moral order of things. Modern society, which, soon after its birth, pulled Plutus by the hair of his head from the bowels of the earth, greets gold as its Holy Grail, as the glittering incarnation of the very principle of its own life.[54]

Here clearly, Marx is a Shakespearean, just as, in other contexts, Freud was. For both social critics, money is not merely a mammon of iniquity to make friends with, but the central organizing principle of societies of ethically inverted values and practices. The young Marx expressed the idea as an alienation of human species-being, that is, as an organization of the totality of human wants and capabilities into a vast abstraction – money – given control over every individual and of society as a whole. The older Marx wrote of the private expropriation of a universal human capability. But both passages are explications of Shakespeare's *Timon of Athens*. And the startling convergence in viewpoints between the nineteenth-century radical socialist and the early seventeenth-century pragmatic Royalist can help us penetrate some of the layers of assumptions about what Shakespeare could and could not have believed and help us see this remarkable play afresh.

TIMON MISANTHROPOS

The falling action of the play, constituting the second of its two main divisions, encompasses what modern editors have designated Acts 4 and 5[55] and is almost entirely by Shakespeare with the exception of two fairly clear interpolations by Middleton and an ambiguous passage at 4.2.1–29 – all three involving the faithful steward Flavius. Although the action builds towards Timon's suicide and the conquest of Athens by Alcibiades, dramatic suspense as such gives way to something more like a series of philosophical dialogues. If there is precedent for this practice elsewhere in Shakespeare, it would be in the middle of *As You Like It* (also set in the wood), when plot development is also sacrificed to a series of encounters of the various characters in a complex discursive dialogue.

In *Timon*, however, Timon is at the center of each of the encounters, and each of the visitors can be considered a dramatic foil designed to throw light on one or another facet of Timon's new misanthropy. Timon

---

[54] Karl Marx, *Capital: A Critical Analysis of Capitalist Production*, ed. Frederick Engels, trans. Samuel Moore and Edward Aveling, 3 vols. (New York: International, 1967), Vol. I, 132–33.

[55] As mentioned previously, Jowett (ed.), *Timon of Athens*, omits the division of the play into acts, numbering them consecutively.

is visited in turn by Alcibiades and his two accompanying prostitutes, by Apemantus, by the Banditti or thieves, by the steward Flavius, by the Poet and Painter, and by two Senators (with Flavius). The procession of these characters recapitulates the major rhetorical figures connected with the central motif of usury built up in the play's first half and thus constructs the diptych-like structure alluded to by many critics. Power, prostitution, diseased sex, Cynicism, theft, and art all parade before the now misanthropic Timon. Several of the encounters re-inforce the satirical condemnation of specific social ills in the play's first half. Alcibiades's prostitutes Timandra and Phrynia, for example, are darkly comic instances of the corrupting power of gold, allegorical figures evoking simultaneously the infections of venereal disease and the socially corrupting influences of the usury which diseased sex has signified.

The Painter and Poet join the procession next. Deciding that Timon is testing his erstwhile friends, they resolve to feign friendship – and art. In this case, as prescient anticipators of commodity futures markets, they attempt to sell the promise of future works:

To promise is most courtly and fashionable; performance is a kind of will or testament which argues a great sickness in his judgement that makes it. (5.1.21–23)

Then the Poet considers the next work he will present to Timon:

I am thinking what I shall say I have provided for him. It must be a personating of himself; a satire against the softness of prosperity, with a discovery of the infinite flatteries that follow youth and opulency. (5.1.26–29)

In *Julius Caesar* the conspirator Decius says of Caesar, 'But when I tell him he hates flatterers; / He says he does, being most flattered' (2.1.207–8). Here the Poet is thinking of applying the same strategy to Timon. The studied ambiguity in scene 1.1 about the status of art – commodity or anti-commodity, vehicle of flattery or of truth – is thus resolved: poetry is revealed as prostitution, one more commodity for sale. And Timon, who has overheard the conversation between the two, includes poetry and painting in his universal scorn and completes its commodification by offering the two his new-found gold. In the next scene, the Senators reveal that civic power too is open to precisely the same corruption.

Three of the visitors, however – Alcibiades, Apemantus, and Flavius – perform another function, measuring for us in their different ways the inadequacy of Timon's misanthropy as a response to corruption. The ending movement of the play re-inforces the diagnosis of profound corruption in Athens, but it undermines Timon's misanthropy as an adequate response to it. The longest of these darkly satirical episodes involves the visit of Apemantus.

Before Timon's change, Apemantus had foreshadowed elements of the bitter misanthropy which Timon ultimately adopts, but after the change, he also offers a contrast. Apemantus helps define the limits of Timon's misanthropy by contrasting it with his own more measured, less logically self-destructing Cynicism – although by the end of the scene his own consistency is also called in doubt.

A character named Apemantus had been mentioned in Plutarch's brief comments on Timon – the only source we can be sure Shakespeare used[56] since he took specific wording from it for the two epitaphs recited at the end of the play. Plutarch had linked Apemantus with Timon as one 'much like to his nature and condition and also followed him in his manner of life'.[57] Shakespeare's Apemantus, as mentioned, is a member of the ancient Cynical branch of philosophy, and we can see admiration for the Cynics in another author from whom Shakespeare borrowed at least once. There is an interesting passage in Montaigne's short essay, 'Of Democritus and Heraclitus' (I, 50), which distinguishes between Diogenes's Cynicism and Timon's misanthropy.[58] In 1605–8, when *Timon* was probably written, Shakespeare would have had access to John Florio's 1603 translation of Montaigne; he certainly had read in Florio's Montaigne by 1611, the date of *The Tempest*, with its verbal borrowing from Florio's translation. In this brief essay Montaigne is exploring the issue of judgment and how multifarious and unsystematizable are the factors it requires to take into account. Near the end of the essay he proposes to consider the contrast between two ancient philosophers and the general stance each took before the world. Both found 'the condition of man vain and ridiculous' but each responded in his own way. Diogenes 'never went out in public but

---

[56] Because the information in Plutarch is sketchy, it seems clear that other sources were used, but it is not obvious which ones. Critics have made the strongest cases for Shakespeare and Middleton's knowledge, directly or indirectly, of Lucian's second-century CE Greek dialogue *Timon, or the Misanthrope*, translated into Latin by Erasmus; and a chapter about Timon in William Painter's 1566 *Palace of Pleasure*. An English academic comedy called *Timon* contains a mock banquet and a faithful servant like Shakespeare and Middleton's version, but it is unclear whether it came earlier or later than their version. Other allusions suggest there was a lost play of *Timon* on the London stages in the 1580s.

[57] Geoffrey Bullough (ed.), *Narrative and Dramatic Sources of Shakespeare,* 8 vols. (London: Routledge and Paul, 1966), Vol. VI, 251.

[58] The relevance of this essay to *Timon* was first pointed out by Willard Farnham, *Shakespeare's Tragic Frontier: The World of his Final Tragedies* (Berkeley, Calif.: University of California Press, 1950), 65–67.

with a mocking and laughing face; whereas Heraclitus, having pity and compassion on this same condition of ours, wore a face perpetually sad, and eyes filled with tears'.[59]

Montaigne writes that he judges Diogenes's stance to be superior, but he clinches his argument not with a reference to Heraclitus, but to the legendary figure of Timon:

Timon wished us ill, passionately desired our ruin, shunned association with us as dangerous, as with wicked men depraved by nature. Diogenes esteemed us so little that contact with us could neither disturb him nor affect him, and avoided our company, not through fear of association with us, but through disdain of it; he considered us incapable of doing either good or evil.[60]

Thus Apemantus, or Cynicism, was a foil for Timon in the already existing material on him before Shakespeare and Middleton took up the legend, and much of the earlier material tended to see Apemantus as positive.[61] The Apemantus of the first half of the play seems to be taken from this mold, as he does much to win over the audience to him even while he alienates us (and his fictional fellows) with his rudeness and verbal aggression. But as the exposition of the play completes its depiction of Timon's foolishness, Apemantus emerges as a voice of perception and moral integrity, particularly in the banquet scene by Middleton when he penetrates the illusion and hypocrisy with his remark:

O you gods! What a number of men eats Timon, and he sees 'em not. It grieves me to see so many dip their meat in one man's blood, and all the madness is, he cheers them up too. (1.2.39–41)

Apemantus continues his double role as unsocial churl and truth-teller in his appearance in the second act. Just like the Fool in *Lear* (and the association may explain why he has a Fool as a companion briefly in a clearly Shakespearean portion of 2.2), even more like Thersites of *Troilus*, he is colored by the negativity of his judgments, a character completely taken up by a certain stance or role, the very opposite of Shakespeare's myriad-minded protagonists who most often engage audiences sympathetically. Instead, he is a voice from Robert Weimann's *platea*, the intermediate zone between audience and the other dramatic characters,

[59] Michel de Montaigne, *The Complete Essays of Montaigne*, trans. Donald M. Frame (Palo Alto, Calif.: Stanford University Press, 1965), 220.
[60] Montaigne, *The Complete Essays*, 221.
[61] A similar distinction, this time between the characters Diogenes and Lucian, was put forth in an anonymous, undated work from the period, *A Dialogue Between Lucian and Diogenes*; see Jowett, Introduction, 76.

part interlocutor, part satirical Chorus. Thus, by the time Apemantus pays his visit to misanthrope Timon in the woods, our expectations are whetted. Timon, it would appear, has joined Apemantus's sect, just as Plutarch had described. Apemantus greets Timon by saying,

> Men report
> Thou dost affect my manners, and dost use them. (4.3.199–200)

Timon's reply outdoes Apemantus's earlier rudeness and takes the Cynic by surprise. He tells Timon this new affect comes from a melancholy brought on by his reversal of fortune, rather than true philosophy. And for that reason, he tells Timon – and it is hard not to intuit a strong measure of self-serving professional pique as well – 'Do not assume my likeness' (4.3.220).

What follows is an intricate dance, akin, as William O. Scott wrote, to the logical puzzle of the liar's paradox.[62] Timon has followed Cynicism to the extent of withdrawing from an artificial society, living a natural, austere life without the comforts of civilization, and cursing men for their hypocrisy. But Cynicism offers an alternative, a mode of life which its disciples can adopt to remain virtuous amid corruption, and an important part of that life involves seeking converts. Timon rejects this aspect of Cynicism with great verbal hostility and begins to question Apemantus's own motives. The debate continues through a few more turns, then ends in an exchange of mutual insults. Once more the effect is darkly comic. The alienation of each man from his society finally transforms a philosophical debate into a schoolboys' mutual taunting contest. But Apemantus, on balance, scores the better points, and he also provides the audience with an aphorism which gets reaffirmed as the rest of the play develops, again distancing and contextualizing Timon's misanthropy:

The middle of humanity thou never knewest, but the extremity of both ends. When thou was in thy gilt and thy perfume, they mocked thee for too much curiosity; in thy rags thou know'st none, but art despised for the contrary. (4.3.307–10)

And he is able to offer Timon what he desperately needs, a friendship based on shared values and perceptions, not flattery and sponging. Timon refuses this offer, as he does all the others, and drives his would-be philosopher-friend away in anger.

---

[62] William O. Scott, 'The Paradox of Timon's Self-Cursing', *Shakespeare Quarterly* 35.3 (Autumn 1984), 290–304.

From this point on, the play turns against misanthropy and even Cynicism as philosophies. Death is the only logical outcome of each, this play implies, and more pragmatic men, the artists and politician-soldiers, are, at least potentially, much more constructive agents in the world than these universalizing philosophers. In the course of the debate, Apemantus says to Timon, 'Thou shouldst desire to die, being miserable' (4.3.255). At the end of the scene, after Apemantus has left and before the Painter and Poet arrive, Timon seems to have seen Apemantus's logic. He realizes that the only logically cogent outcome of his misanthropy is suicide. Even being a 'beast among the beasts' involves him in corruption and domination, as he had earlier proven in his argument against Apemantus (4.3.330–44).

Thus Apemantus's encounter with Timon in the woods, while it makes its own philosophical points, has comic aspects which relativize and distance the alienation from society of each of these deep-seeing, foul-speaking characters. In contrast, Timon's two faithful friends, Alcibiades and Flavius, lead us in a different direction. Both treat Timon's misanthropy as a kind of madness or disease into which Timon has fallen and ask their companions to take it likewise. Alcibiades repeats this idea, as we will see below, in the very last speech of the play.

In short, it is to a certain point only that Timon takes the audience in his great invectives early in Act 4 denouncing the transformative power of money. As he begins to universalize his anger, to become 'Misanthropos, hater of Mankind', and as we begin to see that such universalism makes no distinctions between true and false friends, the satire of the play is turned against the satirist, the denouncer is implicitly denounced – or pitied as stricken with madness – because of the absurdity of his own blanket condemnations.

Early in his exile, Timon prays:

> The gods confound – hear me, you good gods all –
> Th'Athenians both within and out that wall!
> And grant, as Timon grows, his hate may grow
> To the whole race of mankind, high and low!
> Amen. (4.1.37–41)

We watch as Timon undergoes such growth. But if we remember the early associations of growth in 1.1. – the world growing as it wears, the spontaneous growth of bounty which proves illusory and destructive, the perverse growth of a usurious loan, even the paradoxical growth of poetry, which 'wears' as it 'uses' – we will be suspicious of the growth wished for by

Timon here. Earlier, in lines by Middleton, the steward Flavius had forced Timon into a concession against his universalizing (4.3.483–530), and in the context of his earlier prayer, it is clear that Flavius and his fellow servants rebuff by example Timon's project of hating mankind 'high and low'. In a short scene apparently penned by Middleton, but echoing themes from *As You Like It* and *King Lear*, the servants form a utopian counter-society and embrace fellowship and communalism in the face of the atomization and individualism of Timon's erstwhile wealthy friends:

> Good fellows all,
> The latest of my wealth I'll share amongst you.
> Wherever we shall meet, for Timon's sake
> Let's yet be fellows. Let's shake our heads, and say,
> As 'twere a knell unto our master's fortunes,
> 'We have seen better days.' (4.2.22–27)

This is in its way an affirmation of the rational moment of Timon's earlier prodigality, its basis in the valuing of human connections over the hoarding of wealth, its assertion of money as only a means, not an end in itself. Immediately following come Shakespearean lines echoing the theme of the good servant and clearly functioning, as does this whole scene, as a counter-point to Timon's unmeasured response to his grief.

Timon's misanthropy, then, is like the poet's inspiration: it 'like the current flies / Each bound it chases' (1.1.25–26). It is a kind of madness recognized as such by the most trustworthy of Timon's friends, Alcibiades and Flavius. As several critics have recognized, this madness of Timon's parallels in many ways that of that other great wielder of universalizing invective against mankind, the mad King Lear of the heath scenes. In a classic of the 1920s the Modernist novelist and painter Wyndham Lewis (whose illustrations of *Timon* in Cubist style are among the greatest of all illustrations to Shakespeare), argued that madness in Shakespearean tragedy always signals an exploration of nihilism – the perception of a God-deserted cosmos in which there are no intrinsic values and in which human nature itself is seen to sway between possibilities of benevolence and malevolence. And Lewis was certainly right to group *Timon of Athens* with *Hamlet*, *Troilus and Cressida*, and *King Lear* as his chief examples of this phenomenon.[63] In this play, as in most of Shakespeare after about 1595, there is no revelation of the voice of God in the emptiness – Ken Jackson's recent Derrida- and Levinas-influenced reading of the play notwithstanding.[64] Instead, like the exiles in the Forest of Arden or on the heath with Lear,

[63] Lewis, *The Lion and the Fox*, 247–56. [64] Jackson, '"One wish"'.

like Richard II in his prison, like Antony and Cleopatra after their defeat, we and the remaining characters of *Timon* are left to our own devices to make what we can out of the unenviable circumstances of life under conditions of modernity. Like so many Shakespearean tragic heroes, Timon chooses suicide – a decision presented as the only logical outcome of his universalizing misanthropy. But his suicide is a singular one – off-stage, undramatic, and accompanied by some of the most lyrical language of the entire play. Timon's last movement is two-fold: it is the culmination of his misanthropy, but at the same time it is the inauguration of a new, aesthetic mode of perception that responds to the critique of misanthropy we have had performed before us.

THE REALIZATION OF THE AESTHETIC

This new theme had been artfully and subtly introduced in the first scene of the play but left to bide its time until the very end. Timon, like Romeo and Juliet, like Antony and Cleopatra, at the end makes of his death – and specifically for Timon his final resting place – a work of art. At the end of the play, in passages entirely written by Shakespeare, he goes beyond misanthropy and into the aesthetic. The play's shift in tone at the very end comes from a marked change in Timon's mood. After one of his most devastating (and nonetheless comic in a Beckettesque mode) expressions of universal hatred – his invitation to all Athenians to use his tree to hang themselves – his focus on death brings him to a different word-tone altogether:

> Come not to me again, but say to Athens,
> Upon the beachèd verge of the salt flood,
> Who once a day with his embossèd froth
> The turbulent surge shall cover, thither come;
> And let my grave-stone be your oracle.
> Lips, let four words go by and language end;
> What is amiss, plague and infection mend.
> Graves only be men's works, and death their gain;
> Sun, hide thy beams, Timon hath done his reign. (5. 1. 204–12)

The sentiment is hardly beneficent, with its references to plague, infection, and graves, but the elegiac tone is new, as is the charged description of the seaside. The same emotional heightening, in fact, is present in each of the descriptions of or allusions to this gravesite by the sea. Alcibiades presents one of them as a moment of his own order-restoring pronouncements in the play's very last scene:

>   yet rich conceit
> Taught thee to make vast Neptune weep for aye
> On thy low grave, on faults forgiven. Dead
> Is noble Timon, of whose memory
> Hereafter more. (5.4.77–81)

Timon's mad misanthropy is preserved in the epitaph which Alcibiades reads, but is then distanced:

> These well express in thee thy latter spirits.
> Though thou abhorest in us our human griefs,
> Scornst our brains' flow and those our droplets
> Which from niggard nature fall. (5.4.74–77)

The result is to create a forgiving frame around the madness, which becomes an aesthetic object, a 'rich conceit' in which Timon's misanthropic vision is both contained and re-contextualized. Timon's passionate denunciations of a corrupted world are affirmed, while his universalizing misanthropy is framed as a kind of madness caused by his great passion.

The aesthetic in this play is thus intermingled not with eros, but with thanatos. This is a strategy that Shakespeare had first deployed in the exquisite ending of *Romeo and Juliet* (see Chapter 5), and which he later varied and applied to *Antony and Cleopatra* (and, with more variations, to the four late romances). The aesthetic here acts as a kind of earthward-turned façade and container of what is represented as transcending human experience, but which is nevertheless accessible to us at the moment of death and in art. In this sense the theme of death in the service of something great – especially of heroes, especially in tragedies – involves Shakespeare in a version of the idea of the sublime as it developed in Enlightenment aesthetics and in Kant – in this context, especially in the sense of an 'elevation' of the mind to a sense of limits perceived and transcended, in something of the way Hegel indicated in his remark that conceptualizing a limit is precisely to transcend it.

Interestingly, in one of the classic Enlightenment discussions of the sublime, John Baillie offers an idea very close to Timon's last state of mind as one of his examples of 'the sublime of the passions'. After considering a number of different emotional states, testing them for their sublimity or lack thereof, he concludes: 'Hence the object of the passion only, not the intenseness of it, renders it great and noble; and hence a contempt of riches, of honours, power, and empire, may be justly reckoned amongst the grand affections.'[65]

---

[65] John Baillie, 'An Essay on the Sublime' (1747), in Andrew Ashfield and Peter de Bolla (eds.), *The Sublime: A Reader in British Eighteenth-Century Aesthetic Theory* (Cambridge University Press, 1996), 87–100; 94.

Earlier, Baillie had allowed, citing the example of Julius Caesar, that the desire for these very things was in itself sublime, and he asks how contempt for them can be equally so. His answer to this, in turn, is to separate the sublime from morality, to claim that his preference for the view of the Stoic philosopher (as he terms it) over the world conqueror is an ethical, not an aesthetic judgment, that both examples, involving opposing subjective stances towards the same great objects, are sublime. Whatever we make of this particular line of argument, what is most apposite in this discussion for *Timon* is the notion of the greatness of the kind of sublime contempt of the ways of the world that we see in the play. If, as Adorno suggests, the sublime is no longer readily available to us in a world in which all phenomena have been leveled as instances of mere monetary value, with the result that nothing can be better than something else except quantitatively,[66] we might also or instead code this moment as an instance of what Adorno calls the aesthetic 'shudder' that takes place, as he describes it, at the point in Beethoven's Ninth Symphony when the opening theme is reprised:

It resonates like an overwhelming 'Thus it is.' The shudder is a response, colored by fear of the overwhelming; by its affirmation the music at the same time speaks the truth about untruth. Nonjudging, artworks point – as with their finger – to their content without its thereby becoming discursive … Shudder, radically opposed to the conventional idea of experience [*Erlebnis*], provides no particular satisfaction for the I; it bears no similarity to desire. Rather, it is a memento of the liquidation of the I, which, shaken, perceives its own limitedness and finitude.[67]

The now anachronistic sublimity, the aesthetic shudder of *Timon*, opens up the ending of the play to such intense, imaginative readings as that of G. Wilson Knight, so impressed by this rare moment of Shakespearean aestheticism that he pronounced it the apex of all that Shakespeare had written.[68] Of course in doing so Knight inserted into this brief, subtle opening a world of post-Romantic aestheticism which is latent at best in Shakespeare's singular poetry. And in the process he lost sight of much of the play's searing social criticism, relevant to Knight's, our own, and Shakespeare's day in different ways. The same might be said of Jackson's stimulating recent article, which opens up from this moment into Derrida's and Levinas's meditations on a religion beneath religion. In recent political criticism, in contrast, the ending of this play really cannot compute; we need an idea of the aesthetic to do it justice. And the

---

[66] Adorno, *Aesthetic Theory*, 240.   [67] *Ibid.*, 245.
[68] Knight, *The Wheel of Fire*, 207.

absence of this concept is an important component in the dismissal of this play by many critics.

Thus, we can say, Timon at the end undergoes one more transition, and it is a transition into art. The agents of this transition are not the Poet and the Painter, who introduce the theme in the play's first scene. When they seek out Timon in the woods, as we have seen, it is in order to display even more unambiguously than before their own mercantilism, their treatment of their art as mere commodities for profit. Instead Timon introduces the last stage of his extraordinary development as a dialectical leap from his own despair and spite. The movement from the climax of his misanthropy in his invitation to mass suicide to the idea of his death as an aesthetic act is almost instantaneous. Apemantus, as we have seen, suggests suicide as a logical consequence of Timon's misanthropy. Timon himself decides to undertake a death which creates a new artwork.

A companion to the poem-within-the-play of scene 1.1, Timon's gravesite embodies and signifies a concept of the aesthetic that manages, like a comic ending, but with a very different affect, to reconcile (while maintaining) the disparate themes and contradictory absolutizing discourses that had been building up around Timon's practice of misanthropy – while, of course, leaving them unresolved conceptually. We have seen that as a philosophy, misanthropy is a universalizing discourse that condemns its own thinker, thereby calling itself into question, and creates a universal night in which all humans, like Hegel's cows, are dark – that is, it has no room for distinctions, degrees, and exceptions. We see it lose its philosophical coherence in the dialogue between Timon and Apemantus in scene 4.3.

But with the device of the gravesite Shakespeare creates a form adequate to contain and qualify the great insights of both Apemantus's Cynicism and Timon's mad misanthropy – without endorsing their unworkable universalism. Timon himself at the end foregoes consistency. The same Timon who had in his misanthropy spurned all human contact and sought only solitude finally bombards the world with a number of last messages: two epitaphs and the gravesite itself. All three of these 'letters to the world' utilize a self-destructing rhetoric that conveys two contradictory messages. Timon hates humanity and wants no notice of his grave. But Timon speaks out to humanity and asserts his presence to us.

Montaigne had noted that the misanthrope is involved in a double bind: 'For what we hate we take seriously. Timon wished us ill, passionately desired our ruin, shunned association with us as dangerous, as with wicked men depraved by nature.'[69] Shakespeare at the end of this play finishes the thought for him. Timon reconciles his impulses by aestheticizing his hate and leaving it as his last gift – this time one resistant to commodification – within a work of environmental art.

This gesture, as I have suggested, lacks the mystical transcendent intentions of full-fledged late nineteenth-century aestheticism. This Shakespearean version of the aesthetic is not necessarily the ultimate, truth-illusion about reality which Nietzsche defined and which has been a potent – and of course much criticized – final resting place of so many works of twentieth-century Modernism. It is more modest and apparently inadequate without the pragmatic accompaniment provided by Alcibiades – the man of action constructed in the play's subplot as some kind of complement or foil to Timon, a Fortinbras to a Hamlet. The contrast is obscure in Middleton's free-floating scene of Alcibiades in the Senate, where he asks for special consideration for a guilty but worthy friend and soldier – a contrast, perhaps, to the universalizations of Apemantus and the misanthropic Timon. In the ending, however, his thematic function emerges more clearly.

Where Timon evolves from misanthropic philosopher to environmental artist, Alcibiades in contrast becomes an agent of reform, along the lines Machiavelli described in *The Discourses* in his account of the earliest days of the Roman republic.[70] Alcibiades ends the play with an instance of that inevitable cycle of republics growing corrupt and requiring the strong arm of a harsh reformer to re-establish their ancient virtues and liberties. The artist can withdraw from the world to pronounce an enigmatic judgment upon it through the alterity of art, but only rarely can she change it. If we want change, the ending seems to suggest, we need politicians, men of action, reformers, like Alcibiades. The vision of the artist can act as a guidepost to the reformer – and also a measure of reform's (inevitable) shortcomings. But the reformer can institutionalize something of the artist's vision, and that seems to be the implication of the coupling of Alcibiades in Athens and Timon in his grave that constitutes the play's final movement.

The play concludes, then, with an extraordinary balance, simultaneously affirming the efficacy of pragmatic politics as Alcibiades enters Athens to 'use the olive with my sword' (5.4.82) and the necessity of art to encompass a fuller vision of human reality and possibility. This coupling

---

[69] Montaigne, *The Complete Essays*, 221.
[70] Niccolò Machiavelli, 'Discourses on the First Ten Books of Titus Livius', in Max Lerner (ed.), *The Prince and the Discourses* (New York: Modern Library, 1950), 124–270; Bk. 1, Chs. 6–90.

suggests another way in which the Shakespearean aesthetic is 'impure' – it is always already incomplete, in need of a supplement, it is insufficient to change the world by itself. Precisely because of those limitations and insufficiencies, however, it is a version of the aesthetic that speaks to us with renewed urgency at the beginning of the twenty-first century at a point in history in which the utopian desires of Modernism to transform and humanize an alienated world have proven to be unfulfillable. In our moment of late modernity, with its new, chastened aesthetics of Postmodernism, we have seemingly arrived where Shakespeare ends this strange and haunting play – with a searing, negative, condemning vision of the social madness of commodity idolatry, coupled with an acceptance of the limits of such judgments in themselves, the need for patience and pragmatism. Shakespeare and Middleton's *Timon* is a quiet masterpiece of great philosophical insight and import that speaks freshly to us almost 400 years after its still mysterious origins.

PART TWO

The aesthetics of death and mourning

CHAPTER 4

Hamlet *as mourning-play*

Allegory has to do, precisely in its destructive furor, with dispelling the illusion that proceeds from all 'given order', whether of art or of life: the illusion of totality or of organic wholeness which transfigures that order and makes it seem endurable. And this is the progressive tendency of allegory.[1]

Walter Benjamin

THE AESTHETICS OF THE *TRAUERSPIEL*

The aesthetic space of *Timon of Athens* – depicting an emptied world ruled over by commodification and devoid of other values – is in many ways *sui generis*. While the play fascinates us with its prescient conceptualization and instantiation of an idea of the aesthetic, it displays other important qualities besides meta-aesthetic ones: impure aesthetics such as I am advocating is not exhausted in recognizing meta-aesthetic moments. It is a means as well of exploring works of art displaying other complex dynamics, notably including the four motifs I highlighted in the Introduction: aesthetic forms expressive of their originating historical eras but projecting non-existing utopian possibilities; subtexts of repressed human desires and concerns; art as human labor at work on given forms, traditions, and contents; and art as a means of representing humanity's relation to the natural world. All of these qualities were apparent in the analyses of *A Midsummer Night's Dream* and *Timon of Athens*, but they were necessarily subordinated to a probing of those works for implied aesthetic ideas.

In this book's second half, however, I will be shifting the focus from the meta-aesthetic and onto other aesthetic qualities. Particularly, in order to complement the discussion of erotic subtexts in *Dream* and of social

[1] Walter Benjamin, *The Arcades Project*, ed. Rolf Tiedemann, trans. Howard Eiland and Kevin McLaughlin (Cambridge, Mass.: Belknap, 1999), 331.

satire in *Timon*, I am turning to issues of death and mourning as important constituents of Shakespeare's art – notably the forms our tradition
has labeled 'tragic' – although that term will have to be qualified and
supplemented, as we will see shortly.

In making this shift, I will be turning less to Adorno's posthumous
Aesthetic Theory and more to one of the earliest aesthetic works in the
Frankfurt School archives, Walter Benjamin's 1928 *The Origin of German
Tragic Drama*. The book is an account of a group of seventeenth-century
German dramas called *Trauerspiele* – dramas little known outside of the
German-speaking world. Benjamin was working new territory in this highly
original work, although he speaks much less directly than would Adorno
forty years later of the concept of the aesthetic in itself. This work is steeped
in the German Romantic-aesthetic tradition even as Benjamin is attempting
to push it forward into ideas we recognize as Modernist and Postmodernist.
Rather than reflecting on the aesthetic *per se*, Benjamin's book takes as its
main task the broadly Hegelian one of defining how the form of artworks
manifests the age in which they are produced,[2] how the form of the allegory
is a fragmented rather than unified one, how death emerges as a central
theme in the case of the *Trauerspiel*, and how an agenda of potential liberation can be glimpsed at extreme moments of works that otherwise seem
to despair through their visions of an empty universe and the finality of
death. The book, then, for all its obscurities, is an important model for the
application of impure aesthetics to the reading of early modern drama and
a quarry of ideas little discussed in Anglo-American Shakespeare studies.

Benjamin does not mention *Timon* in his book, although its empty-
world motif fits in well with his descriptions of the *Trauerspiel*. But he
does continually reference another Shakespearean drama, *Hamlet*, as the
Shakespearean work closest in form to the baroque plays he studied. His
Trauerspielbuch, as he called it, is now recognized as a master-work of
twentieth-century critical theory, but it has been discussed in Shakespeare
studies on only a few occasions.[3]

There are reasons for this relative neglect, including the difficulties
of its theoretical language and the unfamiliar originality of its method.

---

[2] Benjamin was critical of Hegel and Hegelianism in many other ways, however, notably of the
Hegelian concept of totality with which he breaks decisively in this work, as will be discussed
below.

[3] Susan Zimmerman, *The Early Modern Corpse and Shakespeare's Theatre* (Edinburgh University
Press, 2005) provides one of the most recent of these few occasions. Zimmerman takes up
Benjamin's description of the German baroque *Trauerspiel* and his claim that Shakespeare's
Hamlet shares many of the genre's features to great effect, arguing that Benjamin had grasped the
larger cultural impact which both the Protestant Reformation and the incipient scientific revolution had on the concept and representation of the body in early modern England. See especially
pp. 13–18. Other works will be noted as the discussion develops.

In addition, neither the examples Benjamin studied of the seventeenth-century *Trauerspiele* nor the term *Trauerspiel* itself has ever had much currency in the English-speaking world. If the book is familiar to readers interested in Benjamin's singular critical theory, it has been largely either because of its 'Epistemo-Critical Prologue', where Benjamin first developed his anti-totalizing concept of the 'constellation', which organizes ideas into selected, interconnected groupings; or through its prescient deconstructing demonstration of how the concept of allegory is a de-valued binary opposite to the privileged term 'symbol', in a relation-ship, Benjamin writes, similar to that of writing to speech.[4]

For readers of Shakespeare, however, the book presents fresh ideas and analysis about Shakespeare's relation to his historical moment and to the dramatic form in which he wrote his non-comic plays. The first half of Benjamin's study after the Prologue is devoted to a multi-faceted argument that the dramatic form of the *Trauerspiel* is fundamentally different from that of ancient Greek tragedy and needs to be distinguished from tragedy proper (*Tragödie* in Benjamin's German). Because of that fundamental distinction, translator Osborne's (or the publisher's) choice of the term 'tragic drama' to render *Trauerspiel* in the book's title is a misleading one. In the translation's text, by way of contrast, the German term is retained exclusively. The German *Trauer* variously means mourning, grief, or sorrow, so that 'mourning-plays' is a common translation for the German. 'Plays of lamentation' is an alternative, and Fredric Jameson suggests 'funeral pageant'.[5] But since for many German critics, before and after Benjamin, *Trauerspiele* were thought of as forms of tragedy, the ambiguity is built into the language,[6] and I will stick to the German form for the most part here with the understanding that Benjamin's sense of the word is meant.

Some Benjaminian sources

Benjamin in this work is both steeped within the ideas and assumptions of German Romanticism and Idealism and a Modernist in search of a

[4] Walter Benjamin, *The Origin of German Tragic Drama*, trans. John Osborne (London: New Left Books, 1977); originally published as *Ursprung des deutschen Trauerspiels* (Berlin, E. Rohwolt, 1928), 159–63. The book was written in the period 1924–25.

[5] Fredric Jameson, *Marxism and Form: Twentieth-Century Dialectical Theories of Literature* (Princeton University Press, 1971), 68.

[6] A similar point about the ambiguity of the relation of the terms *Tragödie* and *Trauerspiel* is made in the thought-provoking study of Benjamin's theory of the *Trauerspiel*, especially in its relations to Nietzsche, Freud, and Lacan, in Julia Reinhard Lupton and Kenneth Reinhard, *After Oedipus: Shakespeare in Psychoanalysis* (Ithaca, NY: Cornell University Press, 1992), 34–59.

break with them. He posits the idea of the allegory as an alternative to the Romantic concept of organic unity that played such a central role in post-Romantic Shakespeare criticism[7] – although he is careful to take his initial notion of the allegory from Idealist and Romantic sources. Already when he was writing this book he had become interested in Marxism, but he rarely steps outside of an idealist and even theological framework in this study. Nevertheless, the result is a document of Marxism, Modernism, and even Postmodernism.[8]

The broad influence of the Hegelian tradition is apparent from the beginning of the book. Benjamin makes it clear in his discussion that among the several critics who have influenced his conception were two Hegelians, Benedetto Croce and Georg Lukács, both of whom had written in different ways about issues of genre and form in critical theory. In his understanding of these issues, he was building on their work. Croce, a developer of Hegelianism and an important source for Gramsci's Marxism, had vigorously critiqued the reliance on the concept of genre in literary and aesthetic theory, arguing that systems of genre were as empty of deeper significance as the arbitrary cataloguing systems of research libraries. Instead, literary artworks were to be seen as singular creations with complex relations to the unfolding of (Hegelian) human history.[9] Croce gives Benjamin warrant to uncouple the *Trauerspiel* from the forms of Attic tragedy and to study it *sui generis*, and he supplies him as well with an idea of art as expression that is a basic premise of the work.

For his specific approach to literary form, however, he was more indebted to the younger, 'Hegelian' Georg Lukács of *Soul and Form* and, especially, of *The Theory of the Novel*. Benjamin drew from Lukács's discussion of tragedy in *Soul and Form*, but the precedent of *The Theory of*

---

[7] See Hugh Grady, '*Hamlet* and the Present: Notes on the Moving Aesthetic "Now"', in Hugh Grady and Terence Hawkes (eds.), *Presentist Shakespeares* (London: Routledge, 2007), 146–50, for a discussion of the turn to organic unity in the late Enlightenment which continues throughout the period of Modernism.

[8] An excellent, multi-facetted introduction to Benjamin's intellectual development and achievement is David S. Ferris (ed.), *The Cambridge Companion to Walter Benjamin* (Cambridge University Press, 2004). On his connections to Romanticism and Modernism (and retrospectively Postmodernism) several essays in this anthology are especially relevant: Michael Jennings, 'Walter Benjamin and the European Avant-Garde', 18–34; Jan Mieszowski, 'Art Forms', 35–53; Howard Caygill, 'Walter Benjamin's Concept of Cultural History', 73–96; Andrew Benjamin, 'Benjamin's Modernity', 97–114; and Rebecca Comay, 'Benjamin and the Ambiguities of Romanticism', 134–51.

[9] The English-language location for the ideas from Croce which Benjamin discusses is Benedetto Croce, *The Essence of Aesthetic*, trans. Douglas Ainslie (London: Heinemann, 1921), 53–54, cited in Benjamin, *Origin*, 43–44 and 237 n.10.

the Novel was more formative for the over-all intellectual framework of his *Trauerspiel* study. In Lukács's analysis of how the novel has differentiated itself from the classical epic to become something qualitatively different, Benjamin found a model for his own differentiation of *Trauerspiel* from tragedy.

For Lukács, the epic is a poetic form of 'integrated' societies, taking its shape within the historico-philosophical context of Hegel's ancient Greece – a place and time:

when the starry sky is the map of all possible paths ... whose paths are illuminated by the light of the stars. Everything in such ages is new and yet familiar, full of adventure and yet their own. The world is wide and yet it is like a home, for the fire that burns in the soul is of the same essential nature as the stars; the world and the self, the light and the fire, are sharply distinct, yet they never become permanent strangers to one another, for fire is the soul of all light and all fire clothes itself in light. Thus each action of the soul becomes meaningful and rounded in this duality: complete in meaning – in sense – and complete for the senses; rounded because the soul rests within itself even while it acts; rounded because its action separates itself from it and, having become itself, finds a centre of its own and draws a closed circumference around itself.[10]

Lukács goes on to deploy a short-hand term for this happy state, and it is 'immanence', the idea being that in the eras when this harmonious connection between self and world is in place, meaning does not have to be searched for; it is implicit in experience itself. In contrast, for this Hegelian aesthete, modernity has long since ceased to have such harmony,[11] and the form of the epic that came to exist in our 'problematic' time is the novel, a form which entered the world in the cosmic irony of *Don Quixote* and then became modernity's most characteristic literary form. The wrenched, frustrated situation of modernity is 'transcendental' rather than immanent because meaning is no longer 'given' in ordinary life, but must be searched for in a world which God has abandoned. The hero of the novel is thrust into a situation of 'transcendental homelessness'[12] and becomes a 'demonic' hero who finds that 'a mere glimpse of meaning is the highest life has to offer, and that this glimpse is the only thing worth the commitment of an entire life, the only thing by which the struggle will have been justified'.[13]

---

[10]   Georg Lukács, *The Theory of the Novel: A Historico-Philosophical Essay on the Forms of Great Epic Literature*, trans. Anna Bostock (Cambridge, Mass.: MIT Press, 1971), 29.

[11]   The turning point, apparently, occurred in Euripidean tragedy which Lukács felt, following Nietzsche, to be different in kind from that of Aeschylus and Sophocles – see Lukács, *The Theory of the Novel*, 40.

[12]   *Ibid.*, 41.   [13]   *Ibid.*, 80.

In Lukács's deployment of a supple, finally indefinable, but dynamic, active, and historicized concept of form in literature, Benjamin found the key to the uniqueness of the form of the *Trauerspiel*. The *Trauerspiel*, Benjamin writes, has been misunderstood by previous German critics as an attempt to revive classical tragedy, and he concedes that there are indeed some external similarities. But the inner forms of the two kinds of drama are profoundly different, precisely because the two separate art-forms have arisen in very different historico-philosophical moments.[14] Attic tragedy, as Lukács, Nietzsche, and Franz Rosenzweig have all argued in their different ways, is a form which has disappeared from the world-stage: 'the modern theatre has nothing to show which remotely resembles the tragedy of the Greeks', Benjamin writes.[15] Attic tragedy is profoundly connected to myth, not history, but a prevailing attempt to universalize tragedy and lift it out of its historical moment has obscured this insight in many late-nineteenth-century German attempts at an aesthetics of tragedy.[16]

Instead, Benjamin argues, it is necessary to grasp the mythic or legendary context and content of Greek tragedy. Borrowing from both Franz Rosenzweig[17] and Lukács, Benjamin situates the tragic hero at a specific point in human history which has been subsequently replaced. It is one in which the tragic hero grasps but remains silent concerning her moral superiority to the gods – a form in which a concept of an unarticulated kind of humanism emerges. Attempts to revive Attic tragedy can reproduce its externals, but never this historically based inner form, Benjamin concludes.

Benjamin and Hegelian 'pre-Marxism'

The German authors of the seventeenth-century baroque dramas on which Benjamin focuses were mistaken, then, in their belief that they were

---

[14] Lupton and Reinhard, *After Oedipus*, 34–59, connect the complex relation of distinction and continuity defined by Benjamin's discussion of the relation of tragedy and *Trauerspiel* to Nietzsche's discussion of the same kind of relation between Attic tragedy and Socratic philosophy in his *The Birth of Tragedy*, to Longinus's discussion of the relation of *The Iliad* and *The Odyssey*, and to Freud's and Lacan's discussions of the differing reactions of male and female children respectively to their 'discovery' of their castrated states.

[15] Benjamin, *Origin*, 101.   [16] *Ibid.*, 100–6.

[17] Franz Rosenzweig, *Der Stern der Erlösung* [*The Star of Redemption*] (Frankfurt, J. Kauffmann, 1921); cited in Benjamin, *Origin*, 243 n. 20. For a very lucid discussion of what Benjamin took from this *apologia* for Judaism by Rosenzweig, see Stéphane Moses, 'Walter Benjamin and Franz Rosenzweig', in Gary Smith (ed.), *Benjamin: Philosophy, Aesthetics, History* (University of Chicago Press, 1989), 228–46.

reviving tragedy, and so are the many critics who have followed them. The *Trauerspiel* is a new form, one very much rooted in its time, and it is consequently developed on completely different historico-philosophical premises. In its most general form it is a European and not merely a German phenomenon. Its two greatest masters for Benjamin are Shakespeare and the Spanish seventeenth-century playwright Pedro Calderón de la Barca, and it is a form which continues to develop, according to Benjamin, up to the plays of Strindberg.[18] A number of critics have also noted that Benjamin's later *apologia* for Bertolt Brecht's epic theatre draws many of its central categories from his discussion of the baroque *Trauerspiel* as well.[19] In short, it is a dramatic form developed in early modernity but continuing to Benjamin's present – and beyond.

Benjamin in the *Trauerspielbuch* is far from being a self-consciously Marxist critic, as his friend the historian of Jewish mysticism Gershom Scholem (1897–1982) has repeatedly insisted. The notion of objective 'ideas' in the 'Epistemo-Critical Prologue', to take one key instance, is essentially Platonic, as Benjamin himself notes.[20] Ideas are objective and 'given' for Benjamin in this book, unlike concepts, which attempt to capture them.[21] And the easy transition from Plato to the story of Adam's naming of the animals and other things of the world in Genesis[22] shows the truth of another of Sholem's contentions, that Benjamin's thought is specifically theological and Judaic in many ways. Indeed, asserts Benjamin scholar Rainer Rochlitz, a portion of the famous obscurity of the 'Epistemo-Critical Prologue' results from Benjamin's attempts to protect himself against entrenched German academic anti-Semitism by disguising his debt to Jewish intellectual traditions.[23]

The idealist and theological tenor of much of the argumentation of *The Origin of the German Tragic Drama* being granted, however, it is also clear that the book formed the basis for much of the originality of Benjamin's later 'Marxist' writings – as well as those of his friend Theodor Adorno, whose entire intellectual development was radically transformed through his reading of Benjamin's *Origin*.[24] The 'pre-Marxist' quality of such

[18] Benjamin, *Origin*, 113.
[19] See Walter Benjamin, *Understanding Brecht*, trans. Anna Bostock (London: New Left Books, 1973).
[20] Benjamin, *Origin*, 30, 36–7, 40.   [21] *Ibid.*, 29–38.   [22] *Ibid.*, 37.
[23] Rainer Rochlitz, *The Disenchantment of Art: The Philosophy of Walter Benjamin*, trans. Jane Marie Todd (New York: Guilford Press, 1996), 33–36.
[24] On the seminal influence of Benjamin on Adorno's most creative work, see Susan Buck-Morss, *The Origin of Negative Dialectics: Theodor W. Adorno, Walter Benjamin, and the Frankfurt Institute* (New York: Free Press, 1977); and Andrew Bowie, *From Romanticism to Critical Theory: The Philosophy of German Literary Theory* (London: Routledge, 1997), 251–65.

idealism (to use a term which is of course a retrospectively constructed figure) is of the same sort as evidenced in Hegel's relation to Marx, Croce's to Gramsci, and Lukács's evolution from Hegelian to Marxist phases. Because of the intimate connections and real continuities between these phases, it is dangerous to attempt to demarcate the 'idealist' from the 'materialist' in all these intellectual evolutions too sharply, although differences between the two phases are apparent. In the case of Benjamin, he continued to value his theory of the *Trauerspiel* throughout his later, Marxist writings, arguing in effect that all it lacked was insight into the connection of the allegorical method he defined for these plays to the rise of commodity production that accompanied it.[25] I would add to that diagnosis the influence of new or revived forms of instrumental rationality in the early modern[26] and new forms of subjectivity dialectically connected with an early modern split between subject and object. But I will return to those issues below.

Benjamin never does attempt a formal definition of the *Trauerspiel*, and this omission is deliberate. He argues that the traditional scholarly procedure of an inductive survey of examples, an isolation of common qualities, and an abstracting definition based on these cannot grasp the inner aesthetic form he is seeking, and he rejects these procedures in favor of one that is more thoroughly historical and dialectical.[27] Croce was correct in his suspicion of the Procrustean nature of traditional genre classifications, but on the other hand, Croce sees (but cannot account for) the apparent exception to this rule, that some traditional aesthetic categories (he names the comic and the tragic) have their place, so long

---

[25] Benjamin wrote in 1938: 'The allegorical mode of apprehension is always built on a devalued world of appearances. The specific devaluation of the world of things, as manifested in the commodity, is the foundation of Baudelaire's allegorical intention'; see Walter Benjamin, 'The Study Begins with Some Reflections on the Influences of *Les Fleurs du mal*', in Walter Benjamin, *Selected Writings*, 4 vols., eds. Howard Eiland and Michael W. Jennings, trans. Edmund Jephcott *et al.* (Cambridge, Mass.: Belknap, 2003), Vol. IV, 95–98; 96. For a lucid discussion of the connection of the theory of allegory in the *Origin* to Benjamin's later Marxist work on Baudelaire, see Susan Buck-Morss, *The Dialectics of Seeing: Walter Benjamin and the Arcades Project* (Cambridge, Mass.: MIT Press, 1991), 177–85.

[26] Benjamin in this work has a conception of a form of rationality within seventeenth-century culture close to Adorno and Horkheimer's concept of modern instrumental reason in his notion that in the empty world of the *Trauerspiele*, political history is treated as a kind of 'natural history', in which there is no connection between morality and the historical (88) and in which there is 'no other historical activity than the corrupt energy of schemers' (88). For a much more detailed exploration of Benjamin's multi-facetted and complex notion of natural history, which extends beyond this particular application, see Beatrice Hanssen, *Walter Benjamin's Other History: Of Stones, Animals, Human Beings, and Angels* (Berkeley, Calif.: University of California Press, 2000).

[27] Benjamin, *Origin*, 42–47.

as they are deployed critically and historically.[28] Benjamin's attempt to surpass Croce is centered in his development of a dialectical concept of *Ursprung* or 'origin' – a historical concept, he asserts, but not to be confused with the ordinary idea of the genesis or very beginnings of a thing, but rather to be thought of in more Hegelian terms, as a changing process which takes place over time and one whose essence, like Hegel's *Begriff,* or concept, only emerges retrospectively, 'in the totality of its history', as Benjamin puts it.[29] At the same time but on another level, it reproduces one of the doctrines of the Kabbalah, to the effect that the Messianic future of humankind is one of recapturing its origin: the status of humanity that already existed before the Fall. In that way the origin of a thing is also its future, if the fallen form is redeemed.[30]

Thus the origin designates the coming into existence of something new, but also the restoration of something lost. It is a kind of dialectical ideal, encompassing (as Benjamin repeatedly insists) extremes or opposites, and emerging in a historical process. It is not an empirical generalization. And because it should be constructed from 'the weakest and clumsiest experiments and in the overripe fruits of a period of decadence'[31] as well as the exemplary, it is well suited to the aesthetically clumsy plays he will work with.

These plays, he writes – the *Trauerspiele* of Gryphius, Opitz, Lohenstein, Harsdörffer, Hallmann, Haugwitz, and several others – have been overshadowed by Shakespeare and overlooked by the Romantics, even though they played an important part in creating a national German literature. The *Trauerspiel's* difficult form has been misunderstood, Benjamin writes, and it had no great exemplar; there was never a German Calderón. The analytic discussion of seventeenth-century dramas that follows is an attempt to instantiate such a dynamic type and to anchor it in the world of neo-Platonic but historically unfolding ideas and essences which make up Benjamin's idealist theoretical frame in this work. But it is relevant to more materialist criticism – like Benjamin's own subsequent work – precisely because the issues of historical development and their relation to inner aesthetic form are issues for materialists as well as idealists.

[28] *Ibid.*, 45.   [29] *Ibid.*, 45–46.
[30] For this interpretation of the influence of the Kabbalah on Benjamin here and below, I am indebted to Richard Wolin, 'An Aesthetic of Redemption: Benjamin's Path to the *Trauerspiel*', *Telos* 43 (Spring 1980), 61–90; 67–68. Much of this material was later incorporated into Richard Wolin, *Walter Benjamin: An Aesthetics of Redemption* (New York: Columbia University Press, 1982).
[31] Benjamin, *Origin*, 46.

The form of allegory

Greek tragedy had disappeared from the world because the intellectual framework in which it originated and developed disappeared in favor of Christian monotheism with a dualistic tendency to separate the empirical and material from the ideal and spiritual. Greek tragedy's promotion of its heroes to a status greater than the divine was no longer tenable in this new world, and the idea of tragedy passed to the Middle Ages as an external form which was reconfigured as a submission to a higher will, a realization that the empirical world is worthless and empty – although it is open to the Messianic transformations of divine history.[32] Medieval drama reflects this epistemic change in developing the new forms of the miracle and morality plays. They can be considered in some ways the first *Trauerspiele*, but the early modern forms differ from them in one crucial respect: the divine comedy of salvation history – always present, explicitly or implicitly in the medieval drama – drops out of the form of seventeenth-century baroque drama – and its analogues in England and Spain. The most typical form of the *Trauerspiel* (that of modernity) is one based on a profane and empty world, and this in turn forms the basis for the most important aesthetic technique of the *Trauerspiel*, which Benjamin calls allegory, using the term in an expanded and unique sense.

Much more than the extended metaphor that it has traditionally been defined as, allegory in this work is for Benjamin a technique and a form whose properties are grounded in the seventeenth-century historico-philosophical moment – although as his later work will make clear, it extends forward at least into the early twentieth century. First, in a conception akin to Lukács's notion of a problematized world of modernity as expressed in the novel's inner form, the allegory assumes that the empirical world is de-valued or empty, so that its objects are free to be used as protean signifiers. The allegory thus constructs a form, Benjamin says, in which 'anything can mean anything else'.[33] This encompasses traditional extended metaphors but is a principle which has several other dimensions as well. In addition and importantly, while the pre-condition for the allegory of the *Trauerspiel* is a sense of a meaningless world, the artwork anchored in this world and reproducing its negative evaluations also and crucially produces a profligate, meaningful aesthetic space of multiple significations.

Second, this allegorical space is emphatically not one of Romantic organic unity. The allegorist fills up aesthetic space through a strategy of the accumulation or agglomeration of a series of fragments: 'For it is

---

[32] *Ibid.*, 112.   [33] *Ibid.*, 175.

common practice in the literature of the baroque', Benjamin observes, 'to pile up fragments ceaselessly, without any strict idea of a goal.'[34] Furthermore, the inner logic of allegory resists any attempts at totalization: 'In the field of allegorical intuition the image is a fragment, a rune ... The false appearance of totality is extinguished.'[35] The dis-unifying, fragmenting qualities of the allegorical extend into several aspects of the *Trauerspielbuch*, including elements of what we would think of as 'style'. For example, Benjamin speaks of the poetry of the *Trauerspiele* as involving a 'breaking up' of sound and meaning, 'so as to acquire a changed and intensified meaning in its fragments'.[36] Baroque allegory deploys a 'disjunctive, atomising principle at work'. in several ways.[37] What is valued in it above all is 'the fragmentary and the chaotic'.[38]

The allegory as defined by Benjamin thus involves 'fragmentation' in more than one sense of the word. The term refers both to the overall non-organic unity created by this poetic trope as well as the individual units – the 'fragmented allegories' – which are 'amalgamated' into a dissonant unity. An emptied world creative of a profligacy of signification and a rejection of organic unity in favor of a (dis-)unity of accumulated fragments – these are the two negative principles which make up the most original and most enabling aspects of Benjamin's singular theory of the baroque allegory.

The epistemic change behind these developments affected all of Europe but took specific theological forms in different places in line with the ebbs and flows of the Reformation and Counter-Reformation. In the German baroque *Trauerspiele*, the authors tended to be either Lutherans or Counter-Reformation Catholics. For the Lutherans, Benjamin asserts, the end of the meritorious status of good works in Luther's theology deprived daily life of some of its meaning, but this was at least partially compensated for in Luther's recommendation of participation in a civic sphere. Benjamin thought that perhaps a residuum of Teutonic pagan fatalism was also at work in these attitudes.[39] And for the Catholics, the Counter-Revolution was an era 'denied direct access to a beyond ... Nothing was more foreign to it than the expectation of the end of the world, or even a revolution ... In philosophical-historical terms its ideal was the acme: a golden age of peace and culture, free of any apocalyptic features, constituted and guaranteed *in aeternum* by the authority of the Church.'[40] This led to a 'strict immanence' – not Lukács's immanence of meaning, but an immanence in the sense of a world cut off from higher meaning.[41]

---

[34] *Ibid.*, 178.   [35] *Ibid.*, 176.   [36] *Ibid.*, 208.   [37] *Ibid.*   [38] *Ibid.*, 209.   [39] *Ibid.*, 138–39.
[40] *Ibid.*, 80.   [41] *Ibid.*

Also crucial to the specific German context for the baroque *Trauerspiele* were the horrors of the Thirty Years War, and its influence led to the unprecedented violence of these plays, as well as to an emphasis on Machiavellian plots and counter-plots in the political sphere.[42] The resulting 'emptying' of the empirical world of value was the most crucial determinant of the new aesthetic form they constituted and the new aesthetic technique those forms utilized: the allegory.

Allegory in Benjamin's sense, then, is not the four-fold system of signifying which was defined and famously exemplified in the late Middle Ages by Dante – although 'ambiguity' or 'multiplicity of meaning' is characteristic of it.[43] But the several specific references to Judaic mystical tradition suggest that a different model of allegory from Dante's is behind many of the qualities of the secular allegory which Benjamin discusses. In the Kabbalah the Torah is subject to a kind of double allegorical interpretation. After Adam and Eve have been driven out of Paradise, human language begins to lose the Adamic, natural correlation between word and thing which it shared with divine language. As Benjamin writes in his early and seminal essay 'On Language as Such and on the Language of Man', 'the Fall marks the birth of the *human word*, in which the [Adamic] name no longer lives intact ... the word must communicate *something* (other than itself)'.[44] The basis for allegory has come into existence, as a quality of fallen language.

In the Kabbalistic traditions on which Benjamin seems to be drawing, the world after the Fall is presided over no longer by the Tree of Life (which ruled over Paradise), but rather by the Tree of the Knowledge of Good and Evil. The Torah after the Fall – the Torah of Exile – gives us the history of suffering characteristic of the new order and is thus open to a reading based on the Tree of the Knowledge of Good and Evil. However, another level of interpretation is implicit in the promise of redemption through a return to origins. The same sacred narratives which portray suffering can also be read in the light of the promise of redemption, and a highly esoteric knowledge of a utopian future revealed.[45] Since for Benjamin works of art share a similar participation in a language which retains traces of its divine origins even in its fallen state (or of an 'objectivity' based on the primal ideas' collective, historical origins, as Benjamin said

[42] *Ibid.*, 95–96.   [43] *Ibid.*, 177.
[44] Walter Benjamin, 'On Language as Such and on the Language of Man', *Reflections: Essays, Aphorisms, Autobiographical Writings*, ed. Peter Demetz, trans. Edmund Jephcott (New York: Harvest, 1979), 327; quoted in Wolin, 'An Aesthetic of Redemption', 71.
[45] Wolin, 'An Aesthetic of Redemption', 67–68.

when he was being more 'materialist'), they too are open to such double interpretation. Thus, for all the emphasis on emptiness and suffering in Benjamin's account of the *Trauerspiele*, they are ultimately susceptible to a redemptory interpretation as well, what Susan Buck-Morss aptly calls 'a dialectical move to a metalevel, at which the contradictory meanings of emblems themselves become an emblem, the sign of *their* opposite'.[46] Benjamin puts it this way:

For it is precisely visions of the frenzy of destruction, in which all earthly things collapse into a heap of ruins, which reveal the limit set upon allegorical contemplation, rather than its ideal quality. The bleak confusion of Golgotha, which can be recognized as the schema underlying the allegorical figure in hundreds of the engravings and descriptions of the period, is not just a symbol of the desolation of human existence. In it transitoriness is not signified or allegorically represented, so much as, in its own significance, displayed as allegory. As the allegory of resurrection.[47]

And a bit further:

And this is the essence of melancholy immersion: that its ultimate objects, in which it believes it can most fully secure for itself that which is vile, turn into allegories; and that these allegories fill out and deny the void in which they are represented, just as, ultimately, the intention does not faithfully rest in the contemplation of bones, but faithlessly leaps forward to the idea of resurrection.[48]

Two recent commentators on Benjamin have downplayed the significance of this allegorical reversal. Susan Buck-Morss describes the *Trauerspiel's* openness to redemption as something Benjamin ultimately criticizes as an error of 'idealism', preparing the way for his materialist turn.[49] And Richard Halpern argues that 'while the ruined fragments of the Baroque landscape do point obscurely to the possibility of redemption at the end of Benjamin's study, this redemption is decisively separated from the realm of the act'.[50] It seems to me, however, to be instead an instance of a double interpretive possibility, a reading of Redemption superimposed onto a still visible 'empty' reading of Exile – a double hermeneutic he retained throughout his 'Marxist' phase and which is explicit in his last work, 'The Theses on History' of 1940. Buck-Morss wrote of Benjamin's discussion of this most radical of allegorical leaps in the *Trauerspiel*: 'In order to remain true to God, the German allegoricists abandon both nature and politics … This "treacherous" [the word is her

---

[46] Buck-Morss, *The Dialectics of Seeing*, 173.   [47] Benjamin, *Origin*, 232.
[48] *Ibid.*, 232–33.   [49] Buck-Morss, *The Dialectics of Seeing*, 174–75.
[50] Richard Halpern, 'Shakespeare *contre* Benjamin', Presentation at the 2004 Modern Languages Association convention, 29 December, 2004.

rendering of the German *treulos*, which was translated as 'faithlessly' in the previous quotation] leap from the mournful spectacle of history as a "sad drama" to the miracle of resurrection, one in the name of allegory, is in a philosophical sense its negation.'[51] In the theological sense, however, it is a paradoxical truth, and I see no sign that Benjamin is troubled by this last dialectical reversal of the general significance of the artwork – which, after all, is only a semblance, not a representation of the real as such. As he has emphasized, allegory is in its essence ambiguous, and one level cannot cancel another.

Allegory and Postmodernism

In its emphasis on the 'emptying' of the world of the *Trauerspiel* to create a space of interchangeable signifiers and in its emphatic rejection of Romantic organic unity, as has been pointed out by several critics, Benjamin's allegorical seems to be something like Paul de Man's textuality, Derrida's *mise en abyme*, Lacan's Symbolic Order, or the *jouissance* of Barthes's deconstructive period – a chain of signifiers linked through the conventions of linguistic structure which substitutes for, indirectly represents, and thereby maps an otherwise unsignifying world through signifiers or symbols which should never be confused with the real – to which they gesture but which they do not and cannot present. He is in that way, as any number of critics claimed in the 1970s and 1980s, something of a de Man-style allegorist[52] or Barthesean semiotician, in that in his model of the baroque allegory he describes a dis-unified, aesthetic-literary space structured by a set of malleable but interconnected signifiers. Affinities of Benjamin with other later critics have also been observed. For example, Susan Zimmerman sees Benjamin's theory of allegory and *Trauerspiel* as intertextual with Bataille's discussion of the erotic, Lacan's transformation from the mirror stage to the Symbolic Order, and Kristeva's theory of the abject,[53] while Julia Reinhard Lupton and Kenneth Reinhard (as mentioned briefly above) see him as providing an important parallel not only to Lacan, but also to Freud and Nietzsche.[54] Benjamin's affinity with the thinking of all these heroes of Postmodernism derives, more than

51 Buck-Morss, *The Dialectics of Seeing*, 175.
52 De Man was an admirer of the early Benjamin's theories of translation and of allegory; see especially Paul de Man, 'Conclusions: Walter Benjamin's "The Task of the Translator"', in Paul de Man, *The Resistance to Theory* (Minneapolis: University of Minnesota Press, 1986), 73–105. I want to thank Christopher Norris for bringing this connection to my attention.
53 Zimmerman, *The Early Modern Corpse*, 3–13.
54 Lupton and Reinhard, *After Oedipus*, 34–59.

from any other quality, from a shared opposition to the notion of a logo-centric system. In the case of Benjamin, as his usage of the term 'allegory' develops and ramifies over the course of the second half of his treatise, the allegory's core meaning of a kind of extended metaphor – the allegory as traditionally defined – enlarges considerably. Its essential characteristics follow not so much from its continuity of imagery, but rather from the fundamental non-identity of signifier and signified in the form, leading to a mode and form of artistic composition of fundamental dis-unification, de-systemization, or fragmentation that inherently resists totalization.

Breaking with Romanticism

This dis-unifying property of the allegory is rooted in Benjamin's discussion of the traditional distinction of the allegory from the symbol, a distinction defined most consequentially for Benjamin by Goethe, whom he critiques for not getting at the heart of the matter.[55] But Benjamin's real target is not so much the few sentences by Goethe that he quotes – to the effect that the allegory tries to find the particular in the general, but the symbol is more true to the nature of poetry by finding the general in the particular.[56] Rather, when Benjamin distinguishes the allegory from the symbol, he is invoking an antithesis to the central Romantic assumption of the organic unity of the artwork – and the cosmos. Samuel Taylor Coleridge – who took so much of his critical doctrine directly from the German Romantics, by way especially of Schelling and A. W. Schlegel – defined the symbol (he was famously contrasting it favorably with a de-valued allegory) as follows: 'It always partakes of the reality which it renders intelligible; and while it enunciates the whole, abides itself as a living part in that unity of which it is the representative.'[57] This definition is but the tip of an iceberg of Romantic doctrines of universal mystical unity made manifest to us by the greatest artworks, like those of Shakespeare, who, as Coleridge writes, was 'himself a nature humanized'.[58] Benjamin's concept of the allegory is defined as an alternative to these notions.

In his attempt to redirect the German Romantic tradition into the service of Modernism and a Modernist concept of the baroque, Benjamin

---

[55] Benjamin, *Origin*, 161.
[56] Johann Wolfgang von Goethe, *Sämtliche Werke* 38, Schriften zur Literatur, 3, 261; quoted in Benjamin, *Origin*, 161.
[57] Samuel Taylor Coleridge, *The Statesman's Manual* (London: Gale and Fenner, 1816), excerpted and reprinted in David Perkins (ed.), *English Romantic Writers* (New York: Harcourt, 1967), 503.
[58] Samuel Taylor Coleridge, 'From Shakespearean Criticism', in Perkins (ed.), *English Romantic Writers*, 500.

quotes from the early-nineteenth-century mythologist Friedrich Creuzer a remark on the allegory which Benjamin believes is far wiser than Creuzer realized. It is important to note these definitions carefully, for they use the terms 'allegory' and, especially, 'symbol', in ways that are at profound cross-purposes with their received meanings in the Anglo-American literary tradition. That tradition, codified by the mid-twentieth-century New Critics, was based on Coleridge, the French Symbolists, and Modernist poet-critics like Eliot and Yeats. In a formula that can still be found today in countless college-level Literature textbooks, the symbol has been conceived of primarily as a special kind of metaphor in which the second term is implied but not expressed. In fact, that sense of the term 'symbol' fits as well, and perhaps better, Benjamin's 'allegory' than his term 'symbol' – especially for the case of the 'fragmented allegories' that he sees dominating the *Trauerspiel* – and understanding that point helps explain why Benjamin later wrote that Baudelaire was a profoundly allegorical poet in the style of the German baroque dramatists.[59] Since the baroque allegories are 'fragments' for Benjamin, they do not extend over the course of the whole poem, but are localized. And in addition, the signified of the allegory is often implied rather than expressed, just as in the case of Baudelaire's (and New Critical) 'symbols'.

The German tradition from which Benjamin is drawing defines these terms in a way that partially overlaps with, partly differs from those Anglo-American senses of the terms. For an example of both the difference and the overlap, Friedrich Creuzer, whose 1819 *Symbolik und Mythologie* Hegel had cited in his discussion of the symbol,[60] saw the symbol as most clearly exemplified in classical Greek sculptures of gods and goddesses.[61] In these the particular indeed signifies the general – the sculpted human figure represents such abstract qualities as divinity and beauty and uni-fies them by embodying them in a single figure. And it does so in a single instant outside of temporality proper. The allegory, by contrast, is both temporal and differentiating – the allegorical sign represents something 'other than itself' in distinction to the 'incarnation' and 'embodiment of the idea' of the symbol. Instead of unity, the allegory works on a principle of fragmentation and differentiation. Consider, for example, the passage

[59] Benjamin, *The Arcades Project*, 324–38 and throughout the discussion of Baudelaire, 228–387; see also Benjamin, 'Paris, the Capital of the Nineteenth Century: Exposé of 1939', *The Arcades Project*, 22–23.

[60] G. W. F. Hegel, *Aesthetics: Lectures on Fine Art*, trans. T. M. Knox, 2 vols. (Oxford: Clarendon, 1975), Vol. I, 310

[61] Georg Friedrich Creuzer, *Symbolik und Mythologie der alten Völker, besonders der Griechen*, 2 vols. (Leipzig, Darmstadt, 1819), Vol. II, 118; cited in Benjamin, *Origin*, 163.

from Christoph Männling's *Schaubühne des Todes, oder Leich Reden*
[*Theatre of death, or funeral orations*] which Benjamin quotes:

> Wer diese gebrechliche Hüten
> wo das Elend alle Echen zieret
> mit einem vernünftigen Wortschlusse wolte begläntzen
> der würde keinen unförmlichen Ausspruch machen
> noch das Zielmass der gegründeten Wahrheit überschreiten
> wann er die Welt nennte einen allgemeinen Kauffladen
> eine Zollbude des Todes
> wo der Mensch die gangbahre Wahre
> der Tod der wunderbahre Handels-Mann
> Gott der gewisseste Buchhalter
> das Grab aber das versiegelte Gewand und Kauff-Hauss ist.
> [Whosoever would grace this frail cottage,
> in which poverty adorns every corner,
> with a rational epitome, would be making no inapt statement
> nor overstepping the mark of well-founded truth
> if he called the world a general store,
> a customs-house of death
> in which man is the merchandise,
> death the wondrous merchant
> God the most conscientious book-keeper
> but the grave the bonded drapers' hall and warehouse.][62]

Rather than an instantaneous evocation or flash of meaning in which the transitory evokes the eternal (as in the symbol as defined here), there is instead an elaborate set of discrete, metonymically associated images, each of which serves as a signifier for one of a set of metonymically connected metaphors. The world is a merchant's shop where men and women are sold under God's supervision to be placed in graves – such is the chilling contention of the passage, and it is an excellent example not only of one specific technique of poetic allegory, but also of the de-valued, empty world which Benjamin stresses is the deeper significance of the baroque allegory. No longer organically unified, nature is open to allegoricization in fragments. The world loses any intrinsic meaning and becomes a set of hieroglyphs open to allegorical interpretation, a kind of script, he says, to be read as needed. The allegorist gives meaning like 'a stern sultan in the harem of objects', or like a sadist who 'humiliates his object and then – or thereby – satisfies it. And that is what the allegorist does in this age drunk with acts of cruelty both lived and imagined.'[63]

[62] Christoph Männling, *Schaubühne des Todes, oder Leich Reden* [*Theatre of death, or funeral orations*], quoted and translated in Benjamin, *Origin*, 159.
[63] Benjamin, *Origin*, 184–85.

Benjamin's theory of the allegory thus proposes a model of an artwork as forming a dis-unified unity, as an agglomeration or collection within a boundary, but without the quasi-mystical unified interconnectedness of Romanticism. The very opening passages of the extended chapter 'Allegory and *Trauerspiel*' speak of this general Romantic tendency: 'The striving on the part of the romantic aestheticians after a resplendent but ultimately non-committal knowledge of an absolute has secured a place in the most elementary theoretical debates about art for a notion of the symbol which has nothing more than the name in common with the genuine notion.'[64] This 'genuine notion', we learn, is the idea of the theological symbol – probably a reference to the idea of an original divine language which I will discuss shortly – which proposes 'the indivisible unity of form and content' but which is distorted when applied to works of art.[65] Benjamin then describes how, in a process of Hegelian false-consciousness formation, the Romantics' 'bad' notion of the symbol generates a 'bad' concept of its dialectical opposite the allegory, one that misunderstands and de-values allegory. Even Yeats, Benjamin writes of a poet he evidently admired, is still under the false impression 'that allegory is a conventional relationship between an illustrative image and its abstract meaning'.[66]

Rather than being involved in the expression of essences, allegory is linked generally to 'the territory of the "rhetorical" arts'[67] – presumably to rhetoric's storehouse of figures specifically. It is often marked by what he calls 'an exuberant use of metaphor',[68] as in an extended (sexual and misogynistic) quotation from the playwright Hallmann, said to be almost 'out of control, and the poetry to degenerate into flights of ideas':[69]

> Die Frauen-List: Wenn meine Schlang' in edlen Rosen lieget
> Und Züngelnd saught den Weissheits-vollen Safft
> Ward Samson ouch von Delilah besieged
> Und Schell bedaub deer überird'schen Krafft:
> Hat Joseph gleich der Juno-Fahn getragen
> Herodes ihn geküsst auff seinem Wagen
> So schaut doch
> wie ein Molch [Dolch?] diss Karten-Blat zerritzt
> Weil ihm sein Eh-Schatz selbst durch List die Bahre schnitzt.
> [Woman's cunning: When my serpent lies in noble roses,
> and, hissing, sucks in the sap of wisdom,
> Samson is vanquished by Delilah
> and quickly robbed of his supernatural strength:

---

[64] *Ibid.*, 159.   [65] *Ibid.*, 160.   [66] *Ibid.*, 162.   [67] *Ibid.*, 177.   [68] *Ibid.*, 198.   [69] *Ibid.*, 199.

If Joseph has carried the banner of Juno
and Herod has kissed him in his chariot,
then look yet how a salamander [dagger?] tears up his card,
because his marriage-treasure herself cunningly carves the bier.][70]

Benjamin speaks at one point of the 'elements from which the new whole is mixed' or 'constructed' – as he corrects himself in the next sentence.[71] The allegory in this larger sense is thus understood not as a specific figural technique but as a recipe for creating artworks in an otherwise meaningless world – artworks, as I have suggested, with hidden Messianic resonance. Benjamin, ever the definer of dialectical opposites, notes that while the method of the allegory presupposes a meaningless world of empty objects, it also empowers them, 'raises them to a higher plane' by giving them aesthetic meanings. The allegorical world is thus 'both elevated and devalued'.[72] And yet it also manages to contain the ambiguities. Not unlike what the New Critics claimed about Donne's paradoxes, but with a distinct emphasis that does not subordinate difference to unity but keeps them in a dialectical relation,[73] Benjamin asserts that allegory is like a kind of holy scripture which aspires to become 'one single and inalterable complex' of meaning.[74]

As Howard Caygill has noted, Benjamin's view of the fallen world here is theological in many ways, although it is simultaneously linguistic. It depends on a traditional Judaic view that language existed in the mind of God before creation, that God used language in order to create, and that human language retains aspects of the divine thought even in its post-Exile form, so that language itself gives us the perspective from which to survey the fallen nature of the world.[75] And that fallen world is one bathed in melancholy. In this view, as Caygill puts it, melancholy 'is less a psychological state than an ontological property of things. For Benjamin it is not humans that are melancholy before physical and creaturely nature, but nature that is melancholy under the gaze of the human.'[76]

[70] Johann Christian Hallmann, *Trauer-, Freuden- und Schäferspiele*, 'Mariamne', I, 449ff, p. 16; quoted and translated in Benjamin, *Origin*, 199–200.
[71] Benjamin, *Origin*, 178.
[72] *Ibid.*, 175.
[73] See Comay, 'Benjamin and the Ambiguities of Romanticism', 141–43, for an illuminating discussion of the dialectical relation between totalization and fragmentation that Benjamin defined in an early essay which influenced much of his subsequent work.
[74] Benjamin, *Origin*, 175.
[75] The key work of Benjamin's laying out these notions is his 1916 essay 'On Language as Such and on the Language of Man', in Benjamin, *Reflections*, ed. Demetz, 314–32.
[76] Caygill, 'Walter Benjamin's Concept of Cultural History', 88.

Allegory, history, and aesthetics

This melancholy world is the locus for the allegory of the *Trauerspiel*. But as a kind of sacred writing, allegory transforms history into something else, into part of the drama's formal setting, aestheticizing and spatializing it: 'the movement from history to nature', Benjamin says, '... is the basis of allegory'.[77] 'In allegory the observer is confronted with the *facies hippocratica* of history as a petrified, primordial landscape', he writes. *Facies hippocratica* is a medical term referring to the characteristic expression of a face at or near death. Benjamin's history is thus linked with death and is unredeemed and full of sorrow, revealing 'the Passion of the world'.[78] The baroque allegory, he asserts, arises in a conflation of nature and history in which history is signified through images of a natural, reified world without organic unity. And as noted briefly above, the treatment of history as a process of nature implies for Benjamin an amoral world whose emptiness is bathed in a generalized, non-specific feeling of guilt. It is his version of the concept of instrumental reason that Horkheimer and Adorno would make so central to the disastrous unfolding of modernity in their *Dialectic of Enlightenment*.

Many of the baroque *Trauerspiele* which Benjamin discusses were set in antiquity, and in them the legacy of antiquity is transformed into a set of allegorical signifiers which make up, 'item for item', the elements that form the aesthetic structure of the play. But in this process, antiquity is transformed into a set of motifs; it is no longer a unified, interconnected culture. In that way, it is revealed to be in ruins, and the play is built from these ruins, and thus 'history has physically merged into the setting' in the form of 'ruins'.[79] 'Allegories are', writes Benjamin, 'in the realm of thoughts, what ruins are in the realm of things.'[80] They disclose a world in decay but they show how the elements of decay can be re-born as new art in a new and different era: 'The exuberant subjection of antique elements in a structure, which, without uniting them in a single whole, would, in destruction, still be superior to the harmonies of antiquity, is the purpose of the technique [of allegory] which applies itself separately, and ostentatiously, to realia, rhetorical figures and rules.'[81]

Because Benjamin's philosophy has so many ramifications and opens up into such monumental issues as the fate of the human race in its long history, the possibilities of a meaningful life, the messianic hope that even the dead might yet be redeemed, it is easy to lose track

[77] Benjamin, *Origin*, 182.   [78] *Ibid.*, 166.   [79] *Ibid.*, 177–78.
[80] *Ibid.*, 178.   [81] *Ibid.*, 179.

of the specifically *aesthetic* dimensions of his thought. But the aesthetic for Benjamin links into all these great issues at the same time as it is grounded in its status as semblance (*Schein*), with its own autonomy from the empirical. The theory of the *Trauerspiel* as allegory is, as I have tried to show, primarily an aesthetic theory, although one that would prove to have crucial philosophical usefulness in Benjamin's and Adorno's later work. Benjamin's dis-unifying concept of the allegory (and its relative, the 'constellation') amended the Hegelian notion of totality which had been central to German aesthetics, to Lukács, and to Stalinist Marxism alike. As Susan Buck-Morss shows in *The Origin of Negative Dialectics*, Benjamin's rejection of Hegelian totality would prove seminal for post-Hegelian Marxism and set an important precedent for late twentieth-century Postmodernist art and philosophy. But as an aesthetic theory, it describes the creation of an autonomous world of semblance which draws its materials from reality and yet transforms them into aesthetic signifiers within aesthetic space. At the same time, above all at the level of its form, the artwork imprints the specifics of its historical moment like a monad. For all the many differences between them, Benjamin's overall approach to the work of art was one that his younger friend Theodor Adorno borrowed from, developed, and never broke with. In Benjaminesque baroque allegory, as in Adorno's *Aesthetic Theory*, the function of artistic form is 'to make historical content … into a philosophical truth'.[82] This process allows for a re-birth, as the work's original charm fades, stripping ephemeral beauty, revealing a truth-content and thereby 'the work stands as a ruin'.[83] Benjamin's *Trauerspiel* is thus both formalist and historicist – with a strong 'presentist' dimension as well.[84]

In what follows, I want to apply some of Benjamin's ideas about the *Trauerspiel* to the Shakespearean work he himself most often references, *Hamlet*. There are many possible ways to do this, given the richness of Benjamin's theory. Here I will be taking my cue from one of several different manifestations of the allegorical form which he describes: the

[82] *Ibid.*, 182.   [83] *Ibid.*

[84] Benjamin's Bolshevik *inamorata* Asja Lacis (a Latvian actress and developer of children's theater) reported that she had questioned Benjamin about the political implications of his work on the little-known *Trauerspiele*, and he had replied that his work 'had a direct connection to very actual problems of contemporary literature', specifically to works of contemporary expressionism; see Asja Lacis, *Revolutionär im Beruf: Berichte über proletarisches Theater, über Meyerhold, Brecht, Benjamin, und Piscator*, ed. Hildegaard Brenner (Munich: Regner and Bernhard, 1971), 43–44; quoted and translated in Buck-Morss, *The Dialectics of Seeing*, 15. And on the early Benjamin's critique of the traditional German concept of cultural history to emphasize the shaping role of the present moment in our encounter with the past, see Caygill, 'Walter Benjamin's Concept of Cultural History', especially 89–95.

small, 'local' sets of images that Benjamin calls 'fragmented allegories' which accumulate into a non-organic unity manifesting an empty world. Since, however, one of the most common characteristics of the *Trauerspiele* Benjamin studied is their lack of a focalizing hero, there is an important way in which Shakespeare's *Hamlet* is not a typical example of the form – a point Benjamin seems to think is so obvious that he doesn't discuss it. But the affinity of Shakespeare's play to the *Trauerspiel* manifests in several other ways, as we shall see.

To be sure, Benjamin's remarks on Shakespeare's *Hamlet* as a kind of *Trauerspiel* are scattered and tangential, never developed into a full reading of the play. It is in fact that lack in the original work that justifies the present attempt. However, I am not trying to produce the reading of the play *Hamlet* that Benjamin might have himself written had he been so inclined, because his work and its critical techniques are very much of his time and place and because his aim was to define, historically and dialectically, a literary genre expressive of its historico-philosophical moment rather than to attempt to isolate and explicate one play. In addition, my attempt, reflecting my own background and training, draws on a tradition of Anglo-American close reading quite different in technique from Benjamin's treatment of textual detail. Situated in a Germanic tradition of criticism, Benjamin's tendency is instead to quote a textual passage after he has made some general critical point which it illustrates – rather than, as I do here, try to explicate some of the finer implications of the wording and imagery. However, the underlying theory enabling my readings derives from Benjamin on the allegory and the *Trauerspiel* – a theory which, as I have indicated, is in important ways intertexual with a Postmodernist Anglo-American technique of close reading but which it in other ways confronts and challenges strongly.

HAMLET AS TRAUERSPIEL

> O proud death,
> What feast is toward in thine eternal cell
> That thou so many princes at a shot
> So bloodily hast struck![85]

[85] William Shakespeare, *Hamlet* 5.2.308–11, *The Norton Shakespeare*, ed. Stephen Greenblatt *et al.* (New York: Norton, 1997). All subsequent quotations from *Hamlet* are from this edition, which is a modified 'conflated' text based on the Folio version, with passages from the second quarto of 1604 that were not included in the Folio text printed indented, italicized and numbered as decimals of the previous Folio lines. I follow this numbering system, but instead of indenting and italicizing unique material from the second quarto, I will indicate in a note if a quoted passage is uniquely from the second quarto.

The *Trauerspiel* as Walter Benjamin conceptualizes it is an aesthetic form which, like all others, expresses truths about the time in which it was constructed. But Benjamin is no new historicist – he is much more Hegelian than that, and his periodization is large-scale. Essentially, the *Trauerspiel* is an expression of modernity, of an era of a profound subject–object split, resulting in a world of objects empty of inherent significance and of a subject who confronts a world that is an alien collection of objects, seeking meaning and significance but within a structure of deferral, a movement from object to object.[86]

Benjamin, as we have seen, drew from Friedrich Creuzer on the distinction between symbolic and allegorical representation: 'The latter signifies merely a general concept, or an idea which is different from itself; the former is the very incarnation and embodiment of the idea.'[87] As Creuzer explains it (in terms Benjamin incorporates), the allegory is therefore based on a process of 'substitution' of one thing for another, whereas the symbol is an embodiment.[88] And allegory's formal logic of substitution, Benjamin suggests, is at work at more than one level of dramatic and poetic form. It tends to create a dramatic preference for externalization rather than internalization, for deferral rather than identity.[89] As Benjamin himself sees, *Hamlet* – despite the celebrated interiority of its hero – is in other ways a perfect example of this structure, which he considers to be profoundly different from that of classical tragedy:

The death of Hamlet, which has no more in common with tragic death than the Prince himself has with Ajax, is in its drastic externality characteristic of the *Trauerspiel*; and for this reason alone it is worthy of its creator: Hamlet, as is clear from his conversation with Osric, wants to breathe in the suffocating air of fate in one deep breath. He wants to die by some accident, and as the fateful stage-properties gather around him, as around their lord and master, the drama of fate flares up in the conclusion of this *Trauerspiel* as something that is contained, but of course overcome, in it.[90]

---

[86] Cf. what Lacan says of the array of objects – the horses, swords, and scabbards – used as bait in the proposal of a duel with Laertes by Osric: 'These precious objects, gathered together in all their splendor, are staked against death. This is what gives their presentation the character of what is called a *vanitas* in the religious tradition. This is how all objects are presented, all the stakes in the world of human desire.' Jacques Lacan, 'Desire and the Interpretation of Desire in *Hamlet*', *Yale French Studies* 55/56 (1977), 30.

[87] Creuzer, *Symbolik und Mytholgie der alten Völker*, Vol. I, 118; quoted and translated in Benjamin, *Origin*, 164.

[88] Benjamin, *Origin*, 164–65.

[89] This characterization of a structure of deferral implied in Benjamin's theory of the allegory is the enabling point for my treating the theory as, on this issue, intertextual with the concept of deferral in Derrida and Lacan, as will be discussed in more detail below.

[90] Benjamin, *Origin*, 136–37.

Like all the *Trauerspiele* and completely unlike the classics of Attic tragedy, *Hamlet* follows a logic of 'fate' – not, for Benjamin, the classical Greek idea of pre-destination, but rather fate in the sense of contingency, chance, or fortune: 'Fate, whatever guise it may wear in a pagan or mythological context, is meaningful only as a category of natural history in the spirit of the restoration-theology of the Counter-Reformation', Benjamin writes. That is to say, it follows not the laws of Providence, but the laws of Nature as an amoral realm – but the amorality itself is an outcome of original sin and the world's fallen condition and thus radiates an aura of guilt as an important part of the punishment for original sin.[91] In addition, like all *Trauerspiele*, *Hamlet* is set in history, not myth. As was the case with the English histories whose form Shakespeare had mastered and surpassed before turning to *Hamlet*, Shakespeare's depiction of the past is at once historicist and presentist, mixing materials from the chronicles he read with detailed attention to and representations of his contemporary world, its language, technology, and mores.[92] In Benjamin's view, however, this use of history is ultimately 'presentist' in its effect. In the *Trauerspiel*, he writes (as we saw above), we witness the *ruins* of history, the surviving material proofs of its autonomous existence, but 'in decay' and manifesting the past within the play's projected present – in short, 'history as a petrified, primordial landscape'.[93] Like the ruins to which Benjamin compares them, signifiers of the past are always at the same time elements of the present. Shakespeare's *Hamlet* is full of archaic matter taken ultimately from historical chronicles like Saxo Grammaticus's *Historica Danica* (c. 1190).[94] But according to Benjamin's insight, we should treat the play's archaic material allegorically, as representing meanings in the present by way of an evocation of a vanished past experienced in an empty present. 'When, as is the case in the *Trauerspiel*, history becomes part of the setting', Benjamin claims, 'it does so as script' – that is, as a set of elements from which another meaning is constructed.[95]

Benjamin's project thus has a historicizing dimension, but history for him is always a construct of our present moment, and he is also deeply

---

[91] *Ibid.*, 129.
[92] See Phyllis Rackin, *Stages of History: Shakespeare's English Chronicles* (Ithaca, NY: Cornell University Press, 1990), 100–3, for a clear analysis of the layers of anachronism within the depiction of the past in the plays of the second historical tetralogy.
[93] Benjamin, *Origin*, 166.
[94] Much of the medieval material almost certainly passed to Shakespeare via the lost *Ur-Hamlet*, which, according to a note in Henslowe's *Diary*, was played by the Chamberlain's Men in June 1594, a time when Shakespeare was certainly a contributing troupe-member. However, the contents of this early version of the play necessarily remain unknown.
[95] Benjamin, *Origin*, 177.

interested in aesthetic issues of form and genre as expressions of historical moments. The 'present' in which he wrote his study is of course relevant as well. His analytic strategy is in some ways rooted in the 1920s, as perhaps the earliest instance of the Modernist project of spatializing the temporal dimensions of the literary text, especially through a strategy of de-narrativization.[96] But in his championing of fragmentation and definition of an anti-totalizing form of aesthetic unity structured through a series of deferrals, Benjamin has Postmodernist dimensions as well, and these prescient Postmodernist features authorize for me an incorporation into Benjamin's theory of later critical concepts. At stake is the critical usefulness of an idea defined in the late 1920s, and inevitably some of its features will require updating. What is remarkable to me, however, is how current much of the discussion remains all these decades after it was written.

One of these Postmodernist features involves a 'temporal' (i.e., nonspatial) structure which I see as crucial to the combination of allegories in *Hamlet* but which Benjamin did not directly address. Benjamin largely avoids reference to the temporal dimension in his discussion of the plays, in common with many of the Modernist-influenced critics who succeeded him and for whom, in their revolt against nineteenth-century realist narrativization, temporal structure was irrelevant. But Benjamin in this work reads drama not for narrative or other temporal elements, but for the work's depiction of 'a world' expressive of its philosophical–historical moment and for its mobilization of objects and motifs – in poetic structure and in stagecraft – that create an allegory, a form, as we have seen, whose overall unity he characterizes as an amalgamation of signifying elements rather than an organic unity – albeit one ultimately forming an aesthetic, dissonant, non-organic 'unity' of fragments with multiple significations. In what follows I want to explore one possible configuration (or constellation) of poetic images and signifying objects creative of a 'world' of this sort in *Hamlet*, an aesthetic space of fragmented allegories characteristic of modernity. However, these fragments, I will argue, participate in the play's forward movement, not at the level of narrative strictly speaking, but as part of the logic of deferral that gives

[96] In that way Benjamin's approach has parallels with the Modernist 'spatial' hermeneutics which G. Wilson Knight applied to *Hamlet* in his *The Wheel of Fire: Interpretations of Shakespeare's Tragedies* (1930; reprinted Cleveland, Oh.: Meridian, 1964), 17–46. It parallels even more closely the equally Modernist and spatializing attempt to define the 'world' of the play in Maynard Mack, 'The World of Hamlet', *Yale Review* 41.4 (June 1952), 502–23. For a discussion of the connections of this spatialization to Modernism, see Hugh Grady, *The Modernist Shakespeare: Critical Texts in a Material World* (Oxford: Clarendon, 1991), 92–108.

structure to the play's development at formal and thematic levels – in a process Benjamin referred to as 'substitution'.

A later, deconstructive tradition encompassing Paul de Man, Jacques Lacan, and Jacques Derrida works in detail parts of the terrain covered briefly here by Benjamin – in distinct but related terms. Drawing on the Judaic idea of language as having become distanced from its divine origins after the Fall and Exile, Benjamin writes that this distancing created the conditions for allegory by opening the fissure between signifier and signified, so that in a sense the allegory is allied to the fallen nature of language.[97] In that way, his view of language, as I mentioned above, has commonalities with that of the later deconstructors. However, for Benjamin the allegorical, with its disjunctive, fragmentizing structural principle, is more a formal, *aesthetic* category, characteristic of a certain kind of art. For the later deconstructors, in contrast, those qualities were those of *textuality* and were not tied particularly to cases of the aesthetic (although these critics of course work primarily if not exclusively with literary and literary-philosophical texts). In addition, Benjamin, as a good Hegelian and pre-Marxist, puts much more emphasis on the historical determinations of the texts he studied. These important differences being granted, however, I think that it is possible to create a certain intertextuality between Benjamin's theory of the allegory and later deconstructive theory. At issue here, as I mentioned, is the concept of 'deferral' as a term for describing the formal logic of a certain chain of signification. The term is not prominent in Benjamin (as we saw above, he speaks rather of 'substitution'), but it appears prominently in Lacan (as one of the terms describing the structure constituting desire in the Symbolic Order of the speaking 'I')[98] and in Derrida (for whom it is one of the components behind his neologism *différance*, along with *differ*, referring among other things to the always incomplete sense of meaning of specific words in statements). In *Hamlet* particularly, as we will see below, the dissonant but unifying formal principle is not so much the strategy of accumulation which Benjamin emphasizes in the German *Trauerspiele* as it is a strategy of deferral or substitution.

---

[97] See Caygill, 'Walter Benjamin's Concept of Cultural History', 88.
[98] See, for example, Jacques Lacan, *Écrits: A Selection*, trans. Alan Sheridan (New York: Norton, 1977), 281, where, in a note introducing his essay 'The Signification of the Phallus', he claims to have rescued Freud's term 'deferred action' or *Nachtrag* 'from the facility from which [it has] since fallen'; see also in Lacan, 'Desire and the Interpretation of Desire in *Hamlet*', 24: 'Thus, for Hamlet, the appointment is always too early, and he postpones it. Procrastination is thus one of the essential dimensions of the tragedy.'

At the same time, the reading will need to take cogniscence of the surging subjectivity at loose within this world, the world-historical character-symbol of the Prince himself as a paradoxical subject–object dominating the play and inducting its audience into the allegorical hunt that informs it. Benjamin is seeking to forge an anti-Romantic, Modernist approach to drama, and like T. S. Eliot, to take one prominent Anglophone Shakespeare critic with interesting parallels and contrasts to him,[99] the problems of Hamlet's subjectivity are seen as manifestations of a Romantic discourse that need to be replaced so that Shakespeare could emerge as a Modernist. Benjamin's concept of the aesthetics of the *Trauerspiel* allows us to displace issues of subjectivity onto the aestheticized objects evoked in the play, and several of the motifs I will examine are allegories of aspects of Hamlet's subjectivity. The play continually presents us with images of dissolving boundaries, or eruptions from one domain to the next – images linked to the theme of Hamlet's 'experiment' in madness and of the overflowing of the afterlife into the play's present. Furthermore, Hamlet's subjectivity is structured through a strategy of deferral, similar to that of the allegory proper. But I will return to this issue at the conclusion of this chapter.

Because of the richness of Benjamin's theory of the allegory, it would be possible to pursue his claim that *Hamlet* is an allegorical *Trauerspiel* in any number of ways. However, one of the most concrete of the possible procedures involves a focus on the 'fragmented allegories' formed by local passages of connected images and by stage effects and stage properties.[100] Here, I will focus on the following allegorical motifs: the Ghost, the tables of memory, the images of the unweeded garden and of the beetling cliff, the satirical book, the play-within-the play, Ophelia's flowers, the graveyard and skull, the King's signet, and the 'fatal stage properties' of the last scene (Laertes's poisoned sword, the pearl, and the poisoned cup)[101] – along with some related minor motifs discussed in passing. These all work in the play as exactly the kind of deferring 'fragmented allegories' that Benjamin discussed for the German plays – and which in Shakespeare's *Hamlet* define different facets of a world of melancholic vision. They are key relay points in the chain of deferrals or substitutions that structure

---

[99] See Grady, *The Modernist Shakespeare*, 2; and Richard Halpern, *Shakespeare Among the Moderns* (Ithaca, NY: Cornell University Press, 1997), 1–14.

[100] See Jonathan Gil Harris and Natasha Korda, 'Introduction: Towards a Materialist Account of Stage Properties', in Harris and Korda (eds.), *Staged Properties in Early Modern English Drama* (Cambridge University Press, 2002), 12–13, for an earlier statement of the relevance of Benjamin's *Origin* to a study of stage-props.

[101] Benjamin, *Origin*, 137.

this extraordinary *Trauerspiel*, and they are each also open to multiple interpretations, just as Benjamin says allegorical images should be. Thus, in its often observed undecidableness, *Hamlet* is quintessentially allegorical, and, as we shall see, this quality becomes radically apparent in the play's ending.

Hamlet as a collection of allegorical fragments or signifying objects, each a small piece of a mosaic representation of a world of melancholy, empty of intrinsic meaning, each interrelated with the others but resisting totalization into organic unity – this is the structure of the play that Walter Benjamin's theory of the allegory implies as we try to understand his view that *Hamlet* is less a tragedy than a baroque mourning-play, a *Trauerspiel*.

The Ghost in the emptied world

Viewed allegorically, the Ghost of Hamlet's father has multiple significations, but here I want to stress his evocation of the motif of a lost world of meaning the absence of which has thrust young Hamlet into a profound melancholy. Benjamin had emphasized the affinity of the baroque motif of melancholy in visual and other artworks to the spirit of the *Trauerspiel*, and he thought that in *Hamlet* the Renaissance had produced the ultimate synthesis of the contradictory elements of its conception of melancholy, split, he thought, between images from antiquity and from the medieval. For Benjamin, Shakespeare in *Hamlet* had succeeded in 'striking Christian sparks from the baroque rigidity of the melancholic, un-stoic as it is un-Christian, pseudo-antique as it is pseudo-pietistic'.[102] Benjamin agrees with an earlier critic who had identified Hamlet as a carrier of all the marks of melancholy and *acedia*,[103] but he differs from him in seeing these classical characteristics as 'overcome in the spirit of Christianity'.[104] Of course in the English-speaking world, Hamlet has long been seen as a type of the melancholy man in one of its darkest modes,[105] and the aura of this icon permeates the play. It is a form of subjectivity represented as the outcome of Hamlet's epochal disengagement from what had been, before the death of his father, a

---

[102] *Ibid.*, 157–58.
[103] Rochus Freiherr von Liliencron, *Wie man in Amwald Musik macht: Die siebente Todsünde* (Leipzig, 1903); cited in Benjamin, *Origin*, 247 n. 51.
[104] Benjamin, *Origin*, 158.
[105] See, for example, A. C. Bradley, *Shakespearean Tragedy: Lectures on Hamlet, Othello, King Lear, and Macbeth* (1904; reprinted. Harmondsworth: Penguin, 1991), 120–26.

meaningful, epic, 'immanent' world.[106] He yearns for death and famously inhabits a world that has become radically de-valued and empty:

This goodly frame, the earth, seems to me a sterile promontory. This most excellent canopy, the air, look you, this brave o'erhanging, this majestical roof fretted with golden fire – why, it appears no other thing to me than a foul and pestilent congregation of vapours. What a piece of work is a man! How noble in reason, how infinite in faculty, in form and moving how express and admirable, in action how like an angel, in apprehension how like a god – the beauty of the world, the paragon of animals! And yet to me what is this quintessence of dust? Man delights not me. (2.2.286–98)

In statements like this one, Hamlet defines himself as a Lukácsian 'demonic hero' in the throes of transcendental homelessness,[107] unable to find in this newly fallen world forms which correspond to his now unfixed but mourning subjectivity, his sense of loss. And while the loss is firmly implanted in his life-experience, and specifically in an Oedipal drama of a father's death, a mother's sexuality, a son's inarticulate longing, it is a philo-sophical one as well, expressive of the larger cultural-historical revolutions of Shakespeare's time. And its reverberations over the next four centuries suggest that it expresses a quality of the times that continues into our own.

Hamlet reacts to the death of his father as the death of an entire worldview. The return of his father as a Ghost – with all the 'ques-tionable' resonances of the mysterious aura created in the ambiguous metaphysics of afterlife assumed in the fiction of the play's aesthetic space – in turn creates a powerful 'hauntology', as Derrida calls it,[108] an effect of presence and non-presence.[109] Among other things, the Ghost embodies Hamlet's sense of the lost world of immanent meaning, and his return asserts the continuing power of that ideal while powerfully evoking its absence. 'Ghosts', Benjamin writes, 'like the profoundly sig-nificant allegories, are manifestations from the realm of mourning; they have an affinity for mourners, for those who ponder over signs and over

---

[106] In this act of periodization, then, simultaneously creative of a present of emptiness and a past of lost meaning, Shakespeare depicts Hamlet as creating what Fredric Jameson has called 'the golden-age effect'; see Fredric Jameson, *Late Marxism: Adorno; Or, The Persistence of the Dialectic* (London: Verso, 1990), 100.

[107] These are terms Lukács applies to the problematic hero of the modern novel in his *Theory of the Novel* (e.g. 41, 86–88, 107) , but they seem to me to apply as well or better to Hamlet as a quint-essential hero of modernity.

[108] Jacques Derrida, *Specters of Marx: The State of the Debt, the Work of Mourning, and the New International*, trans. Peggy Kamuf (New York: Routledge, 1994), 10.

[109] Cf. Lacan, 'Desire and the Interpretation of Desire in *Hamlet*', 50–52, who famously interprets the Ghost as an uncanny ideal Phallus 'bound to nothing', which 'always slips through your fingers'.

the future.'[110] More recently Stephen Greenblatt echoes something of this sentiment in his own terms, seeing theatrical ghosts – and especially Shakespeare's – as signifying something important about the function of the theater as art: 'Ghosts, real or imagined, are good theater – indeed … they are good for thinking about theater's capacity to fashion realities, to call realities into question, to tell compelling stories, to punctuate the illusions that these stories generate, and to salvage something on the other side of disillusionment'.[111]

As Greenblatt points out, the curious emphasis on memory in the Ghost's instructions to the Prince is closely related to this function, but I will here pursue the meaning of memory in relation to the play's structure of deferral rather than, *pace* Greenblatt, its evocation of the rites of discountenanced Catholic prayers for the dead.

Hamlet's interior conflict throughout the play suspends him in an indeterminate, intermediate mental space up until his final moments. This indeterminate zone is a kind of earthly Purgatory in a different, more allegorical sense than the one defined by Stephen Greenblatt – but one parallel to the apparent daytime dwelling place of his father's spirit. It is the purgatory of one 'crawling between heaven and earth' (3.1.128). In this way the play's many allusions to Purgatory serve an allegorical purpose signifying Hamlet's terrestrial condition. He is marked for death – he wears black in his electrifying first scene in the court of Denmark, and arguably throughout the entire play – although the weeds are but the 'outwards show', 'the trappings and the suits of woe' (1.2.85–6). He is doing penance, he is full of guilt for obscure deeds, past and future. His 'wit' (i.e. his intelligence), as he tells Rosencrantz and Guildenstern, is truly 'diseased' (3.2.294), profoundly out of ease.

Not only a Melancholic, he is a Malcontent, a figure radically alienated from the world he inhabits. Death is a refuge from all this that calls to him several times in the play, above all in the famous 'To be or not to be' soliloquy, and at the very end, as he approaches it. It is the salvation that will put a terminus on his sentence in purgatory, 'a consummation devoutly to be wished'. *Hamlet* lives up to Benjamin's designation of 'mourning-play' far more directly than many other examples of the genre. Its aesthetic space is structured by its hero's mourning of the loss of father – and world.[112]

---

[110] Benjamin, *Origin*, 193.

[111] Stephen Greenblatt, *Hamlet in Purgatory* (Princeton University Press, 2001), 200.

[112] Cf. Lacan, 'Desire and the Interpretation of Desire in *Hamlet*', who states: 'from one end of *Hamlet* to the other, all anyone ever talks of is mourning' (39).

The tables of memory

'Adieu, adieu, Hamlet. Remember me' (1.5.91), the Ghost tells the Prince, and he famously echoes the phrase in soliloquy:

> Remember thee?
> Ay, thou poor ghost, while memory holds a seat
> In this distracted globe. Remember thee?
> Yea, from the table of my memory
> I'll wipe away all trivial fond records,
> All saws of books, all forms, all pressures past,
> That youth and observation copied there,
> And thy commandment all alone shall live
> Within the book and volume of my brain,
> Unmix'd with baser matter. (1.5.95–104)

To remember his (assigned but questionable) duty to revenge is somehow to strike a blow of restoration of what has been lost. But, as the oldest and truest cliché of all says, it can't. It can't bring back the dead, and it can't restore a world that is now revealed as an illusion of youth to be 'wiped away' from the table of memory. Hamlet is implicitly thus given a symbolic, ambiguous task of restoration along with the material one of slaying Claudius, and the rest of the play unfolds as he attempts first to elude, then to accomplish his bi-fold assignment in a series of artfully concocted deferrals. Jan Kott in particular has stressed the 'external', 'imposed' nature of the tasks assigned, not only to Hamlet, but to Fortinbras, Laertes, and Ophelia as well.[113] In the end, Hamlet accomplishes the retribution at a bodily level (he kills Claudius), but he does not accomplish a symbolic restoration. Instead, through a series of contingent improvisations he changes the world but cannot restore what has been lost, and he leaves us mourning his own new absence from the world, initiating a new phase of 'hauntology' in the quite different figure of the dead Prince Hamlet whose story must be told, has been told, will be told.

In a recent article, Peter Stallybrass and several collaborators have shed considerable light on the nature of the 'table' or 'tables' Hamlet refers to in the passage just quoted and which he also physically writes on (1.5.110). It was a set of papers coated with plaster, sometimes blank, sometimes bound together with calendars, almanacs, or other reference material and widely used in Shakespeare's London as an *aide-mémoire* on which it was possible to write and then later rub out notations to create

[113] Jan Kott, *Shakespeare Our Contemporary*, trans. Boleslaw Taborski (New York: Doubleday, 1964), 60–61.

space for additional notes.[114] And it is precisely the action of erasing and over-writing that Hamlet evokes in his figure comparing the table to his memory. Margaret Ferguson had earlier pointed out a pervasive motif in the play of the Prince's propensity to 'materialize' various tropes by taking them literally.[115] In this case, after referring to metaphoric tables, Hamlet turns to physical ones. Thus both his words and his action with a stage-property create a fragmentary allegory of a kind of memory (for example, rote memory) that is external to the self, needing to be 'set down', and thus suggesting the absence of a truly interior memory that took to heart what the Ghost has just told him.[116] But the image shifts in the following sentence to one of a book rather than a table, suggesting a more permanent and interiorized memory within Hamlet's brain, now said to be 'a book and volume'. Though there is an associative link of similarity between the plastered table and the book and volume – both of these things are media for written language – one is erasable, the other is not.[117] As with so many other of Hamlet's equivocations, the difference is deeply expressive of different possibilities in the future: whether Hamlet's memory will prove a transitory table or a more permanent book, whether the Ghost's commands (and his/its version of reality) will remain an external, alienated task, or be assimilated, taken within Hamlet's (protean) sense of self – these issues, whose centrality will become apparent in the scenes of Hamlet's 'antic disposition' and dilatory tactics to come, are posed for the audience and readers in this brief and fragmentary allegory amidst the 'wild and whirling words' (1.5.137) of Hamlet's agitated reactions to the Ghost's revelations. But it is part of the formal characteristic of the *Trauerspiel*, as we saw earlier,

---

[114] Peter Stallybrass, Roger Chartier, J. Franklin Mowery, and Heather Wofe, 'Hamlet's Tables and the Technologies of Writing in Renaissance England', *Shakespeare Quarterly* 55.4 (Winter 2004), 379–419.

[115] Margaret W. Ferguson, '*Hamlet*: Letters and Spirits', in Patricia Parker and Geoffrey Hartmann (eds.), *Shakespeare and the Question of Theory* (New York: Methuen, 1985), 292–309; 292.

[116] I draw here from Marjorie Garber, *Shakespeare's Ghost Writers: Literature as Uncanny Causality* (New York: Methuen, 1987), 147–53. Garber in turn has taken the distinction between two types of memory from Hegel, via Paul de Man, 'Sign and Symbol in Hegel's *Aesthetics*', *Critical Inquiry* 8.4 (Summer 1982), 761–75. De Man borrows the distinction in Hegel between an internal, self-reflective kind of memory (*Erinnerung*) and external, rote memory (*Gedächtnis*), associating the first kind with symbol, the second kind with allegory. Garber ties de Man's and Hegel's distinction to *Hamlet* and Hamlet's change from an initial state of internalized, 'symbolic' memory in the first soliloquy to one of externalized, 'allegorical' memory in need of being written down when he turns to his tables after seeing the Ghost (pp. 148–51). Garber goes on to discuss Jacques Derrida's use of the same distinction to define the work of mourning as requiring a substitution of *Erinnerung* by *Gedächtnis* and claims that is precisely what Hamlet does when he writes on his tables (pp. 152–53).

[117] See Stallybrass *et al.*, 'Hamlet's Tables', 414–16, for a similar distinction.

to favor allegory over symbol, writing over voiced language, and deferral over fulfillment. *Hamlet*, it seems clear, hews closely to this norm.

The unweeded garden and the beetling cliff

The motif of the emptiness of the world under the gaze of Hamlet's depressed, melancholic vision is enunciated, as we have seen, in Hamlet's first conversation with Rosencrantz and Guildenstern, but he is there recapitulating a theme already announced in his first soliloquy, a revelation of a state of mind that had been kept at least partially occluded in the preceding court scene – where Hamlet seemed to be lively, witty, and manic. Despite his protestation that he knows not 'seems' (1.2.76), it is clear that his claim of having 'that within which passeth show' (1.2.85), is equivocal, encompassing deception as well as depth of feeling. For he has not fully revealed either his wish for self-dissolution or the extent of his depression:

> O, that this too too solid flesh would melt,
> Thaw, and resolve itself into a dew,
> Or that the Everlasting had not fixed
> His canon 'gainst self-slaughter! O God, God,
> How weary, stale, flat and unprofitable
> Seem to me all the uses of this world!
> Fie on't, ah fie, fie! 'Tis an unweeded garden
> That grows to seed; things rank and gross in nature
> Possess it merely. (1.2.129–37)

The image of the garden evokes the early modern ideal of nature as a realm that must be cultivated, adapted by human labor to satisfy human needs, pruned of excess, governed, disciplined, dominated.[118] The well-tended garden is one of its most common expressions, one used by artists and poets alike, one signaled in the great interest in gardens of the period. Shakespeare had memorably used the image of the garden for a brief but telling political allegory in *Richard II*, and it recurs elsewhere in his own works – it is, Caroline Spurgeon tells us, the most frequent vehicle for Shakespeare's allusions to nature.[119] Here it functions as well as a kind of implied political allegory, providing the first hint of the theme of the something rotten in Denmark, akin to the hidden ulcers and impostures

---

[118] Stephen Greenblatt, *Renaissance Self-Fashioning: From More to Shakespeare* (University of Chicago Press, 1980), 157–92, provides a useful discussion of this motif, especially in the passages on the razing of the Bower of Bliss in Spenser's *The Fairie Queene*, 170–73.

[119] Caroline Spurgeon, *Shakespeare's Imagery: And What It Tells Us* (Cambridge University Press, 1935; 1966), 86–91, 164–65.

that form a well-known image-pattern in the play.[120] But its most obvious allegorical application at this point in the play is a psychological one, a theme to which Hamlet will return several times: the unweeded garden suggests a corruption of a female sexuality now unregulated by the social norms of marriage and patriarchy of the lost world of the past:

> Must I remember? Why, she would hang on him
> As if increase of appetite had grown
> By what it fed on, and yet within a month –
> Let me not think on't; frailty, thy name is woman –
> ...
> O, God, a beast that wants discourse of reason
> Would have mourned longer! – married with mine uncle,
> My father's brother, but no more like my father
> Than I to Hercules; within a month,
> ...
> ...O most wicked speed, to post
> With such dexterity to incestuous sheets! (1.2.143–57)

And finally, such a concept of female frailty is implicitly extended to encompass the entire history of humanity in the fallen world – the unweeded garden suggests the Garden of Eden after the Exile, and constitutes an indictment of the world and time out of joint, the age of emptied meaning and Machiavellian behavior in politics, sexuality, and commerce. 'In allegory the observer is confronted with the *facies hippocratica* of history as a petrified, primordial landscape', Benjamin observes in a passage I quoted above and whose concrete application to the play can be seen here. History has become nature – a degraded, empty nature, much as Benjamin suggested was the case for the *Trauerspiel* generally.[121] But, as we will see below, in the very emptiness of this transformation there lies the suggestion of redemption, Benjamin would insist – of a restoration that Hamlet perceives if he cannot fathom how to bring about.

A related but quite differently inflected allegory of the susceptibility of human nature to corruption is given in the striking images of vertiginous danger in Horatio's warning to Hamlet not to follow the beckoning Ghost:

> What if it tempt you toward the flood, my lord,
> Or to the dreadful summit of the cliff
> That beetles o'er his base into the sea,
> And there assume some other horrible form

[120] Spurgeon, *Shakespeare's Imagery*, 133–34, 316–21.   [121] Benjamin, *Origin*, 182.

> Which might deprive your sovereignty of reason
> And draw you into madness? Think of it.
> The very place puts toys of desperation,
> Without more motive, into every brain
> That looks so many fathoms to the sea
> And hears it roar beneath. (1.4.50–55.4)[122]

The roaring sea is a figure for madness, the absence of reason, a chaos that can result if the boundaries within the 'little world' of human mentality are dissolved through too intimate a contact with the fearful figure of the Ghost. Reason might plunge, like Hamlet himself in Horatio's mind's eye, from 'the dreadful summit of the cliff', the open boundary of sanity, into the flood of the fearful unknown. The beetling cliff might also suggest another potent emblem that Hamlet will peer into later in the play, the skull which figures both the seat of reason and the inevitability of death, that 'undiscover'd country from whose bourn / No traveller returns'(3.1.81–82).

The threatened dissolution of the self suggested in these allegorical fragments is a theme that plays throughout the drama, beginning with Hamlet's first remark in soliloquy 'that this too too solid flesh would melt / Thaw and resolve itself into a dew!' (1.2.129–30), and providing much of its psychological power.[123] This threat helps prepare the audience as well for the ambiguities of Hamlet's 'antic disposition' (1.5.176–87), that feigning of madness to which I will turn next.

The satirical book as allegory

We watch Hamlet's antic disposition on display above all with Polonius, with the hidden Claudius behind the arras and Hamlet reading a satirical book – a book which serves to suggest another fragmented allegory (2.2.168–220) – and serves as well as a gloss to Hamlet's earlier metaphor of memory as a book within his mind. This book serves as a very unobtrusive metonymy to reference a number of different strands of the play. In the first instance, it helps establish Hamlet's status as a scholar, a university student on leave from Wittenberg. And Hamlet reports the book to be a satire, the work of 'a satirical slave' (2.2.196),

---

[122] The final four lines of this passage are unique to the second quarto.
[123] Cf. Janet Adelman, *Suffocating Mothers: Fantasies of Maternal Origin in Shakespeare's Plays* excerpted and reprinted in Susanne L. Wofford, (ed.), *Williiam Shakespheare: Hamlet* (Boston, Mass.: Bedford, 1994). 256–82; 273. Adelman argues that these images take their origin 'in the earliest stages of emergent selfhood, when the nascent self is most fully subject to the mother's fantasied power to annihilate or contaminate'.

and this reference serves as a metatheatrical one casting light on the satirical properties of the play *Hamlet* and prefiguring for us the more sustained metatheatrical moments of the inset play to come. Two final significations are more subtle than these.

The physical object of the book recalls for us Hamlet's earlier characterization of his new mind-set after the revelations of the Ghost, one in which all 'baser matter' had been expunged and only the Ghost's commands lived within the 'book and volume of my brain' (1.5.104). The 'jump' between the two metaphoric vehicles Hamlet employs to express the comparison – the jump from erasable plastered tables to a more permanent book that I discussed above – posed, as we have seen, the question of interpretation that dominates the next few scenes of intrigue in the play. Will Hamlet's memory of the Ghost's injunction to revenge remain external to his sense of self, or will he incorporate it permanently within a new consciousness of self and situation in the light of the revelation of Claudius's murder and usurpation?

The appearance of the physical book in 2.2, in a setting in which Hamlet is being spied on by his enemies, tested for his true intentions, and engaged in bandying with Polonius in a dialogue dominated by obscure puns and *double entendres*, is attention-getting as a possible reference to Hamlet's earlier comparison of book and brain. For the book is ambiguously and simultaneously both external and internal to Hamlet's consciousness. As the work of a 'satirical slave' who has set down things that in all decency should have remained unsaid, as Hamlet points out to Polonius, the book is kept at a distance from Hamlet's own intentionality. But no audience needs an informing Ghost to understand the sly malice and irony in Hamlet's words to this tedious old fool. Looked at this way, the distance between the book and Hamlet himself is the distance between a ventriloquist and his puppet – it is illusory. Even Polonius detects the illusion, in his famous remark that there is method in this madness – although at the same time he writes it off as the happy and poignant effect of Hamlet's love-sickness. The hidden Claudius, we soon learn, is not so taken in, at least after he has witnessed Hamlet's insulting behavior towards Ophelia and Hamlet's not-so-veiled threats against himself in the last part of the scene. The overall effect, however, is puzzling and ambiguous, just like the book as an allegorical signifier. At the end we are simply uncertain about the state of Hamlet's mind. But Claudius's perspicuity certainly raises that fundamental interpretive problem of Hamlet's distance from the insanity he is supposedly feigning.

The motif of pretended madness is one of the most memorable components of Kyd's *The Spanish Tragedy*, that block-buster theatrical and book-trade hit of the 1580s. Beyond that it seems to have founded the subgenre of the Elizabethan-Jacobean revenge-tragedy and supplied Shakespeare with many of his most atmospheric theatrical devices in this play: a ghost and multiple evocations of an afterlife, madness and near madness, prevalent Machiavellian deception within a royal court, a context of international politics, uncertainty and mystery as to how to proceed and perceive, soliloquies, treachery, a wronged heroine, suicide, a play-within-a-play (along with other metatheatrical allusions) and an ending with bodies piled on the stage.[124]

In *The Spanish Tragedy*, however, as any number of previous commentators have noted, there is a clear purpose to Don Hieronimo's feigned madness – it provides a 'cover' giving him access to his court enemies, who assume his debility renders him harmless.[125] And to make sure no one in the audience misperceives the feigning as genuine, Kyd provides a commentary from his allegorical frame-characters Andrea and Revenge, who assure us just before the beginning of Act 4 that Revenge is alive and well although he has been sleeping and that 'poor Hieronimo / Cannot forget his son Horatio'.[126] In contrast, in Shakespeare's play, it is precisely Hamlet's feigning that arouses Claudius's suspicions that he knows something about the murder – or that in any case he is too dangerous to be allowed to live. Thus many readers or viewers of the play have suspected that Hamlet is not completely in control of his antic disposition, that the appearance of madness has in his case become the thing itself, at least at moments,[127] and the recurrent images of dissolution reinforce this supposition. It is only after Hamlet's return from his aborted sea-voyage that he seems truly to have 'taken in' the Ghost's

---

[124] I draw this list from Hugh Grady, *Shakespeare, Machiavelli, and Montaigne: Power and Subjectivity from 'Richard II' to 'Hamlet'* (Oxford University Press, 2002), 245. Most of these effects are prominent characteristics of the German baroque *Trauerspiele* Benjamin studied as well, and I note in passing that we might argue accordingly that Kyd and Marlowe founded the early modern (as opposed to medieval) English *Trauerspiel* in Benjamin's sense.

[125] The same is true of the 1626 adaptation of *Hamlet* in German, *Tragoedia: Der Bestrafte Brudermord oder: Prinz Hamlet aus Dännemark* [*Tragedy: Fratricide Punished; or, Prince Hamlet of Denmark*], trans. Horace Howard Furness, in Horace Howard Furness (ed.), *A New Variorum Edition of Shakespeare: Hamlet,* 2 vols. (Philadelphia, Pa.: Lippincott, 1877; reprinted 1905), Vol. ɪɪ, 121–42 – obviously a baroque *Trauerspiel* as Benjamin defines the term, complete with allegorizing double title, in which Hamlet says after seeing the Ghost, 'Horatio, I will so avenge myself on this ambitious man and adulterer and murderer that posterity shall talk of it for ever. I will now go, and, feigning madness, wait upon him until I find an opportunity to effect my revenge' (1.6. 180–83).

[126] Thomas Kyd, *The Spanish Tragedy*, ed. David Bevington (Manchester University Press, 1996), 3.15.

[127] See Furness (ed.), *A New Variorum Edition,* Vol. ɪɪ 195–235, for a series of excerpts from some thirty-nine critics debating the insanity issue from 1780 to 1876.

injunction. Before that – even after he proclaims the end of his previous
doubts at the conclusion of *The Mousetrap* – he always defers the moment of
revenge, and in that sense the Ghost's injunction seems to be always external
to him, always something to put off, or to find substitutes for.

All these considerations, involving scenes both before and after
Hamlet is presented to us reading a book in 2.2, suggest that the book
is an ambiguous figure, and one that shifts its meaning as the theme of
Hamlet's memory unfolds. We should recall that in *The Spanish Tragedy*,
Hieronimo is also presented, in the words of the stage direction at the
beginning of scene 3.13, 'with a book in his hand', one which apparently
is intended to be a plausible source for the several lines of Latin verse
he quotes, as he informs the audience of his plans for revenge. Hamlet's
book, however, instead supplies him with matter – or pretended matter –
for a curious cat-and-mouse game with Polonius:

> POLONIUS: What do you read, my lord?
> HAMLET: Words, words, words.
> POLONIUS: What is the matter, my lord?
> HAMLET: Between who?
> POLONIUS: I mean, the matter you read, my lord.
> HAMLET: Slanders, sir: for the satirical slave says here that
>   old men have grey beards, that their faces are wrinkled,
>   their eyes purging thick amber or plum-tree gum, and
>   that they have a plentiful lack of wit, together with most
>   weak hams. All which, sir, though I most powerfully
>   and potently believe, yet I hold it not honesty to have it
>   thus set down, for yourself, sir, should be old as I am –
>   if like a crab you could go backward. (2.2.191–202)

Beyond its ambiguous evocation of memory, the book serves here as
a prop for and as an emblem of Hamlet's de-stabilizing language, one
in which words are ends in themselves, meaning is always multiple, and
insults are delivered without, Hamlet blithely and disingenuously suggests, being really intended. But the language which seems unstable here
is capable of being instrumentalized, we will learn a bit later in the play,
when Hamlet uses his knowledge of writing a 'fair' hand to create an
instrument of execution for Rosencrantz and Guildenstern.

Even at this point in the story, the unstable properties of Hamlet's
language are given an instrumental dimension, as part of the greater
intrigue going on in this part of the play, when indirections are employed
to find directions out. As well as ambiguously evoking 'the book and
volume of my brain' as the permanent depository of memory, this book is

in addition a means of pretense and a means of deferral. It is a sign, like
Hamlet's earlier reversion to writing on erasable tables (after he had used
the image of an indelible book as a metaphor for his memory), that the
Ghost's injunction has not really been assimilated, that Hamlet is doing
something other than sweeping to his revenge 'with wings as swift / As
meditation or the thoughts of love' (1.5.29–30). An important intimation
of Hamlet's investment in deferral is that, singularly, *Hamlet* is a revenge-
tragedy in which a revenge-plan is never articulated. The jousting with
Polonius seems instead to be a substitute for or deferral of such a plan –
like others to come. Hamlet's memory remains extraneous, unintegrated
into Hamlet's now clearly decentered self.

Hamlet's metadramatic turn: The Mousetrap

With the appearance of the players from the city – who arrive just as
Hamlet is trying to gauge the danger posed to him by Rosencrantz and
Guildenstern – *Hamlet* takes an unprecedented turn. *The Spanish Tragedy*
had ended with its own spectacular play-within-the-play, a bravura court
performance in which what were apparently stage deaths are revealed
at the end as the real thing, the play thus emerging as Hieronimo's
well-wrought instrument of revenge. In *Hamlet* Shakespeare instead
situates the inset play in his drama's center and makes of it the dramatic
turning point. Hamlet momentarily steps back from the role of troubled
intriguer to show the audience his connoisseurship of plays, acting, and
dramatic poetry. He indeed makes the play his instrument: 'The play's
the thing', he exults, 'Wherein I'll catch the conscience of the King'
(2.2.581–82). But instead of being an instrument of violence, as in Kyd,
it is in *Hamlet* an empirical probe, a means to move from uncertainty to
knowledge.

Ever since John Dover Wilson's 1935 *What Happens in 'Hamlet'*,[128] critics
have been at pains to point out that Claudius's actions when he orders the
play to be given over are ambiguous, susceptible to being seen as either
the startling of a guilty thing (as Hamlet and Horatio assume) or as the
prudence of a man who has just witnessed a blatant affront to his and his
Queen's dignity, an accusation of murder and lust, and a palpable threat
against his person as well. For all that, however, the play soon establishes
the correctness of Hamlet's and Horatio's surmise, the correctness of the
Ghost on at least the central point that Claudius has murdered King

[128] John Dover Wilson, *What Happens in 'Hamlet'* (Cambridge University Press, 1935), 154–57.

Hamlet, when we are presented with the isolated figure of King Claudius confessing his guilt and trying to repent of his sin. Theodor Adorno has pointed out how human rationality can never gain direct access to the real, that it at best constructs concepts and attempts to 'place' aspects of the real 'under' them. However, Adorno argues, science has at least that adequacy to the real that allows technology to dominate nature.[129] Hamlet's play *The Mousetrap*, for all the uncertainties that its performance entailed, has that same imperfect but pragmatic adequacy.

In other ways, however, the play's metadrama is de-stabilizing and creative of aesthetic effects. By drawing attention to the art of playing, the play of course exposes itself as playing, as artifice, as art. As Robert Weimann puts it, '*The Mousetrap* itself becomes a peculiar "trap of *sa-voir*", a self-conscious vehicle of the drama's awareness of the functional and thematic heterogeneity of mimesis itself.'[130] Hamlet had developed this theme, and inserted it back inside the fictional frame of the play, with another *a fortiori* argument about the greater urgency and dignity of his own situation as opposed to that of a mere actor in 'a fiction, in a dream of passion' (2.2.529). But the play continually overflows the boundaries of its own fictionality. In a few moments we hear Hamlet and the players passionately denouncing the children's drama that was undercutting the revenues of the Chamberlain's Men and the other adult actors of London, followed by a passage which steps outside of the fictional space of the narrative to name its own purposes, aesthetic and social:

> for any thing so overdone is from the purpose of playing, whose end, both at the first and now, was and is, to hold as 'twere the mirror up to nature, to show virtue her own feature, scorn her own image, and the very age and body of the time his form and pressure. (3.2.18–22)

It is, as Weimann says, a 'mimesis of mimesis',[131] a vertiginous assertion of the nature of art as semblance, as a 'mirror' that alludes to but is Other than the society which gave it birth. And *The Mousetrap* is of course itself a kind of allegory, one in which the apparent signified of an 'image of a murder done in Vienna' (3.2.233) becomes in turn a signifier of the

---

[129] Theodor Adorno, *Negative Dialectics,* trans. E. B. Ashton (New York: Continuum, 1983), 135–207.
[130] Robert Weimann, 'Mimesis in *Hamlet*', in Patricia Parker and Geoffrey Hartman (eds.), *Shakespeare and the Question of Theory* (New York: Methuen, 1985), 275–91; 279. Weimann is using the term *mimesis* in a complex but classically rooted sense to refer to the artwork's property of reflecting without exactly reproducing empirical reality. He does not reference Adorno and Benjamin's sense of the term discussed above in the Introduction.
[131] Weimann, 'Mimesis in *Hamlet*', 281.

murder of old King Hamlet.[132] At moments like this, Hamlet's own account of himself as a player within a de-valued world plays within our memory and establishes a metadramatic quality to all his actions. The term 'antic' which Hamlet had employed to describe his deceptive actions to come has itself roots in a world of playing – according to the *Oxford English Dictionary*, it comes from a meaning of the term as a clown-like fantastick in plays. Weimann in fact counts six different 'uses of mimesis which Hamlet relates to' – as theorist, critic, dramatist, director, chorus, and actor.[133]

Benjamin sees the meta-aesthetic quality of motifs like this as of the essence of the baroque:[134] 'The Renaissance explores the universe; the baroque explores libraries. Its meditations are devoted to books', Benjamin writes.[135] *Hamlet*'s play-within-the-play, like those of *A Midsummer Night's Dream* and *The Tempest*, is a de-stabilizing 'baroque' technique, one that expresses the principle of the empty world that the various allegorical fragments of these plays had relied on for specific, local dramatic and poetic effects. It is the moment of the play, too, in which the unfixed subjectivity of the role-shifting Hamlet is inscribed within an explicitly aesthetic context, but this point needs fuller development, and I will return to it below.

Allegorical deferral and the prayer scene

After he has conversed with the Ghost, Hamlet acts like the character-type in the German baroque *Trauerspiele* which Benjamin calls 'the Intriguer'.[136] However, we would have to say he is an Intriguer oddly committed to deferral. When Hamlet's recourse to drama as a political instrument reaches its climax with apparent success, as Claudius experiences a moment of panic and ends the performance, the success does not end Hamlet's series of deferrals. In an action which has puzzled several generations of interpreters, Hamlet, right at his moment of triumph, stumbles onto a clear, unimpeded opportunity to kill Claudius at his prayers, only to decide the moment is not right.

Hamlet's explicitly expressed motivation for foregoing his momentary advantage is one of the moments of the play when its archaic, medieval

---

[132] Cf *Ibid.*   [133] *Ibid.*, 283.

[134] The identification of Shakespeare as a baroque figure was common in Germany in this era, as can be seen in the well-known work by German critic Levin Ludwig Schücking, *The Meaning of Hamlet*, trans. Graham Rawson (New York: Barnes and Noble, 1966; originally published as *Der Sinn des Hamlet*, 1935).

[135] Benjamin, *Origin*, 140.   [136] *Ibid.*, 95–6, 125, 127, 228.

material surfaces in Hamlet's own subjectivity.[137] The reason he gives for
the deferral is as savage as the preceding imagery of hell and night. His
decidedly un-Christian desire not just to execute his father's murderer
and Denmark's usurper but to damn him as well is at once highly
expressionistic and theologically puzzling. Eighteenth-century critics
were shocked and dismayed by Hamlet's passion here. Samuel Johnson,
for example, found Hamlet's explanation for his delay 'too horrible to be
read or to be uttered'.[138] Beginning with the Romantics, critics tended to
discount these words, arguing that they are a cover for Hamlet's hesitation
to kill. In the twentieth century, a critic like J. Dover Wilson, who was
attempting to recreate an authentically 'Elizabethan' *Hamlet*, thought
that Hamlet's explanation for foregoing revenge would not have shocked
the original audience, and although it might be 'discordant ... with our
scale of values, does not detract from our general sense of the nobility and
greatness of the man'.[139]

But taking a completely different tack, Arthur McGee argued several
decades later that these Catholic resonances were signals to the original
audience that Hamlet's mission was flawed, that the Ghost was entrapping
him, successfully tempting him to effectuate his own damnation at
a moment of weakness.[140] And deliberately willing the damnation of
another was a grievous sin for both Catholic and Protestant theologians,
so that Hamlet seems in that light to be courting the loss of his own
soul.

But it is impossible, I believe, to map such moments – the executed
order of 'not shriving time allowed' for Rosencrantz and Guildenstern
is another very similar one – into a key to the play's overall significance. Rather, we might say, they are moments of 'madness', the archaic
material expressive of primal emotions and extreme stress. In that way,
these moments function as fragmented allegories in Benjamin's sense – in
this case, they are fragments that evoke feeling and atmosphere; they are
evocative of the rage and cold resolve of a revenge-hero, moments when

[137] Phillipe Ariès, *The Hour of Our Death*, trans. Helen Weaver (New York, Knopf, 1981), 297–321,
argues that the Renaissance was a period in which both Protestant and Catholic teachers tended
to criticize the previous age's emphasis on the disposition of the soul at the moment of death,
casting doubt on death-bed conversations and repentance, and emphasizing that a person's
entire life was relevant to her salvation. In that sense Hamlet's and the Ghost's preoccupation
with the state of the soul at the moment of death was medieval and anachronistic.

[138] Samuel Johnson, 'Notes on Shakespeare's Plays: "Hamlet"', *The Yale Edition of the Works of
Samuel Johnson*, 17 vols., Vol. VIII: *Johnson on Shakespeare*, ed. Arthur Sherbo (New Haven,
Conn.: Yale University Press, 1968), 990.

[139] Wilson, *What Happens in 'Hamlet'*, 102.

[140] Arthur McGee, *The Elizabethan Hamlet* (New Haven: Yale University Press, 1987).

Hamlet is not far from Hieronimo or Marlowe's Barabas. We see a world not only emptied of meaning but open to the forces of hell and damnation as well. Significantly, Hamlet situates the moment in a direful nighttime:

> 'Tis now the very witching time of night,
> When churchyards yawn, and hell itself breathes out
> Contagion to this world. Now could I drink hot blood,
> And do such bitter business as the day
> Would quake to look on. (3.2.358–62)

It is as if, at this moment, Hamlet has plunged over the beetling cliff into madness, and yet the feeling it evokes is as much relief at his apparent resolution as horror at its savagery. Again, as in the allegory of the beetling cliff, the images depict boundaries giving way, borders dissolving: graves 'yawn' and hell 'breathes out / Contagion'. The image of drinking hot blood is a kind of inverted, diabolical Eucharist. Hamlet seems suspended between two different moral frames; from one perspective (Christian) he is damning himself, but from another (Machiavellian and Roman) he is empowered: he is finally preparing himself for the bloody necessities of carrying out his princely duty. Of course, what follows from this vivid dramatic build-up is – another deferral, perhaps the most ambiguous one of all.

But however we evaluate the seriousness and ethics of Hamlet's fervent wish for the damnation of Claudius, we can see the incident as also making an important point in the play's investigation of knowledge. Hamlet had just affirmed the possibility of reading Claudius's subjectivity by studying his external actions as he watched the play, and he carries on the same project here. In this case, however, we learn that the Prince has erred in his judgment. Claudius is unable to undertake a meaningful reformation and instead chooses to keep the effects gained by his murder rather than relinquish them in repentance. The incident thus marks an important qualification to the possibility of reading another's interiority by external appearances, returning us to the play's generally skeptical, Montaignean epistemology.[141] And it is one of the most remarkable of the play's several moments of deferral of revenge.

Still following the logic of deferral, Hamlet proceeds from this postponement of revenge to an encounter with his mother, in which he tries to share with her his vision of the fallen world and her contribution to it. In the intimacy of the lady's chamber, for the first time in the play he enacts (rather than imagines) the violent spirit of the revenge-hero – only, of course, finding the wrong hidden target and slaying Polonius, another

---

[141] I want to thank Susan Wells for suggesting this reading of this incident.

substitute, in error. Without realizing it, he has slain Ophelia as well, who becomes the play's most unambiguous subject of madness in the famous fourth-act scenes of her disordered mourning.

More images of dissolution and corruption

When Laertes re-appears soon after Ophelia's first mad-scene, the allegorical motif of dissolving boundaries that had previously been centered on Hamlet is transferred to the social level, as Laertes leads a mob to confront Claudius:

> The ocean, overpeering of his list,
> Eats not the flats with more impetuous haste
> Than young Laertes, in a riotous head,
> O'erbears your officers. The rabble call him lord,
> And, as the world were now but to begin,
> Antiquity forgot, custom not known,
> The ratifiers and props of every word,
> They cry 'Choose we! Laertes shall be king.'
> Caps, hands, and tongues, applaud it to the clouds,
> 'Laertes shall be king, Laertes king!'' (4.5.96–105)

Rosencrantz, Guildenstern, and Claudius himself have sounded the motif of the sovereign's centrality to the welfare of the kingdom's population in lines that rehearse the logic of reasons of state requiring the removal of, and, as Claudius later states, the execution of Hamlet in deference to the King's safety (3.3.1–26 and 4.1.11–14).

But the dissolving of the state's authority seems already to be well in process when Laertes bursts through the door as the unhesitating revenge-hero that Hamlet himself could not be. Only he is himself soon inducted into the general corruption of Denmark when Claudius convinces him that Hamlet, not King Claudius, is the author of Polonius's death. An allegory of this process is provided as the two intriguers imagine, first the anointing with poison of Laertes's sword – the emblem of his masculine honor – and then an envenoming of a chalice of wine – an emblem of pleasure, reward, and female sexuality now made a vehicle of death (4.7.116–37). The occasion for the treacherous fencing match will be provided by Claudius's mention of the praise of Laertes's swordsmanship by the significantly named gentleman of Normandy, Lamord – a name, as several commentators have noted, that simultaneously evokes the French *la mort* (death) and the Latin *amor* (love). The aura of these stage-prop allegories in the final scene is a climactic signifier of the corruption of family, sexuality, and the state that is the dominating characteristic of this play's world.

Ophelia's allegorical bouquet

While Hamlet passively if warily accepts a hasty conveyance to England, Ophelia evokes the motif of madness in scenes which have since become iconic for their allegorical effect, in paintings and in allusions like Mary Pipher's *Reviving Ophelia*, a study of suicides by adolescent females. In another image of dissolving open boundaries, Ophelia's madness is presented as a kind of dissolution of maidenly decorum, the spilling over of repressed psychic materials brought on by the two shocks she suffered in losing first her lover, second her father – a coupling that is also a textbook instantiation of the play's uncanny psychoanalytic acumen. And like virtually everything in this play, her madness is a manifestation of mourning – and an aestheticizing of it:

> Thought and affliction, passion, hell itself
> She turns to favour and to prettiness. (4.5.188–89)

This is Laertes's comment on Ophelia's allegory of the herbs and flowers, a carefully designed miniature of the play's larger motifs: rosemary for remembrance, pansies for thoughts, fennel for flattery, columbines for sexual betrayal,[142] and rue for sorrow (4.5.175–84). For herself there is a homely daisy, and violets, the signifier of faithfulness, all withered at the death of Polonius – here a displacement for the changeable Hamlet.

This motif shares in the self-referential 'baroque' quality of the inset play that Benjamin alludes to in his observation, quoted above, that 'The Renaissance explores the universe; [but] the baroque explores libraries.'[143] While some might see this meta-aesthetic device as more properly a symbol than an allegory, inasmuch as it seems to embody the entire play, it should also be clear that the 'embodiment' is multiple and shifting, never achieving the kind of classical focus that the German Romantics saw as the crucial quality of its idea of a symbol. The device instead is a linked series of allegorical 'substitutions' which aestheticize elements of the play without unifying them.

This allegorical bouquet is thus the aestheticizing instrument of the kind of poetic sea-change Ariel will sing about in his famous

---

[142] According to G. R. Hibbard (ed.), *Hamlet* by William Shakespeare (Oxford University Press, 1987), 307–8, nn.181–5.

[143] Benjamin, *Origin*, 140.

song of *The Tempest* ('Full fathom five thy father lies'). The emotions represented by herbs or flowers summarize for us much about both Hamlet the character and *Hamlet* the play: the Prince's struggle to remember, the 'pale cast of thought' that sicklies o'er resolution, the flattery of the court, the betrayal of Gertrude. In turning these to favor and prettiness, Ophelia enacts the aesthetic ritual of transformation that is at the heart of so much of Shakespeare's 'fourth-act pathos' in the Jacobean tragedies (if I may revert to traditional genre classification for the moment) and the late romances. Desdemona with her ballad of the maid of Barbary, Antony and Cleopatra hearing the flute-playing of Antony's retreating guiding spirit, Perdita's flowers in *The Winter's Tale*, the masque in *The Tempest* – all of these involve an element of self-conscious aesthetic practice and the use of words and images to embody feeling-tones in a patterned, 'framed' manner creative of a meta-aesthetic effect. All of them are also allegorical fragments in Benjamin's extended usage of the term. Madness, death, eros, and aesthetic signification itself all seem to be interrelated in these famous Shakespearean moments – as they will be in so much European art of the eras to come. And as Benjamin reminds us, the emptied world of the *Trauerspiel*, one productive of free-floating, protean objects which can come to stand for anything at all, is one of the richest aesthetic forms for this combination, as *Hamlet* shows us.

The rich description of Ophelia's ambiguous death by drowning – was it suicide or the negligence of her madness? – follows up and extends the mood of her allegory of the flowers. It portrays the outcome of an extended stay on the very boundary between two different elements, water and air – 'But long it could not be' (4.7.155). She is surrounded by more allegorical flora, this time again mingling death and the erotic:

> Of crow-flowers, nettles, daisies, and long purples,
> That liberal shepherds give a grosser name,
> But our cold maids do dead men's fingers call them.
>
> (4.7.140–42)

The allegories of the graveyard scene

But it is in the great graveyard scene – that piece of comic relief that adds new social and thematic dimensions to the play and serves to mark yet another stage of Hamlet's uncertain mental evolution, encompassing such contradictory qualities as his nearness to madness, his continuing ability to see through the surfaces of things to their hidden natures, his fascination with death – that the most iconic allegorical moment of the play takes place. Earlier I cited Margaret Ferguson's insight into the logic of 'materialization' of figures of speech that is a motif of Hamlet's own thought processes. At this point in the analysis, it should be clear that such a tendency is one of the play as a whole, and that it is a tendency toward visual allegories. We saw the method at work earlier when Hamlet no sooner discoursed on the table of memory than he turned to his material tables and physically wrote upon them. As a lead-in to the grave-yard scene, we should recall Hamlet's direful description of his state of mind after the revelations of *The Mousetrap*, 'When churchyards yawn, and hell itself breathes out / Contagion to this world' (3.2.378–79). At the graveyard we witness such a yawning grave, but instead of demons, we meet two clowns, figures of such harmony-in-discord, such ambiguous but potent significance, that they formed the models for Beckett's exist-ential clowns Estragon and Vladimir in *Waiting for Godot* 350 years later. The change of pace provided by these two deconstructive delvers is one of the great surprises – and great moments – of the play. They force us to re-think everything we have seen so far. Momentarily we leave behind our direct access to the deadly Machiavellian statecraft we have been immersed in and enter a plebeian world where death is commonplace, the world of politics a distant set of gossiped-about events, and social cor-ruption is manifested directly in the rottenness of corpses: 'I' faith, if a be not rotten before a die – as we have many pocky corses nowadays, that will scarce hold the laying in – a will last you some eight year or nine year: a tanner will last you nine year' (5.1.152–54). In the light of their carnivalesque vision, death is revealed to us as also a moment of a life which continues in the community as it is extinguished in the indi-vidual.[144] And the gallows-humor of the two clowns adds an element of the grotesque to the play's exploration of death and corruption and provides a point of view distanced from the political intrigue we have been immersed in – one that provides Hamlet with a context for coming to terms with death as a physical, corporeal reality shared by all men and women regardless of their social estate – an inevitable triumph of nature over history and society. The first part of the scene reaches its greatest intensity when the singing, intoxicated digger throws up a skull which Hamlet contemplates in a self-defining moment of *memento mori*. Unexpectedly, in a quintessentially Shakespearean moment, the skull

[144] See Michael D. Bristol, '"Funeral Bak'd Meats": Carnival and the Carnivalesque in *Hamlet*', in Wofford (ed.), *Hamlet*, 348–67.

achieves an identity – that of old King Hamlet's Fool, Yorick, whom
Prince Hamlet describes, like a figure of Melancholy studying the transi-
ence of Mirth, to Horatio:

a fellow of infinite jest, of most excellent fancy. He hath borne me on his back
a thousand times; and now, how abhorred my imagination is! My gorge rises at
it. Here hung those lips that I have kissed I know not how oft. Where be your
gibes now, your gambols, your songs, your flashes of merriment, that were wont
to set the table on a roar? Not one now to mock your own grinning? Quite chap-
fallen? (5.1.171–78)

The comic interlude, these lines announce, is over and is now
incorporated as merely a build-up to this epiphany. The skull is the
simplest, but also the most emotionally powerful of the play's allegorizing
objects. The moment must have been iconic in the original performances
as a visual invocation of a Stoic and medieval Christian practice of
meditating on death; it is even more iconic now, as providing the most
common of all of Hamlet's representations in the visual arts. Beyond this
identification of Hamlet with an ancient moment of wisdom, the skull
also signifies and focuses other motifs of the play – notably, rottenness,
death, and the extinguishing of mirth. These feelings and concepts seem
to be 'taken in' by Hamlet as he holds and studies the skull, in marked
contrast to the externalizing logic of his earlier reaction to the Ghost's
command. In a sense we can say he has finally found an object which
truly corresponds to his vision of the world, with which in some sense he
can identify. The universality of death which Hamlet begins to compre-
hend concretely will form the basis for his subsequent acceptance of the
Ghost's order, hereafter seen also as an acceptance of death.

The allegorical signet

When Hamlet narrates his adventures on the ship to England, another
signifying object proves to be a crucial part of the whole series of events
and substitutions:

> I had my father's signet in my purse,
> Which was the model of that Danish seal;
> Folded the writ up in the form of th'other,
> Subscribed it, gave't th'impression, placed it safely,
> The changeling never known. (5.2.50–54)

The word 'signet' derives from the French *signe* (sign) and forms in the
first instance one more link in the *Trauerspiel*-like chain of allegorical

fragments relating to externalization, writing, substitution, and deferral. But the signet is also an emblem of the royal power of Hamlet's father, and the fact that Hamlet is in possession of it (as we learn for the first time), is new and meaningful, paralleling Prince Hal's picking up his father's crown in the famous scene in *2 Henry IV.* In both cases, the Prince does not thereby become King – King Henry, we recall, was not really dead, and of course Claudius remains very much enthroned in Denmark. Rather, in each case the Prince begins to act like a King, to imagine being King. Hamlet conspicuously takes action against a sea of troubles for the first time in the play when he discovers the plot of death against him and opposes it. Again like Prince Hal, Hamlet acts the true Prince by counterfeiting, by forging new documents that defer his own death and that designate as his substitutes his old schoolmates Rosencrantz and Guildenstern – 'not shriving time allowed', as we saw earlier, an allusion which makes the two also substitutes for Claudius. But in an important sense, Hamlet here is impersonating not his father, but Claudius, and the instrument of his stratagem is not really the official Danish seal, but a substitute, albeit one that 'was the model of that Danish seal', his father's personal signet.

The signet is thus a very complex allegorical trope, with strong psychoanalytic resonances relating to sons, fathers, and empowerment. Lacan unaccountably neglected this particular object in his bravura reading of the play, instead seeing Ophelia, the Ghost, and Claudius's person as momentarily embodying at different points in the play the idealized Phallus, then seeing Hamlet's stabbing of Claudius near the end of the play as the moment when Hamlet finally addresses his real target, the Phallus that is at once Claudius and an idealized signifier.[145] But what of this emanation of his idealized father and taskmaster, the sign that holds the power of life and death, that allows Hamlet to be at once his father, his father's usurper, and himself as dutiful son? Without attempting to place this complex and contradictory sign precisely within Lacan's infernal machinery of terms, we can say that the signet is both paternal and kingly, an instrument of Hamlet's new level of activity in the world, and thus an emblem of a new-found agency and new sense of identity as a purposeful actor; that, like the crown passed from King to Prince at the moment of succession, it confers both identity with the father and the supplanting of the father. But it manages to do all this, as I mentioned, through feigning, through substituting, through role-playing. In a play with its much-quoted

[145] Lacan, 'Desire and the Interpretation of Desire in *Hamlet*', 50–51.

advice from foolish Polonius about being true to self, Hamlet here seems to affirm a very anti-essentialist idea of the self, a very performative one. But I will return to these issues in a separate section below.

The signet is thus a strategic relay point in the chain of deferrals and substitutions that have played through the text up to this point. At every previous moment when action is deferred – when Hamlet bandies with Polonius and the others, when he insults Ophelia, when he contrives a play as the way to settle his doubts, when he by-passes the praying Claudius, when he seeks to convert his mother to go against her new husband, when he kills Polonius, when he forges the orders of execution of Rosencrantz and Guildenstern, when he grapples with Laertes in Ophelia's grave – in all these instances, a logic of displacement – in many ways working at a formal, rather than an unconscious level – can be discerned. Hamlet's revenge-passions (and secret identifications) are clearly deflected from their true target Claudius and re-directed to some substitute for Claudius. This logic of displacement is itself a part of the aura of the royal signet Hamlet uses – he turns it in the first instance not directly against Claudius, but against two of his instruments. But then things change. For the first time in the play, he is also striking a blow against Claudius by thwarting his execution plans and then by escaping from the ship and contriving a way back to Denmark. In his forging of the letters in a 'fair' hand – the elegant style that made the forgery appear authentic – Hamlet also re-directs the art of writing from what it had been in the gesture of the writing tables (an externalization of memory) to become an instrument of political intrigue and of his own agency. In this play of absences and ghosts, this turning point is narrated rather than dramatized, but it marks a crucial change in Hamlet's conduct.

Although Hamlet's substitution of letters takes place before the graveyard scene, Shakespeare postponed the narration of it until after it had taken place, after Hamlet had courted 'madness' one last time in his 'tow'ring rage' against a Laertes who claimed to love his sister extravagantly and whom Hamlet clearly took as a rival for his dead beloved. His actions are puzzling, and they provoke the only sustained expression of regret that Hamlet makes throughout the entire play:

> But I am very sorry, good Horatio,
> That to Laertes I forgot myself;
> For by the image of my cause, I see
> The portraiture of his. I'll court his favours.
> But sure, the bravery of his grief did put me
> Into a tow'ring passion. (5.2.76–81)

But the leap into the grave with the provocative cry of 'This is I, / Hamlet the Dane' is itself a brief expressive allegory. Hamlet joins Laertes and Ophelia in the grave – they are all marked for death, one already dead, the other two exisiting in the boundaries between the 'prison' of Denmark and the realm of death, corruption, and uncontained hell-fire. This scene is properly positioned *before* Hamlet takes up the signet-seal because it shows us a Hamlet still subject to his passions, his interior self marked by open borders and hence to 'madness', and still involved in a logic of deferral. But it is capable of being retrospectively 'redeemed', seen to be compatible with the newly active, more focused Hamlet of the adventures of his aborted passage to England (which we only learn about after this scene) because Hamlet has now 'taken in' the reality of his own death, has asserted himself in his claim to be 'the Dane' as his father's successor and the enemy of his usurping uncle, and has become the restored lover of a young woman he had previously seemed to dismiss and denigrate. His actions in short, in this light, are not madness but noble anger, based on a renewed sense of his inherited place in the Symbolic Order of his society. Like so much in the play, this scene can be read in multiple ways.

Catastrophe and redemption

While *Hamlet* surpasses the limitations of the typical *Trauerspiel* in its dominating, complex hero, it follows the logic of the *Trauerspiel* in its conclusion. I have already quoted Benjamin's praise of the contingent, accidental quality of Hamlet's death as one quintessentially suited to the form's disenchanting view of the world. But he also calls attention to the prevalence of mass death at the end of these plays, 'the form of a communal fate, as if summoning all the participants before the highest court'.[146] With four bodies piled on the stage at the end (joining four off-stage), *Hamlet* certainly fits this aspect of Benjamin's chosen genre. And there is something in the attempt to assign guilt and innocence in these closing moments, too – Laertes's and Hamlet's mutual forgiveness, Laertes's and Horatio's condemnations of Claudius and commendations of Hamlet, with a discreet silence about the Queen – that is reminiscent of court proceedings in a mode quite foreign, as Benjamin underlines, to classical tragedy.

But it was also a characteristic of the radical allegorizing methodology of Benjamin's baroque *Trauerspiele*, we recall, that despite the preponderance

---

[146] Benjamin, *Origin*, 136.

of emptiness and melancholy in the representation of the world in nearly every detail, they were also susceptible – usually near their ending points – to a vertiginous allegorical reversal in which redemption is glimpsed amidst the gloom as a possibility, as an alternative mode of perception of the underlying nature of the world. Benjamin has described such a structure, as we have seen, as one borrowed from seventeenth-century religious emblems:

The bleak confusion of Golgotha, which can be recognized as the schema under-lying the allegorical figure in hundreds of the engravings and descriptions of the period, is not just a symbol of the desolation of human existence. In it transitoriness is not signified or allegorically represented, so much as, in its own significance, displayed as allegory. As the allegory of resurrection.[147]

As we also have seen previously, Susan Buck-Morss refers to this moment in Benjamin's allegorical interpretation as 'a dialectical move to a metalevel, at which the contradictory meanings of emblems themselves become an emblem, the sign of *their* opposite'.[148] Such a possibility swims into view within *Hamlet* when the Prince himself unexpectedly, for the first time, begins to speak of Providence. 'Why, even in that was heaven ordinant' (5.2.49), he tells Horatio in explaining the lucky coincidence of his having his father's seal – that complex symbol of coming of age and replacing the father – with him. And Providence becomes a central theme for Hamlet as he prepares for the fight against Laertes with the forebod-ing about his heart – a foreboding he puts aside with this reply:

Not a whit. We defy augury. There's a special providence in the fall of a sparrow. If it be now, 'tis not to come. If it be not to come, it will be now. If it be not now, yet it will come. The readiness is all. Since no man has aught of what he leaves, what is't to leave betimes? (5.2.157–61)

This is very likely the moment Benjamin had in mind when he praises Shakespeare for being able to strike 'Christian sparks from the baroque rigidity of the melancholic, un-stoic as it is un-Christian, pseudo-antique as it is pseudo-pietistic'.[149] In this moment Hamlet himself, we might say, becomes something of an allegorist in a redemptory mode, finding a means to read the play's externalized, *Trauerspiel*-like succession of contingencies and accidents as part of a hidden divine drama – and inviting us to do the same. And yet at the end of the play, Horatio avoids these terms and speaks instead of bloody contingencies, in the same

---

[147] *Ibid.*, 232.   [148] Buck-Morss, *The Dialectics of Seeing*, 173.
[149] Benjamin, *Origin*, 157–58.

mode Benjamin himself evinced in defending Shakespeare's treatment of Hamlet's death as something accidental and contingent. If Hamlet offers us, near the end, as a means of reconciling himself to the unknown, a theory of divine Providence (that, as we will see below, can also be read as an affirmation of a kind of free-flowing subjectivity), Horatio remains outside of Paradise, still in an unweeded garden, as he speaks:

> Of carnal, bloody, and unnatural acts,
> Of accidental judgments, casual slaughters,
> Of deaths put on by cunning and forced cause;
> And, in this upshot, purposes mistook
> Fall'n on th'inventors' heads. (5.2.325–29)

The play thus presents us with these two alternative interpretive frames. Hamlet dies, as Benjamin notes, contingently – 'as the fateful stage-properties gather around him, as around their lord and master'.[150] He is referring to those images of poisoned honor, sexuality, and statecraft – the poisoned sword and chalice, this last enhanced with a 'union' or pearl that, when Hamlet alludes to it in the act of pouring the poisoned wine down Claudius' throat, seems to symbolize both death and sex.[151] But he is also pictured by Horatio, after all this darkness, as a soul ascending to heaven with an angelic squadron leading him on. In short, in the event-packed concluding moments of *Hamlet*, there is a careful balance between a motif of continuing emptiness and another, contradictory one of redemption and even triumph, an establishment if not of ideal justice, than at least of an exemplary self-sacrifice that gives the lie to the play's darkest intimations about human nature through the counter-example of Hamlet's life and death.

This balance is maintained in the play's concluding words, given to the ambiguous Fortinbras, the 'delicate and tender prince, / ... with divine ambition puffed' (4.4.9.38–9.39),[152] who speaks Hamlet's second and final epitaph:

> Bear Hamlet like a soldier to the stage,
> For he was likely, had he been put on,
> To have proved most royally; and, for his passage,
> The soldiers' music and the rites of war
> Speak loudly for him.
> Take up the body. Such a sight as this
> Becomes the field, but here shows much amiss. (5.2.340–46)

---

[150] *Ibid.*, 137.

[151] 'Is thy union here? / Follow my mother' (5.2.279–80), Hamlet tells Claudius.

[152] These phrases about Fortinbras are exclusively in the second quarto.

Jan Kott, in his milestone reading of *Hamlet* as fulfilling a
Shakespearean – and *Trauerspiel*-like – pattern of 'the Grand Mechanism',
of one iron age succeeded by another, interpreted Fortinbras as a young
tyrant-to-be who inaugurates a new cycle of empty history,[153] and
numerous productions of the play in recent decades have followed suit,
portraying Fortinbras's return as that of an invading army taking power.
Although this conception is close to the spirit of Benjamin's *Trauerspiel*
at one level, it misses something important at another. Of all the
Machiavellian intriguers of the play, Fortinbras is the only one Hamlet
admired at all, and his endorsement of his candidacy for the throne of
Denmark just before his death re-inforces his admiration with emphasis.
To be sure, the world of *Hamlet* remains dark at the end the play, as empty
of essential meaning at the end as it was at the beginning, and Fortinbras
is at best only a well-meaning but very worldly politician, a player in the
Machiavellian games of statecraft who sends thousands to their deaths
over an eggshell. He is no Hamlet senior, no epic, idealized ruler of a
kingdom of immanent meaning – but neither is he Claudius, the hidden
serpent, murderer, adulterer, and usurper. He is, as I said above, simply
the best the fallen world has to offer, and Hamlet's endorsement of him
shows him as politically active, a participant in the Machiavellian arts of
political-natural history till the end – in short, someone now thinking
like a King even though he has come to understand the emptiness of such
thinking.

What Kott's eye-opening reading of the end of the play misses is, of
course, the glimpse of redemption, the fleeting moment of reversal when
the series of deferrals, of bloody accidents and contingencies, come briefly
into focus as the façade of some providence, of some moment when the
fallen world is also an emblem of its own possible redemption. Hamlet
never succeeded in setting a time out of joint aright. But he did finally face
up to the imperious demands of his Ghost-father, allowing the perturbed
spirit to rest and freeing the throne of Denmark of a usurper – at the cost
of undertaking his own journey into the unknown country – and taking
five more-or-less innocent by-standers with him as well. The last moments
of the play leave us with images both of a Hamlet open to the forces of
hell and damnation and a picture of him with angels bearing him to his
final rest.

And then this depressed and dilatory revenge-hero is proclaimed 'most
likely, had he been put on, / To have proved most royally'. Contrary

---

[153] Kott, *Shakespeare Our Contemporary*, 51–65.

to a great number of critics, I do not think this is to be taken as irony; it is rather part of the process of rapid, even say hasty, apotheosis and ennoblement in which Hamlet is inscribed at the play's closing moments, to balance the diabolic associations of Hamlet's words after seeing Claudius at prayer. It is not irony, but doubleness. The dark world continues, but we have all also experienced the fervent wish that it might be otherwise, that the immanent world might somehow be restored. In Hamlet's fierce depression, there burnt the desire for such a transformation, and we have been given his vision, his desire – which is ultimately, of course, all art can ever give us. In Benjamin's own words, the *Trauerspiel*'s allegories 'fill out and deny the void in which they are represented'[154] – proclaiming themselves to be – to gloss what Benjamin implies but leaves unsaid here – that remarkable thing, an aesthetic and utopian object. Such an impossible combination of contrary perceptions is what we are left with at the end of this perfect *Trauerspiel*, which, as Benjamin also says, at once completes and abolishes the form. 'A major work', Benjamin writes, 'will either establish the genre or abolish it; and the perfect work will do both.'[155] He seems to have, precisely, *Hamlet* in mind. While much of the play is firmly rooted in Kyd's and Marlowe's theatrical practice and while it clearly forms part of the developing genre that Benjamin calls baroque *Trauerspiel*, the play is finally *sui generis*. Nothing before or after it compares to it, even among the works of Shakespeare himself.

POST-SCRIPT: *HAMLET*, SUBJECTIVITY, AND AESTHETICS

The Benjaminesque approach to *Hamlet* I have elaborated seems to give us an instance of that proverbial paradox, a *Hamlet* without the Prince of Denmark. But this initial impression is deceptive, and in fact I believe Benjamin's insights into the allegorical form of the *Trauerspiel* and of *Hamlet* specifically also have applications to the problem of Hamlet as a character, or to put it differently, to the construction of Hamlet as a simulacrum of a new form of subjectivity in the early modern. Hamlet's subjectivity shares the structure of Benjamin's allegorical form: both are based on deferment and resist organic unity. Instead of what the Scottish Enlightenment essayist William Richardson thought he had discovered in the character Hamlet – a 'ruling principle'[156] – there is a set of behaviors

---

[154] Benjamin, *Origin*, 232–33. [155] *Ibid.*, 44.
[156] William Richardson, 'On the Character of Hamlet' (1774), in Brian Vickers (ed.), *Shakespeare, the Critical Heritage: 1774–1801*, Vol. VI (London: Routledge, 1981), 121–24.

that cannot be integrated. This is not quite the same thing as saying, as
did both Francis Barker and Terry Eagleton in the 1980s, that at the heart
of Hamlet is precisely 'nothing'.[157] Of course there is *something* (or the
aesthetic semblance of something), but the something is mobile, unfixed,
like the play of objects in the text. I discussed these dynamics of subjectivity in a previous book in terms of the interplay of Machiavellian and
Montaignean discourses.[158] In the different context supplied here, I want
briefly to recapitulate and ramify that analysis in more Benjaminesque
terms, as the outcome of *Hamlet*'s situation in the emptied world of early
modernity.

The emptied world and alienated subject

Benjamin, as we have seen, views *Hamlet* as a perfect example of the
Trauerspiel, one which simultaneously fulfills and undoes its genre. Most
obviously, unlike any of the German baroque plays which Benjamin
discusses, *Hamlet* is constructed around its central character, and his
melancholic vision permeates the play as a whole rather than being
confined within his subjectivity. This dominance of a central character
makes *Hamlet* in this way more like the Attic tragedies than the German
Trauerspiele, which tended to have multiple central characters rather than
one focusing figure. The object-dominated, otherwise empty aesthetic
space of the play is also the space of Hamlet's own subjectivity. In that
sense it is like the German expressionist dramas which Benjamin saw as
the modern descendants of the *Trauerspiele.* To put it another way, the
same emptying of the world that lets objects serve as signifiers decen-
ters Hamlet's subjectivity by alienating him from the world, allowing
the free play of his melancholic subjectivity within that fallen world. As
we have seen, the death of Hamlet's father is a shock which causes the
young Prince to lose his previous worldview of epic, immanent meaning,
to create an idealized past associated with and represented by his dead
father, and to plunge him into a meaninglessness which Shakespeare, here
and elsewhere in his works, sees as akin to, or a form of, madness.[159]

---

[157] Francis Barker, *The Tremulous Private Body: Essays in Subjection* (London: Methuen, 1984), 36–37
and Terry Eagleton, *William Shakespeare* (Oxford: Blackwell, 1986), 72. See Grady, *Shakespeare,
Machiavelli, and Montaigne,* 252–65 for an earlier critique of Barker and Eagleton on these
issues.
[158] Grady, *Shakespeare, Machiavelli, and Montaigne,* 243–65.
[159] Besides *Hamlet,* madness as the name for the mental state resulting from a loss of worldview and
identity can be seen in *King Lear* and *Timon of Athens,* as well as being a subtext in *The Comedy
of Errors. Othello* and *Macbeth* are border-line examples as well. See Wyndham Lewis, *The Lion*

In the terms of our own day, it is a form of 'disinterpellation'. Louis Althusser famously (and problematically) links Lacanian psychology and a Marxist theory of ideology in his idea that we form our identities in ideology through what he called 'interpellation' or 'hailing'. The term sardonically refers to a police hailing of an individual who takes on or internalizes the identity provided by an accusation of wrong-doing, the idea being that all of us form our concept of self within the prevailing conceptual framework of dominant ideologies.[160] What is less than clear in Althusser, however, is how we ever escape them. Shakespeare, as I have argued in a previous book, seemed to have a version of the idea of interpellation in the instance of young Prince Hal. The Prince at the end of *2 Henry IV* finally takes on the ideological role of King which he is in flight from throughout Part 1 and most of Part 2.[161] Shakespeare surpasses Althusser, however, in that he presents some of the complexities of identity-formation which the French theorist never addresses, by emphasizing Hal's resistance to interpellation and his ability to undertake a number of histrionic roles which defer the moment of dynastic destiny.

Hamlet's resistance to unified subjectivity

In the last part of *Richard II*, as in *Hamlet*, the focus is on this resistance. Richard becomes disinterpellated when he loses his title and his power and embraces what he calls in his jail-cell 'nothing' – the status of having no fixed identity, the state of open-ended subjectivity and theatricality.[162] The same process is on display in the case of Rosalind in *As You Like It* and to some extent in the other comic cross-dressing heroines of *The Merchant of Venice* and *Twelfth Night* – as well as in the misidentified twins in *The Comedy of Errors* and *Twelfth Night*. And we see darker versions of the same process in the abused Othello and in *King Lear's* Edgar.

Hamlet, however, is the play in which disinterpellation leading to unfixed subjectivity is most central to the entire drama. That Hamlet's

---

and the Fox: The Role of the Hero in the Plays of Shakespeare (London: G. Richards, 1927), 248–51, for a pioneering statement of the link in Shakespeare between madness and meaninglessness or nihilism.

[160] Louis Althusser, 'Ideology and Ideological State Apparatuses: Notes towards an Investigation', in Louis Althusser, *Lenin and Philosophy and Other Essays*, trans. Ben Brewster (New York: Monthly Review Press, 1971), 127–86.

[161] Grady, *Shakespeare, Machiavelli, and Montaigne*, 180–204.

[162] William Shakespeare, *Richard II, The Norton Shakespeare*, ed. Greenblatt *et al.*, 5.5.31–41. I discuss this motif in Grady, *Shakespeare, Machiavelli, and Montaigne*, 106–8.

melancholy has led to a loss of a previous self and an entrance onto
uncharted waters is one of Ophelia's most perceptive observations:

> O what a noble mind is here o'erthrown!
> The courtier's, soldier's, scholar's eye, tongue, sword,
> Th'expectancy and rose of the fair state,
> The glass of fashion and the mould of form,
> Th'observed of all observers, quite, quite down! (3.1.149–53)

Hamlet himself confirms the diagnosis in his first conversations with
Rosencrantz and Guildenstern (2.2.219–362), and he embarks on a search
to understand his own inner life, the play of his own subjectivity, in the
series of remarkable soliloquies that are one of the glories of the play.
From the time of his first interaction with Ophelia after seeing the Ghost
and taking on his ambiguous 'antic disposition', he is continually trying
and failing to find his 'self' in his own actions – and lack of action:

> Am I a coward?
> Who calls me villain, breaks my pate across,
> Plucks off my beard and blows it in my face,
> Tweaks me by th' nose, gives me the lie i' th' throat
> As deep as to the lungs? Who does me this?
> Ha? 'Swounds, I should take it; for it cannot be
> But I am pigeon-livered and lack gall
> To make oppression bitter, or ere this
> I should 'a' fatted all the region kites
> With this slave's offal. Bloody, bawdy villain!
> Remorseless, treacherous, lecherous, kindless villain!
> O, vengeance! –
> Why, what an ass am I? Ay, sure, this is most brave,
> That I, the son of the dear murderèd,
> Prompted to my revenge by heaven and hell,
> Must, like a whore, unpack my heart with words,
> And fall a-cursing, like a very drab,
> A scullion! (2.2.548–65)

Hamlet's remarkable response to these self-accusations, as we have
seen, is a dramatically singular one. Having berated himself for bandying
with words instead of deeds, he embraces words more closely in becoming a dramatist – to put on a play to catch the conscience of the King. In
embracing theatricality, Hamlet affirms rather than ends his role-playing,
his protean self, and tries on one more new identity. In the lead-up to
the performance he is, as Ophelia notes with continued perspicacity, as
good as a chorus. We watch him proceed to undertake additional roles

in what follows – a confessor to his wayward mother; a witty coiner of grotesqueries and a humanist philosopher of death in the graveyard; an impassioned lover and mourner of Ophelia; a diplomatic secretary, for-ger, and intriguer; a swordsman and courtier. Like the play's fragmented allegories, Hamlet himself is continually filling up the empty theatrical space with his many roles, none of which can be said to embody that goal of Polonius's pseudo-wisdom, a true self. Rather, we have to say, Hamlet's decentered self is radically unfixed, existing only within the process of deferred identification that is his condition throughout the play.

The character Hamlet seems at the end, as we have seen, to take comfort in a concept of Providence that appears like a surprising and bright lantern in the darkness that fills up the rest of the play. It is, Benjamin would have argued, an opening into the final allegorical reversal inherent in the aesthetics of the *Trauerspiel*, the moment when dark events are seen to embody concealed utopian possibilities. Providence is the name Hamlet gives to the play of accidents, disasters, purposes mistook, and violence that makes up the play's narrative structure of deferral. In the end, the purpose proposed to him by the questionable Ghost has indeed been accomplished, and the throne of Denmark is purged of its usurper – through a series of apparent accidents and spontaneous reactions to them. Hamlet's brief references to Providence constitute the play's only opening to a way out of the empty world and the empty theatricalizing with which Hamlet has filled it, a glimpse of an otherwise completely hidden God. Rather than replacing the vision of emptiness, however, it merely co-exists with it in the play's complex ending, as we have seen.

But another way to interpret Hamlet's desperate embrace of the idea of Providence is seeing it as another allegory – one that signifies the free-flow of subjectivity, the endless chain of deferrals, which has shaped the play's aesthetic form. Rather than achieving a final, definitive identity, Hamlet embraces his own unfixedness under the sign of Providence. The same form of 'nothing' in search of meaning that propelled Hamlet's erring quest and crooked pathways has also constituted the aesthetic object which we contemplate at the end.

Hamlet's *resistance to unity*

The character Hamlet, like the play itself, resists the act of totalization through which Romantic criticism, with its ideal of organic unity, would have contained it. Benjamin's alternative concept of unity, his non-totalizing concept of allegory, is a much better figure for encompassing the famous aesthetic and psychological difficulties of the play and the character.

Jean-Paul Sartre liked to say that we humans become essences rather than existences only at the moment of death, when all our deferrals are brought to a final close. But Hamlet's essence, even in death, remains ambiguous, unfocused. We cannot pluck out the heart of his mysteries any more than could Rosencrantz and Guildenstern. Horatio portrays him as a kind of saint of an iron-age world, and Fortinbras proclaims him a soldier and worthy would-be King. As witnesses of this play's fictions, we may doubt both of these claims: we have seen moments in Hamlet's last months that are neither saintly nor kingly.

This play, with a moment of disinterpellation at its beginning, the play-within-the-play at its dramatic and thematic center, and an uncompromising enigmaticalness at its end, embodies non-conceptual art and subjectivity rather than any definitive 'solution' to its mysteries. The rest, therefore, is silence – a silence that leaves the play's many enigmas, its revelation of an emptied world that just might harbor some unrealized potential for redemption, sounding for us.

CHAPTER 5

Beautiful Death in Romeo and Juliet

> All creation is really a re-creation of a once loved and once whole, but now lost and ruined object, a ruined internal world and self. It is when the world within us is destroyed, when it is dead and loveless, when our loved ones are in fragments, and we ourselves in helpless despair – it is then that we must re-create our life anew, reassemble the pieces, infuse life into dead fragments, re-create life.[1]
>
> Hanna Segal

If *Hamlet* is, as Walter Benjamin suggests, Shakespeare's consummate exploration of death, melancholy, and mourning in a world seen as having become valueless, *Romeo and Juliet* explores a different context for and a differently inflected idea of death: its connections with desire. *Romeo and Juliet* has commonalities with the form of the *Trauerspiel* above all in the central role that chance and contingency (Benjamin's 'fate') play in its denouement, but it does not display the melancholic vision of a completely empty world that dominates *Hamlet*. It is another Shakespearean *sui generis* play, one that sees in death different aesthetic possibilities from those of the *Trauerspiel* proper. The play sets up a dynamic dialectic between desire – which dominates its largely comedic first half – and death – which dominates the second. But if the second half seems something of a *Trauerspiel*, it is one with a good deal more positivity about desire than is typical of the genre as described by Benjamin, so that the play magnifies the utopian potentialities of *Trauerspiel* to a much higher degree than is typical of the form. Death in this play is cruel and destructive of eros, but it is also the 'mother of beauty' (in Wallace Stevens's apt phrasing) and the means of a healing of a social rift. As in *Hamlet*'s very end, mimetic death is enshrined in an idealizing language of mourning and loss in an intense aesthetic moment and is made aesthetically self-reflective through the golden statues of the two lovers which both families agree to construct – an

---

[1] Hanna Segal, 'A Psychoanalytic Approach to Aesthetics', in *The Work of Hanna Segal: A Kleinian Approach to Clinical Practice* (New York: Jason Aronson, 1981), 190.

artwork that is also a sign of the end of their feud. Death and desire in this play turn out to be in many ways opposites rather than, as so many critics have argued, the former being the true goal of the latter.

Death and desire have long been linked and in several different ways, not least because both of these *sine qua non*s of human existence have served as fundamental, trans-cultural themes of aesthetic works from the ancient world to the present. Both of them would seem to be limit cases for cultural materialist theories of anti-essentialism because it is impossible either to find or imagine any human culture in which they were not fundamental, essential givens of human existence.[2] At the same time, these biological essentials have always already been embedded in the myriad varieties of human cultures, imbricated within social power arrangements, understood and experienced in different ways as parts of the narratives of the culturally formed life-world. Within Western culture, both death and desire display varied histories, as the *Annales* School in particular has famously shown. Not surprisingly, Shakespeare presents both of these elemental themes in the myriad variety for which he is famous. Having given some attention to the link of eros to art and poetry in Chapter 2, I want to turn now to the connections of thanatos to art. If anything, the theme of death is even more pervasive in Shakespeare's oeuvre than that of desire, and it is impossible in this short space to treat the issue comprehensively.[3] After a few brief generalizations, then, I will turn to *Romeo and Juliet* as a crucial instance of Shakespeare's treatment of death and its links to the aesthetic and to desire; it is a work that in fact comes up in several general discussions of the connections of death and desire in Western culture, as we will see. And it is an early, but already consummate example of how mimetic death is used by Shakespeare to create and heighten meaning and beauty in works of art.

---

[2] See Hugh Grady, 'Tragedy and Materialist Thought', in Rebecca Bushnell (ed.), *A Companion to Tragedy* (Oxford: Blackwell, 2005), 128–44 for a fuller discussion of these limits.

[3] An early work by Theodore Spencer, *Death and Elizabethan Tragedy: A Study of Convention and Opinion in the Elizabethan Drama* (Cambridge, Mass.: Harvard University Press, 1936), attempts to survey attitudes toward death in the English drama between 1588 and 1620, with Shakespeare a prominent example. Spencer argues that the period was characterized by a clash between Christian, medieval views of death centered on the afterlife and Renaissance revivals of classical attitudes towards death as primarily the end of a meaningful life. He argues that both views seem to co-exist, their contradictions more apparent in hindsight than in their own day. In addition, he thinks that Shakespeare is not the best example of the age's attitudes because his talent for characterization made death less impactful than in other dramatists' work. The book seems dated by its rigidly Buckhardtian binary opposition between 'medieval' and 'modern', by its method of gathering and organizing materials through the technology of the index card, and by its avoiding the complicated cases.

SHAKESPEARE'S SECULAR DEATHS AND THE AESTHETIC

While *Hamlet* presents us with an ambiguous, Catholic afterlife, its focus was squarely on this side of paradise, a world profoundly out of joint. Elsewhere in the histories and tragedies, death is almost never presented solely in the religious context which the culture of Shakespeare's age normally supplied for it. Instead, classical-pagan or romantic contemporary beliefs and values surround it. Heroic suicide, as Othello and Romeo and Juliet (in their actions) and Horatio (in his speech) show us, is hardly confined to the Roman plays.[4] In short, death in Shakespeare's plays is primarily secular. It is in fact transformed by the artwork in which it was represented into an aesthetic rather than a religious experience. The mimetic deaths of central characters with whose fate we are emotionally involved create a mourning-effect projected onto all that we have associated with the lost characters, bathing them in a light of beauty, imbuing them with lost significance. Their deaths resonate with us in our world, rather than in their supposed fates in an afterlife. And this imagined mourning is a powerful resource of aesthetic production. In short, Shakespeare's treatment of death throughout his works – and nowhere more outstandingly than in *Romeo and Juliet* – is part of the secularizing, modernizing dynamics characteristic of his great plays and productive of a prescient Shakespearean version of the aesthetic.

More than three centuries after Shakespeare, another poet expressed a similar idea of the relation between death and art in memorable terms. 'Death is the mother of beauty', wrote Wallace Stevens in his celebrated lyric 'Sunday Morning', and his claim has resonated with subsequent readers. But the relation of death to beauty – or to art or the aesthetic, as I will inflect Stevens's phrase in what follows – is hardly a simple one. That death, along with sexual love, is one of art's most repeated themes is a commonplace whose significance is elusive. 'Death … is the other of everything known; it threatens the meaning of discourses. Death is hence irreducibly heterogeneous to homologies; it is not assimilable', writes Denis Hollier,[5] expressing what is a great deal of the problem with writing about death – it is overwhelming, final, terrifying, comforting,

---

[4] For a contrary view, see Spencer, *Death and Elizabethan Tragedy*, 173–79. Spencer sees the plays' treatment of suicide as falling into two categories: those with Roman settings, which approve of suicide, and those with Christian settings, which disapprove of it. The latter would necessarily include *Romeo and Juliet, Hamlet,* and *Othello* – 'Christian' plays which have characters with 'Roman' attitudes toward suicide, as I see it.

[5] Denis Hollier, *Against Architecture: The Writings of Georges Bataille,* trans. Betsy Wing (Cambridge, Mass.: MIT Press, 1989), 36; quoted in Jonathan Dollimore, *Death, Desire and Loss in Western Culture* (New York: Routledge, 1998), 339 n.3.

and ultimately incomprehensible. And yet art, like its cousin religion, has been fascinated with the theme of death in every era recorded, and Shakespeare's work represents an impressive *summa* of treatments of the theme.

As I argued briefly in the Introduction, if we can speak of a 'content' of the aesthetic, it would have to involve those two basic and biological human data, thanatos and eros, our mortality and our eroticism,[6] for art invokes each in myriad ways that defy simple generalization. Stevens's insight draws on the millennia-old *carpe diem* tradition, in which the inevitability of death creates a kind of categorical imperative for sexual pleasure. Stevens enlarges this tradition by in turn linking the erotic to the aesthetic:

> Death is the mother of beauty; hence from her,
> Alone, shall come fulfillment to our dreams
> And our desires. Although she strews the leaves
> Of sure obliteration on our paths,
> The path sick sorrow took, the many paths
> Where triumph rang its brassy phrase, or love
> Whispered a little out of tenderness,
> She makes the willow shiver in the sun
> For maidens who were wont to sit and gaze
> Upon the grass, relinquished to their feet.
> She causes boys to pile new plums and pears
> On disregarded plate. The maidens taste
> And stray impassioned in the littering leaves.[7]

This leads to the next stanza's question: 'Is there no change of death in paradise?' If beauty emerges only under the pressure of humanity's universal death sentence, how can beauty be possible in the absence of death? A series of rhetorical questions suggests the impossibility of this, and so the haunting phrase is repeated:

---

[6] As discussed in the Introduction, Georges Bataille would add a third biological fundamental, excrement, which manifests itself aesthetically in satire. Bataille argues that death, sex, and excrement are disclosures of human links to the material and tend to be excluded from 'civilized' human self-understanding but return in hidden form in works of art. See Georges Bataille, *Erotism: Death and Sensuality*, trans. Mary Dalwood (San Francisco, Calif.: City Light Books, 1957). The larger theoretical context for these ideas is Georges Bataille, *The Accursed Share*, trans. Robert Hurley, 3 vols. (New York: Zone Books, 1991, 1993). I concentrate on love and death here as most prominent in Shakespeare and especially in *Romeo and Juliet*.

[7] Wallace Stevens, 'Sunday Morning', in Richard Ellman and Robert O'Clair (eds.), *Modern Poems: A Norton Introduction*, 2nd edn. (New York: Norton: 1989), 150–53; verse v: ll.3–13). Subsequent quotations from the poem are from this edition and are referenced through stanza and line numbers.

> Death is the mother of beauty, mystical,
> Within whose burning bosom we devise
> Our earthly mothers waiting, sleeplessly. (VI: 13–15).

This is obscure, but suggests that the mysticalness of religion is aesthetic – 'we devise' – but the aesthetic is 'natural' (i.e., not divine), originating in a human creativity born in a desperate dance in defiance of death's universality.

THE PSYCHOANALYSIS OF DEATH

Psychoanalysis has long linked death and the aesthetic, with Freud famously arguing in his 'Three Caskets' essay that the wish for death empowers the folk tales which in turn underlie Shakespeare's *The Merchant of Venice* and *King Lear*.[8] Other theorists have connected the aesthetic more specifically to the act of mourning. For example, Jacques Lacan, in his essay on *Hamlet* mentioned in the previous chapter, links mourning not only to Oedipal desire, but to the structure of the play *Hamlet* itself. And if we turn to Kleinian psychoanalyst Hanna Segal's essay 'A Psychoanalytic Approach to Aesthetics', we find a similar argument about the need for a period of mourning after early childhood experiences, an act of mourning connected not just to *Hamlet* but to artistic creativity more generally.[9] The terminology shifts to the registers of Melanie Klein's object relations theory, and Segal's account is less firmly rooted in the Oedipal drama *per se* than Lacan's. Segal emphasizes a stage in infant development Klein called 'the depressive condition', reached when the child ceases to experience her mother, father, and others as 'part objects' and begins to see them as 'real persons'.[10] But the outcome is similar to the one Lacan described. In the new, holistic dynamics of this phase, the infant's aggressive impulses continually destroy in fantasy the loved object, resulting in feelings of loss and a desire for restoration and re-creation.[11] This is the situation, according to Segal, out of which the aesthetic impulse arises, from a need for the artist to create 'a world of his own'.[12]

Marcel Proust is Segal's prototype of the artist here. She is struck particularly by a remark of one of Proust's characters, the painter Elstir, who says: 'It is only by renouncing that one can re-create what one loves'. Segal takes this idea as her leitmotiv and concludes, in words

[8] Sigmund Freud, 'The Theme of the Three Caskets' (1913); reprinted in Dan Latimer (ed.), *Contemporary Critical Theory* (San Diego, Calif.: Harcourt, 1989), 489–99.
[9] Segal , 'A Psychoanalytic Approach to Aesthetics', 185–206.   [10] *Ibid.*, 186–87.   [11] *Ibid.*, 187.
[12] *Ibid.*, 187–88.

I used as the epigraph to this chapter, that all artistic creation 'is really a re-creation of a once loved and once whole, but now lost and ruined object, a ruined internal world and self'.[13] With her emphasis on the fragmentation of the world in the act of mourning , she seems to echo crucial elements of Benjamin on the *Trauerspiel* – or to put it differently, reveals a psychoanalytical dimension within Benjamin.[14] But in this psychoanalytic reading, allegory would come into existence at a developmental stage in individual history rather than in socio-philosophical history, as both Benjamin and Adorno emphasize. Nevertheless Benjamin's vision of the fragmented allegory as a form expressive of an empty world has clear affinities with Segal's account of the origins of the artistic impulse.

Many psychoanalytic theorists, and not just Segal, posit the aesthetic as a breach in a narrow rationality and an embodiment of the drives of desire, often a desire for death. This includes Julia Kristeva, whose well-known comments on *Romeo and Juliet* in this connection I will discuss below.[15] However, all the Shakespearean texts considered up to this point – *A Midsummer Night's Dream*, *Timon of Athens*, and *Hamlet* – could also be taken as examples of these psychoanalytic processes and be seen as further evidence that aesthetic form creates a separation from the world of the Law in an artwork in which the Law is partially suspended by eros and thanatos.

The great weakness of the psychoanalytic theories, however, is their difficulty in accounting for historical difference in some of the categories they employ, like subjectivity and transgression – and even changing reactions to death itself. But supplemented with diachronic methodologies, they are valuable analytic tools. Aesthetic theory has need of psychoanalysis in many ways, not least of all the various observations on mourning and the aesthetic of Segal, Kristeva, and Jacques Lacan (whose analysis of *Hamlet* I discussed briefly in Chapter 4).[16] Indeed, in this context *Hamlet* particularly seems to represent not only the results of mourning and aesthetic creativity, but the very process itself. Hamlet is an artist seeking the restoration of a great loss, finding his moment of greatest satisfaction

---

[13] *Ibid.*, 190.
[14] For an informative discussion of Benjamin's familiarity with and critiques of both Freud and Jung, see Sarah Ley Roff, 'Benjamin and Psychoanalysis', in David S. Ferris (ed.), *The Cambridge Companion to Walter Benjamin* (Cambridge University Press, 2004), 115–33.
[15] Julia Kristeva, *Revolution in Poetic Language*, in Toril Moi (ed.), *The Kristeva Reader* (New York: Columbia University Press, 1986), 120. The Kleinian tradition has been worked into Julia Kristeva's linguistic–psychoanalytic analysis of the dynamics of literary creation, in a rich synthesis with Lacan as well as several others, and with a distinct emphasis on the death-wish.
[16] Jacques Lacan, 'Desire and the Interpretation of Desire in *Hamlet*', *Yale French Studies*, 5556 (1977), 24–52.

not in the final and non-restorative killing of his uncle/himself, but in the re-staging of the moment of loss in the play-within-the-play and in a logically endless series of deferments of the fulfilling of his desire, deferments which reach their terminus only through contingency and chance.

THE HISTORY OF DEATH

These psychoanalytic insights into the relation of death, mourning, and a posited death-wish within art find some support in the well-known work by *Annales* School historian Philippe Ariès, who in two different books attempted to periodize attitudes toward death in the Western world.[17] According to Ariès, the High Middle Age was an era of the co-existence of life and death, as churchyard and cemetery burials within cities replaced the classical practice of burial outside of city walls. Death was, as Ariès puts it, 'tamed' in this era, robbed of many of its terrors. It was an era when death was defined, under the influence of Christian theology, as a ritualized passage to an afterlife, typically involving deathbed prayers and sacraments in the presence of family and friends. These deathbed practices, in fact, survived until the end of the nineteenth century, but other attitudes toward death slowly evolved over this period, as the earlier medieval view of death as a common fate uniting the community gave way, after the twelfth century, to new views which emphasized the separate fates of individuals at the end of life. The eleventh and twelfth centuries put more emphasis on the Last Judgment and the definition of the particular judgment; there was a new interest in macabre themes in art and physical decomposition, a return of funeral inscriptions and a certain personalization of tombs.[18]

In this context (see chapter 4, n. 137), *Hamlet*'s anachronistic emphasis on the fate of the soul at the moment of death can be seen as an attempt to re-create a pre-Reformation set of cultural assumptions about death for 'atmospheric' purposes. But a more characteristically early modern set of attitudes toward death, if Ariès is correct, can be found in the earlier play *Romeo and Juliet*. For one of the novelties of artworks from the fifteenth through the seventeenth centuries, Ariès argues, is that within a larger set of continuities with the late medieval, a new trend becomes marked, especially in the baroque era, when death becomes eroticized. One sees it

---

[17] Philippe Ariès, *Western Attitudes Toward Death: From the Middle Ages to the Present,* trans. Patricia M. Ranum (Baltimore, Md.: Johns Hopkins University Press, 1974; and *The Hour of Our Death,* trans. Helen Weaver (New York: Knopf, 1981).

[18] Ariès, *Western Attitudes Toward Death,* 28–29.

in visual arts and in literature – and Ariès alludes briefly to Shakespeare's
Romeo and Juliet in this connection, seeing its graveyard scene as an
example of the practices of a later baroque theater.[19] He describes the
linkage of death and desire in terms borrowed from Georges Bataille's
Erotism:

Like the sexual act, death was henceforth increasingly thought of as a
transgression which tears man from his daily life, from rational society, from
his monotonous work, in order to make him undergo a paroxysm, plunging
him into an irrational, violent and beautiful world. Like the sexual act death
for the Marquis de Sade is a break, a rupture. This idea of rupture is something
completely new.[20]

The baroque fascination with death as a metaphor for sexual ecstasy
was, Ariès argues, largely unconscious in origin, related (as the allusion
to de Sade in the above quote might suggest) to sadistic impulses
within eroticism.[21] Ariès sees in this development a response at the level
of something like a collective unconscious to an unfolding dialectic of
enlightenment. Like Horkheimer and Adorno before him, but displaying
perhaps more of a residual faith than they in what he calls the 'progress'
of humanity which necessitated this historical development,[22] he sees in
Sade's sexual practices an embodiment of and development from what
becomes the ruling mentality of Western modernity: a will to domination
and mastery of nature. However, as Ariès argues, this 'bulwark erected
against nature had two weak spots, love and death, through which a little
of the savage violence [of nature] always leaked. Human society took great
pains to reinforce these weak spots'.[23] Thus nature and society are separate
realms but, as he puts it, they are separate but with a certain symmetry –
custom and tradition had rhythms that are like the natural, particularly
the liturgical calendar with its panoply of holidays and carnivals (and of
course Shakespeare famously reproduces this 'symmetry', in his festive
comedies and tragedies – including *Romeo and Juliet*). But within the
overall symmetry, boundaries were still maintained, since holidays,
with their licensing of sex and violence, opened up the boundaries only
temporarily.[24]

The sixteenth- and seventeenth-century 'baroque' moment in the history of death came about when this symmetry broke down as part of
the processes of modernization. Under the pressure of Reformation and
Counter-Reformation, as Ariès puts it, the walls cracked, and a new

[19] *Ibid.*, 56–57.   [20] *Ibid.*, 57–58.   [21] Ariès, *The Hour of Our Death*, 370.   [22] *Ibid.*, 393.
[23] *Ibid.*   [24] *Ibid.*, 394.

association between love and death emerged: 'The order of reason, work, and discipline gave way before the assault of love and death, agony and orgasm, corruption and fertility' – first in the realm of imagination, then in the real.[25] That is, sexuality and death came to be seen more as irruptions of the natural into the human world, transcendent of human society, rather than immanent, cyclical patterns in both realms. For Ariès this is one of the cultural impulses underlying the new Western spirit of expansion and imperialistic domination. As Ariès sees it,

The savagery of nature invaded the city of man just as the latter was preparing to colonize nature by expanding the frontiers of technological advancement and rational organization. It is almost as if society, in its effort to conquer nature and the environment, abandoned the old defense system that had surrounded sex and death, and nature, which had apparently been conquered, surged back *inside* man, crept in through the abandoned fortification and made him savage again.[26]

The reference is primarily to the nineteenth century, but the diagnosis has clear application as well to the beginnings of colonialism in the early modern.

Within Shakespeare's *Romeo and Juliet* we will see something of this historical development enacted, as the play moves from a 'comic' opening which in many ways celebrates a civil society echoing the rhythms of the natural world, to a 'tragic' (or, as we will see, more properly *Trauerspiel*-like) second half in which both desire and death are forces which disrupt and challenge that order 'like the lightning which doth cease to be / Ere one can say it lightens' (2.1.161–62).[27]

As Jonathan Dollimore has noted, however, Ariès's intricate weaving of a number of different narrative strands – this one beginning in the early medieval, that one in the eleventh and twelfth centuries, this one ending with the late medieval, that one lasting up to the nineteenth-century – is often confusing and in particular short on analyses of what causes underlie the complexly intertwined changes.[28] In the case of Ariès's 'baroque' period in the Western narrative of death practices, we are dealing with a change within a set of continuities, connected to an all too briefly sketched notion of some kind of collective unconscious at work in the widespread linkages of sex and death in the era's art and literature.

[25] *Ibid.*, 395.   [26] *Ibid.*
[27] William Shakespeare, *Romeo and Juliet*, *The Norton Shakespeare*, ed. Stephen Greenblatt *et al.*: (New York: Norton, 1997). This and all subsequent citations of Shakespeare in this chapter are from this edition and will be given parenthetically in the text.
[28] Dollimore, *Death, Desire and Loss in Western Culture*, 63.

Ariès defines the baroque as the pre-eminent era when the desire–death connection (posited by an ancient tradition and articulated in new terms in the twentieth century by voices as diverse as Freud, Denis de Rougemont, and Julia Kristeva) finds its strongest expression – but he is largely silent on why this might be so beyond the briefly sketched ideas I summarized above.

All this should serve as a caution against too much reliance on Ariès's narrative in all its details – even though the insight that death, too, has its history, and that we can trace a set of large-scale changes in attitudes toward it and practices in regards to it, is seminal. Instead, I want to look at the evidence provided by one highly significant source, *Romeo and Juliet*. In the course of that investigation, I believe, we will discover that the treatment of death in this work owes as much to aesthetics as it does to cultural history *per se*. As elsewhere in Shakespeare, the death of characters in whom the audience has emotionally invested leads to a kind of mourning, a mourning that, as psychoanalytic theory suggests, creates an aura of beauty and immanent meaning surrounding that which is being mourned. In that way, mimetic death is a powerful tool of aesthetic creation.

LOVE-DEATH, OR *LIEBESTOD*

This is perhaps the point to say something about the concept of *Liebestod* (love-death), the ancient idea that death is in fact the true object of erotic desire – a theme hauntingly evoked in Wagner's *Tristan und Isolde* and in the medieval romances behind it – and one that has been connected to *Romeo and Juliet* several times.[29] Its best-known analyst is the French writer Denis de Rougemont,[30] but it is an idea that has found other

---

[29] See Denis de Rougemont, *Love in the Western World*, trans. Montgomery Belgion (Princeton University Press, 1983), 89–92; Julia Kristeva, *Tales of Love*, trans. Leon S. Roudiez (New York: Columbia University Press, 1987), 209–33; Ariès, *Western Attitudes Toward Death*, 56–57. De Rougemont's views on *Romeo and Juliet*, or the importance to it of the idea of *Liebestod* which he introduced, were discussed by Shakespeare critics well before the writings of the psychoanalytic critics I focus on here. For example, M. M. Mahood critiqued the idea that *Romeo and Juliet* is a good example of the theme in her *Shakespeare's Wordplay* (London: Methuen, 1957), 56–65, while Roy W. Battenhouse, *Shakespearean Tragedy: Its Art and Its Christian Premises* (Bloomington, Ind.: Indiana University Press, 1969), 108–10, invoked de Rougemont's description of *Liebestod* to buttress his argument that the play exposes and implicitly criticizes the two lovers as erotic idolaters.

[30] See de Rougemont, *Love in the Western World*. De Rougemont attempted a radical critique of the Western tradition of love that began with the medieval Troubadours, entered into early Renaissance Italy, and found its classic expression in Petrarch's sonnets to Laura. This tradition, as de Rougemont saw it, replicated in a secular sphere the twelfth-century Cathars' heretical error of identifying materiality with evil, valuing in desire not its completion but rather a state of continual unrest, of desire as longing. The result was that secular love was given a religious

twentieth-century proponents in Freud, Kristeva, and, at least in part, Jonathan Dollimore, who discusses all three of these earlier theorists. Dollimore traces a long (but not unanimous) tradition, beginning in ancient Greek lyric poetry, continuing in Roman literature (from where it migrated to Augustine and other Church fathers), and into much of the medieval and early modern periods. It extends in the twentieth century to Freud and beyond. There has thus been a continual 2,500-year tradition that has understood death to be the ultimate outcome of desire, in many ways its ultimate truth. To be sure Dollimore is highly skeptical of this long tradition linking death and sexuality; he notes how this linkage was put to the ideological work of promoting an acceptance of sexual acts leading to death in the AIDS epidemic within the gay community. But he does think, along with de Rougemont and Kristeva, that Shakespeare's *Romeo and Juliet* is part of the tradition linking desire and death.[31]

I think, on the contrary, that skepticism ought to be extended to this claim concerning *Romeo and Juliet* as well. Certainly Shakespeare is by no means a stranger to this tradition – Dollimore establishes this clearly.[32] Several of the sonnets and powerful passages in *Hamlet, Othello, Measure for Measure*, and elsewhere must surely be seen as eloquent moments of this tradition. However, contrary to Dollimore, de Rougemont, and Kristeva, I do not believe that *Romeo and Juliet* is among Shakespeare's works that participate in this tradition of seeing death as the secret content of desire, except at specific moments for local effects. Yes, the play is nothing but a powerful exploration of the human experiences of both desire and death in aesthetically charged language and dramatic structure. But, along with Shakespeare's later exploration of the same themes in *Antony and Cleopatra, Romeo and Juliet* celebrates and cherishes desire as an essential life-force, mourns its loss in premature death, and encloses both of its elemental themes in self-conscious aesthetic patternings that fashion a symbolic triumph of desire over death in an idealized aesthetic sphere. Thus, rather than a lamenting over death-in-desire, both of these plays create kinetic dialectics between death and desire, in which each of these human basics asserts its triumph and then its defeat in endless aesthetic oscillation. *Romeo and Juliet* thus represents the defeat of death by desire

---

importance – a burden it could not bear and which could never be satisfied except through death, and thus the theme of love-death, or *Liebestod*, became prominent in our literature and expresses a little understood secret about Western love: its ultimate aim is not fulfillment, but constant longing culminating in death. Modern beliefs about love, de Rougemont argued, stem from this tradition and condemn us to unhappiness.

[31] Dollimore, *Death, Desire and Loss in Western Culture*, 108–13.
[32] *Ibid.*, 102–16.

crystallized in art at the same time that it recognizes and mourns both the cruelty of chance and the inevitability of death. In this reading, desire is the very opposite of death, a life-force that is self-sustaining and indefinite, and death is a cruel accident visited on these lovers, not because of the essential nature of desire but instead from the contingencies of power and patriarchy. The death that is so prominent an atmospheric, poetic, and dramatic theme at the end of the play is the enemy of love – but the mother of beauty, as Stevens had it. The death of the lovers is a loss mourned jointly by both the feuding families and conducive to the healing of the breach between them. And it is a loss memorialized by the two families in artworks that crystallize the moment of shared loss, of goodness gone from the world. Finally, it is a loss which creates a kind of mourning within the audience, creative of a sense of beauty and longing.

ROMEO AND JULIET IN CRITICAL HISTORY

Romeo and Juliet has been a wildly popular play, but it has had a checkered *critical* history because it so resolutely resists many readers' preconceptions, not only about death and desire, but about Aristotelian tragedy. Neoclassical critics, as might be expected, found any number of 'faults' among what they saw as the play's many 'beauties'. For example, in 1710 an early commentator, Charles Gildon, although in generally positive remarks, faulted the play as 'far from Dramatic Perfection'.[33] As time went on, the play's 'tragic' downfall was often seen to have been brought about through accident rather than fatality or character, and so to have violated tragic norms and the supposed moral mission of the theater, as Henry Home argued in 1762.[34]

An influential twentieth-century version of this position was H. B. Charlton's treatment of the play in his 1948 *Shakesperian Tragedy*. Charlton – an ardent admirer of A. C. Bradley's criticism and an opponent of the 'new criticism' of T. S. Eliot and I. A. Richards – saw the play as a new departure for Shakespeare from the earliest tragedies (*Titus Andronicus, Richard III,* and *Richard II)* as Shakespeare searched for a viable tragic form. As Charlton sees it (in an argument about as far from Benjamin's notions of the aesthetic value of early modern *Trauerspiele* as can be imagined), Shakespeare attempted to import 'the half-barbarian,

---

[33] Charles Gildon, 'Remarks on the Plays of Shakespeare', in Nicholas Rowe (ed.), *The Works of Mr. William Shakespeare,* 7 vols. (1710; reprinted New York, AMS Press, 1967), 369–71.

[34] Henry Home, Lord Kames, *Elements of Criticism,* 2 vols. (1762; reprinted New York: Garland, 1971), Vol. II, 380–81.

half Roman deities of Fate and Fortune' in place of 'the whole universe of God's justice, vengeance, and providence' implied by the Christian setting,[35] with the result that the attempt cannot carry and fails to sustain itself. What gets produced for Charlton is an affecting play full of great poetry, but one that is a failure to the extent it was an attempt to 'grasp ... the foundations of tragedy'.[36]

Even though Samuel Johnson praised the play, and Romantics like Schlegel and Hazlitt were captivated by its treatment of the power of innocent love,[37] Charlton's diagnosis – it was quite similar to Bradley's briefly worded judgment on the play – has been echoed by large numbers of critics. Many of them have found good reasons for the play's popularity with the larger public and have acknowledged its beauties and power, but it is just as common to read that *Romeo and Juliet* lacks depth, profundity, or insights into life and death – that it is not a 'deep' tragedy – or as Bradley puts it, *'Romeo and Juliet* ... is a pure tragedy, but it is an early work, and in some respects an immature one.'[38] And partially in response to these complaints, a significant number of critics have attempted to 'save' the play by reading its plot as embodying various moral judgments – as condemning and punishing the Capulets and Montagues for their feud or by showing the folly of immature passion – in effect using conventional moral commonplaces to produce a specious 'maturity' for the play.[39]

But if the play does indeed violate the patterns of Aristotelian tragedy, it does not follow that these violations are 'faults' or marks of superficiality. Instead they link the play to the *Trauerspiel* tradition. To be sure, *Romeo and Juliet* is no unalloyed *Trauerspiel* any more than it is an unalloyed tragedy. In any case, the use of the generic term 'tragedy' in literary studies is too institutionalized and too widespread for a term like *Trauerspiel* to replace it. Clearly, however, elements of the received ideas of tragedy – fatality and tragic flaw pre-eminently[40] – are irrelevant to several of the works which Shakespeare's fellows inserted into the section of the Folio devoted to

[35] H. B. Charlton, *Shakesperian Tragedy* (Cambridge University Press, 1948), 50–51.   [36] *Ibid.*, 61.
[37] Samuel Johnson, 'Notes on Shakespeare's Plays: "Romeo and Juliet"', *The Yale Edition of the Works of Samuel Johnson*, Vol. VIII:, ed. Arthur Sherbo (New Haven, Conn.: Yale University Press, 1968), 956–57; August Wilhelm Schlegel, *A Course of Lectures on Dramatic Art and Literature*, ed. A. J. W. Morrison, trans. John Black, revised edn. (1846; reprinted New York: AMS, 1965), 400–1; William Hazlitt, *Characters in Shakespeare's Plays and Lectures on the English Poets* (London: Macmillan 1903), 83–94.
[38] A. C. Bradley, *Shakespearean Tragedy: Lectures on 'Hamlet', 'Othello', 'King Lear' and 'Macbeth'* (1904; Harmondsworth: Penguin, 1991), 21.
[39] See, for example, Battenhouse, *Shakespearean Tragedy*, 102–30.
[40] Harry Levin critiqued the notion of the tragic flaw (*hamartia*) cogently years ago; see Harry Levin, *The Question of Hamlet* (New York: Viking, 1959), 133–36.

'Tragedies'. Benjamin's notion of a *Trauerspiel* tradition separate from the tragic one can teach us something about such instances. In addition, whatever the play's 'tragic' qualities, it is clear (as many previous critics have noted) that the tragedy develops out of an initial set of scenes that are remarkably like those of Shakespeare's romantic comedies, in tone, plot, and theme.

THE COMIC ELEMENTS OF *ROMEO AND JULIET*

As in most of the comedies, love is, as Evelyn Gajowski eloquently puts it, at the center of the play – love defeated by power and patriarchy, but triumphant in a precisely aesthetic, utopian sphere.[41] Adorno would have agreed, writing in a brief but insightful comment on the play:

In *Romeo and Juliet* Shakespeare was not promoting love without familial guardianship; but without the longing for a situation in which love would no longer be mutilated and condemned by patriarchal or any other powers, the presence of the two lost in one another would not have the sweetness – the wordless, imageless utopia – over which, to this day, the centuries have been powerless; the taboo that prohibits knowledge of any positive utopia also reigns over artworks.[42]

The comic beginning provides the development of the love between the two young people that achieves 'the sweetness – the wordless, imageless utopia' – of which Adorno speaks, and sets the groundwork for the catastrophes to come. It is the powerful sense of love that lingers within the audience and provides much of the poignancy as we watch accident and death overtake innocence and good will. Thus, the association of death and eros insisted on over and over in the final scenes is framed against one of the most powerful representations of *possibility*, of what might have been, ever written. This utopian moment stays with us even as we mourn its impossibility in the world we know.

Romeo and Juliet is not as centrally meta-aesthetic as the play which was written very near it, *A Midsummer Night's Dream*, nor even as much as *Hamlet* – although it does contain two important meta-aesthetic moments, the Queen Mab speech and the ending, with its allusion to immortalizing golden statues for the dead lovers. But there is a kinship to the comic *Midsummer Night's Dream* in many other ways (it was written either just before or after that play) in its lyrical intensity; its interest

[41] Evelyn Gajowski, *The Art of Loving: Female Subjectivity and Male Discursive Traditions in Shakespeare's Tragedies* (Newark, Del.: University of Delaware Press, 1992), 26–50.
[42] Theodor Adorno, *Aesthetic Theory*, ed. Gretel Adorno and Rolf Tiedemann, trans. Robert Hullot-Kentor (Minneapolis, Minn.: University of Minnesota Press, 1997), 247.

in representing and exploring love, desire, and their social impact; and in its references to fairies, illusion, and dreaming in Mercutio's great Queen Mab speech. The big difference between the two plays is the emphasis on the occurrence of death in *Romeo and Juliet* and death's presence in *A Midsummer Night's Dream* only in a comic, parodic rustic play. The double suicide of the two eponymous characters binds up the play and frames it in something of the way in which Timon's death does (in its invocation of an aestheticized gravesite). In *Romeo and Juliet* gold statues of the two lovers near a joint grave serve a similarly meta-aesthetic function. (5.3.298–303). But this moment is overshadowed by the more properly social theme of the healing of a family feud that completes the form of the work and resolves its central themes, while the whole sad tale is given an understated Providential aura – or, for audiences without faith in any Providential influence in history, in an aura of aesthetic heightening and formalization. The balance at the ending is fragile and exceedingly complex, as a number of more recent critics have seen.

The opening, comic half of the play is pre-occupied with the theme of desire. Everyone remembers that when we first meet Romeo, he is in the throes of an unrequited love for the shadowy Rosaline – a figure who never appears on stage, but only in Romeo's fervid imagination. Momentarily the play seems to de-value Romeo's subjective state in something of the way the love-drops in *A Midsummer Night's Dream* depict love as an arbitrary, unreasonable aberration of vision and judgment. Mercutio's set-piece description of Queen Mab is part of this motif. Queen Mab personifies imagination and performs precisely the task of providing imagined objects of desire for a panoply of social agents, pointedly including lovers:

> And in this state she gallops night by night
> Through lovers' brains, and then they dream of love;
> O'er courtiers' knees, that dream on curtsies straight;
> O'er ladies' lips, who straight on kisses dream,
> Which oft the angry Mab with blisters plagues
> Because their breaths with sweetmeats tainted are.
> …
> This is the hag, when maids lie on their backs,
> That presses them and learns them first to bear,
> Making them women of good carriage. (1.4.71–94)

'Thou talk'st of nothing', Romeo replies (1.4.96), alluding both to the nothing of imagined images and to the vagina in an Elizabethan witticism. And in this moment of the play, the two are indeed closely linked. Mecutio recapitulates the ideas on imagination of Duke Theseus in *Dream*, who also recognizes the role of erotic desire in poetic creation, although, of course, in a skeptical, debunking mode. But as in that companion play considered more broadly, *Romeo and Juliet* recognizes the counter-factual status of imagination while still positively celebrating its ability to model for us objects of our desire, utopias which manifest the radical *lack* of the world. In that way, Queen Mab personifies not only the imagination in general, but the poetic-dramatic imagination on display here, and this speech takes its place among a series of distancing, *mimesis*-conscious moments (the Prologue, the well-known internal sonnets, and the golden statues) that signal aesthetic self-consciousness.

But at first the skeptical mode pre-dominates, and we hear even Romeo articulating it in a rare moment of self-knowledge concerning his obsession with the evanescent Rosaline:

> Love is a smoke made with fume of sighs,
> Being purged, a fire sparkling in lovers' eyes;
> Being vexed, a sea nourished with lovers' tears.
> And what is it else? A madness most discreet,
> A choking gall and a preserving sweet. (1.1.183–87)

The images suggest suffering and ardor, but also a self-conscious resistance to love itself, one repeatedly urged by a deflating, satirical Mercutio.

Another comic element is the strong communal presence in the play.[43] Up until the first meeting of the couple, the play is dominated by the vivid depiction of Veronese civil society, presided over by a well-meaning prince, rent by an ancient feud between two wealthy households. This, in fact, is the emphasis of the play's much-quoted opening Prologue, 'Two households, both alike in dignity / In fair Verona, where we lay our scene' (ll. 1–2), and the impression is under-lined by the lively, bawdy humor and the quarrel and fighting between servants of the two households in 1.1, before we even hear of Romeo. The play represents a civil space with density enough to provide a social context to a couple's young love and marriage. We are involved in the reproduction of Veronese society, and marriage is a means to that end – as it appears to be as well in the fairies' blessing at the end of

---

[43] This is an aspect of the play defined clearly in Susan Snyder, '"Romeo and Juliet": Comedy into Tragedy', *Essays in Criticism* 20.4 (October 1970), 391–402; 400–1.

Dream. We are never allowed to forget for long the power of this social context, especially as Romeo and Juliet themselves resolve to transgress it in the cause of their mutual passion. We hear it repeatedly in the admonitions of Juliet's parents, the final 'tilt' toward Paris rather than Romeo of Juliet's beloved Nurse, and even in the rationale given by Friar Lawrence for his extraordinary and transgressive aid to the couple, when he envisions the union of the two as means to overcome the long-standing feud.

In short, the play up until the death of Mercutio is remarkably comic and community-valuing, in both tone and structure, with only Romeo's melancholy and the young men's threat of violence presaging something different to come. On the whole things proceed very much on a par with Shakespearean romantic comedies past and future,[44] with two different but interacting sets of actions in contrasting styles: a 'high' romantic plot in which the man is educated by his Lady out of a self-defeating Petrarchan narcissism into a love relation of mutuality and equality; and a series of 'low' scenes involving buoyant, witty anti-Romantic, deflating dialogue asserting the realities of bodily sexuality, communal and family interests, and male friendship with homoerotic overtones.

This second set of scenes (it is not quite a 'subplot') makes up the play's vivid civil space, representing a society which is, as a generation of feminist critics have rightly asserted, a thoroughly patriarchal one, where the subjective preferences of a daughter must be secondary to the economic interests of the father, in which women generally are only tokens in an exchange among men, and in which men assert family and individual status with violence. Patriarchal power is represented in this play as a controlling force in which the forbidden love of the two protagonists gets defined, and it is a space that to this day is irresistible to directors for updating, the Shakespearean words or plot inserted into social milieus as diverse as Leonard Bernstein's Westside Manhattan or Baz Luhrman's indeterminate US Hispanic Verona Beach. The love story, as these adapters and directors, as well as any number of critics have asserted, has a strong social dimension implicitly critical of the patriarchal regulation of desire and the masculine violence of city life. It is a love story, as Stephen Greenblatt writes, which presents us with the 'inescapability of the social'.[45]

---

[44] Perhaps the earliest argument for this now common view of the play is Snyder, '"Romeo and Juliet": Comedy into Tragedy', 391–402.
[45] Stephen Greenblatt, Introduction to *Romeo and Juliet*, *The Norton Shakespeare*, ed. Greenblatt *et al.*, 865–71; 869.

UTOPIAN LOVE AND NATURE

It is within this carefully sketched civic space – a representation of early modern European urban life that is capable of constant updating – that the legendary love of Romeo and Juliet is kindled, and it is precisely love that challenges the power of the social. Desire is re-situated from Romeo's solipsistic Petrarchan discourse on Rosaline into a mutual, ritualized, and still idealistic (but also frankly sexual) utopian language in which female subjectivity is given equal weight to that of the male,[46] in contradiction to a society in which the two sexes are far from equal. The words spoken about Juliet by a Chorus introducing the second act make this contrast explicit:

> And she as much in love, her means much less
> To meet her new belovèd anywhere.
> But passion lends them power, time means, to meet,
> Temp'ring extremes with extreme sweet. (2.0.11–14)

The gender roles in the first meeting are the stereotypical ones of an aggressive man, a reluctant, slowly yielding woman, as Romeo approaches and touches Juliet first and uses religious imagery to steal the first, then the second, kiss – with the dialogue, as is well known, constituting an internal sonnet:

> If I profane with my unworthiest hand
> This holy shrine, the gentler sin is this:
> My lips, two blushing pilgrims, ready stand
> To smooth that rough touch with a tender kiss. (1.5.90–93)

It should be noticed, however, that in Juliet's more modest rejoinder, she in fact offers her hand instead of drawing away:

> Good pilgrim, you do wrong your hand too much,
> Which mannerly devotion shows in this.
> For saints have hands that pilgrims' hands do touch,
> And palm to palm is holy palmers kiss. (1.5.94–97)

And as almost every actress I have ever seen playing the role realizes, there is a clear invitation in her further reply, 'Then have my lips the sin that they have took' (1.5.105). In short, the traditional gender relations are first put on display, then subtly undermined, and finally dissolved in explicit claims of mutuality and equality. That is the first way in which Romeo and Juliet's love is utopian in Ernst Bloch's sense, socially counter-factual

---

[46] I am summarizing points made in much greater detail in Gajowski, *The Art of Loving*, 26–50.

but fueled by desire in a relationship of negation to the real and offering an implicit critique of the real. In this case, patriarchy and its oppressions are highlighted in the utopian transgression of the two lovers.

Similarly, the representation of love is utopian in its all-sweeping transformation of the subjectivities of each of the pair, so that for each a new perceptual world is created that amounts to a revolution in perception through a transvaluation of love to a supreme value. We hear this most distinctly in Romeo's swift renunciation of Rosaline:

> Did my heart love till now? Forswear it, sight,
> For I ne'er saw true beauty till this night. (1.5.49–50)

Juliet as well has her moment of subjective revolution – and an important early enunciation in the play hinting at the coming of death as the outcome of this desire:

> If he be married,
> My grave is like to be my wedding bed. (1.5.131–32).

The young couple's utopian desire to transcend their social situation reaches one of its most intense expressions in Juliet's famous speech on names:

> Deny thy father and refuse thy name,
> Or if thou wilt not, be but sworn my love,
> And I'll no longer be a Capulet.
> …
> 'Tis but thy name that is my enemy.
> Thou art thyself, though not a Montague.
> What's Montague? It is not hand, nor foot,
> Nor arm, nor face, not any other part
> Belonging to a man. O, be some other name!
> What's in a name? That which we call a rose
> By any other word would smell as sweet. (2.1.76–86)

This fantasy of abolishing the received social order that is an inextricable feature of our very sense of self – notions that Lacan has theorized, but which Shakespeare investigated over and over throughout his works, and nowhere more intently than in the other two plays of 1595, *Richard II* and *A Midsummer Night's Dream*[47] – is here invoked in order to investigate a different facet of its complex meaning. Richard II's plunge into a

---

[47] See Hugh Grady, *Shakespeare's Universal Wolf: Studies in Early Modern Reification* (Oxford: Clarendon, 1996), 156–7, for a discussion of this motif in *King Lear*; and Grady, *Shakespeare, Machiavelli, and Montaigne: Power and Subjectivity from 'Richard II' to 'Hamlet'* (Oxford University Press, 2002) for an investigation into its ramifications throughout the Henriad.

kind of namelessness, when he is stripped of his title and identity, is the climactic moment of his tragedy, and Shakespeare memorably symbolizes it when Richard calls for a mirror to find his self, then shatters the mirror in recognition that that self is gone.

In the dramatic context in which Juliet's lines appear in this play, however, the fantasy of an escape from the Symbolic Order differs from Richard's fall into a new and terrifying free flowing, identity-shifting subjectivity. It is rather an exhilarating fantasy of freedom, a mental act annihilating an oppressive world of constraint and prohibition. And as Friar Lawrence discerns when he hears of Romeo's mental and emotional revolution, it is the kind of wish that may contain the seeds of a possible social renovation:

> In one respect I'll thy assistant be;
> For this alliance may so happy prove
> To turn your households' rancour to pure love. (2.2.90–92)

In the balcony scene – certainly one of the best-known episodes of any narrative in the world – the intensity increases, the theme of all-transforming love at first sight is made plausible against all odds, and lines that every schoolgirl and schoolboy know crystallize for us an experience of intense pleasure in the idealized, passionate declarations of the couple. If we can manage to look anew at dialogue that has achieved such familiarity that it is almost dead to us conceptually (though it continues to dazzle us with its sounds and affect), we can notice a Shakespearean technique that Ralph Waldo Emerson thought was among Shakespeare's greatest accomplishments: the casual, almost organic linkage of the world of human life to that of nature. As Emerson put it in his remarks on Shakespeare in 1835, 'The power of the Poet depends on the fact that the material world is a symbol or expression of the human mind and part for part. Every natural fact is a symbol of some spiritual fact.[48] Previewing ideas that would be developed at greater length in his famous little book *Nature* (published anonymously in September, 1836, ten months after his Shakespeare lectures), Emerson is celebrating Shakespeare's works as exemplifying the profound connections between the natural world and the human mind which are central to Emerson's philosophy – as they would be to later aesthetics-influenced French Symbolist poets. Emerson notes that there are many proverbial examples, but he is taken with the

---

[48] Ralph Waldo Emerson, 'Shakspear' [First Lecture], in *The Early Lectures of Ralph Waldo Emerson*, 3 vols., ed. Stephen E. Whicher and Robert E. Spiller (Cambridge, Mass.: Belknap Press of Harvard University Press, 1966), Vol. I, 289.

way Shakespeare created innumerable instances that are entirely his own: 'His imperial muse tosses the creation like a bauble from hand to hand to embody any capricious shade of thought that is uppermost in his mind. Open any page grave or gay and you shall find this despotism of the imagination summoning the elements at will to illustrate his momentary thought.'[49]

Friar Lawrence, in his opening monologue, is one of the carriers of this theme in *Romeo and Juliet*. He is an herbalist, a pre-modern scientist of the natural order in which nature, rather than being stripped of value and re-conceived as an empty realm of materials for manipulation, is instead a realm of beauty with gifts useful for human life as well; for the Friar, nature is a two-fold mother, associated with both death and sexual reproduction:

> The earth, that's nature's mother, is her tomb.
> What is her burying grave, that is her womb,
> And from her womb children of divers kind
> We sucking on her natural bosom find,
> Many for many virtues excellent,
> None but for some, and yet all different. (2.2.9–14)

As the Friar goes on he seems to become something of a pre-modern Natural Law theorist, with, at the very end, a naturalistic Machiavellian side:

> For naught so vile that on the earth doth live
> But to the earth some special good doth give;
> Nor aught so good but, strained from that fair use,
> Revolts from true birth, stumbling on abuse.
> Virtue itself turns vice being misapplied,
> And vice sometime's by action dignified.
>
> (2.2.17–22)

Here, the Friar is not unlike those leveling gardeners of *Richard II*, who also saw the processes of nature mirrored in the human realm, but inflected so as to include the ideologically dangerous instances of revolution and the overthrow of monarchs.[50] Here the Friar describes a natural order of which sex and death are inalienable parts – nature has both 'womb' and 'tomb'; in fact the rhyme and the metaphoric 'logic' of the passage implies that these are simply two aspects of the same natural process and rhythm: 'What is her burying grave, that is her womb.' This is

[49] Emerson, 'Shakspear' [First Lecture], 292.
[50] See Grady, *Shakespeare, Machiavelli, and Montaigne*, 75–79.

the 'pre-modern' attitude toward death which Ariès defined as dominant throughout the medieval periods, and it suggests that the 'comic' half of the play achieves much of its atmosphere by invoking an archaic sense of a human world imitating and accommodating the natural. But the phrasing also opens up the 'modern' possibility that the play's emotionally ambivalent, bittersweet ending will attempt to exploit: the natural rhythms of love and death, irrupting into a violent, conflict-ridden world in the transformative eros of Juliet and Romeo, can overturn a social order that 'Revolts from true birth'. The tomb of their death becomes the womb of a new, regenerated order. In short, *Romeo and Juliet*, like several Shakespearean histories and tragedies to come, inscribes a transformation we recognize as one between the pre-modern and the modern within the compass of one play. We move from a 'comic', 'pre-modern' world of harmony between the social and the natural, into a 'tragic' (more properly, as we will see, *Trauerspiel*-like), 'modern', and dissociated one. As Ariès suggests, the meaning of sex and death changes as we move from one era to the other, and *Romeo and Juliet* displays this change as a shift in genre halfway through its plot. The harmony between sex and death described by Friar Lawrence becomes the rupture in the social fabric brought about first by Romeo and Juliet's transgressive, mutual passion, and then by the deaths Romeo becomes involved in. But as we will see, the potential for harmony never completely disappears from this play in the way it does in, say, *Hamlet* or *King Lear*. Love and death never lose their status as 'natural' in this play, although the play's 'social' seems to reject the first and pre-empt the naturalness of the second when events turn tragic. In the end, however, some version of a healing of the breach between the natural and the social is clearly asserted – precisely, as we will see, through the mediation of art.

As in the play's seamless plot-line itself, the transition from the first state to the second is subtle and fluid. The utopian interpenetration of the natural and human realms is celebrated early in the development of Romeo and Juliet's love, in phrases like, 'It is the East, and Juliet is the sun. …' or even in Juliet's counter-pointing observation,

> It is too rash, too unadvised, too sudden,
> Too like the lightning which doth cease to be
> Ere one can say it lightens. (2.1.160–62)

Too familiar to have elicited much attention, all these linkages of the human and the natural worlds take us deep into one of the key components of the aesthetic, an idealizing vision of what might be, and perhaps once was: a harmonization of the natural and the social worlds, an interpenetration and mutual influence. Here sexual desire is at once acknowledged, linked to the highest human values, and held up as a piece of the natural within humanity that links us with a larger domain.

It is this linkage, I believe, rather than the revelation of the hatred within love that Julia Kristeva has claimed to find,[51] that is behind the following lines of Juliet (to which I will return below):

> Come night, come Romeo; come, thou day in night,
> For thou wilt lie upon the wings of night
> Whiter then new snow on a raven's back.
> Come gentle night; come, loving, black-browed night,
> Give me my Romeo, and when I shall die
> Take him and cut him out in little stars,
> And he will make the face of heaven so fine
> That all the world will be in love with night
> And pay no worship to the garish sun. (3.2.17–25)

But to understand this issue, we should first get a sense of the radical generic change the play undergoes in the scene (3.1) just before Juliet speaks these lines, when the latent violence we have been artfully introduced to amid the comic happenings spills out on a hot July day and results in two rapid deaths – and a wrecking of the comic momentum we seem to have been carried on to that point.

THE TURN TO *TRAUERSPIEL* AESTHETICS

After the death of Mercutio and the swift avenging of that death by a Romeo suddenly pulled back into the patriarchal world he had seemed to escape through his utopian relationship, everything changes abruptly. This play, which had seemed so much like a romantic comedy in the making, suffers a shift in tone and becomes something of a *Trauerspiel* in its second half – a *Trauerspiel* rather than a tragedy because of its marked contingencies, its lack of a tight cause-and-effect plot, and a lack of the sense of the tragic ending emerging from the protagonists' *hamartia* or flaw. After the deaths and Romeo's banishment, the play's world becomes much like the one described by Benjamin as the defining feature of this genre of developing modernity: it is an empty panoply of objects, its immanent meaning lost. Particularly after each of the two lovers believes the other dead, the world becomes completely devoid of meaning for

---

[51] Kristeva, *Tales of Love*, 209–33.

them, and death becomes a grim substitute for the love and meaning now missing from the world. A cluster of allegorical objects, in stage props and in imagery, begins to emerge throughout the mournful dialogue. The poison which the despairing Romeo procures from the Apothecary is one such allegorical object. Forbidden by an idealizing Law but available nonetheless because of the poverty and desperation of its possessor, it emblematizes the cruel world of arbitrary authority, misplaced values, and hostility to love which Romeo has bitterly discovered. At the same time, the poison is the potion that will restore the two lovers, the gift of nature which will be used to overthrow that world through restorative death: 'Come, cordial and not poison, go with me / To Juliet's grave, for there must I use thee' (5.1.85–86).

The miscarried letter is another silent allegory, embodying the motifs of accident and chance, an infected world, and the insufficiency of good intentions, but embodying as well the failed possibility of success and happiness. Similarly ambiguous are the rosemary and the flowers of the aborted wedding (4.4) which become signifiers of mourning when Juliet's apparent death overwhelms her household and her would-be husband Paris, maintaining their ambiguity for an audience aware that the appearance of death is only an appearance. When we enter the climactic churchyard and tomb scene, we are surrounded by other ambiguous but meaningful chance objects – the tomb itself, containing both death and resurrection, decay and rebirth; the crowbars and swords, instruments of human ingenuity and skill in play against greater natural forces; and any number of allegorizing personifications with similar qualities, like Romeo's impassioned lines to the earth of the grave, which echo but contrast with the Friar's earlier, celebratory invocations of nature's bounty in a transformed mode:

> Thou detestable maw, thou womb of death,
> Gorged with the dearest morsel of the earth,
> Thus I enforce thy rotten jaws to open,
> And in despite I'll cram thee with more food. (5.3.45–8)

There is a similar allegorical attempt to find meaning and beauty in the (apparent) death of Juliet:

> Beauty's ensign yet,
> Is crimson in thy lips, and in the cheeks,
> And death's pale flag is not advancèd there.
> …
> Why art thou yet so fair? Shall I believe
> That unsubstantial death is amorous,

And that the lean abhorrèd monster keeps
Thee here in dark to be his paramour? (5.3.94–105)

Lines like these have provided evidence to those critics who identify the play as an early instance of what Ariès calls the baroque moment in the history of death. That was the era, Ariès argues, that linked death with sexuality as disturbing irruptions of the natural into a human world now advancing along the modernizing path of the dialectic of enlightenment. But such moments turn out on examination to be local and momentary and are finally subordinated to and incorporated within a larger series of explorations of the relation of desire to death.

THE DARK SIDE OF DESIRE

The graveyard scene is the moment when the play's exploration of the links between love and desire seem to approach the idea of *Liebestod* when death looms as the outcome of the two lovers' great desire. Three of the twentieth-century theorists of *Liebestod* mentioned above – de Rougemont, Kristeva, and Ariès – in fact put *Romeo and Juliet* squarely within this tradition, as noted above. But I believe all three of these related readings of the play ignore to their peril the aesthetic embedding and revaluation that takes place when these themes undergo Shakespearean negotiations from culture to art. From a distance de Rougemont, Ariès, and Kristeva seem plausible. But when we are immersed in the play these theories lose some of their persuasive power precisely because we are dealing with death and desire in mediated forms, as *mimesis* or semblance with multiple meanings. Death in the final scenes of *Romeo and Juliet* is represented as at once natural *and* the accident of a cruel world in the context of forces beyond love's control. Desire is ecstatic and utopian, too good for the world in which it is immersed, but in no sense self-corrupting or merely a delusive mask for the death-wish. The two are kept separate conceptually, even when they are linked together in inspired conceits.[52] A metaphor, of course, is not an identity; nor is it a figure with one single correct interpretation.

Kristeva's diagnosis in particular deserves some exploration. It is undeniable that there is a startling violence in the image evoked by Juliet in her wish that Romeo could be cut into little stars, and this is Kristeva's most striking piece of evidence of a hatred within love in the play. But it is a violence mediated through art, a rhetorical *chiaroscuro* that charms

---

[52] The title-page of the first quarto edition of 1597 refers to the play as 'an excellent conceited tragedy'.

us with its baroque union of opposites, its violent wit, and its passionate declaration of love and admiration heightened, not undercut, by the violence. The context of the remark is a soliloquy by a Juliet yearning for her first sexual union with her love:

> Gallop apace, you fiery-footed steeds,
> Towards Phoebus' lodging. Such a waggoner
> As Phaëton would whip you to the west
> And bring in cloudy night immediately.
> Spread thy close curtain, love-performing night,
> That runaways' eyes may wink, and Romeo
> Leap to these arms, untalked of and unseen. (3.2.1–7)

In that context the violence resonates more with the urgency of desire than with a desire for murder. We are reminded of two of the most memorable couplets in Andrew Marvell's 'To His Coy Mistress':

> And now let us sport us while we may
> And now, like amorous birds of prey,
> Rather at once our time devour
> Than languish in his slow-chapped power.

In the final scenes of the play, when we are surrounded by the aura of death and decay, we witness a miracle-not-to-last of resurrection and re-animation that, like the flickering of Cordelia's breath at the end of *King Lear*, teases us with the prospect of what might have been even while it denies it. But because this is, precisely, an aesthetic representation of death rather than death itself, the fantasy of what-might-have-been has a perduring power that allows for a complex emotional state, divided between mourning and a sense of fulfillment – an apotheosis of Romeo and Juliet, a condemnation of the world that made their union impossible, and a healing suggestive of some limited amelioration from out of the catastrophe. It is through art – and this theme is expressed at the end, as I mentioned, in the image of the golden statues that each family promises will be erected in memory of them – that Romeo and Juliet are crystallized as ideal lovers whose union indicts a world that could not countenance them.

THE ANTAGONISM OF DESIRE AND DEATH

The motif pointed to by commentators as different as Ariès, de Rougemont, Kristeva, and Dollimore – the metaphorical equation of sexuality and death – plays through in an accelerating series of references throughout the play, beginning with Friar Lawrence's rhymed linkage of 'womb' and 'tomb' in his introductory soliloquy discussed above. At that point, as we have seen, the equation is based on the natural cycle of life and death and would seem to suggest that the Catholic setting of the play, with its continual references to the cycle of the year's feast days, is evoking the older medieval tradition of seeing life and death as natural, co-existing, co-dependant processes, as Ariès defines it. It is only in the play's second half that the equation of death and sexuality as extraordinary and rupturing processes, taking their subjects outside of ordinary life, begins to assert itself. And death wears many faces besides erotic ones in this second half, many of them evoking the fearfulness of putrescence, like Juliet's imaginings just before taking the potion:

> How if, when I am laid into the tomb,
> I wake before the time that Romeo
> Come to redeem me? There's a fearful point!
> …
> Or, if I live, is it not very like
> The horrible conceit of death and night,
> Together with the terror of the place –
> As in a vault, an ancient receptacle
> Where for this many hundred years the bones
> Of all my buried ancestors are packed;
> Where bloody Tybalt, yet but green in earth,
> Lies fest'ring in his shroud, where, as they say,
> At some hours in the night, spirits resort –
> Alack, alack, is it not like that I,
> So early waking – what with loathsome smells,
> And shrieks like mandrakes torn out of the earth,
> That living mortals, hearing them, run mad –
> Oh if I wake, shall I not be distraught,
> Environèd with all these hideous fears,
> And madly play with my forefathers' joints,
> And pluck the mangled Tybalt from his shroud,
> And in this rage, with some great kinsman's bone
> As with a club, dash out my desp'rate brains? (4.3.29–53)

Here are powerful, frightening images associated with death in a very different key from that of the erotic. In the end, Juliet overcomes her fears and takes the drink, in an instance of desire outweighing the fear of death's grim sights. She here makes good an earlier promise made to the Friar, one that perhaps led him to conceive of his ill-fated scheme:

> Or hide me nightly in a charnel-house,
> O'ercovered quite with dead men's rattling bones,

> With reeky shanks and yellow chapless skulls;
> Or bid me go into a new-made grave
> And hide me with a dead man in his tomb –
> Things that, to hear them told, have made me tremble –
> And I will do it without fear or doubt,
> To live an unstained wife to my sweet love. (4.1.81–88)

Another instance when death is thematized as the opposite of desire can be seen when Romeo uncomprehendingly notices the colors of life in Juliet's face that are the signs that 'death's pale flag is not advancèd there'. The following fragmented allegory of death as a monster keeping Juliet alive to be his paramour is disturbing, but it is no acceptance of death as the end of desire, but a defying of this:

> For fear of that I still will stay with thee,
> And never from this pallet of dim night
> Depart again. Here will I remain,
> With worms that are thy chambermaids. (5.3.106–9)

For Romeo at this point, death is not embraced like a lover; it is accepted as the dreary outcome of a world that rejects and expels utopia:

> O, here
> Will I set up my everlasting rest,
> And shake the yoke of inauspicious stars
> From this world-wearied flesh. Eyes, look your last.
> Arms, take our last embrace, and lips, O you
> The doors of breath, seal with a righteous kiss
> A dateless bargain to engrossing death. (5.3.109–15)

Thus, while there are moments when both Romeo and Juliet seem to articulate the ancient theme of embracing death like a sexual act, the bringing together of these two opposites, desire and death, creates a complex ambiguous aesthetic effect of the kind Benjamin referred to in his insistence on the ambiguity of the allegory.[53] Romeo's reaction to the news of Juliet's death is one such moment.

The scene begins with Romeo alone on stage, recounting to the audience a strange but, as he thinks, joyful dream:

> I dreamt my lady came and found me dead –
> Strange dream, that gives a dead man leave to think! –
> And breathed such life with kisses in my lips

---

[53] It of course can also be described in the terms of one of Empson's types of ambiguity, or through the New Critical description of a metaphysical conceit as defined by American New Critics like Cleanth Brooks. All of these, including Benjamin, are defining a new Modernist interpretive paradigm valuing ambiguity.

That I revived and was an emperor.
Ah me, how sweet is love itself possessed
When but love's shadows are so rich in joy! (5.1.6–11)

This is the context for Romeo's next soliloquy in which he is resolved for death in the form of an assignation with Juliet: 'Well, Juliet, I will lie with thee tonight' (5.1.34).

In the back-and-forth movement constituted by Romeo's shifting interpretation of the images of his own dream, we can see a movement of despair to joy and back to despair. Romeo's consciousness of himself dead, then revived by Juliet's kisses, is another such movement. Like those favorite images of Metaphysical poetry, the Phoenix and the Easter story, death appears fearful at first, only to be revealed as a necessary condition for, even itself an allegory of resurrection. As the context changes in the wake of news of Juliet's (apparent) death, Romeo's interpretation shifts as well, and he imagines himself dead beside the dead Juliet. What had seemed revivification in his first interpretation (shared life) becomes instead shared death. And for the audience, two other interpretations are possible, though at different points in the play. At this moment, when the audience is aware that Juliet's death is only apparent, the dream could presage the revivification of Romeo's spirits by the revived Juliet. And at the moment of Romeo's premature suicide, if we recall the dream, we can re-interpret it yet again, as a foreshadowing of the possibility missed, when Romeo might have reversed the roles in the dream by kissing his young bride to a phoenix-like re-awakening.

For all these *Trauerspiel*-like qualities, however, what makes this play a much less typical *Trauerspiel* than *Hamlet* is not only the comic first half, so different in tone and affect from the second – although seamlessly flowing into it – but also the final ending moments, in which the deaths of the two principals are revealed not to have left a completely empty world after all, but rather, as Friar Lawrence had hoped, have become the means for the reconciliation of the two feuding families and the healing of the civil breach in the lifeworld of Verona. It is as if the hidden moment of redemption, implicit in the allegory's despair and emptiness for Benjamin, has all but obliterated the sense of emptiness and despair that in *Hamlet*, for example, clearly lingered even as two set speeches memorialize his passing and attempt to restore something of a shattered world. *Romeo and Juliet* is not an unalloyed example of what Benjamin means by the designation *Trauerspiel* as *Hamlet* by and large is. It is instead a nearly unique synthesis of comedy and *Trauerspiel*, a structure to which Shakespeare returned only once or twice (in *Antony and Cleopatra* and perhaps *Timon of Athens*) if we exclude the more up-beat late Romances. But in all these plays, the ending completes the catastrophic denouement of death and defeat, only to show death as containing what we might call 'aesthetic' possibilities – the survival after death of aesthetic representations of the lovers that grant them the kind of immortality which Shakespeare promised his beloved in the Sonnets. In *Timon* (see Chapter 3) this aesthetic memorial is embodied in the gravesite/environmental artwork which he bequeaths to the world against the grain of his misanthropy. In *Antony and Cleopatra*, it is the very legend of the two lovers, embodied meta-aesthetically in the play we are watching. And in *Romeo and Juliet*, it is the two golden statues which the grieving parents promise to erect –

> MONTAGUE: But I can give thee more,
>   For I will raise her statue in pure gold,
>   That whiles Verona by that name is known
>   There shall no figure at such rate be set
>   As that of true and faithful Juliet.
> CAPULET: As rich shall Romeo's by his lady's lie,
>   Poor sacrifices of our enmity. (5.3.297–303)

– and again, in the play itself, which has become 'the most famous love story in the world'.

This ending is thus a re-assertion of the utopian desire for harmony between the natural and the human that is so evident in the play's first half, which presents a pre-modern era of harmony (or potential harmony, since Verona's tranquility is clearly endangered by the feud and the culture of violence of the young men). But in the second half it moves to what Ariès called a 'baroque' moment: first, when Romeo and Juliet's love alienates them from their lifeworld, making them indifferent to the ties of family and friends, and again, when the violence of the feud leads to the deaths of Mercutio and Tybalt. But at the same time that love and violence disrupt the world and radically de-value it, they also prepare for a healing of it, as Friar Lawrence in particular notes in a passage I quoted above.

Thus *Romeo and Juliet* is a far less dark play than either *Hamlet* or *Timon of Athens*, in that it draws back at the end from its most *Trauerspiel*-like moments to find meaning and a measure of redemption in the deaths of the two principals. It is in fact the health of its recognition of larger social bonds and issues that keeps it from being the kind of revelation of *Liebestod* that several critics, as we have seen, found in it. But it is a perfect play, a powerful poetic and dramatic accomplishment that demonstrates

Shakespeare's prescient grasp of desire, death, and the aesthetic interacting in an emerging modernity.

ROMEO AND JULIET AS ART

When analysts like Ariès, de Rougemont, Kristeva, and even Dollimore find in *Romeo and Juliet* an anatomy of a desire whose dark side – whether as sadism (Ariès), hatred (Kristeva), or misplaced religiosity (de Rougemont) – ultimately leads not to life, but to death, they are responding to one latent interpretive schema for conceptualizing the narrative of a mutual love thwarted and ending in twin suicides. In such an interpretation the play becomes a dark tragedy revealing the self-destructive qualities of eros (or the ultimate triumph of a death-drive over it).

Such an interpretation, however, is unsatisfying to me – and, I'm sure to many other readers and viewers of this often underrated early Shakespearean masterpiece. It fails to capture the play's strong assertion of the reality of *other possibilities*, of the role of chance and accident in the fatal denouement – of the play's refusal to be, in fact, an Aristotelian tragedy of *hamartia*. Numerous critics have attempted to read the play in this way, and they inevitably diminish its impact with an imposition of moralizing judgments and insensitivity to the play's utopian spirit. They fail, finally, to grasp the crucial importance of this play's *aesthetic* qualities, its status as *other* than reality, its creation of a counter-factual space in which we can vicariously experience and clarify our desires and needs. It is a space in which love and desire persist even when they are represented as defeated by larger forces. Like all works of art, *Romeo and Juliet* is ultimately a gift to us of an imagined reality in complex positive and negative relation to the (changing) world around us – a gift for the world but not entirely of the world.

The representation of death within the aesthetic space of the play is highly complex and multi-faceted. All five of the deaths in the play – those of Mercutio, Tybalt, Paris, Romeo and Juliet – are losses mourned as such by grieving survivors, and surely one of the play's themes (highly relevant to our own times, of course) is an indictment of street violence as a waste of youth and a blight on communities. The deaths of Romeo and Juliet share in this, but in the case of these two passionate, transcendence-seeking lovers, the deaths signify in more complex ways. We mourn the passing of their goodness from the world, but we (via 400 years of subsequent critical reception and reproduction) apotheosize them, make them emblems of highly valued accomplishments: the intensity of

their love survives their death for us, and that is the source of the sense
of an off-setting satisfaction in the midst of the vicarious mourning we
undertake for these two saints of love. If all art is a mourning, it is also a
consolation within mourning, a way to carry with us the possibilities that
reality has repressed but not really killed. 'What is true in art is something
non-existing', writes Adorno,[54] and that is one of the essential points to
understand about the representation of desire and death in *Romeo and
Juliet*. At the same time the alterity of art is an alterity 'bearing witness
that that world itself should be other than it is',[55] and that, too, is one of
the qualities of the gift that this play represents. Death both defeats and is
defeated by desire in this play, and that kinetic ambiguity is only possible
within aesthetic space.

[54] Adorno, *Aesthetic Theory*, 131.   [55] *Ibid.*, 177.

Conclusion: the critical present

> What was once true in an artwork and then disclaimed by history is
> only able to disclose itself again when the conditions have changed
> on whose account that truth was invalidated: Aesthetic truth con-
> tent and history are that deeply meshed ... Tradition is to be not
> abstractly negated but criticized without naïveté according to the
> current situation: thus the present constitutes the past. Nothing is
> to be accepted unexamined just because it is available and was once
> held valuable; nor is anything to be dismissed because it belongs to
> the past.[1]
>
> Theodor Adorno

Walter Benjamin's Kabbalistic idea of double hermeneutics – part oriented
to the past under the aegis of the Tree of Knowledge, part oriented to the
future, under the aegis of the Tree of Life (see above, Chapter 4) – can
also provide us with a way of thinking about the situation of the theory
of impure aesthetics argued here. Benjamin saw interpretation as always
involving two contradictory but unified impulses. I want to conclude this
book with a similar strategy.

Elements of the revival of aesthetic theory advocated in this book
clearly look to the past for their inspiration – to Immanuel Kant and the
Enlightenment and Romantic origins of aesthetic theory; to Hegel's and
Marx's insertion of art into larger narratives of human development and
liberation; to Theodor Adorno's and Walter Benjamin's attempts, beginning in the 1920s, to forge an aesthetics open to history, politics, and
the possibilities of human liberation; to the Postmodernist theories of the
recent past, with their development of hermeneutics based on an opening
up of the text to its own repressed possibilities; and of course, this book
involves a backward glance at implied concepts and analyses of William
Shakespeare, who seems to have developed an implicit theory of aesthetics

---

[1] Theodor Adorno, *Aesthetic Theory,* ed. Gretel Adorno and Rolf Tiedemann, trans. Robert Hullot-
Kentor (Minneapolis, Minn.: University of Minnesota Press, 1997), 40–41.

very near the earliest emergence of that constellation of modernity –
entailing secularism, instrumental rationality, and a commodity-based
economy – which was required before a modern theory of the aesthetic
could emerge.[2]

But all these moments of the past re-assert themselves now in the early
twenty-first century precisely because the moment seems to have arrived
in contemporary cultural development for a revival that looks ahead to
future critical developments based on them, but going beyond them.
In my 1992 *The Modernist Shakespeare* I describe in the last chapter the
emergence of a set of new critical practices that defined themselves largely
in political terms but which, I argue, also represents the emergence of a
new Postmodernist aesthetics.[3] This argument is harder to make fifteen
years later, in the wake of changes in the meaning of 'the Postmodern'
in the meantime, but I believe it urgently needs to be updated for our
current situation.

In the 1980s, 'Postmodernism' primarily referred to changes in artistic
production, to aesthetics in that sense of the word. Hal Foster's influential
anthology *The Anti-Aesthetic*, with its insights into the commonalities
of newer critical methods and the newer artistic practices of the times,[4]
and Fredric Jameson's milestone, much re-printed definition of a new
Postmodernist aesthetic, beginning in the late 1940s but coming into its
own in the 1980s,[5] were highly influential treatments of the idea of an
aesthetic Postmodernism that had come into being after a break with a
now defunct Modernism. The term entered the 'higher' registers of mass
discourse, attached itself to specific late-1980s and early-1990s aesthetic
practices, and, in the way of such things, its 'collapse' was announced in
an exhibit in Albany, New York by artist Ellen Levy in 1995.[6] By 2004, it
was necessary to use the past tense when writing about Postmodernism in

---

[2] See Mark Robson, 'Defending Poetry, or, Is there an Early Modern Aesthetic?' in John J. Joughin
and Simon Malpas (eds.), *The New Aestheticism* (University of Manchester Press, 2003), 119–30;
120–27, for a cogent argument that the development of aesthetic theory is dependant on the larger cultural development of modernity. Robson rightly critiques several of my earlier works for
discussing modernity without direct reference to aesthetics. I hope this current work makes up
for that previous neglect.

[3] Hugh Grady, *The Modernist Shakespeare: Critical Texts in a Material World* (Oxford: Clarendon,
1991), 210–46.

[4] Hal Foster (ed.), *The Anti-Aesthetic: Essays on Postmodern Culture* (Port Townsend, Wash.: Bay,
1983).

[5] Fredric Jameson, *Postmodernism; or The Cultural Logic of Late Capitalism* (Durham, NC: Duke
University Press, 1991).

[6] See Vivien Raynor, 'Worlds Falling Apart and Getting Hooked Up', *The New York Times*, January 8,
1995; www.nytimes.com, Archives, accessed June 20, 2007. Ellen Levy's show, at the State
Museum, was entitled 'The Collapse of Postmodernism'.

the art pages of *The New York Times*: 'Call it an attitude, a phase or a fad, but postmodernism did at least one good, big thing. It rained hard on the mostly white, mostly male, by-invitation-only party that had long been Western art.'[7]

Meanwhile, as a reaction to the less cautious theoretical claims of followers of (what had been called) the poststructuralist theory of Jacques Derrida, Michel Foucault, Jean Baudrillard, Jean-François Lyotard, and others set in, writers like Christopher Norris and Terry Eagleton sought to distance themselves from the radical uncertainties and absolutist skepticism that was adopted by many poststructuralist theorists,[8] and they (and many others) began to speak of such criticism as 'Postmodernist' rather than 'poststructuralist'.[9] Slowly and subtly 'Postmodernism' became a pejorative in these writers' usages, as Eagleton, Norris, and others argued variations of the idea that Postmodernist theory led merely to an apolitical refusal of knowledge and, as Christopher Norris has it, a merely 'aesthetic' stance vis-à-vis the world.[10]

While I am certainly sympathetic to Norris's and Eagleton's preferences for pragmatic political knowledge and action and less jargon-filled writing, I believe much of their case is being made against a straw man construct, inasmuch as the actual body of criticism underwritten by 'Postmodernist' theory has been in fact the most explicitly political and position-taking criticism in the 100-year-old history of academic literary-critical writing. Nevertheless, the critique has led to a pronounced negative coloration of the term and a shift in meaning from an aesthetic to a theoretical register.

It would not really be accurate to say that English studies from the 1990s to today has positively embraced this negative conception of critical Postmodernism. For one thing, the critiques of both Eagleton and Norris are themselves dependent for much of their argumentation on Postmodernist critical concepts. In addition, an examination of journals

---

[7] Holland Cotter, 'Pumping Air into the Museum, So It's as Big as the World Outside', *The New York Times*, April 30, 2004; www.nytimes.com, Archives, accessed June 21, 2007.
[8] The key work leading to this second strand of meanings for the term Postmodernism is Jean-François Lyotard, *The Postmodern Condition: A Report on Knowledge*, trans. Geoff Bennington and Brian Massumi (Minneapolis, Minn.: University of Minnesota Press, 1984) which, as the subtitle suggests, addresses issues of the evolution of intellectual history rather than aesthetic changes *per se*.
[9] Christopher Norris, *The Truth about Postmodernism* (Oxford: Blackwell, 1993) and Terry Eagleton, *After Theory* (New York: Basic, 2003).
[10] 'The aesthetic moves to centre stage as the focal point for everything that challenges, eludes, or subverts the truth-claims of enlightenment critique', he complains about a tendency in the thought of Michel Foucault; see Norris, *The Truth about Postmodernism*, 60.

and bookstalls in the field will uncover innumerable studies couched in the theoretical concerns of the broad poststructuralist theory of the 1980s, with its emphases on deconstructing gender, race, class, sexuality, and colonialism. There is perhaps a certain resurgence of more 'traditional' scholarly methods (they never really disappeared), but much – indeed, probably most – of the profession is still working the terrain opened up by the critical revolutions of twenty to thirty years ago.

One result of these developments is that the idea of a postmodernist *aesthetic* revolution has been largely forgotten about, since the term *globalization* replaced *postmodern* as the buzzword of cultural theory sometime in the mid- to late 1990s.[11] Another result has been that very few critical practitioners debate the larger significance or truth-value of the underlying theories they continue to make use of. This development has been called the rise of 'Post-theory' – apparently the last in the series of 'posts' that defined the field of literary studies since the introduction of the terms Postmodernism and poststructuralism in the 1980s. Critics within this tendency *use* theory, but they do not *create, critique*, nor *develop* it. And so the debatable idea that the Postmodernist critical revolution has led the field into a dead-end of self-undermining absolutist skepticism, producing an unacceptable 'Postmodernism', has monopolized the recent evolving meanings of the term in the absence of much counter-argumentation, even while 'Postmodernism' in this sense of the word (designating the array of poststructuralist theories that have provided the tools of the literary and cultural criticism of the last thirty years) continues very much to dominate the field, albeit without much in the way of an underlying theoretical justification.

I have argued in this book for a different critical outcome: one that broadly accepts rather than broadly rejects the hermeneutic methods of the poststructuralist or Postmodernist critical revolution as a *de facto* cultural development that is *aesthetic* in nature and represents a kind of cultural *donnée* of our era; and one that values a continued theoretical discussion and critique of literary and cultural theory. Thus, I do not mean to dismiss the various critiques (and indeed self-critiques) of Derrida, Foucault, Lyotard, and Baudrillard – critiques that have put their fingers on significant theoretical problems in this body of theory. But it is to advocate not throwing out the baby of significant theoretical advancements with the bathwater of the *lacunae* and weaknesses that

---

[11] Of course this forgetting is a relative one. The term *Postmodernism* continues to have aesthetic meanings, for example, in Fredric Jameson's work and in that of the many he has influenced.

call for further critique and development of the art. For all the intricate philosophical and theoretical argumentation behind the competing claims of the various theoretical grand masters, the outcome of their appropriation by a generation of cultural workers in literary and cultural study has been a revolutionary paradigm-shift in how we approach the interpretation of texts. We have in effect suspended the classical aesthetic assumption of organic unity and replaced it with a Postmodernist aesthetics of disunity. We have done so, as Fredric Jameson has brilliantly argued over a sustained number of works since his milestone *Postmodernism; or, The Cultural Logic of Late Capitalism*, in complex dialectical interaction with a rapidly evolving culture of commodified images now dominating daily life throughout the 'developed' world – and producing a complex series of reactions within it and in the 'underdeveloped' world. As Jameson has argued, the new Postmodernist condition has not resulted from any fundamental revolution in the lifeworld, but from an intensification and extension of already existing systemic mechanisms. For all the 'posts-' involved in its discourses, the Postmodern has never claimed to be Postcapitalist. In our era of unfettered free markets, we have witnessed an increased and accelerated colonization of traditional lifeworlds by commodification and an intensification of mass media's hold over popular consciousness – in the process creating such new forms as religious fundamentalisms propagating themselves through access to the new media and marketing techniques of late capitalism. And although the economic crisis unfolding globally as this book goes to press suggests this era may be ending, of course something of the same process has propelled the image and influence of that global icon William Shakespeare to unprecedented centrality in world culture, creating such unusual hybridizations as Baz Luhrman's brilliant, pumped-up *William Shakespeare's Romeo + Juliet*, or versions of Shakespeare performed in the style of traditional Asian theatrical forms.

For a long time, however, it has seemed to me that as powerful and progressive as much of the Postmodernist revolution has been, the classical poststructuralist 'anti-humanist' approaches to subjectivity of Derrida, of Foucault, and of Althusser represent a succumbing to this culture of commodification rather than a resistance to it. David Hawkes has been particularly eloquent on this point:

> Once we admit that such postmodern phenomena as the objectified subject, the autonomy of representation, the impossibility of teleology, and the disappearance of the referent are effects of commodity fetishism, then postmodern ideology begins to look decidedly unappetizing. When we recall that

commodity fetishism involves the triumph of dead labour over living labour, the postmodern world begins to seem positively sinister.[12]

Unfortunately as well (from my point of view), this weakness in a central strand of Postmodernist thought has been the occasion for a recently revived 'traditionalist' assault on critical theory that sees no alternative to this form of anti-humanism but the traditional 'liberal humanism' of the 1940–1970 'Modernist' period of literary criticism.[13] But to me and many others, the rug has so long been pulled out from underneath this mid-century construct that any revival could only be based on a willful ignorance of the series of devastating critiques that have been patiently mounted against it over the last thirty years.

More promising (because more willing to critique and develop rather than jettison literary and cultural theory) are two recent works which call for a re-vitalization of the traditional categories of humanism and liberal individualism respectively, Andy Mousley's *Re-Humanising Shakespeare*[14] and Peter Holbrook's *Shakespeare's Individualism*.[15] Both of these somewhat different works attempt to recuperate 'traditional' ideas but within an informed discussion of the theoretical consequences involved, and both are more sensitive to aesthetic issues than the last generation of theoretical works.

Not unlike these last two books, but in distinction to the traditionalists, I am arguing here that precisely the related categories of the subjective and the aesthetic need to be positively developed within contemporary critical and cultural theory – specifically from the point of view of the poststructuralist/Frankfurt School critique of totality, commodity fetishism, and 'centered' consciousness. For this task the recent work of Andrew Bowie, which I summarized and discussed briefly in the introductory chapter, represents a crucial contribution. Bowie takes us with him in a new look at the epistemology and aesthetics of Immanuel Kant and his immediate philosophical and literary successors in the late Enlightenment and early Romantic periods, arguing that Kant had built his cases for agency and for aesthetics more strongly than the first

[12] David Hawkes, *Ideology*, 2nd edn. (London: Routledge, 2003), 170.
[13] See, for example, John Lee, *Shakespeare's 'Hamlet' and the Controversies of Self* (Oxford: Clarendon, 2000), and Richard Levin, *Looking for an Argument: Critical Encounters with the New Approaches to the Criticism of Shakespeare and his Contemporaries* (Madison, NJ: Fairleigh Dickinson University Press, 2003).
[14] Andy Mousley, *Re-Humanising Shakespare: Literary Humanism, Wisdom, and Modernity* (Edinburgh University Press, 2007). Mousley is at the time of writing editing a special issue of *Shakespeare: A Journal* on the related theme of Shakespeare and the Meaning of Life.
[15] Peter Holbrook, *Shakespeare's Individualism* (Cambridge University Press, forthcoming).

generation of Postmodernist theorists had assumed. And Kant's great successors in this tradition turn out to be Theodor Adorno and Walter Benjamin, who, building on crucial concepts from Kant – along with others from Hegel, Marx, Nietzsche, and Freud – each and in concert critique aspects of classical Kantian aesthetics ('pure' formalism, 'organic' unity) while retaining its sense of art as autonomous from the social reality it represents and of subjectivity as a bulwark against commodity culture's threat to reify all of human experience. In this respect the 'New Aestheticism' developed in recent years in Britain deserves great credit for bringing precisely this project to the floor – a project of advancing Postmodernist theory and practice by a return-with-a-difference to subjectivity and aesthetics.[16]

Within Shakespeare studies, the work of John J. Joughin has been exemplary in bringing the thinking of the new aestheticism into the field. In addition to his work as co-editor of *The New Aestheticism*, Joughin has authored a number of studies using its ideas to advance our understanding of Shakespeare's writings as artworks in our present. Joughin was perhaps the first Shakespearean operating from within the critical premises of literary and cultural theory to make the case that it is not simply an anachronism to speak of aesthetic ideas implied in Shakespeare's texts, and he did so convincingly in a reading of *The Winter's Tale* in 2000. He has continued to make this case in his essay on *Hamlet* adaptations in *The New Aestheticism* anthology, and I have already referenced his ground-breaking essay on *A Midsummer Night's Dream*'s Bottom above in Chapter 2. Joughin's work has been a valuable inspiration for my present effort.[17]

Similar impulses have developed in recent years in the United States, and they have come into new prominence of late with the efforts of Marjorie Levinson, President of the Modern Languages Association in 2006, to feature works of what she terms a 'new formalism', both through the program of the 2006 MLA convention in Philadelphia and in a survey

---

[16] See Joughin and Malpas (eds.), *The New Aestheticism* for a varied collection of essays making the case for a return to an aesthetics incorporating the newer critical methodologies of the recent past.

[17] See John J. Joughin, 'Shakespeare, Modernity and the Aesthetic: Art, Truth and Judgement in *The Winter's Tale*' in Hugh Grady (ed.), *Shakespeare and Modernity: From Modern to Millennium* (London: Routledge, 2000), 61–84; '*Lear*'s Afterlife', *Shakespeare Survey* 55 (2002): 67–81; 'Shakespeare's Genius: *Hamlet*, Adaptation, and the Work of Following', in Joughin and Malpas (eds.), *The New Aestheticism*, 131–50; 'Bottom's Secret …', in Ewan Fernie (ed.), *Spiritual Shakespeares* (London: Routledge, 2005), 130–56; and 'Shakespeare's Memorial Aesthetics', in Peter Holland (ed.), *Shakespeare, Memory and Performance* (Cambridge University Press, 2006), 43–62.

of the field published in the March 2007 issue of *PMLA*. The movement originated a good deal earlier than that, however. Douglas Bruster writes that the earliest use of the term 'new formalism' can be traced to a 1989 MLA session organized by early modern scholar-critic Heather Dubrow,[18] and Dubrow remains an important developer of its ideas.[19] A special issue of *Modern Language Quarterly* in 2000 presented articles defining several versions of the tendency, and Mark David Rasmussen's 2002 critical anthology *Renaissance Literature and Its Formal Engagements* was a milestone collection of documents promulgating 'the new formalism' within Shakespeare and early modern studies.[20]

The trend continues with a variation in a very recent critical anthology edited by Stephen Cohen, *Shakespeare and Historical Formalism*, whose Introduction advocates an investigation of form promised but not actually carried out by the politically inflected criticism of the new historicism. Cohen thus calls for a critical synthesis not unlike my own here – albeit a synthesis described as an encounter between new historicism and new formalism, without reference to Adorno or Benjamin.[21]

While I am sympathetic to this approach, and more broadly with Levinson's (and others') championing of what is in many ways a call for a return to the aesthetic congruent with my own, I find myself uncomfortable with the term 'new formalism' because, as should be clear, I do not think it is the form of art *per se* which needs re-emphasis, so much as the complex relation of the formed artwork with the social reality from which it draws its materials. As Adorno has emphasized, the 'content' of art, as much as the 'form', needs attention. By framing this critical development in terms of 'reinstat[ing] the problematic of form',[22] Levinson is in danger of succumbing to the very idea of 'form as an inherent as opposed to interactional or historically contingent property of the work' she warns against in her essay.[23]

---

[18] Douglas Bruster, *Shakespeare and the Question of Culture: Early Modern Literature and the Cultural Turn* (New York: Palgrave, 2003), 169.

[19] See Heather Dubrow, *A Happier Eden: The Politics of Marriage in the Stuart Epithalamium* (Ithaca, NY: Cornell University Press, 1990); *Shakespeare and Domestic Loss: Forms of Deprivation, Mourning, and Recuperation* (Cambridge University Press, 1999); 'Guess Who's Coming to Dinner? Reinterpreting Formalism and the Country House Poem', *Modern Languages Quarterly* 61.1 (March 2000), 59–72; and *The Challenges of Orpheus: Lyric Poetry and Early Modern England* (Baltimore, Md.: Johns Hopkins University Press, 2007).

[20] Mark David Rasmussen (ed.), *Renaissance Literature and Its Formal Engagements* (New York: Palgrave, 2002).

[21] Stephen Cohen, Introduction, in Stephen Cohen (ed.), *Shakespeare and Historical Formalism* (New York: Ashgate, 2007), 1–27.

[22] Marjorie Levinson, 'What is New Formalism?', *PMLA* 122.2 (March 2007) 558–69; 561.

[23] *Ibid.*, 567.

As Levinson construes the field of the new formalism, it is a 'mixed bag',[24] containing two different 'strains': 'activist' and 'normative'. The latter is, in my own terms, an Apollonian aesthetic, one that focuses on literariness as such and emphasizes its connections to Kant and the old New Critics. Much closer to the kind of aesthetics advocated here is the strain Levinson calls 'activist', which looks to Fredric Jameson and Theodor Adorno for some of its key concepts and sees form as a dynamic, 'productive' principle, mediating the historical contexts in which it was constructed.[25] All in all, however, the new formalism is one more sign that the profession is ready to move on from its nearly thirty-year sojourn in historicism.

THE TURN TO 'RETURNS'

Although this work is minimally involved in its details, one of the most significant developments in the larger field of literary studies in the last few years has resulted from a gradual assimilation of the late work of Jacques Derrida. In a remarkable set of new and relatively more accessible essays, Derrida set an agenda for a new stage of critical theory through what he called a 'return' to 'religion' – encompassing as well a return to such previously deconstructed key words as 'presence', 'spirituality', and 'aesthetics'.[26] All of these terms had been contaminated by the metaphysics of presence, but in the last period before his untimely death, Derrida made a number of attempts to recuperate their value while redefining their meaning in the light of his earlier deconstructions. The details are far beyond the scope of this brief discussion, but Derrida's re-engagement with formerly dismissed categories is clearly an important precedent for contemporary attempts to refunction the idea of the aesthetic for the twenty-first century.

We find a similar impulse in Fredric Jameson's recent call for a 'return' to the utopian – in his argument that in the recent climate of widespread acceptance of unregulated free markets, oppositional politics will need to re-engage with the idea of the utopian – and learn lessons from history and from recent political developments to carry forward into the changing political environment in the aftermath of the economic collapse

---

[24] *Ibid.*, 562. [25] *Ibid.*, 559–61.
[26] See Herman Rapaport, *Later Derrida: Reading the Recent Work* (New York: Routledge, 2003) for a good overview of Derrida's work since his 'ethical turn' in dialogue with Emmanuel Levinas in the 1980s. A convenient selection of essays from this period is Jacques Derrida, *Acts of Religion*, ed. Gil Anidjar (London: Routledge, 2002).

of late 2008 – such as that Jameson finds in Hegel's criticism of the French Terror:

Hegel, whose sympathies with the French revolution were already profound and considerable, was also capable of proposing a historically original post-Enlightenment 'solution' to the problem of religion and so-called irrationalism. The mistake of the Revolution, he argues, was to have insisted on the elimination of its cultural antithesis; and the result of this insistence was the Terror. Hegel's dialectic on the other hand suggests (it is a whole political program) that we need to go all the way through religion and come out on the other side: absorbing all its positive features – it is after all in this period culture and desire, the very content of the premodern superstructure as such – in order to combine them with an Enlightenment impulse no longer menaced by reduction to instrumental reason and the narrower forms of bourgeois positivism.[27]

A similar 'return' with a difference can be seen in the recent development within Shakespeare studies of new forms of criticism which can be described under the labels 'presentism' and 'green' or Ecocriticism – allies, as I see it, of 'the new aestheticism' and 'impure aesthetics'.

ECOCRITICISM

Despite the fact that they have seldom been clearly articulated, contemporary 'green' or Ecocriticism has pronounced commonalities with and connections to (impure) aesthetics. Shakespearean critic Jonathan Bate, for instance, alludes to this connection at several points in his chapter on *The Tempest* and elsewhere in his 2000 work *The Song of the Earth*[28] – although the main inspiration for his version of Ecocriticism has clearly been the writings of Wordsworth and the German and British Romantics rather than Shakespeare. But, as demonstrated by Bate and other Ecocritics, the ideal of a harmonization of the human world with the natural, or of the deconstruction of the human/natural binary opposition, is as central to Ecocriticism as it is to post-Kantian aesthetics – most especially to Theodor Adorno's unfashionable and persistent championing of the thesis that every work of art worthy of the name projects (and ultimately fails in) a reconciliation with nature that is an inextricable part of the beautiful.[29] 'Art', he writes, is 'the afterimage of human repression of nature, [it] simultaneously negates this repression

[27] Fredric Jameson, *Archaeologies of the Future: The Desire Called Utopia and Other Science Fictions* (London: Verso, 2005), 65.
[28] Jonathan Bate, *The Song of the Earth* (Cambridge, Mass.: Harvard University Press, 2000), 68–93.
[29] Adorno, *Aesthetic Theory*, 61–78, especially 63; and 273–75.

through reflection and draws close to nature ... In the semblance of the restoration of the mutilated other to its own form, art becomes the model of the unmutilated.'[30]

It is not surprising that Adorno has already been recognized by some green critics as an important source of ideas. Bate mentions Adorno in this context,[31] as does Lawrence Coupe, who, in his General Introduction to a critical anthology on Ecocriticism, also speaks of a 'return' to a concept of nature with roots in Romanticism (and also in Eastern spirituality).[32] But with its organizing idea that the ecological movement has strong links to the literary Romanticism of William Wordsworth, the collection in several instances touches on the links between the aesthetic and the ecological movement, and it re-prints a dense excerpt from Adorno's *Aesthetic Theory*, the section in which Adorno discusses the concept of natural beauty and its relation to works of art.[33]

In Shakespeare studies, 'green' criticism is still young, but it is rapidly developing. Gabriel Egan's *Green Shakespeare* is the first monograph to have appeared in the field, and this work enacts its own version of the theme of a 'return', in Egan's case a return to an idea of nature that had been undermined in the 'linguistic turn' of Postmodernism but can be reconceptualized by new scientific developments:

In curious ways, the new ideas about nature and animals have analogues in old ideas expressed in Shakespeare's plays, and for the New Age fringe of ecopolitics this suggests that the entire eighteenth century Enlightenment was a mistake of hyper-rationality. However, we do not have to adopt such an irrationalist stance in order to think and act ecopolitically and ecocritically, because the latest developments in science and philosophy (representing the heights of rationality) also return us to the same fundamental problems of human existence regarding our relations one with another, and with nature and the animals, that the plays dramatize.[34]

Green criticism seems to be of increasing interest in Shakespeare studies. There have been seminars on the subject at the Shakespeare Association of America's Annual Meetings of 2002 and 2006, the British Shakespeare Association Conference of 2005, and the World Shakespeare Conference of 2006. Growing interest in the topic is evidenced by Sharon O'Dair's report that while in 2002 only eight participants signed up for

[30] *Ibid.*, 288.   [31] Bate, *Song of the Earth*, 119–24 and throughout.
[32] Lawrence Coupe, General Introduction, in Lawrence Coupe (ed.), *The Green Studies Reader: From Romanticism to Ecocriticism* (London: Rouledge, 2000), 1–8.
[33] Adorno, *Aesthetic Theory*, 61–62, 65–66, 73–74; reprinted as 'Nature as "Not Yet"', in Coupe (ed.), *The Green Reader*, 81–83.
[34] Gabriel Egan, *Green Shakespeare: From Ecopolitics to Ecocriticism* (London: Routledge, 2006), 3.

that year's Shakespeare Association of America seminar on Shakespeare and Ecocriticism, in 2006 at the SAA Annual Meeting a similarly titled seminar attracted twenty.[35] Several articles by such critics as Simon Estok[36] and Sharon O'Dair[37] have already appeared, and others are in process as I write. In all these forums it has been apparent that the central aesthetic issue of the relationship between humanity and nature is a central issue of green criticism as well.

PRESENTISM AND AESTHETICS

The 'presentist' movement within Shakespeare studies with which I have been associated in recent years is another critical tendency of the present that shares values with the 'impure aesthetics' I am working with here – although not every practising presentist would necessarily embrace it. 'Presentism', as Terence Hawkes and I construed the term, was meant to be broad, providing a 'big tent' for a large array of contemporary critical practices that share the assumption that the critic's own situation in our cultural present is a resource for, rather than an impediment to, a productive and insightful reading of Shakespeare – or indeed, other writings in and out of the critical 'canon'. Its primary motivation was our shared perception that the 'new materialism' (see the Introduction above for this argument) was rapidly evolving into an anti-political and anti-aesthetic critical methodology that threatened to negate thirty years of the field's self-education in cultural theory.[38] The 'new materialism' as

---

[35] Sharon O'Dair, 'Slow Shakespeare; or, Reversing Our Crimes Against Nature', in Karen Raber and Ivo Kamps (eds.), *Early Modern Ecostudies*, forthcoming. My thanks to Sharon O'Dair for providing me with a pre-publication typescript of her article.

[36] See Simon Estok, 'Teaching the Environment of *The Winter's Tale*: Ecocritical Theory and Pedagogy for Shakespeare', in Lloyd Davis (ed.), *Shakespeare Matters: History, Teaching, Performance* (Newark, Del.: University of Delaware Press, 2003), 177–90; Estok, 'Sangtae beapung eui hangae rul numerseogee [Pushing the Limits of Ecocriticism: Environment and Social Resistance in *2 Henry IV* and *2 Henry VI*]', *Shakespeare Review* (Seoul) 40: (2004), 631–58; and Estok (ed.), Special Cluster on Shakespeare and Ecocriticism, *Interdisciplinary Studies in Literature and the Environment (ISLE)*, 12:2 (2005), 109–17.

[37] See Sharon O'Dair, '*The Tempest* as *Tempest*: Does Paul Mazursky "Green" William Shakespeare?', *Interdisciplinary Studies in Literature and the Environment (ISLE)* 12.2 (Summer 2005), 165–178; 'Horror or Realism? Filming "Toxic Discourse" in Jane Smiley's *A Thousand Acres*', *Textual Practice* 19.2 (June 2005), 263–82; 'A way of life worth preserving? Identity, Place, and Commerce in Big Business and the American South', *Borrowers and Lenders: The Journal of Shakespeare and Appropriation* 1.1 (Spring 2005), www.borrowers.uga.edu/borrowers/archive; 'Toward a Postmodern Pastoral: Another Look at the Cultural Politics of *My Own Private Idaho*', *Journal x* 7 (Autumn 2002), 25–40.

[38] See Hugh Grady and Terence Hawkes, 'Introduction: Presenting Presentism,' in Hugh Grady and Terence Hawkes (eds.), *Presentist Shakespeares* (London: Routledge, 2007), 1–5.

we saw it – despite some exceptional figures within it who resisted this anti-theoretical trend, like Peter Stallybrass and Gil Scott Harris – was providing cover for a revival of the discredited idea of an 'objective' past that is transparently open to our modern sensibilities. We welcomed any critics who shared that idea and offered the simple but consequential idea that criticism today should interrogate its own historicist inclinations – and deepen them through reflection on what it is in our present culture and situation that structures our appropriation and valorization of texts of the past like Shakespeare's. We specifically argued that recent criticism's neglect of the aesthetic dimensions of Shakespeare was one result of the field's focus on historicism and called for 'new approaches' to aesthetics as part of a developing Presentist critical practice.[39]

Terence Hawkes – who should be given the lion's share of the credit for developing and promoting critical 'presentism' in Shakespeare studies – is an astute practitioner of the art of criticism whose essays themselves are Postmodernist artworks which embed the interpretation of Shakespearean texts in a kaleidoscope of changing contexts so that, as in many pieces of contemporary performance art, it becomes impossible to separate the changing artwork from the contexts in which it takes its meaning. Hawkes's reader of Shakespeare becomes a co-creator of an exhilarating, multi-faceted, politically charged, and disunified Postmodernist art-work, and in that sense his works are fully within today's new aesthetics, even though Hawkes has not been inclined to discuss aesthetic theory directly. He has, however, used the figure of the performativity of jazz as an analogue to both critical practice and to the art of drama itself,[40] and this analogy is an aesthetic one in important ways.

Some other Presentists more directly appropriate aesthetic theory into our writings. Ewan Fernie should be mentioned as someone who has taken up this 'aesthetic' version of presentism and is developing it into a critical theory related to but somewhat different in its details from my own work and that of the British New Aestheticists.[41] Partly inspired by a critical relationship with Levinas and the late Derrida, partly by an increasing commitment to a more phenomenological encounter with the literary text, Fernie has advanced the interesting thesis that *all* art

---

[39] Grady and Hawkes, 'Introduction: Presenting Presentism', in Grady and Hawkes, eds., *Presentist Shakespeares*, 4.
[40] Terence Hawkes, *Shakespeare in the Present* (London: Routledge, 2002), 124–26.
[41] Ewan Fernie, 'Shakespeare and the Prospect of Presentism', *Shakespeare Survey* 58 (2005), 169–84; 'Action! *Henry V*', in Grady and Hawkes (eds.), *Presentist Shakespeares*, 96–120; and 'The Last Act: Presentism, Spirituality, and the Politics of *Hamlet*, in Ewan Fernie (ed.), *Spiritual Shakespeares* (London: Routledge, 2005), 186–211.

238 *Conclusion*

forms, to the extent that they operate as works of art, unfold within the present. 'It is time', Fernie writes, 'after new historicism, to recover the creativity and agency that blaze in the Shakespearean text as the promise of human possibility. Creativity is the best-known and most obvious face of art. How can we ignore it?'[42] This is an idea which I think is fully compatible with the Adorno–Benjamin aesthetic theory discussed here – indeed, Benjamin himself suggested something similar in the epigrammatic language of his celebrated essay, 'The Work of Art in the Age of Mechanical Reproduction':

The uniqueness of a work of art is inseparable from its being embedded in the fabric of tradition. This tradition itself is thoroughly alive and extremely changeable. An ancient statue of Venus, for example, stood in a different traditional context with the Greeks, who made it an object of veneration, than with the clerics of the Middle Ages, who viewed it as an ominous idol. Both of them, however, were equally confronted with its uniqueness, that is, its aura.[43]

Feminist and gender studies also have clear Presentist principles – both of these critical methods make use of contemporary theory and sensibility to re-illumine the works and cultural assumptions about sexuality and gender of the past. These connections are explored in a new collection of essays edited by Evelyn Gajowski, *Presentism, Gender, and Sexuality in Shakespeare*, a wide-ranging critical anthology with contributions from both feminism and gender studies and illustrating the radical presentness of the way we construct the meaning of Shakespeare.[44] While cultural politics is more central to this collection than aesthetics, several of the essays, particularly the four focused on performance on stage and screen, also address issues of form, genre, and the interplay of ideology and art.

Cary diPietro is another Presentist critic who raises the relevance of new aesthetic categories, in his case through a very consequential re-engagement with the theories of Fredric Jameson within a larger re-opening of inquiry into the complex story of the impact of aesthetic Modernism on the twentieth-century's Shakespeare.[45] In this multi-facetted work, DiPietro complicates and enriches our understanding of the interactions of cultural 'moments' with the construction of Shakespearean meaning – and of aesthetics in the more general sense as that medium in which

[42] Fernie, 'Shakespeare and the Prospect of Presentism', 183.
[43] Walter Benjamin, 'The Work of Art in the Age of Mechanical Reproduction', in Walter Benjamin, *Illuminations*, ed. Hannah Arendt, trans. Harry Zohn (New York: Schocken, 1969), 217–51; 223.
[44] Evelyn Gajowski (ed.), *Presentism, Gender, and Sexuality in Shakespeare* (New York: Palgrave, 2009).
[45] Cary DiPietro, *Shakespeare and Modernism* (Cambridge University Press, 2006).

Shakespearean meaning is formed – organizing his study in an intricate but well-wrought intertexuality of such figures as George Bernard Shaw, Sigmund Freud, Frank Harris, T. S. Eliot, Virginia Woolf, and a number of theatrical productions. DiPietro demonstrates with new materials the thesis that art is always of the 'now', always complexly implicated in an ever-changing historical landscape – and shows us again that if Shakespeare, as Ben Jonson had it, was 'not of an age but for all time', he has been in all time(s) constantly re-invented and re-interpreted in the complex shifting of how we conceptualize art in every era.

SHAKESPEARE AS ART

Hegel made a convincing case in his aesthetic theory that there can be no limits to the subject matter of art, that art history is – in a sense that can survive outside of Hegel's Idealist framework – simply the search of the mind and spirit of collective humanity to find forms adequate to our always evolving historical development. But this most Idealist of all philosophers since Plato needs to be corrected in this instance with the materialist observations of Georges Bataille, that art – and particularly literary art – seems to recur constantly to three fundamental bodily functions of sexual reproduction (the comic), of digestive elimination (the satirical), and of death itself (the tragic). Thus while there are no limits to what art can use as the material of its forms, there are recurring themes and pre-occupations, all connected to the bodily limits of human exist-ence and experience. The works of Shakespeare examined here are clear illustrations of all of these contradictory statements, as we can see in the infinite variety of Shakespeare's writing – but also in the pervasive spirit of sexuality in the comedy of *A Midsummer Night's Dream*, in the corrosive, aggressive, and intellectually probing satirical-comical-tragical spirit of *Timon of Athens*, and in the death-obsessed aesthetics of *Hamlet*. Finally (in this study), *Romeo and Juliet* seems to show aspects of all of these – although satire (to be found in the inspired wit of Mercutio) is faintest of all in this young work. But in this often underrated early masterpiece, Shakespeare managed simultaneously to affirm the beauty of nature and desire, the ineluctability of death, the vulnerability of humanity to its own creations, culture, and science – and the power of art to represent all this so that we can both think and feel the immensity of existence. A 'return' to these themes can and should hold an important place on the agenda of a myriad-minded Shakespeare studies in its next phase as it defines itself once again in terms of a constantly changing present.

Bibliography

Adelman, Janet, *Suffocating Mothers: Fantasies of Maternal Origin in Shakespeare's Plays*, excerpted and reprinted in Wofford (ed.), *Hamlet*, 256–82.

Adorno, Theodor W., *Aesthetic Theory*, ed. Gretel Adorno and Rolf Tiedemann, trans. Robert Hullot-Kentor, Minneapolis, Minn.: University of Minnesota Press, 1997.

'Letter to Walter Benjamin, 5 June 1935', in Theodor W. Adorno and Walter Benjamin, *The Complete Correspondence, 1928–1940*, ed. Henri Lonitz, trans. Nicholas Walter, Cambridge, Mass.: Harvard University Press, 1999.

Minima Moralia: Reflections from Damaged Life, trans. E. F. N. Jephcott, London: New Left Books, 1974.

'Nature as "Not Yet"', in Lawrence Coupe (ed.), *The Green Studies Reader: From Romanticism to Ecocriticism*, London: Routledge, 2000, 81–83.

Negative Dialectics, trans. E. B. Ashton, New York: Continuum, 1983.

Notes to Literature, ed. Rolf Tiedemann, trans. Shierry Weber Nicholsen, 2 vols., New York: Columbia University Press, 1991, 1992.

Agnew, Jean-Christophe, *Worlds Apart: The Market and the Theater in Anglo-American Thought, 1550–1750*, Cambridge University Press, 1986.

Alighieri, Dante, *La Vita Nuova*, trans. D. G. Rossetti, in *The Portable Dante*, ed. Paolo Milano, New York: Viking, 1947.

Althusser, Louis, 'A Letter on Art in Reply to André Daspre', in Louis Althusser, *Lenin and Philosophy and Other Essays*, trans. Ben Brewster, New York: Monthly Review Press, 1971, 221–27.

'Ideology and Ideological State Apparatuses: Notes towards an Investigation' in Louis Althusser, *Lenin and Philosophy and Other Essays*, trans. Ben Brewster, New York: Monthly Review Press, 1978, 127–86.

Ariès, Philippe, *The Hour of Our Death*, trans. Helen Weaver, New York: Knopf, 1981.

Western Attitudes Toward Death: From the Middle Ages to the Present, trans. Patricia M. Ranum, Baltimore, Md.: Johns Hopkins University Press, 1974.

Armstrong, Isobel, *The Radical Aesthetic*, Oxford: Blackwell, 2000.

Baillie, John, 'An Essay on the Sublime' (1747), in Andrew Ashfield and Peter de Bolla (eds.), *The Sublime: A Reader in British Eighteenth-Century Aesthetic Theory*, Cambridge University Press, 1996, 87–100.

Balibar, Étienne and Pierre Macherey, 'On Literature as an Ideological Form', in Terry Eagleton and Drew Milne (eds.), *Marxist Literary Theory*, Oxford: Blackwell, 1996, 275–95.

Barber, C. L., *Shakespeare's Festive Comedy: A Study of Dramatic Form and its Relation to Social Custom*, 1959; reprinted Cleveland, Oh.: Meridian, 1967.

Barkan, Leonard, *The Gods Made Flesh: Metamorphosis and the Pursuit of Paganism*, New Haven, Conn.: Yale University Press, 1986.

Barker, Francis, *The Tremulous Private Body: Essays in Subjection*, London: Methuen, 1984.

Bataille, Georges, *The Accursed Share*, trans. Robert Hurley, 3 vols., New York: Zone Books, 1991, 1993.

Erotism: Death and Sensuality, trans. Mary Dalwood, San Francisco, Calif.: City Light Books, 1957.

Bate, Jonathan, *The Genius of Shakespeare*, London: Picador, 1997.

The Song of the Earth, Cambridge, Mass.: Harvard University Press, 2000.

Battenhouse, Roy, 'Falstaff as Parodist and Perhaps Holy Fool', *PMLA* 90.1 (Jan. 1975), 32–52.

Shakespearean Tragedy: Its Art and Its Christian Premises, Bloomington, Ind.: Indiana University Press, 1969.

Benjamin, Andrew, 'Benjamin's Modernity', in Ferris (ed.), *The Cambridge Companion to Walter* Benjamin, 97–114.

Benjamin, Walter, *The Arcades Project*, ed. Rolf Tiedemann, trans. Howard Eiland and Kevin McLaughlin, Cambridge, Mass.: Belknap, 1999.

'Edward Fuchs, Collector and Historian', in Walter Benjamin, *Selected Writings*, 4 vols., ed. Howard Eiland and Michael W. Jennings, trans. Edmund Jephcott, Howard Eiland, *et al.*, Cambridge, Mass.: Belknap, 2002, Vol. III, 260–302.

'Letter to Theodor W. Adorno, 17 July, 1931', in Henri Lonitz (ed.), *The Complete Correspondence, 1928–1940*, Cambridge, Mass.: Harvard University Press, 1999.

'On Language as Such and on the Language of Man', in Walter Benjamin, *Reflections: Essays, Aphorisms, Autobiographical Writings*, ed. Peter Demetz, New York: Harcourt Brace Jovanovich, 1978, 314–32.

'On the Mimetic Faculty,' in Walter Benjamin, *Reflections: Essays, Aphorisms, Autobiographical Writings*, ed. Peter Demetz, New York: Harvest, 1979, 333–36.

The Origin of German Tragic Drama, trans. John Osborne, London: New Left Books, 1977; originally published as *Ursprung des deutschen Trauerspiels*, Berlin: E. Rowohlt, 1928.

'Paris, the Capital of the Nineteenth Century: Exposé "of 1939"' in Benjamin, *The Arcades Project*, ed. Tiedemann, Cambridge, Mass.: Belknap, 1999, 22–23.

'The Study Begins with Some Reflections on the Influences of *Les Fleurs du mal*', in Walter Benjamin, *Selected Writings*, ed. Howard Eiland and Michael W. Jennings, 4 vols., Cambridge, Mass.: Belknap, 2003, Vol. IV, 95–98.

Understanding Brecht, trans. Anna Bostock, London: New Left Books, 1973.

'The Work of Art in the Age of Mechanical Reproduction', in Walter Benjamin, *Illuminations*, ed. Hannah Arendt, New York: Schocken, 1969, 217–51.

Bernstein, Jay, *The Fate of Art: Aesthetic Alienation from Kant to Derrida and Adorno*, Cambridge: Polity Press, 1992.

Bloch, Ernst, *The Principle of Hope*, trans. Neville Plaice, Stephen Plaice, and Paul Knight, Cambridge, Mass.: MIT Press, 1986; trans. of *Das Prinzip Hoffnung*, 3 vols., Berlin: Aufbau-Verlag, 1954–59.

The Utopian Function of Art and Literature: Selected Essays, trans. Jack Zipes and Frank Mecklenburg, Cambridge, Mass: MIT Press, 1988.

Bloom, Harold, *Shakespeare: The Invention of the Human*, New York: Riverhead, 1998.

Bonnard, George A., 'Shakespeare's Purpose in *Midsummer-Night's Dream*', *Shakespeare Jahrbuch* 92 (1956), 268–79.

Bourdieu, Pierre, *Distinction: A Social Critique of the Judgement of Taste*, trans. Richard Nice, Cambridge, Mass.: Harvard University Press, 1984.

Bowie, Andrew, *Aesthetics and Subjectivity: From Kant to Nietzsche*, 2nd edn., Manchester University Press, 2003.

From Romanticism to Critical Theory: The Philosophy of German Literary Theory, London: Routledge, 1997.

Bradley, A. C., *Shakespearean Tragedy: Lectures on 'Hamlet', 'Othello', 'King Lear', and 'Macbeth'*, 1904; reprinted Harmondsworth: Penguin, 1991.

Brandes, Georg, *William Shakespeare: A Critical Study*, trans. William Archer and Diana White, 2 vols., New York: F. Ungar, 1963.

Bristol, Michael D., ' "Funeral Bak'd Meats": Carnival and the Carnivalesque in *Hamlet*', in Wofford (ed.), *Hamlet*, 348–67.

Bruster, Douglas, *Drama and the Market in the Age of Shakespeare,* Cambridge University Press, 1992.

Shakespeare and the Question of Culture: Early Modern Literature and the Cultural Turn, New York: Palgrave, 2003.

Buck-Morss, Susan, *The Dialectics of Seeing: Walter Benjamin and the Arcades Project*, Cambridge, Mass.: MIT Press, 1991.

The Origin of Negative Dialectics: Theodor W. Adorno, Walter Benjamin, and the Frankfurt Institute, New York: Free Press, 1977.

Bullough, Geoffrey (ed.), *Narrative and Dramatic Sources of Shakespeare*, 8 vols., London: Routledge and Paul, 1957–75.

Burckhardt, Jacob, *The Civilization of the Renaissance in Italy*, trans. S. G. C. Middlemore, Harmondsworth: Penguin, 1990.

Burke, Kenneth, *Language as Symbolic Action: Essays on Life, Literature, and Method*, Berkeley, Calif.: University of California Press, 1966.

Callaghan, Dympna, 'Comedy and Epyllion in Post-Reformation England', *Shakespeare Survey* 56 (2003), 27–38.

Shakespeare Without Women: Representing Gender and Race on the Renaissance Stage, London: Routledge, 2000.

Caygill, Howard, 'Walter Benjamin's Concept of Cultural History,' in Ferris (ed.), *The Cambridge Companion to Walter Benjamin*, 73–96.

Chambers, E. K., *William Shakespeare: A Study of Facts and Problems*, 2 vols., Oxford: Clarendon, 1930, Vol. 1.

Charlton, H. B., *Shakesperian Tragedy*, Cambridge University Press, 1948.

Charney, Maurice, Introduction to *Timon of Athens*, in *The Complete Signet Shakespeare*, ed. Sylvan Barnet, New York: Harcourt, 1972.

Chorost, Michael, 'Biological Finance in Shakespeare's *Timon of Athens*', ELR 21 (1991), 349–70.

Clark, Michael (ed.), *Revenge of the Aesthetic: The Place of Literature in Theory Today*, Berkeley, Calif.: University of California, 2000.

Cohen, Stephen, Introduction, in Stephen Cohen (ed.), *Shakespeare and Historical Formalism*, New York: Ashgate, 2007, 1–27.

Coleridge, Samuel Taylor, *Coleridge's Shakespearean Criticism*, ed. Thomas Raysor, 2 vols., Cambridge, Mass.: Harvard University Press, 1930, Vol. 1.

'From Shakespearean Criticism', in David Perkins (ed.), *English Romantic Writers*, New York: Harcourt, 1967, 496–502.

The Statesman's Manual, London: Gale and Fenner, 1816, excerpted and reprinted in David Perkins (ed.), *English Romantic Writers*, New York: Harcourt, 1967, 496–502.

Comay, Rebecca, 'Benjamin and the Ambiguities of Romanticism', in Ferris (ed.), *The Cambridge Companion to Walter Benjamin*, 134–51.

Cooper, David E. (ed.), *Aesthetics: The Classic Readings*, Oxford: Blackwell, 1997.

Cotter, Holland, 'Pumping Air into the Museum, So It's as Big as the World Outside', *The New York Times*, April 30, 2004; www.nytimes.com, Archives.

Coupe, Lawrence, General Introduction, in Lawrence Coupe (ed.), *The Green Studies Reader: From Romanticism to Ecocriticism*, London: Routledge, 2000, 1–8.

Creuzer, Georg Friedrich, *Symbolik und Mythologie der alten Völker, besonders der Griechen*, 2 vols., Leipzig, Darmstadt, 1819.

Croce, Benedetto, *The Essence of Aesthetic*, trans. Douglas Ainslie, London: Heinemann, 1921.

D[avies], A[nthony], '*Timon of Athens*', in Michael Dobson and Stanley Wells (eds.), *The Oxford Companion to Shakespeare*, Oxford University Press, 2001.

Dawson, Anthony B. and Gretchen E. Minton (eds.), *Timon of Athens*, by William Shakespeare and Thomas Middleton, Arden Shakespeare Third Series, London, Arden, 2008.

de Man, Paul, 'Conclusions: Walter Benjamin's "The Task of the Translator"' in *The Resistance to Theory*, Minneapolis, Minn.: University of Minnesota Press, 1986, 73–105.

The Rhetoric of Romanticism, New York: Columbia University Press, 1984.

'Sign and Symbol in Hegel's *Aesthetics*', *Critical Inquiry* 8.4 (Summer 1982), 761–75.

de Rougemont, Denis, *Love in the Western World*, trans. Montgomery Belgion, Princeton University Press, 1983.

Dent, R. W., 'Imagination in *A Midsummer Night's Dream*', *Shakespeare Quarterly* 15 (1964), 115–29; reprinted in Kehler (ed.), '*A Midsummer Night's Dream*', 85–106.

Derrida, Jacques, *Acts of Religion*, ed. Gil Anidjar, London: Routledge, 2002.
  Specters of Marx: The State of the Debt, the Work of Mourning, and the New International, trans. Peggy Kamuf, New York: Routledge, 1994.

Desmet, Christy, 'Disfiguring Women with Masculine Tropes: A Rhetorical Reading of *A Midsummer Night's Dream*', in Kehler (ed.), '*A Midsummer Night's Dream*', 299–329.

Dewey, John, *Art as Experience*, New York: Minton Balch, 1934.

DiPietro, Cary, *Shakespeare and Modernism*, Cambridge University Press, 2006.

Dobson, Michael, 'Shakespeare as a Joke: The English Comic Tradition, *A Midsummer Night's Dream* and Amateur Performance', *Shakespeare Survey* 56 (2003), 117–25.

Dollimore, Jonathan, 'Art in Time of War: Towards a Contemporary Aesthetic', in John J. Joughin and Simon Malpas (eds.), *The New Aestheticism*, Manchester University Press, 2003, 36–50.
  Death, Desire and Loss in Western Culture, New York: Routledge, 1998.
  Radical Tragedy: Religion, Ideology and Power in the Drama of Shakespeare and his Contemporaries, 3rd edn., Durham, NC: Duke University Press, 2004.

Draper, John W., 'The Theme of "Timon of Athens"', *Modern Language Review* 29.1 (Jan., 1934), 20–31.

Dubrow, Heather, *A Happier Eden: The Politics of Marriage in the Stuart Epithalamium*, Ithaca, NY: Cornell University Press, 1990.
  The Challenges of Orpheus: Lyric Poetry and Early Modern England, Baltimore, Md.: Johns Hopkins University Press, 2007.
  'Guess Who's Coming to Dinner? Reinterpreting Formalism and the Country House Poem', *Modern Languages Quarterly* 61.1 (March 2000), 59–72.
  Shakespeare and Domestic Loss: Forms of Deprivation, Mourning, and Recuperation, Cambridge University Press, 1999.

Dutton, Richard and Jean E. Howard (eds.), *A Companion to Shakespeare's Works*, 4 Vols, Vol. 1: *The Tragedies*, Oxford: Blackwell, 2003.

Eagleton, Terry, *After Theory*, New York: Basic, 2003.
  Ideology: An Introduction, London: Verso, 1991.
  The Ideology of the Aesthetic, Oxford: Blackwell, 1990.
  Sweet Violence: The Idea of the Tragic, Oxford: Blackwell, 2003.
  William Shakespeare, Oxford: Blackwell, 1986.

Egan, Gabriel, *Green Shakespeare: From Ecopolitics to Ecocriticism*, London: Routledge, 2006.

Eliot, T. S., 'Dante', in *The Sacred Wood: Essays on Poetry and Criticism*, London: Methuen, 1920; reprinted New York: Barnes and Noble, 1960, 159–71.
  'The Metaphysical Poets', in *Selected Essays*, New York: Harcourt, 1950, 241–50.

Elliott, Robert C., *The Power of Satire: Magic, Ritual, Art*, Princeton University Press, 1960.

Ellis-Fermor, Una, '"Timon of Athens": An Unfinished Play', *The Review of English Studies* 18 (July 1942), 270–83.

Emerson, Ralph Waldo, 'Shakspear' [First Lecture], in *The Early Lectures of Ralph Waldo Emerson*, 3 vols., ed. Stephen E. Whiches and Robert E. Spiller, Cambridge, Mass.: Belknap, 1966, Vol. i, 289–292.

Empson, William, *The Structure of Complex Words*, 3rd edn., London: Chatto & Windus, 1951.

Engle, Lars, *Shakespearean Pragmatism: Market of his Time*, University of Chicago Press, 1993.

Estok, Simon, 'Sangtae beapung eui hangae rul numerseogee [Pushing the Limits of Ecocriticism: Environment and Social Resistance in 2 Henry IV and 2 Henry VI]', *Shakespeare Review* (Seoul) 40 (2004), 631–58.

   'Teaching the Environment of *The Winter's Tale*: Ecocritical Theory and Pedagogy for Shakespeare', in Lloyd Davis (ed.), *Shakespeare Matters: History, Teaching, Performance*, Newark, Del.: University of Delaware Press, 2003, 177–90.

Estok, Simon (ed.), Special Cluster on Shakespeare and Ecocriticism, *Interdisciplinary Studies in Literature and the Environment (ISLE)* 12:2 (2005), 109–17.

Farnham, Willard, *Shakespeare's Tragic Frontier: The World of his Final Tragedies*, Berkeley, Calif.: University of California Press, 1950.

Ferguson, Margaret W., '*Hamlet*: Letters and Spirits', in Patricia Parker and Geoffrey Hartmann (eds.), *Shakespeare and the Question of Theory*, New York: Methuen, 1985, 292–309.

Fernie, Ewan, 'Action! *Henry V*', in Grady and Hawkes (eds.), *Presentist Shakespeares*, 96–120.

   'The Last Act: Presentism, Spirituality, and the Politics of *Hamlet*', in Ewan Fernie (ed.), *Spiritual Shakespeares*, London: Routledge, 2005, 186–211.

   'Shakespeare and the Prospect of Presentism', *Shakespeare Survey* 58 (2005), 169–84.

Ferris, David S. (ed.), *The Cambridge Companion to Walter Benjamin*, Cambridge University Press, 2004.

Foster, Hal (ed.), *The Anti-Aesthetic: Essays on Postmodern Culture*, Port Townsend, Wash.: Bay, 1983.

Freedman, Barbara, 'Dis/Figuring Power: Censorship and Representation in *A Midsummer Night's Dream*', in Kehler (ed.), '*A Midsummer Night's Dream*', 179–215.

Freud, Sigmund, 'The Theme of the Three Caskets' (1913), reprinted in Dan Latimer (ed.), *Contemporary Critical Theory*, San Diego, Calif.: Harcourt, 1989, 489–99.

Frye, Northrop, *Anatomy of Criticism: Four Essays*, New York: Atheneum, 1968.

Fumerton, Patricia, *Cultural Aesthetics: Renaissance Literature and the Practice of Social Ornament*, University of Chicago Press, 1991.

Furness, Horace Howard (ed.), *A New Variorum Edition of Shakespeare: Hamlet*, 2 vols., Philadelphia, Pa.: Lippincott, 1877; reprinted 1905.

Gajowski, Evelyn, *The Art of Loving: Female Subjectivity and Male Discursive Traditions in Shakespeare's Tragedies*, Newark, Del.: University of Delaware Press, 1992.

Gajowski, Evelyn (ed.), *Presentism, Gender, and Sexuality in Shakespeare*, New York: Palgrave, 2009.

Garber, Marjorie, *Shakespeare's Ghost Writers: Literature as Uncanny Causality*, New York: Methuen, 1987.

Garner, Shirley Nelson, '*A Midsummer Night's Dream*: "Jack Shall Have Jill; / Naught Shall Go Ill"', in Kehler (ed.), '*A Midsummer Night's Dream*', 127–44.

Gervinus, G. G., *Shakespeare Commentaries*, trans. F. E. Bunnett, revised edn., London: Smith, Elder, 1877.

Gheeraert-Graffeuille, Claire, '"Call you me fair? That 'fair' again unsay": La beauté et ses monstres', in Gheeraert-Graffeuille and Vienne-Guerrin (eds.), *Autour du 'Songe d'une nuit d'été'*, 273–74.

Gheeraert-Graffeuille, Claire and Nathalie Vienne-Guerrin (eds.), *Autour du 'Songe d'une nuit d'été' de William Shakespeare*, Rouen: Publications de l'Université de Rouen, 2003.

Gildon, Charles, 'Remarks on the Plays of Shakespeare' (1710), in *Shakespeare: The Critical Heritage*, ed. Brian Vickers, 6 vols., London: Routledge, 1974– 1981, Vol. II, 226–62.

'Remarks on the Plays of Shakespeare', in *The Works of Mr. William Shakespeare*, ed. Nicholas Rowe, 7 vols., 1710; reprinted New York, AMS Press, 1967, 369–71.

Gohlke, Madelon, '"I Woo'ed Thee with my Sword": Shakespeare's Tragic Paradigm', in Murray M. Schwartz and Coppélia Kahn (eds.), *Representing Shakespeare*, Baltimore, Md.: Johns Hopkins University Press, 1980, 170–87.

Grady, Hugh, 'Falstaff: Subjectivity between the Carnival and the Aesthetic', *Modern Language Review* 96.3 (July 2001), 609–23.

'*Hamlet* and the Present: Notes on the Moving Aesthetic "Now"', in Grady and Hawkes (eds.), *Presentist Shakespeares*, 141–63.

'Introduction: Shakespeare and Modernity', in Grady, *Shakespeare and Modernity*, 1–19.

The Modernist Shakespeare: Critical Texts in a Material World, Oxford: Clarendon, 1991.

'On the Need for a Differentiated Theory of Subjectivity', in John J. Joughin (ed.), *Shakespeare and Philosophy* (London: Routledge, 2000), 34–50.

'Renewing Modernity: Changing Contexts and Contents of a Nearly Invisible Concept', *Shakespeare Quarterly* 50.3 (Fall 1999), 268–84.

Shakespeare, Machiavelli, and Montaigne: Power and Subjectivity from 'Richard II' to 'Hamlet', Oxford University Press, 2002.

'Shakespeare Studies, 2005: A Situated Overview', *Shakespeare: A Journal* 1.1 (2005), 102–20.

Shakespeare's Universal Wolf: Studies in Early Modern Reification, Oxford: Clarendon, 1996.

'Tragedy and Materialist Thought', in Rebecca Bushnell (ed.), *A Companion to Tragedy*, Oxford: Blackwell, 2005, 128–44.

Grady, Hugh (ed.), *Shakespeare and Modernity: From Early Modern to Millennium*, London: Routledge, 2000.

Grady, Hugh and Terence Hawkes, 'Introduction: Presenting Presentism,' in Grady and Hawkes (eds.), *Presentist Shakespeares*, 1–5.

Grady, Hugh and Terence Hawkes (eds.), *Presentist Shakespeares*, London: Routledge, 2007.

Greenblatt, Stephen, *Hamlet in Purgatory*, Princeton University Press, 2001.

Introduction to *Romeo and Juliet*, in William Shakespeare, *The Norton Shakespeare*, ed. Greenblatt *et al.*, 865–71.

Learning to Curse: Essays in Early Modern Culture (New York: Routledge, 1990).

Renaissance Self-Fashioning: From More to Shakespeare, University of Chicago Press, 1980.

Shakespearean Negotiations: The Circulation of Social Energy in Renaissance England (Berkeley, Calif.: University of California Press, 1988).

Will in the World: How Shakespeare Became Shakespeare, New York: Norton, 2004.

Habermas, Jürgen, *Knowledge and Human Interests*, trans. Jeremy Shapiro, Boston, Mass.: Beacon, 1971.

The Philosophical Discourses of Modernity, trans. Frederick Lawrence, Cambridge, Mass.: MIT Press, 1987.

Society and Human Interests, trans. Jeremy Shapiro, Boston, Mass.: Beacon, 1971.

Hadfield, Andtew, *Shakespeare and Republicanism*, Cambridge University Press, 2005.

Halio, Jay L., *Shakespeare in Performance: A Midsummer Night's Dream*, 2nd edn., Manchester University Press, 2003.

Hall, Stuart, Introduction to 'Formations of Modernity', in Stuart Hall, David Held, Don Hubert, and Kenneth Thompson (eds.), *Modernity: An Introduction to Modern Societies*, Oxford: Blackwell, 1996, 3–18.

Halpern, Richard, *Shakespeare Among the Moderns*, Ithaca, NY: Cornell University Press, 1997.

'Shakespeare *contre* Benjamin', Presentation at the 2004 Modern Languages Association Convention, December 29, 2004.

Hanssen, Beatrice, *Walter Benjamin's Other History: Of Stones, Animals, Human Beings, and Angels*, Berkeley, Calif.: University of California Press, 2000.

Harris, Jonathan Gil, 'The New New Historicism's *Wunderkammer* of Objects', *European Journal of English Studies* 4.3 (2000), 111–23.

Sick Economies: Drama, Mercantilism and Disease in Shakespeare's England, Philadelphia, Pa.: University of Pennsylvania Press, 2004.

Harris, Jonathan Gil and Natasha Korda, 'Introduction: Towards a Materialist Account of Stage Properties', in Jonathan Gil Harris and Natasha Korda (eds.), *Staged Properties in Early Modern English Drama*, Cambridge University Press, 2002, 1–31.

Hawkes, David, *The Faust Myth: Religion and the Rise of Representation*, New York: Palgrave, 2006.

Ideology, 2nd edn., London: Routledge, 2003.

Idols of the Marketplace: Idolatry and Commodity Fetishism in English Literature, 1580–1680, New York: Palgrave, 2001.

Hawkes, Terence, 'Band of Brothers', in Grady and Hawkes (eds.), *Presentist Shakespeares*, 6–26.

Meaning by Shakespeare, London: Routledge, 1992.

Shakespeare in the Present, London: Routledge, 2002.

Hazlitt, William, *Characters of Shakespeare's Plays and Lectures on the English Poets*, London: Macmillan, 1903.

Hedrick, Don, 'Advantage, Affect, History, *Henry V*', *PMLA* 118.3 (May 2003), 470–87.

'Male Surplus Value', *Renaissance Drama* 31 (2002), 85–124.

Hegel, G. W. F., *Aesthetics: Lectures on Fine Art*, trans. T. M. Knox, 2 vols., Oxford: Clarendon, 1975.

Hendricks, Margo, 'Obscured by Dreams: Race, Empire, and Shakespeare's *A Midsummer Night's Dream*', *Shakespeare Quarterly* 47 (1996), 37–60.

Hibbard, G. R. (ed.), *Hamlet*, by William Shakespeare, Oxford University Press, 1987.

Holbrook, Peter, *Shakespeare's Individualism*, Cambridge University Press, forthcoming.

Holdsworth, R. V., Middleton and Shakespeare: The Case for Middleton's Hand in *Timon of Athens*, Diss., University of Manchester, 1982.

Hollier, Denis, *Against Architecture: The Writings of Georges Bataille*, trans. Betsy Wing, Cambridge, Mass.: MIT Press, 1989.

Home, Henry, Lord Kames, *Elements of Criticism*, 2 vols., 1762; reprinted New York: Garland, 1971.

Hopkins, Lisa, *Writing Renaissance Queens: Texts by and about Elizabeth I and Mary, Queen of Scots*, Newark, Del.: University of Delaware Press, 2002.

Horkheimer, Max and Theodor Adorno, *Dialectic of Enlightenment: Philosophical Fragments* (1944), ed. Gunzelin Schmid Noerr, trans. Edmund Jephcott, Stanford, Calif.: Stanford University Press, 2002.

Hunt, Maurice, 'A Speculative Political Allegory in *A Midsummer Night's Dream*', *Comparative Drama*, 34 (2000–1), 423–53.

Jackson, Ken, '"One wish" or the Possibility of the Impossible: Derrida, the Gift, and God in Timon of Athens', *Shakespeare Quarterly* 52.1 (Spring 2001), 34–66.

Jackson, MacDonald P., '"A Wood Near Monte Athena": Michael Hoffman's *A Midsummer Night's Dream*', *Shakespeare Newsletter* 49 (Summer 1999), 29, 37–38, 44, 48.

Studies in Attribution: Middleton and Shakespeare, Jacobean Drama Studies 79, Salzburg studies in English Literature, Salzburg: Institut für Anglistik und Amerikanistik Universität Salzburg, 1979.

Jameson, Fredric, *A Singular Modernity: Essay on the Ontology of the Present*, London: Verso, 2002.

Archaeologies of the Future: The Desire Called Utopia and Other Science Fictions, London: Verso, 2005.

The Cultural Turn: Selected Writings on the Postmodern, 1983–1998, London: Verso, 1998.

Late Marxism: Adorno; Or, The Persistence of the Dialectic, London: Verso, 1990.

Marxism and Form: Twentieth-Century Dialectical Theories of Literature, Princeton University Press, 1971.

The Political Unconscious: Narrative as a Socially Symbolic Act, Ithaca, NY: Cornell University Press, 1981.

Postmodernism; or The Cultural Logic of Late Capitalism, Durham, NC: Duke University Press, 1991.

Jennings, Michael, 'Walter Benjamin and the European Avant-Garde', in Ferris (ed.), *The Cambridge Companion to Walter Benjamin*, 18–34.

Johnson, Samuel, 'Notes on Shakespeare's Plays: *"Hamlet"*', *The Yale Edition of the Works of Samuel Johnson*, 17 vols., Vol. VIII: *Johnson on Shakespeare*, ed. Arthur Sherbo, New Haven, Conn.: Yale University Press, 1968, 990.

'Notes on Shakespeare's Plays: *"Romeo and Juliet"*', *The Yale Edition of the Works of Samuel Johnson*, 17 vols., Vol. VIII: *Johnson on Shakespeare*, ed. Sherbo, 956–57.

Joughin, John J., 'Bottom's Secret …', in Ewan Fernie (ed.), *Spiritual Shakespeares*, London: Routledge, 2005, 130–56.

'Lear's Afterlife', *Shakespeare Survey* 55 (2002), 67–81.

'Shakespeare's Genius: *Hamlet*, Adaptation, and the Work of Following', in Joughin and Malpas (eds.), *The New Aestheticism*, 131–50.

'Shakespeare's Memorial Aesthetics', in Peter Holland (ed.), *Shakespeare, Memory and Performance*, Cambridge University Press, 2006, 43–62.

'Shakespeare, Modernity and the Aesthetic: Art, Truth and Judgement in *The Winter's Tale*' in Grady (ed.), *Shakespeare and Modernity*, 61–84.

Joughin, John J. and Simon Malpas (eds.), *The New Aestheticism*, Manchester University Press, 2003.

'The New Aestheticism: An Introduction', in Joughin and Malpas (eds.), *The New Aestheticism*, 1–19.

Jowett, John, Introduction, in William Shakespeare and Thomas Middleton, *The Life of Timon of Athens*, ed. John Jowett, Oxford University Press, 2004, 1–154.

'Middleton and Debt in *Timon of Athens*', in Linda Woodbridge (ed.), *Money and the Age of Shakespeare: Essays in New Economic Criticism*, New York: Palgrave, 2003, 219–35.

'Shakespeare, Middleton, and Debt in *Timon of Athens*', Presentation, Annual Meeting, Shakespeare Association of America, April 2001, Miami, Fla.

Kahn, Coppélia, '"Magic of Bounty": *Timon of Athens*, Jacobean Patronage, and Maternal Power', *Shakespeare Quarterly*, 38.1 (Spring 1987), 34–57.

Kant, Immanuel, *Critique of Judgment* (1790), trans. Werner S. Pluhar, Indianapolis, Ind.: Hackett, 1987.

Kehler, Dorothea, 'A Midsummer Night's Dream: A Bibliographic Survey of the Criticism', in Kehler (ed.), 'A Midsummer Night's Dream', 3–76.

Kehler, Dorothea (ed.), 'A Midsummer Night's Dream': Critical Essays, New York: Garland, 1998.

Kernan, Alvin, The Cankered Muse: Satire of the English Renaissance, New Haven, Conn.: Yale University Press, 1959.

Kerrigan, William, Hamlet's Perfection, Baltimore, Md.: Johns Hopkins, 1994.

Klein, Karl, Introduction, William Shakespeare, Timon of Athens, ed. Karl Klein, Cambridge University Press, 2001, 1–66.

Knight, G. Wilson, The Wheel of Fire: Interpretations of Shakespeare's Sombre Tragedies, London: Oxford University Press, 1930; reprinted Cleveland, Oh.: Meridian, 1964.

　The Wheel of Fire: Interpretations of Shakespearean Tragedy, with Three New Essays, revised edn., London: Methuen, 1949.

Kott, Jan, Shakespeare Our Contemporary, trans. Boleslaw Taborski, Garden City, NY: Doubleday, 1964.

Kristeva, Julia, Revolution in Poetic Language, in Toril Moi (ed.), The Kristeva Reader, New York: Columbia University Press, 1986, 89–136.

　Tales of Love, trans. Leon S. Roudiez, New York: Columbia University Press, 1987.

Kyd, Thomas, The Spanish Tragedy, ed. David Bevington, Manchester University Press, 1996.

Lacan, Jacques, 'Desire and the Interpretation of Desire in Hamlet', Yale French Studies, 55/56 (1977), 11–52.

　Écrits: A Selection, trans. Alan Sheridan, New York: Norton, 1977.

Lacis, Asja, Revolutionär im Beruf: Berichte über proletarisches Theater, über Meyerhold, Brecht, Benjamin, und Piscator, ed. Hildegaard Brenner, Munich: Regner and Bernhard, 1971.

Lake, David J., The Canon of Thomas Middleton's Plays: Internal Evidence for the Major Problems of Authorship, Cambridge University Press, 1975.

Laroque, François, '"I see a voice": Les voix du Songe: De la synesthésie au mystère', in Gheeraert-Graffeuille and Vienne-Guerrin (eds.), Autour du 'Songe d'une nuit d'été' de William Shakespeare, 119–35.

Lee, John, Shakespeare's 'Hamlet' and the Controversies of Self, Oxford: Clarendon, 2000.

Lefebvre, Henri, Critique of Everyday Life, trans. John Moore, London: Verso, 1991.

Leibniz, Gottfried Wilhelm, Freiherr von, 'The Monadology', trans. George Montgomery with revisions by Albert R. Chandler, in The Rationalists, Garden City, NY: Dolphin, 1960, 455–71.

Levin, Harry, The Question of Hamlet, New York: Viking, 1959.

　'Shakespeare's Misanthrope', Shakespeare Survey 26 (1973), 89–104.

Levin, Richard, Looking for an Argument: Critical Encounters with the New Approaches to the Criticism of Shakespeare and his Contemporaries, Madison, NJ: Fairleigh Dickinson University Press, 2003.

Levine, George (ed.), *Aesthetics and Ideology*, New Brunswick, NJ: Rutgers University Press, 1994.

Levine, Laura, 'Rape, Repetition, and the Politics of Closure in *A Midsummer Night's Dream*', in Valerie Traub, M. Lindsay Kaplan, and Dympna Callaghan (eds.), *Feminist Readings of Early Modern Culture*, Cambridge University Press, 1996, 210–28.

Levinson, Marjorie, 'What is New Formalism?', *PMLA* 122.2 (March 2007), 558–69.

Lewis, Wyndham, *The Lion and the Fox: The Role of the Hero in the Plays of Shakespeare*, London: G. Richards, 1927.

Lifshitz, Mikhail, *The Philosophy of Art of Karl Marx*, ed. Angel Flores, trans. Ralph B. Winn, New York: Critics Group, 1938; reprinted London: Pluto, 1973.

Loesberg, Jonathan, *A Return to Aesthetics: Autonomy, Indifference, and Postmodernism*, Stanford University Press, 2005.

Lonitz, Henri, 'Editor's Afterword', in Theodor W. Adorno and Walter Benjamin, *The Complete Correspondence, 1928–1940*, ed. Henri Lonitz, Cambridge, Mass.: Harvard University Press, 1999.

Lukács, Georg, *History and Class Consciousness: Studies in Marxist Dialectics*, trans. Rodney Livingstone, Cambridge, Mass.: MIT Press, 1971.

    Soul and Form, trans. Anna Bostock, Cambridge, Mass.: MIT Press, 1974.

    The Theory of the Novel: A Historico-Philosophical Essay on the Forms of Great Epic Literature, trans. Anna Bostock, Cambridge, Mass.: MIT Press, 1971.

Lupton, Julia Reinhard and Kenneth Reinhard, *After Oedipus: Shakespeare in Psychoanalysis*, Ithaca, NY: Cornell University Press, 1992.

Lyotard, Jean-François, *The Postmodern Condition: A Report on Knowledge*, trans. Geoff Bennington and Brian Massumi, Minneapolis, Minn.: University of Minnesota Press, 1984.

McGee, Arthur, *The Elizabethan Hamlet*, New Haven, Conn.: Yale University Press, 1987.

Machiavelli, Niccolò, 'Discourses on the First Ten Books of Titus Livius', in Max Lerner (ed.), *The Prince and the Discourses*, New York: Modern Library, 1950, 103–540.

Mack, Maynard, 'The World of Hamlet', *Yale Review* 41.4 (June 1952), 502–23.

McLuskie, Kathleen, '"Your Imagination and not Theirs": Reception and Artistic Form in *A Midsummer Night's Dream*', in Gheeraert-Graffeuille and Vienne-Guerrin (eds.), *Autour du 'Songe d'une nuit d'été'*, 31–43.

Mahood, M. M., *Shakespeare's Wordplay*, London: Methuen, 1957.

Maley, Willy, *Nation, State and Empire in English Renaissance Literature: Shakespeare to Milton*, New York: Palgrave Macmillan, 2003.

Mallin, Eric, 'Emulous Factions and the Collapse of Chivalry: *Troilus and Cressida*', *Representations* 29 (Winter 1990), 145–79.

Marcuse, Herbert, *The Aesthetic Dimension: Toward a Critique of Marxist Aesthetics*, trans. Herbert Marcuse and Erica Sherover, Boston, Mass.:

Beacon, 1978; orig. pub. as *Die Permanenz der Kunst: Wider eine bestimmte Marxistische Aesthetik*, Munich: Karl Hanser Verlag, 1977.

Marx, Karl, *Capital: A Critique of Political Economy*, ed., Frederick Engels, trans. Samuel Moore and Edward Aveling, 3 vols., New York: International, 1967.

A Contribution to the Critique of Political Economy, ed. Maurice Dobb, trans. S. W. Ryazanskaya, New York: International, 1970.

The Economic and Philosophic Manuscripts of 1844, ed. Dirk Struik, trans. Martin Milligan, New York: International, 1964.

'Marx: The Utopian Reflex', from letter to Arnold Ruge, in Maynard Solomon (ed.), *Marxism and Art: Essays Classic and Contemporary*, New York: Knopf, 1973.

Mauss, Marcel, *The Gift: The Form and Reason for Exchange in Archaic Societies*, trans. W. D. Halls, New York: Norton, 1990.

Mieszowski, Jan, 'Art Forms', in Ferris (ed.), *The Cambridge Companion to Walter Benjamin*, 35–53.

Miola, Robert S., 'Timon in Shakespeare's Athens', *Shakespeare Quarterly* 31 (Spring 1980), 21–30.

Montaigne, Michel de, *The Complete Essays of Montaigne*, trans. Donald M. Frame, Palo Alto, Calif.: Stanford University Press, 1965.

Montrose, Louis, *The Purpose of Playing: Shakespeare and the Cultural Politics of the Elizabethan Theatre*, University of Chicago Press, 1996.

'"Shaping Fantasies": Figurations of Gender and Power in Elizabethan Culture', *Representations* 1.2 (Spring 1983), 153–82.

Moses, Stéphane, 'Walter Benjamin and Franz Rosenzweig', in Gary Smith (ed.), *Benjamin: Philosophy, Aesthetics, History*, University of Chicago Press, 1989, 228–46.

Mousley, Andy, *Re-Humanising Shakespare: Literary Humanism, Wisdom, and Modernity*, Edinburgh University Press, 2007.

Mowat, Barbara A., 'Nicholas Rowe and the Twentieth-Century Shakespeare Text', in Tetsuo Kishi, Roger Pringle, and Stanley Wells (eds.), *Shakespeare and Cultural Traditions: The Selected Proceedings of the International Shakespeare Association World Congress, Tokyo, 1991*, Newark, Del.: University of Delaware Press, 1994.

Muir, Kenneth, 'Timon of Athens and the Cash Nexus,' *Modern Quarterly Miscellany I* (1947); reprinted in Kenneth Muir, *The Singularity of Shakespeare and Other Essays*, Liverpool University Press, 1977, 56–75.

Muldrew, Craig, *The Economy of Obligation: The Culture of Credit and Social Relations in Early Modern England*, Basingstoke: Macmillan, 1998.

Nietzsche, Friedrich, *The Birth of Tragedy and the Genealogy of Morals*, trans. Francis Golffing, New York, Anchor, 1956.

Norris, Christopher, *The Truth about Postmodernism*, Oxford: Blackwell, 1993.

O'Dair, Sharon, 'A way of life worth preserving? Identity, Place, and Commerce in Big Business and the American South', *Borrowers and Lenders: The Journal of Shakespeare and Appropriation* 1.1 (Spring 2005), www.borrows.uga.edu/borrows/archive.

'Horror or Realism? Filming "Toxic Discourse" in Jane Smiley's *A Thousand Acres*', *Textual Practice* 19.2 (June 2005), 263–82.

'Slow Shakespeare; or, Reversing Our Crimes Against Nature', in Karen Raber and Ivo Kamps (eds.), *Early Modern Ecostudies*, forthcoming.

'*The Tempest* as *Tempest*: Does Paul Mazursky "Green" William Shakespeare?', Special Cluster on Shakespeare and Ecocriticism, *Interdisciplinary Studies in Literature and the Environment (ISLE)* 12.2 (Summer 2005), 165–78.

'Toward a Postmodern Pastoral: Another Look at the Cultural Politics of *My Own Private Idaho*', *Journal x* 7 (Autumn 2002), 25–40.

Olson, Paul A., '*A Midsummer Night's Dream* and the Meaning of Court Marriage', *ELH* 24 (1957), 95–110.

Orgel, Stephen, *Imagining Shakespeare: A History of Texts and Visions*, New York: Palgrave Macmillan, 2003.

Parker, Patricia, *Shakespeare from the Margins: Language, Culture, Context*, University of Chicago Press, 1996.

Paster, Gail Kern and Skiles Howard (eds.), *A Midsummer Night's Dream: Texts and Contexts*, Boston, Mass. and New York: Bedford, 1998.

Patterson, Annabel, *Shakespeare and the Popular Voice*, Oxford: Blackwell, 1989.

Pepys, Samuel, *The Diary of Samuel Pepys*, ed. Robert Latham and William Matthews, 11 vols., Berkeley, Calif.: University of California Press, 1979.

Rackin, Phyllis, *Stages of History: Shakespeare's English Chronicles*, Ithaca, NY: Cornell University Press, 1990.

Raman, Shankar, *Framing India: The Colonial Imaginary in Early Modern Culture*, Stanford University Press, 2001.

Rapaport, Herman, *Later Derrida: Reading the Recent Work*, New York: Routledge, 2003.

Rasmussen, Mark David (ed.), *Renaissance Literature and Its Formal Engagements*, New York: Palgrave, 2002.

Raynor, Vivien, 'Worlds Falling Apart and Getting Hooked Up', *The New York Times*, 8 Jan., 1995; www.nytimes.com, Archives.

Regan, Stephan (ed.), *The Politics of Pleasure: Aesthetics and Cultural Theory*, Philadelphia, Penn.: Open University Press, 1992.

Reid, Robert L., '*The Fairy Queen*: Gloriana or Titania?', *The Upstart Crow* 13 (1993), 16–32.

Richardson, William, 'On the Character of Hamlet' (1774), in *Shakespeare, the Critical Heritage*, 6 vols., Vol. VI: *1774–1801*, ed. Brian Vickers, London: Routledge, 1981, 121–24.

Rimbaud, Arthur, *Complete Works*, trans. Paul Schmidt, New York: Harper & Row, 1974.

Letter to Georges Izambard, 13 May 1871, in Rimbaud, *Oeuvres*, 344.

Letter to Paul Demeny, 15 May 1871, in Rimbaud, *Oeuvres*, 344–50.

Oeuvres, ed. Suzanne Bernard, Paris: Garnier Frères, 1960.

Rimbaud: Complete Works, Selected Letters, trans. Wallace Fowlie, University of Chicago Press, 1966.

Robson, Mark, 'Defending Poetry, or, Is there an Early Modern Aesthetic?' in Joughin and Malpas (eds.), *The New Aestheticism*, 119–30.

Rochlitz, Rainer, *The Disenchantment of Art: The Philosophy of Walter Benjamin*, trans. Jane Marie Todd, New York: Guilford Press, 1996.

Roff, Sarah Ley, 'Benjamin and Psychoanalysis', in Ferris (ed.), *The Cambridge Companion to Walter Benjamin*, 115–33.

Rosenzweig, Franz, *Der Stern der Erlösung* [*The Star of Redemption*], Frankfurt: J. Kauffmann, 1921.

Rubin, Gayle, 'The Traffic in Women: Notes on the "Political Economy" of Sex', in Rayna R. Reiter (ed.), *Towards an Anthropology of Women*, New York: Monthly Review Press, 1975, 157–210.

Rudich, Norman, 'Coleridge's "Kubla Khan": His Anti-Political Vision', in Norman Rudich (ed.), *Weapons of Criticism: Marxism in America and the Literary Tradition*, Palo Alto, Calif.: Ramparts, 1976, 215–41.

Ryan, Kiernan, *Shakespeare*, 3rd edn., New York: Palgrave, 2002.

　　'*Troilus and Cressida*: The Perils of Presentism', in Grady and Hawkes (eds.), *Presentist Shakespeares*, 164–83.

Schaper, Eva, 'Taste, Sublimity, and Genius: The Aesthetics of Nature and Art', in P. Guyer (ed.), *The Cambridge Companion to Kant*, Cambridge University Press, 1982.

Schiller, Friedrich, *On the Aesthetic Education of Man: In a Series of Letters*, trans. Reginald Snell, New York: Ungar, 1965.

Schlegel, August Wilhelm, *A Course of Lectures on Dramatic Art and Literature*, ed. A. J. W. Morrison, trans. John Black, revised edn., London: Henry G. Bohn, 1846; reprinted New York: AMS, 1965.

　　Lectures on Dramatic Art and Literature, ed. A. J. W. Morrison, trans. John Black, London: George Bell, 1892.

Schücking, Levin Ludwig, *The Meaning of Hamlet*, trans. Graham Rawson, New York: Barnes and Noble, 1966; originally published as *Der Sinn des Hamlet*, 1935.

Scott, William O., 'The Paradox of Timon's Self-Cursing', *Shakespeare Quarterly* 35.3 (Autumn 1984), 290–304.

Scragg, Leah, 'Shakespeare, Lyly and Ovid: The Influence of "Gallathea" on "A Midsummer Night's Dream"', *Shakespeare Survey* 30 (1977), 125–34.

Segal, Hanna, 'A Psychoanalytic Approach to Aesthetics', in *The Work of Hanna Segal: A Kleinian Approach to Clinical Practice*, New York: Jason Aronson, 1981, 185–206.

Shakespeare, William, *The Norton Shakespeare*, ed. Stephen Greenblatt *et al.*, New York: Norton, 1997.

　　Timon of Athens, ed. Karl Klein, Cambridge University Press, 2001.

Shapiro, James, *A Year in the Life of William Shakespeare: 1599*, New York: HarperCollins, 2005.

Shell, Marc, *Money, Language, and Thought*, Baltimore, Md.: Johns Hopkins University Press, 1982.

Sidney, Sir Philip, *A Defence of Poetry* (1595), in Brian Vickers (ed.), *English Renaissance Literary Criticism*, Oxford: Clarendon, 1999, 336–91.

Sinfield, Alan, 'Cultural Materialism and Intertextuality: The Limits of Queer Reading in *A Midsummer Night's Dream* and *The Two Noble Kinsmen*', *Shakespeare Survey* 56 (2003), 67–78.

Singer, Alan, *Aesthetic Reason: Artworks and the Deliberative Ethos*, University Park, Penn.: Pennsylvania State University Press, 2003.

Slights, William W. E., '"*Genera mixta*" and "Timon of Athens"', *Studies in Philology* 74. 1 (1977), 36–62.

Snyder, Susan, '"Romeo and Juliet": Comedy into Tragedy', *Essays in Criticism* 20.4 (October 1970), 391–402.

Soderholm, James (ed.), *Beauty and the Critic: Aesthetics in an Age of Cultural Studies*, Tuscaloosa, Ala.: University of Alabama Press, 1997.

Solomon, Maynard (ed.), *Marxism and Art: Essays Classic and Contemporary*, New York: Vintage, 1974.

Spencer, T. J. B., '"Greeks" and "Merrygreeks": A Background to *Timon of Athens* and *Troilus and Cressida*', in Richard Hosley (ed.), *Essays on Shakespeare and Elizabethan Drama in Honor of Hardin Craig*, Columbia, Mo.: University of Missouri Press, 1962, 223–33.

Spencer, Theodore, *Death and Elizabethan Tragedy: A Study of Convention and Opinion in the Elizabethan Drama*, Cambridge, Mass.: Harvard University Press, 1936.

   Shakespeare and the Nature of Man, New York: Macmillan, 1942.

Spenser, Edmund, *The Faerie Queene*, ed. Thomas P. Roche and C. Patrick O'Donnell, Harmondsworth: Penguin, 1979.

Spurgeon, Caroline, *Shakespeare's Imagery: And What It Tells Us*, Cambridge University Press, 1935; 1966.

Stallybrass, Peter, Roger Chartier, J. Franklin Mowery, and Heather Wofe, 'Hamlet's Tables and the Technologies of Writing in Renaissance England', *Shakespeare Quarterly* 55.4 (Winter 2004), 379–419.

Stevens, Wallace, 'Sunday Morning', in Richard Ellman and Robert O'Clair (eds.), *Modern Poems: A Norton Introduction*, 2nd edn., New York: Norton: 1989, 150–53.

Taylor, Gary and John Lavagnino (eds.), *Thomas Middleton: The Collected Works*, Oxford Univeristy Press, 2007.

Thomson, Patricia, 'The Literature of Patronage, 1580–1630', *Essays in Criticism* 2.3 (July 1952), 267–84.

Traub, Valerie, 'The (In)Significance of "Lesbian" Desire in Early Modern England', in Jonathan Goldberg (ed.), *Queering the Renaissance*, Durham, NC: Duke University Press, 1994, 62–83.

Ulrici, Hermann, *Shakespeare's Dramatic Art; And His Relation to Calderon and Goethe*, trans. A. J. W. Morrison, London: Chapman, 1846.

Ure, Peter, *William Shakespeare, the Problem Plays: 'Troilus and Cressida', 'All's Well That Ends Well', 'Measure for Measure', 'Timon of Athens'*, revised edn., London: Longmans Green, 1964.

Vial, Claire, 'De la fée épique à la fée elfique: Oberon, de *Huon de Bordeaux* au *Midsummer Night's Dream*', in Patricia Dorval (ed.), *Shakespeare et le Moyen-Âge*, Paris: Société Française Shakespeare, 2002, 203–22.

Vickers, Brian, *Shakespeare, Co-Author*, Oxford University Press, 2002.

Vyvyan, John, *Shakespeare and Platonic Beauty*, London: Chatto and Windus, 1961.

Weimann, Robert, *Author's Pen and Actor's Voice: Playing and Writing in Shakespeare's Theatre*, ed. Helen Higbee and William West, Cambridge University Press, 2000.

'Mimesis in *Hamlet*', in Patricia Parker and Geoffrey Hartman (eds.), *Shakespeare and the Question of Theory*, New York: Methuen, 1985, 275–91.

Whitney, Charles, 'Ante-aesthetics: Towards a Theory of Early Modern Audience Response', in Grady (ed.), *Shakespeare and Modernity*, 40–60.

Williams, Gary Jay, *Our Moonlight Revels: 'A Midsummer Night's Dream' in the Theatre* (Iowa City, Ia: University of Iowa Press, 1997).

Williams, Raymond, *Marxism and Literature*, Oxford University Press, 1977.

Wilson, Edmund, *To the Finland Station: A Study in the Writing and Acting of History*, 1940; reprinted Garden City, NY: Doubleday, 1953.

Wilson, John Dover, *What Happens in 'Hamlet'*, Cambridge University Press, 1935.

Wofford, Susanne L. (ed.), *William Shakespeare: Hamlet*, Boston, Mass.: Bedford, 1994.

Wolin, Richard, 'An Aesthetic of Redemption: Benjamin's Path to the Trauerspiel', *Telos* 43 (Spring 1980), 61–90.

Walter Benjamin: An Aesthetics of Redemption, New York: Columbia University Press, 1982.

Young, David P., *Something of Great Constancy: The Art of 'A Midsummer Night's Dream'*, New Haven, Conn.: Yale University Press, 1966.

Zimbardo, R.A., 'Regeneration and Reconciliation in *A Midsummer Night's Dream*', *Shakespeare Studies* 6 (1970), 35–50.

Zimmerman, Susan, *The Early Modern Corpse and Shakespeare's Theatre*, Edinburgh University Press, 2005.

Index

Lightning Source UK Ltd.
Milton Keynes UK
UKHW012349260220
359412UK00001B/5